VISUAL QUICKSTART GUIDE

DREAMWEAVER
CS4

Learn Dreamweaver CS4
the Quick and Easy Way!

**FOR WINDOWS
AND MACINTOSH**

**TOM NEGRINO
DORI SMITH**

VISUAL QUICKSTART GUIDE

DREAMWEAVER CS4

FOR WINDOWS AND MACINTOSH

Tom Negrino
Dori Smith

 Peachpit Press

Visual QuickStart Guide
Dreamweaver CS4 for Windows and Macintosh
Tom Negrino and Dori Smith

Peachpit Press
1249 Eighth Street
Berkeley, CA 94710
510/524-2178
510/524-2221 (fax)

Find us on the Web at www.peachpit.com
To report errors, please send a note to errata@peachpit.com
Peachpit Press is a division of Pearson Education

Editor: Nancy Davis
Production editor: Rebecca Winter
Proofreader: Tracy D. O'Connell
Compositor: WolfsonDesign
Indexer: Valerie Haynes Perry
Cover design: Peachpit Press

ISBN 13: 978-0-321-57352-0
ISBN 10: 0-321-57352-8

9 8 7 6 5 4 3 2 1

Printed and bound in the United States of America

To our son, Sean Smith,
with love from Mom and Dad

Special Thanks to:

Our wonderful (and wonderfully patient and cheerful) editor, Nancy Davis, who pulled this book together, made it better, and encouraged us when we were flagging.

Virginia DeBolt, who contributed several chapters to previous editions, which we have built upon in this revision. Her work was terrific, and we are grateful for her help. Thanks also to Virginia for the use of her photographs in Chapters 7, 8, and 14.

Thanks to Rebecca Winter, for her excellent production work.

Thanks to the book's compositor, Owen Wolfson, and thanks to Valerie Haynes Perry for the index.

Thanks to Peachpit's Nancy Ruenzel for her support.

Dori would like to thank the Wise-Women's Web community (www.wise-women.org) for their help and support, for contributing their years of Dreamweaver expertise, and for being the best darn Web-related mailing list around.

Of course, our gratitude to the members of the Adobe Dreamweaver CS4 team for creating a terrific product.

In Tom's office, the soundtrack for this book included music from my Pandora and Rhapsody subscriptions, and lots more bouncy pop music.

TABLE OF CONTENTS

Chapter 7: Styling Page Content   **183**

Chapter 8: Positioning Page Content   **219**

Chapter 9: Managing Styles   **255**

Chapter 10: Inserting Tables   **271**

TABLE OF CONTENTS

INTRODUCTION

Welcome to *Dreamweaver CS4 for Windows and Macintosh: Visual QuickStart Guide*! Adobe Dreamweaver has long (under its previous name, Macromedia Dreamweaver) been the premier visual tool for Web site developers, allowing you to build great-looking Web pages and smoothly running Web sites. Dreamweaver's ease-of-use takes much of the pain out of creating Web sites, without sacrificing flexibility. It's possible to use Dreamweaver to create terrific Web sites without knowing much about HTML, CSS, and JavaScript (though you will create better Web sites if you familiarize yourself with at least the basics of these languages).

Dreamweaver is a rich, powerful, and deep program, and at first glance, it can be a bit intimidating. We've written this book as a painless introduction to Dreamweaver and its features, and with our help, you will use Dreamweaver to build an excellent Web site.

Using this book

We've organized the different elements of building Web sites with Dreamweaver CS4 into chapters, and within each chapter are numbered, step-by-step directions that tell you exactly how to accomplish various tasks. You don't have to work through the entire book in order, but it is structured so the more complex material builds on the earlier tasks.

We start with an overview of Dreamweaver, move on to setting up your Web site and creating your first Web page, then discuss how to add content and interactivity to your pages. Finally, we show you how to work with HTML code and manage your Web site.

When we first decided to write this book, we wanted to take a fresh look at Dreamweaver—at how people use it, and how people *should* use it. Throughout the book, we've tried to show you how to use Dreamweaver using its most modern features, rather than using some of the features that are still in the program, but are "old school." Specifically, we'll show you how to apply styles and position your page elements using Cascading Style Sheets, rather than older, obsolete methods. If you don't know what that means, don't worry; it's all explained in Chapters 7 through 9.

✔ Tips

- Throughout the book we've included many tips that will help you get things done faster, better, or both.

- Be sure to read the figure captions, too; sometimes you'll find extra nuggets of information there.

- When we're showing HTML, CSS, or JavaScript code, we've used this `code font`. We also use the code font for Web addresses.

- You'll also find sidebars (with gray backgrounds) that delve deeper into subjects.

For keyboard commands, we've included Mac keyboard shortcuts in parentheses immediately after the Windows shortcut, like this:

To open the Find & Replace dialog, press Ctrl-F (Cmd-F).

While writing this book, we've made the assumption that you're familiar with the basics of using Windows or Mac OS X. You don't need to be a computer expert by any means, but you shouldn't be stumped by concepts like selecting text, using menus, clicking and dragging, and using files and folders. Naturally, you should be familiar with Web surfing and how to use a Web browser to view a Web site.

Getting the most from Dreamweaver

Dreamweaver is a professional-class tool, and it provides professional results. Dreamweaver allows you to build Web sites visually, without needing to know the details of HTML, CSS, and JavaScript. But to best use Dreamweaver, you will still need some fundamental knowledge of what these languages are, and how they work together to make up a Web site. Similarly, you will find it helpful to know basic things such as what a Web page is and what a Web server does.

Where necessary, throughout this book we explain what you'll need to know about HTML, CSS, and JavaScript to work with Dreamweaver. But there is much more to say about these subjects, and there are thousands of books devoted to that job. In fact, we wrote one of the most popular books on JavaScript. You'll find information about that book, as well as some of our favorite Web design and development books written by other authors, listed in Appendix A.

A note for our M⸻ls

If you've flipped through ⸻ you probably noticed that the vast majority of the screenshots were taken on machines running Windows (mostly Windows Vista). That doesn't mean that the book (or its authors) don't welcome Dreamweaver users on the Mac. Far from it; in fact, both of us are primarily Mac users, and we are frequent contributors to *Macworld* magazine and other Mac-oriented publications.

However, our crack research department tells us that most Dreamweaver users are running the program on Windows machines, so we have included screenshots that will reflect the experience of the majority of our readers. Happily, Dreamweaver (and especially Dreamweaver CS4) works almost identically on both platforms. In the few cases where there are differences, we've included separate procedures for Windows and for Mac users.

There is one other thing that we *haven't* done in this book that we have done in our previous Mac books. We are no longer telling Mac users to Control-click to bring up a contextual menu (which we sometimes call shortcut menus in this book). Instead, we've adopted right-click, because Apple now ships its multiple-button mouse (which it calls Mighty Mouse) with all of its computers that come with a mouse. If you still have one of the old Apple mice with a single button, just mentally substitute Control-click wherever you see right-click in the book. Better yet, we suggest that you get any USB or wireless mouse with multiple buttons and a scroll wheel. It will really increase your productivity.

Th

We'...on Web site for
this...at:

http://www.dreamweaverbook.com

On this site, you'll find news about the book and links to other online resources that will help you use Dreamweaver CS4 more productively. If we discover any mistakes in the book that somehow got through the editing process, we'll list the updates on the site, too.

If you have any questions, please first check the FAQ (Frequently Asked Questions) page on the companion Web site. It's clearly marked. If you've read the FAQ, and your question isn't answered there, you can contact us via email at dwcs4@dreamweaverbook.com. We regret that because of the large volume of email that we get, we cannot, and will not, answer email about the book sent to our personal email addresses. We can only guarantee that messages sent to the dwcs4@ dreamweaverbook.com email address will be answered. Unfortunately, due to the danger of computer viruses being spread with e-mail attachments, we cannot accept any messages with attachments.

Let's get started

Every journey begins with a first step, and if you've read this far, your journey with Dreamweaver has already begun. Thanks for joining us, and let's get started building your great Web site.

—*Tom Negrino and Dori Smith,*
  September 2008

INTRODUCTION

INTRODUCING DREAMWEAVER

1

Welcome to the world of Dreamweaver! The premiere Web design and development tool from Adobe may appear a little daunting at first, so this chapter shows you what's what and what's where. Once you understand what all the parts of its interface do, you'll soon find that Dreamweaver is an invaluable application for creating and maintaining Web sites.

In this chapter, you'll learn about the Dreamweaver Welcome screen and document window. Then you'll see the plethora of toolbars and panels included with the software: the menu bar, the Document toolbar, the Style Rendering toolbar, and the Standard toolbar. The Status bar, Property Inspector, other panels, and the Insert panel are next, and then you'll learn about the included workspace layouts, and how to set up your own custom workspace. Finally, there's a summary of the new features in Dreamweaver CS4.

A Quick Tour of Dreamweaver

In this section, you'll learn about the different windows, panels, pages, views, toolbars, and inspectors that make up the Dreamweaver experience. Whether you're a novice to Web design, an experienced pro who's new to Dreamweaver, or someone who primarily wants to know what's new in Dreamweaver CS4, this will bring you up to speed.

The Welcome screen

The first time you launch Dreamweaver, you'll see the Welcome screen, as shown in **Figure 1.1**. This page (which changes based on what you've recently done in Dreamweaver) is your starting point for both creating and modifying pages and sites. If you close all your open Dreamweaver windows, the Welcome screen reappears.

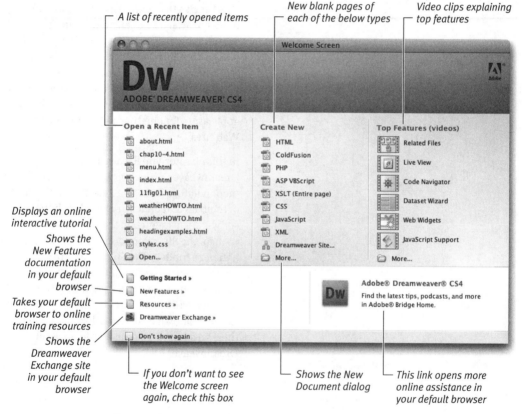

Figure 1.1 Dreamweaver's Welcome screen will soon become familiar—but if you don't want to see it, you can make it go away.

The Welcome screen consists of several sections:

- **Open a Recent Item:** This section contains a list of the nine most recently opened items in Dreamweaver. If you've opened fewer than nine, it shows just that number; if you've never used Dreamweaver, it appears with just a button showing an "Open" folder; clicking the button displays the Open dialog, just as if you had chosen File > Open.

- **Create New:** If you want to create a new page or site, this is the column for you. Choosing one of these options creates a new HTML, ColdFusion, PHP, ASP VBScript, XSLT, CSS, JavaScript, or XML file. You can also create a new Dreamweaver site. And lastly, you can choose "More" which will display the New Document dialog (**Figure 1.2**) about which we'll learn more later.

- **Top Features (videos):** If you're the type of person who likes video training, these clips open in your default browser and give you an overview of some of the new features in Dreamweaver CS4. This section may change from time to time, as Adobe updates the video selection.

- **Getting Started:** Choosing this option gives you, as it says, a quick tour of Dreamweaver's functionality. You'll see a short online tutorial on Adobe's Web site.

- **New Features:** This opens the online new features documentation using your default browser.

- **Resources:** If, despite having this book, you still want further training, you can follow this link to find additional resources on Adobe's site.

continues on next page

Figure 1.2 The New Document dialog offers a multitude of choices.

◆ **More Help:** If you want to learn more about working with Dreamweaver and its associated programs, the link at the bottom-right corner of the window takes you to Adobe's Web site for more help resources.

◆ **Dreamweaver Exchange:** Dreamweaver is built with an extensible architecture—that is, it's easy to add functionality to Dreamweaver that wasn't included when it shipped. That's done through a technology called extensions, which are bits of software that extend Dreamweaver's capabilities.

You can get additional extensions through the Adobe Dreamweaver Exchange at www.adobe.com/exchange/dreamweaver/. Some of them have an additional charge, and some are free, but it's worth checking out what's available when Dreamweaver alone doesn't scratch your itch. See Appendix B for more information about extending Dreamweaver.

◆ **Don't show again:** Adobe knows that while some people love the Welcome screen, other people aren't so fond of it. Throughout this book, you'll see many examples of how you can personalize your copy of Dreamweaver so that it works just the way you want it to. Here, you can choose to never see the Welcome screen again.

If you reconsider, though, it's easy to bring back the Welcome screen: in Dreamweaver, choose Edit (Windows)/ Dreamweaver (Mac) > Preferences > General > Document Options, and check the "Show Welcome Screen" box.

Figure 1.3 Windows users will see the Default Editor dialog the first time they launch Dreamweaver.

Editor Setup (Windows only)

If you've just launched Dreamweaver for the first time, and you're using Windows, you'll see a dialog before the Welcome screen (**Figure 1.3**). The Default Editor dialog lets you choose which file types you want to tell Windows to assign to Dreamweaver as the primary editor. In other words, when you double-click on a file with one of the listed extensions, Dreamweaver will launch to edit the file.

Many of these file types are types that are used with kinds of Web sites that we won't be covering in this book, but unless you have a preference for a different editing program, there's no harm in clicking the Select All button in the dialog. You should make sure that at least the JavaScript, Cascading Style Sheets, and Extensible Markup Language choices are selected. The Default Editor only appears the first time you run Dreamweaver.

The menu bar

The Dreamweaver menu bar looks about like what you'd expect to see on your platform. There is one big difference between the Windows menu bar (**Figure 1.4**) and the Mac menu bar (**Figure 1.5**): the latter also contains a "Dreamweaver" menu. On it are the "About Dreamweaver," "Keyboard Shortcuts," and "Preferences" menu options. On Windows, the first can be found under Help, and the latter two under Edit. And of course, the Windows menu bar is part of the Dreamweaver window, while on the Mac the menu bar is always at the top of the screen.

The other big difference is that on Windows, the Layout, Extend Dreamweaver, Site, and Workspace menus, and the Search online help field, which together are called the Application Bar, appear as part of the menu bar. On Mac, these appear in a separate toolbar below the menu bar.

✔ Tip

■ On Mac, you can turn the Application Bar off (and recover some valuable vertical screen real estate) by choosing Window > Application Bar. Since the Application Bar contains items that you probably won't use every day (and are also available via the regular menu bar), hiding it is usually a good idea.

Figure 1.4 The Dreamweaver menu bar on Windows.

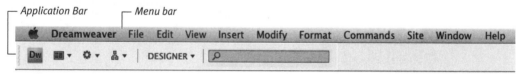

Figure 1.5 The Dreamweaver menu bar on a Mac, which includes an additional "Dreamweaver" menu and the Application Bar below.

A QUICK TOUR OF DREAMWEAVER

The document window

Now that you've opened a file, you see the document window and all its surrounding panels, inspectors, etc. (**Figure 1.6**). It may look busy and cluttered at first, but you'll soon learn your way around.

The document window shown here is a blank white Web page, ready for you to add your design and content. If you want, you can just click inside the window and start typing away! The details of creating a Web page are covered in Chapter 3.

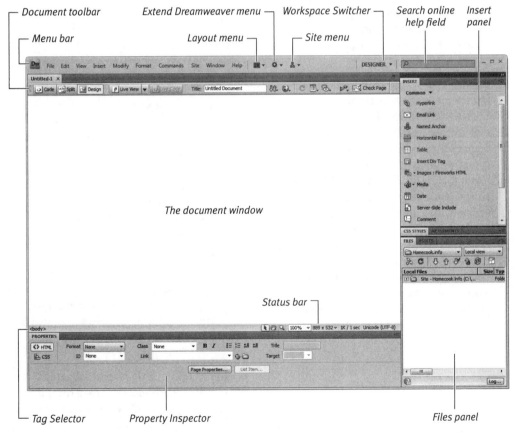

Document toolbar   Extend Dreamweaver menu   Workspace Switcher   Search online help field   Insert panel

Menu bar   Layout menu   Site menu

The document window

Status bar

Tag Selector   Property Inspector   Files panel

Figure 1.6 This shows your basic vanilla Dreamweaver document window, but you can modify it to fit your work habits.

If you have multiple files open at once (a fairly common occurrence), you'll see a row of tabs across the top of the document window (**Figure 1.7**). To go from one file to another, just click the name of the file you want to edit.

Don't like tabs? Dreamweaver lets you get rid of them:

◆ **Windows:** When you open a document in Dreamweaver, click the Restore Down button (**Figure 1.8**) in the top-right corner of the document window (*not* the one in the Dreamweaver window). Once one document has been moved into its own window, all the others automatically move, too. To go back to the original, click the Maximize button (which has replaced the Restore Down button) in the top-right corner of the document window.

◆ **Mac:** Tabs are the normal interface in Windows, so Windows users have to manually lose the tabs any time they want to do without them. Mac users, though, only got tabs with Dreamweaver 8. Because of that, Dreamweaver allows Mac users to choose whether to get rid of tabs permanently (older Dreamweaver/Mac behavior), to force windows to always show tabs (Windows behavior), or to open documents in tabs, but only when two or more documents are open (new Dreamweaver/Mac behavior). These can be set by going to Dreamweaver > Preferences > General > Document Options and choosing your preferred combination of "Open documents in tabs" and "Always show tabs."

Figure 1.7 Switch from document to document by clicking the tab with the document name.

Figure 1.8 On Windows, the Restore Down button changes Dreamweaver from a tabbed view to a multiple document view.

Hey, This Looks Different...

If you've used previous versions of Dreamweaver, you'll notice that things look pretty different in Dreamweaver CS4. That's because this version of Dreamweaver uses OWL, the OS Widget Library. This is a user interface construction kit that Adobe uses to provide what they call the Adobe Look and Feel to their applications. First introduced with Adobe Creative Suite 3, OWL was initially applied to certain long-time Adobe programs, notably Photoshop, Illustrator, and InDesign, plus Flash, which had been recently acquired from Macromedia. In CS4, the other applications formerly owned by Macromedia, including Dreamweaver, Fireworks, and Contribute, get the OWL treatment.

The idea of OWL is to unify the user interface across all of the Adobe applications, so that when you move from one program in the Creative Suite to another, you don't have to adjust to each program's idiosyncrasies.

Part of the updated OWL look is a grayscale look for panels and toolbars, with button icons inside them turning to color when you roll over them with the cursor. If you want, you can set a preference to always display the button icons in color; choose View > Color Icons.

The Document toolbar

Below any document tabs you have open, you'll find the Document toolbar (Windows: **Figure 1.9**, Mac: **Figure 1.10**). The Document toolbar itself consists of three parts:

◆ **View mode buttons:** These let you choose between Design, Code, and Split views of your document. This area also includes the new Live View and Live Code buttons. See "Using document views" for more on what each of these does and when you'd want to choose each. Live Code is discussed in Chapter 17, "Editing Code."

◆ **The page title:** Every page needs a descriptive title, and here's where you'll change yours. The page title, and how it differs from the name of a page itself, will be covered in Chapter 3, "Building Your First Page."

◆ **Miscellaneous buttons:** These contain everything from a "preview in browser" button, to a button to validate content, to a button to show additional visual aids inside Dreamweaver itself.

Figure 1.9 The Document toolbar on Windows.

Figure 1.10 The Document toolbar on a Mac.

Using document views

The four document views allow you to
choose which version of the document you
want to see:

◆ **Design: Figure 1.11** shows a typical
Web page in the Design view. This mode,
known as WYSIWYG (What You See
Is What You Get), allows you to get an
idea of how your page will appear when
viewed in a browser. For the most part,
almost everything you want to do in
Dreamweaver can be done in the Design
view, and this book will be entirely about
what you can do here (except for Chapter
17, "Editing Code").

Figure 1.11 A simple Web page displayed in the Design view.

◆ **Code: Figure 1.12** shows the exact same page in the Code view. Here's what the underlying markup and tags look like. While Chapter 17 will cover the ins-and-outs of tags, many people work quite well with Dreamweaver without ever using the Code view. Note that in the Code view, you get a new toolbar at the left side of the document window, with specialized tools to work with code.

continues on next page

Figure 1.12 The same Web page displayed in the Code view.

◆ **Split: Figure 1.13** shows the same page, again, in the Split view. If you can't decide whether you want to look at Code or Design, Split lets you have the best of both, with code on the top, and the WYSIWYG view below. It's a great way to start to learn about markup, and it's also handy for control freaks who want to tweak their tags to be just so, and simultaneously see how their design looks. You can resize the amount of space taken up by each of the two views by dragging the split bar between the two panes up or down.

Split bar

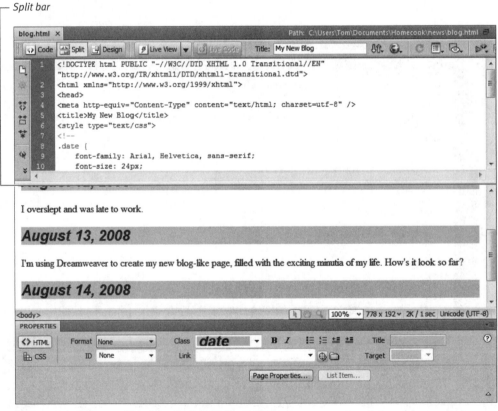

Figure 1.13 And the same Web page, displayed in the Split view.

Figure 1.14 Live View allows you to see how a page looks in Dreamweaver's regular editing mode (top) and how it would look rendered in a browser (bottom). Note how in Live View, the table shows CSS styling, as well as its Ajax-driven ability to sort the table by clicking its column headings.

◆ **Live View:** This is one of the new features in Dreamweaver CS4, and it's perfect for giving you a good idea of what pages powered by JavaScript or other code will look like in a browser. In previous versions, you could only see the static version of a page in Dreamweaver; to see the dynamic view, you needed to view the page in a separate Web browser. With Live View, a browser engine (the cross-platform WebKit, the engine used by Apple's Safari browser) is built into Dreamweaver, and clicking the Live View button displays the page using WebKit in the document window (**Figure 1.14**).

Other toolbars

If you right-click in a blank part of the Document toolbar, you'll see that there are two other bars that aren't enabled by default:

◆ **Style Rendering bar:** If you've set up your CSS stylesheets so that your pages appear differently in, for example, a screen view versus a page designed for printing, this is what you'll use to switch between the two style renderings. Most of the time, you'll just want the default screen view. The button at the far-right end of the bar works a little differently: it toggles the page between a view that includes the rendered CSS styles and a view with CSS styles turned off (**Figure 1.15**).

◆ **Standard bar:** While Adobe refers to this bar as "standard," it's actually used to make Dreamweaver feel more like a word processing application (**Figure 1.16**). Some examples of what it contains—New, Open, Save, Print, Cut, Copy, Paste—give you an idea of what's here. As with the Style Rendering bar, the chances are that Adobe's default for these toolbars (off) is what you'll want to use.

You can turn off any of these three toolbars if you want the cleanest possible layout (for instance, if you're working on a very small screen). To turn them back on, choose View > Toolbars, and select the ones you want to see again.

Figure 1.15 The Style Rendering toolbar allows you to view the page with and without any attached CSS Styles.

Figure 1.16 The little-used Standard toolbar gives you access to functions such as Save, Copy, Paste, and Undo.

Rubber Soul	1965
Revolver	1966
Sgt. Pepper's Lonely Hearts Club Band	1967
Magical Mystery Tour	1967
The Beatles	1968
Yellow Submarine	1969

`<body> <table#theTable> <tr> <td>`

Figure 1.17 The tag selector makes it easy to select all the contents of a tag.

Figure 1.18 The controls on the right-hand side of the Status bar.

592w

536 x 196 (640 x 480, Default)

600 x 300 (640 x 480, Maximized)

760 x 420 (800 x 600, Maximized)

795 x 470 (832 x 624, Maximized)

955 x 600 (1024 x 768, Maximized)

Edit Sizes...

Figure 1.19 Use this pop-up menu to choose the dimensions of your document window.

The Status bar

The Status bar is the bottom-most part of the document window. It's often also referred to as the *tag selector*, although that's really the correct name for just the left-most part. Click anywhere in a document, and the tag selector shows you the current tags based on the current location of the cursor. You can then click any of the tags in the tag selector (**Figure 1.17**) to select everything contained within that tag. Clicking the <body> tag always selects the entire contents of the page.

The right-most side of the Status bar contains more controls (**Figure 1.18**). The Select, Hand, and Zoom tools let you (respectively) select objects on the page, scroll around the page, and zoom into the page. The next control shows the current zoom percentage of the page. After that is the window size currently being displayed; click this to get a pop-up menu of available window sizes (**Figure 1.19**). Next is an estimate of how long it would take a browser to download this page. If you don't like the default values for these last two controls, you can change either or both by selecting "Edit Sizes" from the pop-up menu. We'll cover this more extensively in Chapter 8. Finally, the status bar tells you the document text encoding for the page. The encoding tells the browser which character set should be used to display the fonts on the page.

The Property Inspector

At the bottom of the screen is the Property Inspector (**Figure 1.20**). Based on what is selected in the document window, different options appear in this inspector; that is, if you've selected some text, you'll see text options, while if you've selected an image, image options appear. The Property Inspector can be used to both view and modify the displayed options. The many uses of the Property Inspector will be covered throughout the rest of the book.

In the lower-right corner of the inspector is an expand/collapse triangle. Depending on its current state, this either expands or collapses the inspector. This lets you choose whether you want to display the extra information shown in the bottom half.

New to Dreamweaver CS4, the Property Inspector now has two tabs, HTML and CSS. Depending on which tab you're on, Dreamweaver will apply properties of that type. For example, if you're on the HTML tab, select some text in the document window, and click the Italic button, Dreamweaver will apply the style using the HTML <em> tag. If you're on the CSS tab of the Property Inspector (**Figure 1.21**), select some text, and click the Italic button, Dreamweaver will walk you through creating a new CSS style rule for the selection.

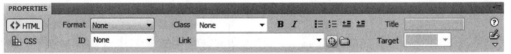

Figure 1.20 The HTML tab of the Property Inspector.

Figure 1.21 The CSS tab of the Property Inspector.

Tab area ┌ Dock header bar

Collapse to Icons button

Panel options button

Collapsed tabs

Figure 1.22 A panel and its parts.

The Panels

Along the right side of the Dreamweaver window are *panels*. In the default installation of Dreamweaver (**Figure 1.22**), the Insert, CSS Styles, AP Elements, Files, and Assets panels are visible and docked (in the default Designer workspace; more about workspaces later in this chapter). Also available, although not visible until you turn them on, are Databases, Bindings, Server Behaviors, Components, Snippets, Tag Inspector, Behaviors, History, Frames, Code Inspector, and Results. These can all be found under the Window menu.

The different panels appear by default in the *dock area* on the right side of the screen. You can move this area to the left side of the screen by dragging the *dock header bar* at the top of the stack of docked panels.

You can hide, show, move, resize, and rearrange panels to fit the way that you work. There are controls on each panel that help you do these things:

◆ At the top of each panel, next to the tab with its name, is a dark gray area. This is the *tab area*. Click and drag this to move the panel to a new location. If you drag the panel out of the dock area, you *undock* the panel (**Figure 1.23**), and the dock header bar appears. To dock the panel again, use the tab area to drag the panel back into the dock area.

◆ Double-clicking the tab area will expand and collapse it to show either the whole panel or just the tab area. You can also resize a panel by clicking and dragging its left or bottom edge.

◆ **Dock header bar:** The bar across the top of an undocked panel is the *dock header bar*. Click and drag the dock header bar to move the panel to a new location. Clicking the close box (Windows) or close button (Mac) closes the panel group; it does not re-dock it. To re-dock, drag the panel back into the dock.

◆ **Collapse to Icons button:** If you want more space to reduce screen clutter and see more of your document window, click the Collapse to Icons button at the upper-right corner of the dock, which shrinks the panels to icons (**Figure 1.24**). To use the iconic panel, click its icon, and the panel appears as a drawer next to the dock (**Figure 1.25**).

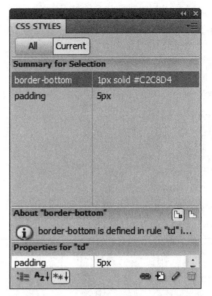

Figure 1.23 An undocked panel has a dock header bar.

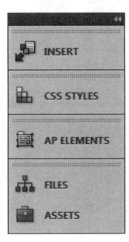

Figure 1.24 If you need more screen space, you can shrink your panels to icons in the dock area.

Figure 1.25 Clicking a panel icon opens the panel in a drawer next to the dock area.

Figure 1.26 Different panels have different menu options, but these are the most common.

◆ **Panel options button:** If you click the panel options button, a menu appears that gives you a variety of options (**Figure 1.26**) based on which panel and tab you're currently on. This example shows the options for the Insert panel. From here, you can hide the labels in the Insert panel, or show its icons in color. The ability to close tabs and move tabs from one panel to another allows you to set Dreamweaver up to work just the way you want it.

✔ Tips

■ Panels have an occasional tendency to go missing. If you've got a situation where the Window menu says a panel is open but you can't find it anywhere, choose Window > Arrange Panels to make all currently open panels visible again.

■ If you want to completely concentrate on working in your document window, you can hide the dock with all of the panels and the Property Inspector by pressing F4, or by choosing Window > Hide Panels. The panels and inspector shrink down to a thin gray strip on the right and bottom edges of your screen called the *reveal strip*. Click on a reveal strip to briefly show the dock or Property Inspector; it will shrink back down after a short delay when you move the cursor away. Press F4 or use the menu choice again to bring the hidden elements back for good.

A QUICK TOUR OF DREAMWEAVER

The Insert panel

In the default Designer workspace, the top panel is the Insert panel (**Figure 1.27**). As you might have guessed, the Insert panel is used to insert content and objects into your Web page.

The Insert panel has eight different categories, which you can switch between with a pop-up menu. You get different tools in each category:

◆ **Common:** This set of objects contains most commonly used objects, such as links and images.

◆ **Layout:** This tab includes divs, tables, and frames: all objects that let you describe how you want to lay out your page.

◆ **Forms:** The Forms set includes form elements such as text fields, buttons, and check boxes.

◆ **Data:** If you're someday going to work with external data such as databases, that's when you'll use the Data set.

◆ **Spry:** Spry is a JavaScript library for designers and developers that allows them to add rich page functionality using Ajax widgets, such as menus, form validation, and tabbed panels. The Spry tab allows you to insert Spry widgets onto your pages, with no coding required.

◆ **InContext Editing:** InContext Editing (ICE) is a hosted service that Adobe introduced with Creative Suite 4. It allows users to make relatively simple edits to their Web pages from a Web browser, with no other software required. In Dreamweaver, the Insert panel allows you to add certain areas to pages to make them available to ICE end users. We'll discuss ICE in more detail in Chapter 16.

Figure 1.27 The Insert panel contains many of the tools you'll use most often to insert objects on your Web pages.

◆ **Text:** The text tab doesn't actually contain objects to insert on the page; instead, it lets you style text that's already on the page.

◆ **Favorites:** This starts off empty, but you can modify it to contain just what you'd like it to have. To do this, choose the Favorites set, and then right-click. You'll be presented with a dialog that allows you to add your most commonly used objects.

✔ Tips

■ The Insert panel is just a different orientation of the Insert bar, which was the staple of all past versions of Dreamweaver. If you're a long-time user and miss the Insert bar, just drag the Insert panel's tab above the document window, and the panel will transform back into the familiar Insert bar (**Figure 1.28**). You lose a little vertical space for your document window, but you get back an old friend.

■ If you're ever wondering what an icon on the Insert Bar does, just move your cursor over it—a tool tip will appear with the icon's name. If there's a small black triangle to the right of an icon that means this object contains related tools and objects. Click the object to view the pop-up menu of choices.

Figure 1.28 If you're an old-school Dreamweaver user, you can turn the Insert panel back into the Insert bar.

Setting Up Your Workspace

It's not just a matter of deciding what you do want to see—setting up your workspace also means figuring out what you *don't* want to see. Given the toolbars *and* all the possible panels *and* the Property Inspector, you can run out of room for the actual Web page you're trying to work on (**Figure 1.29**). In Dreamweaver's parlance, a *workspace* is an arrangement of panels, the dock, the document window, and the Property Inspector. Here's how to set up a workspace that works for you.

Figure 1.29 Not all the tools and panels are visible, but this is already an unusable workspace.

Figure 1.30 The Workspace Switcher makes it easy to change between workspace layouts.

The Included Workspace Layouts

Dreamweaver CS4 introduces new preset workspaces that look and work the same on Windows and Mac, and are designed for different classes of users:

◆ App Developer

◆ App Developer Plus

◆ Classic

◆ Coder

◆ Coder Plus

◆ Designer (the default workspace)

◆ Designer Compact

◆ Dual Screen

These workspaces rearrange the document window, panels, and Property Inspector to work more efficiently for each type of user.

The Dual Screen layout isn't associated with a kind of user; rather it attempts to make the best of your hardware. If you're lucky enough to have two (or more) monitors, the Dual Screen layout attempts to make the most of all of them. For example, the document window is expanded to cover the whole primary monitor, and the panels are moved onto the secondary monitor.

You switch between the different layouts with the Workspace Switcher in the Application Bar (**Figure 1.30**). Just choose from the pop-up menu to switch between workspaces.

SETTING UP YOUR WORKSPACE

Saving custom layouts

Chances are that the workspaces that come with Dreamweaver aren't likely to be exactly what you want. No problem! You can save your own workspaces.

To save a custom workspace:

1. Set up your layout just the way you want it. Show or hide panels, and drag them to where you want.

2. From the Workspace Switcher menu, choose New Workspace.

   The New Workspace dialog appears (**Figure 1.31**).

3. Enter a name for your custom workspace, then click OK.

   Your new workspace appears at the top of the Workspace Switcher menu.

✔ Tip

■ If at any point you've added, deleted, and moved around panels and documents to the point where everything's all over the place, you can always go back to the original layout for any workspace by first choosing it from the Workspace Switcher menu, then choosing Reset [workspace name] from the same menu.

To delete or rename a custom workspace:

1. If you later decide that you don't want a custom workspace any more, or want to give it another name, you can change it. From the Workspace Switcher menu, choose Manage Workspaces.

   The Manage Workspaces dialog appears (**Figure 1.32**).

2. Select the workspace you want to change, then delete or rename your custom layout (but you can't do this to any of the included layouts).

Figure 1.31 Give your new custom workspace a name.

Figure 1.32 The Manage Workspaces dialog lets you rename or delete your custom layouts.

Managing windows

You may want your documents to open in tabs sometimes and in their own windows sometimes. It's easy to go back and forth between these two options and to set your documents to appear just the way you want them. It's a little different on each platform:

To manage windows (Windows):

◆ Starting with the default tabbed layout (**Figure 1.33**), choose Window > Cascade. Your document windows appear in a cascade: each slightly lower and to the right of the one behind it (**Figure 1.34**).

or

continues on next page

Figure 1.33 The default tabbed layout that you've seen before.

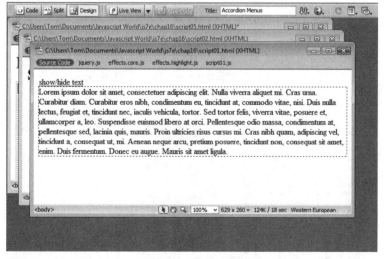

Figure 1.34 Your three document windows, displayed in a cascade.

◆ Starting with the default tabbed layout (Figure 1.33), choose Window > Tile Horizontally. Your document windows appear tiled horizontally, with the available space split evenly between them (**Figure 1.35**).

or

◆ Starting with the default tabbed layout (Figure 1.33), choose Window > Tile Vertically. Your document windows appear tiled vertically, with the available space split evenly between them (**Figure 1.36**).

Figure 1.35 Your three document windows, tiled horizontally.

Figure 1.36 Your three document windows, tiled vertically.

✔ Tips

- To return to the tabbed window view, click the Maximize button in the top-right corner of any document. This puts all open windows back in their place.

- There's one good reason to have your documents opened in separate windows: it's the only way a Windows user can use the pop-up menu of available window sizes (Figure 1.19).

- Having trouble getting from document to document because one is behind another? All open documents are available for the choosing at the bottom of the Window menu.

To manage windows (Mac):

◆ Starting with the default tabbed layout (**Figure 1.37**), choose Window > Cascade. Your document windows appear in a cascade, each slightly lower and to the right of the one behind it (**Figure 1.38**).

or

◆ Starting with the default tabbed layout (Figure 1.37), choose Window > Tile. Your document windows appear tiled vertically, with the available space split evenly between them (**Figure 1.39**).

Figure 1.37 The default tabbed layout, on the Mac.

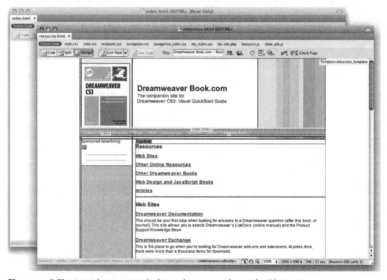

Figure 1.38 The two document windows, in a cascade on the Mac.

✔ Tips

- To return to the tabbed window view, choose Window > Combine as Tabs. This puts all open windows back in their places. This command isn't available in the Windows version, as the Maximize button in each window serves the same purpose.

- Having trouble getting from document to document because one is behind another? The Window menu has a list of all open documents, as well as Next Document and Previous Document commands, so you can use it to choose the file you want.

- Note that on Windows, you have a choice of horizontal or vertical window tiling, but on the Mac, the only tiling option is vertical.

Figure 1.39 The two document windows, tiled vertically on the Mac.

What's New in Dreamweaver CS4

If you've used Dreamweaver before, you'll notice that while some things look similar, some things also look very different. A comprehensive description of all the new features in Dreamweaver CS4 would take up an entire chapter, so here are just a few of the highlights:

◆ In this chapter, you've already seen four of the new features in Dreamweaver: the panel-centric **Adobe look and feel**; **Live View,** allowing you to see how your page will look without previewing in a browser; the **CSS tab** in the Property Inspector, to make it easier to create CSS styles; and support for the **InContext Editing** Web page editing service. See Chapter 16 for more on the InContext Editing support.

◆ **Improved Photoshop integration:** Dreamweaver CS3 introduced integration with Photoshop, with a copy and paste workflow from Photoshop into Dreamweaver. Dreamweaver CS4 improves that workflow by making .psd (Photoshop) images that you place into Dreamweaver a SmartObject. Changes that you make to the .psd file in Photoshop automatically update the image in Dreamweaver. There's more about this integration in Chapter 16.

◆ **Spry widgets and effects:** You know all those cool Ajax effects you see on Web pages these days? Now you can add many of them to your own sites in Dreamweaver, even if you know nothing about JavaScript. See Chapter 14 for more details. Of course, if you *want* to learn more about JavaScript, we suggest you pick up one of our other books, *JavaScript & Ajax for the Web, Seventh Edition: Visual QuickStart Guide.*

◆ Modern Web pages often have several supporting files that help make up the page. For example, what appears to the user as a single Web page may actually consist of an HTML file, a CSS file, and a JavaScript file. The new **Related Files** feature adds a bar with the names of these supporting files under the documents tab (**Figure 1.40**). You'll learn more about using the Related Files feature in Chapter 7.

◆ If you're a coder, there are two new features for you. The **JavaScript Extractor** makes it easy to remove JavaScript from an HTML page and write it out to an external .js script file. And the **Code Navigator** allows you to easily drill down to a related code source that affects the current selection. For example, if you have a separate CSS or JavaScript file, you can use the Code Navigator to open the external file and jump to the relevant part of the file. You'll learn more about the Code Navigator in Chapter 7, and more about the JavaScript Extractor in Chapter 17.

Related Files

Figure 1.40 The new Related Files bar makes it easy to switch to files that are attached to the current document, such as CSS or JavaScript files.

STARTING
YOUR FIRST SITE

2

Dreamweaver is all about building Web sites. Sure, it has all of the tools you need to create great Web pages. But the basic building block is the site, not the page. You need to define a site in Dreamweaver, which will then be the container for all of the files and folders that will make up your Web site.

When you build sites, you start by creating and testing the site on your local machine. Then, when the site is ready, you will send it over the Internet to your Web server, where it will go live for the world to see. Dreamweaver has all the tools you'll need to create the site, work with its files and folders, and then transfer it to the Web server. That's what we'll be covering in this chapter. So let's get started!

Understanding Local and Remote Sites

Dreamweaver CS4 can do a great job of helping you manage all the files and folders that make up your Web site, but for the best results, you'll need to use the program's site management tools to set up and maintain the site. First, you need to understand some of the terminology Dreamweaver uses for sites. You'll want to build and test your Web site within a single folder on your hard disk, which Dreamweaver calls the *local root folder*. This folder contains all of the files and folders that make up the site. For example, let's say that you're building a company site that has two sections in it, one for product information (called products), and the other for information about the company (called companyinfo). Each of the two sections gets its own folder. These folders are located inside the local root folder (which in this example we're calling MyCompany). Because each section shares some of the same graphic images, there is also an images folder in the local root folder. The site structure would look something like **Figure 2.1**. With one exception, each of the Web pages that you build for the site will go into either the products or companyinfo folder. The exception is the main site page (the one that people see when they load your site in their browsers). That's called the *index page*, and it usually goes in the local root folder (which is also called the *local site*).

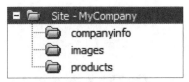

Figure 2.1 The top folder here is the local root folder, which contains all of the files and folders that make up the Web site.

After you build the pages for your site, you will use Dreamweaver to copy all of the files and folders (usually over the Internet) to the Web server. Dreamweaver replicates the folder structure from your hard disk on the Web server, so the site's structure and all of the links between the pages are preserved. Dreamweaver refers to the copy of the site on the Web server as the *remote site*. The remote site should always be a mirror image of your local site, and Dreamweaver has tools that can synchronize the two sites (you'll learn more about that later in this chapter and in Chapter 18).

✔ Tips

- Strictly speaking, you don't have to create all of your site's files within the local root folder. But if you do not, Dreamweaver will often put up dialogs complaining that files aren't in a local site, and you'll lose access to very useful Dreamweaver features, such as the ability to automatically update all links to a file that has been moved to another location in the site. We strongly recommend that you always build your pages in a local site, and keep all of the elements that make up those pages in the local root folder.

- If you were using Dreamweaver's ability to work with sites built using a database, you could have a third copy of your site on a testing or staging server.

Static versus Dynamic Sites

There are two main kinds of Web sites that you can create in Dreamweaver: *static* sites, where you build all of the pages of the site on your local machine, then upload them to the Web server; and *dynamic* sites, in which all the pages are created from information drawn from a database. The content from a dynamic page is created when the user loads the page. Many e-commerce sites are dynamic sites; for example, when you go to Amazon.com and see pages that greet you by name and offer personalized recommendations, those pages are created and served just for you, based on the programming of Amazon's database.

We're covering how to build static sites with Dreamweaver in this book. When we run into options that Dreamweaver offers to work with dynamic sites, we'll mention that, but we generally will not cover those options in detail in this book.

Creating the Local Site

Because the process of setting up your local and remote sites has many steps, Dreamweaver provides a handy Site Definition dialog that walks you through the process. Once you're familiar with setting up local and remote sites, the Site Definition dialog provides Basic and Advanced modes. The Basic mode (**Figure 2.2**) uses many screens, like a Wizard, which is a friendlier way of entering all the needed information. The Advanced mode (**Figure 2.3**) allows you to enter information on one screen with several categories, and provides more detailed options in each category.

You'll use the Site Definition dialog to create both the local and remote sites. In this section, however, we'll just create the local site. See "Defining the Remote Site," later in this chapter, for instructions on how to tell Dreamweaver about the remote site.

Figure 2.2 The Basic mode of the Site Definition dialog walks you through the information that you need to enter to define a site.

Figure 2.3 Once you've used Dreamweaver for a while, you'll be ready to define sites or make changes using the Site Definition dialog's Advanced mode.

Figure 2.4 Click the Dreamweaver Site link in the Welcome screen to begin creating your site.

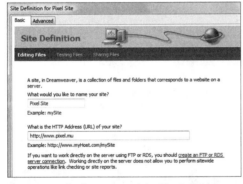

Figure 2.5 In the first screen of the Site Definition dialog, enter the name and Web address of your site.

To create the local site:

1. In the Dreamweaver Welcome screen, click the Dreamweaver Site link (**Figure 2.4**).

   The Site Definition dialog appears, set to the Editing Files screen of the Basic tab.

   or

   Choose Site > New Site.

   The Site Definition dialog appears, set to the Advanced tab.

2. If the dialog is set to the Advanced tab, click the Basic tab, which switches the dialog to show the Editing Files screen. Then, in the field under "What would you like to name your site?", enter the name.

   The site name is only for your reference; it won't be visible to users of the site.

3. In the field under "What is the HTTP Address (URL) of your site?", enter the Web address of your site including the leading http:// (**Figure 2.5**).

4. Click Next.

   The Editing Files, Part 2 screen appears.

5. Dreamweaver asks, "Do you want to work with a server technology such as ColdFusion, ASP.NET, ASP, JSP, or PHP?" Click the button next to "No, I do not want to use a server technology."

   Server technologies such as the ones listed are used for sites that have pages that are generated *dynamically*, that is, the contents of the page are drawn from a database when the user requests the page. Using server technologies is beyond the scope of this book; instead, we'll be creating *static* pages.

6. Click Next.

   The Editing Files, Part 3 screen appears (**Figure 2.6**).

continues on next page

CREATING THE LOCAL SITE

7. Dreamweaver asks, "How do you want to work with your files during development?" Click the button next to "Edit local copies on my machine, then upload to server when ready (recommended)."

The other choice, "Edit directly on server using local network," is for specialized situations where your Web server is on the local network, rather than accessible over the Internet.

8. On the same screen, Dreamweaver asks, "Where on your computer do you want to store your files?" Click the folder icon to the right of the text field, which brings up a dialog titled "Choose local root folder for site sitename," and browse to the folder on your hard disk that contains all of the files for your site.

On Windows, select the folder in the dialog and click Open, then click the Select button.

or

On Macintosh, select the folder in the dialog and click the Choose button.

The dialog closes and you will return to the Site Definition dialog.

9. Click Next.

The Sharing Files screen appears (**Figure 2.7**).

10. From the pop-up menu labeled "How do you connect to your remote server?", choose None.

In this case, we are only creating the local site. If you want to continue on and define the remote site, go to step 4 in "Defining the Remote Site," later in this chapter.

11. Click Next.

The Summary screen appears (**Figure 2.8**).

12. Click Done.

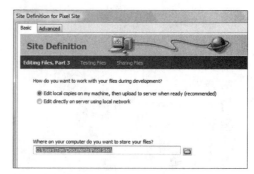

Figure 2.6 Next, you'll need to tell Dreamweaver where to put your local site folder.

Figure 2.7 For now, we won't connect to a remote server, so None is the correct choice.

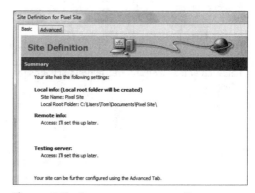

Figure 2.8 The Summary screen recaps the information you entered.

Getting Yourself Organized

Before you dive deeper into Dreamweaver, it's useful to spend some time deciding the structure and design of your site. In fact, this is a great time to push away from the computer and pick up a much older design tool: a pencil and pad of paper. While a primer on site design would take up much more space than we have in this sidebar (indeed, entire books are devoted to the subject), before you begin building your site with Dreamweaver, consider the following, then sketch out your designs.

◆ What do your customers need from your site? Your site's visitors are your customers. Create your sites for them, not for you. Customers can visit your site for a variety of reasons: to purchase something, to get information or entertainment, or to be part of a community. Sites centered on your customer's needs are sites that visitors will return to. Sites driven by company structure, or by the designer's ego—not so popular.

◆ What is the best structure and navigation for your site? Site structure is generally like an upside-down tree, or an organization chart. The index page is the main trunk, and branches off to folders with other pages inside (and often other folders with their own pages). On your pad, add the main folders that you'll create from the index page (the home page of your site). Your structure will also determine the site navigation you choose. Again, put yourself in the place of the customer, and imagine what they'll need to get around your site. Remember that they may not enter your site at your home page, so make sure the navigation is clear and consistent throughout the site.

Take the time to work out your customer's needs, and then the site's structure and navigation, on paper before you start creating things in Dreamweaver. You'll end up saving time by avoiding dead ends and wasted effort. To learn more, see Appendix A for our suggestions of some good Web design books.

Defining the Remote Site

The remote site lives on your Web server, and it is the destination for the files and folders from the local site on your computer's hard disk. Dreamweaver can connect to your Web server in several ways. The most common connection, called *FTP*, is used when your server resides on the Internet or on your company's intranet. Another way to connect is called *SFTP*, for Secure FTP. A third way to connect is via a protocol called *WebDAV* (see the sidebar "What's FTP, SFTP, and WebDAV?").

Before you begin creating a connection to the remote site, you need to ask your network administrator for some information about the Web server you're using. You will need:

◆ The connection type, which will be FTP, SFTP, or WebDAV

◆ The FTP, SFTP, or WebDAV address for your server

◆ The login (sometimes called the username) for the server

◆ The password associated with the login

◆ The folder's path on the server that contains your Web site

Once you gather this information, you're ready to define the remote site in Dreamweaver. You'll begin by editing the site definition.

✔ Tip

■ Dreamweaver offers two other ways to connect to remote sites, RDS and Microsoft Visual SourceSafe (Windows only), which are used for database-backed sites, and will not be discussed in this book.

What's FTP, SFTP, and WebDAV?

If you've never done any Web site maintenance before, you might be baffled by the term *FTP*. It stands for "File Transfer Protocol," and it's a common method for transferring files (such as Web pages and images) between two computers connected to the Internet. Web servers often use FTP to send files between the server and the computer of whomever is maintaining the Web site. In order to do this, the server machine runs an *FTP server* program in addition to the Web server software. Normally you need a program called an *FTP client* on your computer to transfer files to and from an FTP server. Dreamweaver has the FTP client functions built in.

One of the drawbacks to FTP is that it is a protocol with no built-in security; all information is sent "in the clear," including your username, password, and the files themselves. The Secure FTP (SFTP) protocol solves this problem by encrypting all information sent between the SFTP client (in this case, Dreamweaver) and the SFTP server.

The WebDAV protocol provides both security and deals with another problem faced by Dreamweaver users: that of ensuring that only one person at a time is modifying a particular Web page. WebDAV locks a file while it is being edited, and releases the lock when the page is completed. Dreamweaver has its own system of locking and unlocking files when you use protocols other than WebDAV; in practice, you won't see a difference in the way Dreamweaver works no matter which connection protocol you select.

Figure 2.9 Begin adding the remote site to your site definition in the Manage Sites dialog.

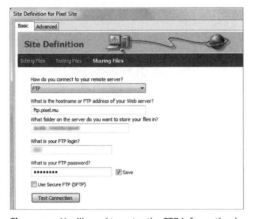

Figure 2.10 You'll need to enter the FTP information in the Sharing Files screen. We've blurred some private information here.

To define the remote site with FTP or SFTP:

1. Choose Site > Manage Sites.

The Manage Sites dialog appears (**Figure 2.9**).

2. Select the site you want, then click Edit.

The Site Definition dialog appears. If you last used this dialog in Basic mode, it will appear still set to that mode. If you last used it in Advanced mode, it will appear that way.

3. If necessary, click the Basic tab, then click the Next button until the Sharing Files screen appears.

4. From the pop-up menu labeled "How do you connect to your remote server?," choose FTP.

The dialog changes to show fields you need to fill in for the FTP connection type (**Figure 2.10**). If you will be making an SFTP connection, choose FTP from the pop-up menu, then check the "Use Secure FTP (SFTP)" check box when the dialog changes to show that option.

5. In the field labeled "What is the hostname or FTP address of your Web server?" enter the hostname or FTP address of your Web server.

The hostname could be a name like www.peachpit.com or ftp.dori.com. It will usually be the name you would enter into a Web browser, without the http://. It must begin with www or ftp, and cannot be just the domain name, such as dori.com. The name should not contain directories or slashes, such as www.negrino.com/books/. You can also enter a numeric IP address in this field, such as 66.39.104.128.

continues on next page

6. In the next field, enter the name of the folder on the Web site that contains your site's files and will serve as the root folder for your site.

    This folder is also called the *host directory*, and is usually a path from the FTP folder to the root folder. Depending on your Web hosting company, this path could be named many different things. Typical host directory names are `htdocs`, `public_html`, or `www/public/docs/`. If you're unsure of the exact name of the host directory, check with your Web hosting company. Sometimes, the FTP host connects to the correct directory automatically, and you can leave the field blank.

7. Enter the FTP login name.

8. Enter the FTP password.

    Don't forget that FTP logins and passwords are case-sensitive on many servers.

9. If you want Dreamweaver to remember the FTP login and password (recommended), make sure the Save check box is selected.

10. Click the Test Connection button to make sure that Dreamweaver can connect successfully to your Web server.

    If Dreamweaver reports an error, check the information you entered.

11. Click Next.

    The Sharing Files, Part 2 screen appears.

Figure 2.11 If you connect to your Web server via WebDAV, you'll need to enter the connection information.

12. Dreamweaver asks, "Do you want to enable checking in and checking out files, to ensure that you and your co-workers cannot edit the same file at the same time?" Click the radio button next to "No, do not enable check in and check out."

    Check in and check out is a useful feature when you are working on the site with others, because it helps keep different people from accidentally editing a page at the same time. We will explore this feature further in Chapter 18.

13. Click Next.

    The Summary screen appears, with the information that you have entered for the local and remote sites.

14. Click Done.

To define the remote site with WebDAV:

1. Choose Site > Manage Sites.

    The Manage Sites dialog appears.

2. Select the site you want, then click Edit.

    The Site Definition dialog appears.

3. If necessary, click the Basic tab, then click the Next button until the Sharing Files screen appears.

4. From the pop-up menu labeled "How do you connect to your remote server?" choose WebDAV.

    The dialog changes to show fields you need to fill in for the WebDAV connection type (**Figure 2.11**).

5. Enter the URL of your WebDAV server.

6. Enter the WebDAV login name.

continues on next page

DEFINING THE REMOTE SITE

7. Enter the WebDAV password.

If you want Dreamweaver to remember the WebDAV login and password (recommended), make sure the Save check box is selected.

8. Click the Test Connection button to make sure that Dreamweaver can connect successfully to your Web server.

If Dreamweaver reports an error, check the information you entered.

9. Click Next.

The Sharing Files, Part 2 screen appears.

10. Dreamweaver asks, "Do you want to enable checking in and checking out files, to ensure that you and your co-workers cannot edit the same file at the same time?" Click the radio button next to "No, do not enable check in and check out."

11. Click Next.

The Summary screen appears, with the information that you have entered for the local and remote sites.

12. Click Done.

DEFINING THE REMOTE SITE

Figure 2.12 It's faster to edit site definitions in the Advanced tab of the Site Definition dialog.

Editing Site Definitions

Once you have created your site definitions, you might need to change them. For example, you might want to change the location of the local root folder, or you may change the path on the remote server. You'll use the Site Definition dialog, but this time we'll use the Advanced tab to get things done a bit faster.

To change a site definition:

1. Choose Site > Manage Sites.

   The Manage Sites dialog appears.

2. Select the site you want, then click Edit.

   The Site Definition dialog appears.

3. If necessary, click the Advanced tab.

   The dialog changes to the Advanced mode (**Figure 2.12**).

4. Choose the category on the left side of the dialog for the kind of change you want to make.

   The right side of the dialog changes to show the options for the category you chose.

5. Make the changes you need to make.

6. Click OK.

EDITING SITE DEFINITIONS

Working with the Files Panel

To work with the files and folders that make up your Web sites, you'll use the Dreamweaver Files panel. This panel allows you to add and delete files and folders; view and change the local or remote sites; and do other maintenance tasks for your sites.

The Files panel appears at the right side of the Dreamweaver window, docked with other panels. By default, the Files panel is at the bottom of the group of panels. The panel consists of a couple of pop-up menus, a toolbar, and the files area below (**Figure 2.13**).

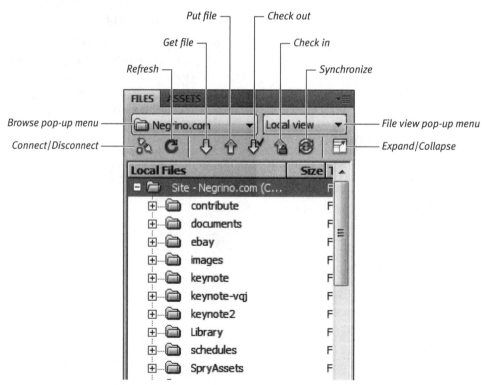

Figure 2.13 The Files panel is your command center for working with files in Dreamweaver.

Figure 2.14 The Browse menu in the Files panel reflects the differences in the Windows (left) and Mac (right) operating systems.

Figure 2.15 If you choose your hard disk from the Browse pop-up menu, you can then navigate to any file or folder on the disk.

Navigating Disks and Sites

The Browse pop-up menu at the top of the Files panel allows you to browse through your hard disk and easily switch between sites that you have defined. The menu looks a bit different on Windows and Mac, reflecting the differences between the operating systems (**Figure 2.14**). On both platforms, sites you have defined appear in the menu as folders.

To browse your hard disk:

1. In the Files panel, choose the disk you want from the Browse pop-up menu.

   The disk's contents appear in the files area (**Figure 2.15**).

2. Navigate to the folder and file that you want.

To switch between defined sites:

◆ In the Files panel, choose the site from the Browse pop-up menu.

Switching Between Local and Remote Views

The File view pop-up menu, next to the Browse pop-up menu, allows you to switch the view in the Files panel between the local and remote sites.

To switch between local and remote views:

1. Choose a site you have defined from the Browse pop-up menu.

   The site's local files appear in the files area, and the File view pop-up menu switches to Local view.

2. From the File view pop-up menu, choose Remote view (**Figure 2.16**).

   Dreamweaver connects to the site (you can tell because the Connect/Disconnect button in the Files panel toolbar will highlight), and the remote files appear in the files area.

✔ Tip

■ The File view pop-up menu has two other choices: Testing server and Repository view. We won't be discussing either of these in this book.

Figure 2.16 To see the files on the remote site, choose Remote view from the File view pop-up menu.

Refreshing Views

When you switch to the local or remote views of a site, Dreamweaver scans the contents of your local or remote site folders and displays the current contents. On occasion, the view you're looking at in the Files panel may become out of date. For example, if you happen to upload or delete items on the remote site with a program other than Dreamweaver, those changes won't be shown in the Files panel. Similarly, if you move files into the local root folder by working on the Windows or Mac desktop, you may need to tell Dreamweaver to rescan and refresh its display of the local site.

To refresh the local or remote view:

1. Choose the site you want to refresh from the Browse pop-up menu.

2. Choose the view (local or remote) you want from the File view pop-up menu.

3. Click the Refresh button in the Files panel toolbar.
   Dreamweaver rescans the site you selected and updates the files area.

Working with Files and Folders

The Files panel is great for organizing all of the files on your site and creating new files and folders. You should do most of your file creation and management in the Files panel, because it can often save you quite a bit of time compared to using another method in Dreamweaver.

For example, you can create a new page by choosing File > New, then choosing the kind of page you want from the New Document dialog, then editing the page. When you save the page, you must navigate to the correct folder in the local site folder, name the page, and then save it. In contrast, to create a new page in a particular folder using the Files panel, you select the folder that you want to contain the page, then choose the New File command as described below.

✔ Tip

- Just because the Dreamweaver files area is reminiscent of the Windows Explorer or Macintosh Finder, don't be fooled into thinking that it is the same, and that you could do your local file management on your computer's desktop. Dreamweaver is designed for working with Web pages, and it can do incredibly useful things, like updating the links on a page to work correctly, even if you move the page that contains the links to a different folder on the site.

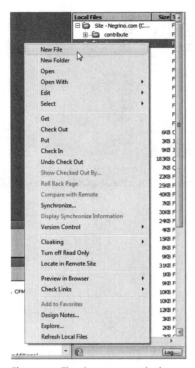

Figure 2.17 The shortcut menu in the Files panel is the fastest way to create a new file or new folder.

Figure 2.18 If you move files that are the target of links, Dreamweaver asks to update the pages that link to the file you moved.

To create a new file or folder:

1. Use the File view pop-up menu to select the local or remote site. You will usually create files or folders in the local site.

2. Right-click a file or folder in the files area. A shortcut menu appears that gives you many options (**Figure 2.17**).

3. From the shortcut menu, choose New File or New Folder.

   The new file or folder appears in the files area. If you selected a folder in step 2, the new file or folder will be created inside the selected folder.

4. The name of the newly created file or folder ("untitled.html" for a file, or "untitled" for a folder) is selected in the Files panel. Type the name you want.

✔ Tip

- You could use the panel options button at the upper-right corner of the Files panel, which gives you a different shortcut menu, but it's easier to use the right-click shortcut menu.

To move files or folders:

1. Select a file or folder in the files area. To move multiple items, Ctrl-click (Cmd-click) to select each of the items you want to move.

2. Drag the selected item(s) to the new location.

   The Update Files dialog appears (**Figure 2.18**).

3. Click Update.

   Dreamweaver updates all of the links in the site that are affected by the move.

To rename files or folders:

1. Select a file or folder in the files area.

2. Click the name of the file or folder.

   or

   Press F2.

   The name becomes highlighted.

3. Type the new name. Don't forget to add the correct file extension for the file that you're renaming. For example, most Web pages have the file extension `.htm` or (preferably) `.html`.

4. Press Enter (Return).

   The Update Files dialog appears.

5. Click Update.

   Dreamweaver updates all of the files in the site that are affected by the renamed file.

To edit files or folders:

1. Right-click a file or folder in the files area.

2. From the resulting shortcut menu, choose the Edit submenu (**Figure 2.19**).

3. Choose one of the items in the Edit menu.

   You can Cut, Copy, Paste, Delete, Duplicate, or Rename the file or folder. If a file operation will affect other files, Dreamweaver may display an "Are you sure?" dialog or the Update Files dialog.

✔ Tip

- Note the shortcut keys listed next to each of the items in the Edit menu. As you become more comfortable working with files in Dreamweaver, using the shortcut keys can save you time.

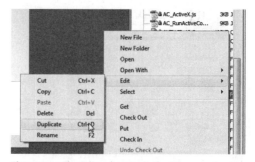

Figure 2.19 The Edit submenu in the Files panel shortcut menu gives you several options for working with files or folders.

Putting and Getting Files

You can copy selected files or folders (or the entire site) between the local and remote sites using the Files panel. The Dreamweaver term for moving an item from the local to the remote site is called *putting* the item; moving the item from the remote to the local site is *getting* the item. If a put or get operation will overwrite a file, Dreamweaver warns you. If you select a folder, Dreamweaver moves the folder and all of the items that it contains. So, if you select the local root folder, you can put the entire site up on the remote server in just a couple of clicks. Sometimes, however, you'll want to use Dreamweaver's site synchronization feature, rather than put or get individual items. See "Synchronizing the Local and Remote Sites," later in this chapter.

To put or get a file or folder:

1. In the Files panel, choose Local view or Remote view from the File view pop-up menu.
   The local or remote view is displayed in the files area.

2. Select the file or folder you want to move.

3. Click the Get file or Put file button in the Files panel toolbar.

4. If any of the files that you're transferring are open and have unsaved changes, Dreamweaver asks if you want to save the files before they are sent. Click Yes, or if there are multiple files, click Yes to All.

5. Dreamweaver may also display a dialog asking if you want to transfer any dependent files. An example of dependent files would be the graphics on the pages that you are uploading. If the dependent files have already been uploaded to the server, click No; there's no reason to reupload files that haven't changed. If you want to transfer dependent files that have changed, click Yes.

Checking files in and out

We'll discuss operations with the Check in and Check out buttons in the Files panel toolbar in Chapter 18.

Expanding the Files Panel

Normally, the Files panel will only show either the local site or the remote site. But if you would like to compare the list of files and folders on both sites, you can do that by expanding the Files panel. This feature works slightly differently on Windows and on Macintosh. On Windows, expanding the Files panel causes it to grow to take over the entire screen, replacing the rest of the Dreamweaver interface. On Mac, expanding the Files panel opens the panel in a new window that allows you to see the remote site on the left and the local site on the right (**Figure 2.20**).

To expand the Files panel:

◆ Click the Expand/Collapse button in the Files panel toolbar.

✔ Tip

■ To collapse the Files panel, click the Expand/Collapse button again.

Figure 2.20 On the Mac, when you expand the Files panel, it opens in a new window, with the remote site on the left and the local site on the right.

Figure 2.21 In the Synchronize Files dialog, you'll need to select the synchronization method you want to use.

Synchronizing the Local and Remote Sites

Having two copies of a Web site—one on your local machine and the other on a Web server—can potentially lead to trouble. It's possible, for example, for you to update several pages on your local site and lose track of just which files you changed. In that case, it might be difficult for you to determine which copy of the site (local or remote) has the latest version of the files. Dreamweaver's Synchronize command compares the local and remote sites and transfers the newer files in either direction.

To synchronize local and remote sites:

1. Click the Synchronize button in the Files panel.

or

Choose Site > Synchronize Sitewide.

The Synchronize Files dialog appears (**Figure 2.21**).

2. From the Synchronize pop-up menu, choose the files you want to update.

Your choices are to synchronize all the files in the site, or just files or folders that you selected in the Local view.

continues on next page

SYNCHRONIZING THE LOCAL AND REMOTE SITES

3. From the Direction pop-up menu, choose how you would like to copy newer files:

▲ **Put newer files to remote** sends newer files from your local site folder to the Web server.

▲ **Get newer files from remote** finds newer files on the Web server, and copies them to your local site folder. This option also copies completely new files that are on the Web server (ones, for example, that may have been placed there by a coworker) to your local site folder.

▲ **Get and Put newer files** synchronizes files both ways. New files on the local site will be transferred to the remote site and vice versa.

4. (Optional) If you want, turn on the "Delete remote files not on local drive" check box.

This is a good option to choose when you've made substantial deletions in the local site (perhaps because you did a big site cleanup). The wording of this option changes depending on what you chose in step 3. If you chose to transfer newer files from the remote site, the wording changes to "Delete local files not on remote server." If you chose to get and put files, this option becomes inactive.

5. Click Preview.

Dreamweaver connects to the remote site, compares the files you chose to synchronize, and then displays the Synchronize dialog (**Figure 2.22**). This allows you to preview the changes that will be made on the site. The Action column in the dialog tells you what Dreamweaver proposes to do to each file.

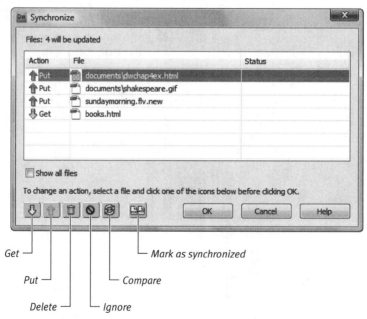

Figure 2.22 You can select actions in the Synchronize dialog that will determine how the files are affected as they are synchronized.

6. If desired, select one or more files in the Synchronize dialog and choose one of the action buttons at the bottom of the dialog. You have the following choices:

▲ **Get** marks the selected files to be retrieved from the remote site.

▲ **Put** marks the selected files to be sent to the remote site.

▲ **Delete** marks the selected files for deletion.

▲ **Ignore** tells Dreamweaver to ignore the selected files for this synchronization.

▲ **Mark as synchronized** tells Dreamweaver to consider the selected files as already synchronized, so no action will be taken.

▲ **Compare** opens the local and remote versions of the file so you can compare their differences.

7. Click OK.

Dreamweaver performs the synchronization.

Cloaking Files and Folders

Not every file or folder in your local site needs to be uploaded to the remote site on the Web server. Dreamweaver allows files and folders to be *cloaked*, which means that they will be exempt from synchronization. This can save you a lot of time. Imagine that you're working on a site that contains large movie files. Cloaking the folder that contains the movie files means that while you're working on other parts of the site, Dreamweaver won't take the time to scan through the folders when synchronizing, and won't upload any of the files. When you're ready to upload the files, uncloak the movies folder and synchronize the local and remote sites.

To cloak a site folder:

1. Right-click a file or folder in the Files panel.

2. From the resulting shortcut menu, choose the Cloaking submenu, then from the submenu, choose Cloak (**Figure 2.23**).

   In the Files panel, Dreamweaver displays the file or folder with a slash through it, indicating that it is cloaked.

✔ Tip

- You can cloak all files of a particular type. Choose Site > Manage Sites, then select the site you're working on. In the Advanced tab of the Site Definition dialog, choose the Cloaking category. Enable the "Cloak files ending with" check box, then enter the file extensions of the kinds of files you want to cloak (**Figure 2.24**).

To uncloak a file or folder:

1. Right-click a cloaked file or folder in the Files panel.

2. From the resulting shortcut menu, choose Cloaking > Uncloak or Cloaking > Uncloak All.

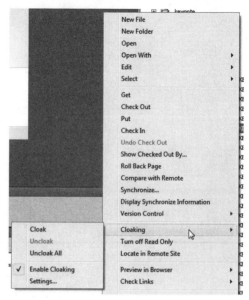

Figure 2.23 Choosing Cloak from the Files panel shortcut menu keeps a file or a folder and its contents from being affected during synchronization operations.

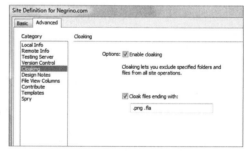

Figure 2.24 The Cloaking category in the Advanced tab of the Site Definition dialog allows you to set particular kinds of files to always be cloaked.

BUILDING YOUR FIRST PAGE

After you've set up your local site, you can begin filling the site with pages. To do that, you'll need to create a page, give it a title, add some content to the page, and save it. To check your work, you should view the page in one or more Web browsers before you upload it to your Web server. Luckily, Dreamweaver makes it easy to view your work in different browsers.

If you need a little inspiration, Dreamweaver offers a variety of sample pages that you can use as a jumping-off point for your own creative efforts. You can also choose from a variety of page designs created entirely with CSS.

In this chapter, we'll also briefly discuss how you add text, images, and links to your pages, although we go into those subjects in much greater detail in Chapters 4, 5, and 6, respectively.

Creating a New Page

The first HTML page that you create in a new site should be the *index page*, which is the page that a Web browser loads automatically when a visitor goes to the site. Depending on how you are naming pages on your site, the index page could have a variety of names, but it is most often named index.html. After you create the index page, you will want to create other pages for the site.

As is often the case with Dreamweaver, there is more than one way to do the task at hand. You can create a new page using the Welcome screen, or you can use the New Document dialog.

Using the Welcome screen

The Welcome screen is the fastest way to create a new HTML page. It appears when you have closed all other document windows.

To create a new page from the Welcome screen:

1. Close any open document windows.

   The Welcome screen appears (**Figure 3.1**). Each of the items in the Welcome screen is a link.

2. In the Create New section, click HTML.

   Dreamweaver creates the new blank HTML page (**Figure 3.2**).

Figure 3.1 Click the links in the Welcome screen to open a recent item, or create a new item.

✔ Tips

- You can also use the Welcome screen to open pages that you recently worked on. Just click the item's name in the Open a Recent Item section of the Welcome screen.

- Clicking ColdFusion or PHP in the Create New section of the Welcome screen also creates an HTML page. Clicking CSS creates a new CSS style sheet. Clicking any of the other choices creates documents designed for different Web programming languages that you would normally work with in Code view.

- If you don't want to use the Welcome screen at all, you can turn it off in Dreamweaver's Preferences. Choose Edit > Preferences (Dreamweaver > Preferences), and click the General category. Then clear the check box next to "Show Welcome screen."

Figure 3.2 A brand-new page in Dreamweaver, showing the Design view.

Using the New Document dialog

The New Document dialog gives you a bit more flexibility than the Welcome screen when creating new documents. Like the Welcome screen, you can create several different types of new documents, plus it allows you to choose the doctype of the new document.

To create a new page from the New Document dialog:

1. Choose File > New, or press Ctrl-N (Cmd-N).

   The New Document dialog appears (**Figure 3.3**), set to the Blank Page tab.

2. Click to choose one of the tabs in the leftmost column.

   The second column changes to show the available items for the tab you selected. The name of this column also changes to match the name of the tab.

3. Click the item you want in the second column.

   If Dreamweaver has a preview image of the item you selected available, it appears in the Preview pane (previews are mostly available for sample pages and templates), with its description below the preview area.

4. (Optional) Some of the kinds of documents you can create in this dialog allow you to declare their doctype, and for those the DocType pop-up menu will be available. Most of the time the default choice is fine, but if you want you can change the doctype from the pop-up menu (**Figure 3.4**).

5. Click Create.

   Dreamweaver creates the new document and displays it in a new window.

Figure 3.3 You'll probably create most of your new pages from the New Document dialog.

Figure 3.4 You can choose from the available doctypes in the New Document dialog.

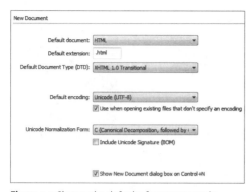

Figure 3.5 Change the defaults for new pages in the New Document category of Dreamweaver's Preferences dialog.

✔ Tips

- If you want to change any of the defaults for a new document, click the Preferences button in the New Document dialog. In the resulting dialog (**Figure 3.5**), you can change the default document type for the New Document dialog; the extension used for that document; the default document type (DTD); and the default character encoding. You can also choose whether or not you want the New Document dialog to appear when you press Ctrl-N (Cmd-N), or if you just want Dreamweaver to create a new default document.

- We'll cover the Blank Template and Page from Template tabs of the New Document dialog in Chapter 15.

Behind the Doctype

If you're not familiar with doctype, it's a declaration at the start of an HTML page that specifies the DTD (Document Type Definition) that is in use for the file. Web browsers use the doctype declaration to determine how the page should be rendered.

By default, Dreamweaver inserts the "XHTML 1.0 Transitional" doctype, and the code it creates is consistent with that standard.

Using Sample Pages

Dreamweaver has many sample pages available, which do some of the work of creating new pages for you. The sample pages are often good jumping-off points for your own pages. After you create a document from one of the sample pages, you can customize and modify it as you wish.

The sample pages come in two categories:

◆ **CSS Style Sheet** chooses external CSS style sheet documents that contain style definitions with a wide variety of looks for your pages. You can click any of the sample style sheets to see a preview and description (**Figure 3.6**).

◆ **Frameset** has 15 premade frameset pages with different frame layouts (**Figure 3.7**). This makes creating framesets considerably easier than doing it by hand.

To create a page from a sample page:

1. Choose File > New, or press Ctrl-N (Cmd-N). The New Document dialog appears.

2. Click the Page from Sample tab in the leftmost column.

   The second column changes to show the available items for the tab you selected. The name of this column also changes to Sample Folder.

3. Click the item you want in the second column.

   The preview image of the item you selected appears in the Preview pane (previews are mostly available for sample pages and templates), with its description below the preview.

4. Click Create.

   Dreamweaver creates the page in a new window.

5. Modify the sample page as you like.

Figure 3.6 Dreamweaver provides many starter CSS Style Sheets, which you can preview in the New Document dialog.

Figure 3.7 You can preview and choose from the predefined framesets.

What Happened to the Starter Pages?

In previous versions of Dreamweaver (8 and CS3), the program included themed *starter pages*, which gave you dozens of prebuilt pages you could use to create whole sites. There were several categories of sites, such as Entertainment, Travel, Spa, and more. Each site type came with a home page and interior pages, all sharing the same basic design. These were useful for quick prototyping of sites, though you would almost always want to use them as jumping-off points for your own page designs. These starter pages have been eliminated in Dreamweaver CS4.

The reason is simple: the starter pages may have been handy, but they were all originally built using tables for layout, and their underlying code was, in the words of one Adobe employee, "scary." Rather than invest developer resources into updating the sample pages into proper CSS layouts, Adobe decided to drop them altogether.

If you're looking for rapid prototyping of sites, one possibility is to download or purchase one of the many available free or inexpensive Dreamweaver templates; a quick Google search for "Dreamweaver templates" will turn up a large selection. When you find one that you like, make sure that its layout is CSS-based, not table-based. It makes no sense to use templates that won't be easy to maintain in the future.

A more robust alternative is WebAssist's (www.webassist.com) SiteAssist Professional, a wizard-based Dreamweaver extension that steps you through the process of creating the layouts, choosing the navigation menu structure, and building the pages for your site (**Figure 3.8**). SiteAssist lets you choose from a wide variety of CSS-based page and navigation bar styles, and it lets you change your mind and redo the site at any time, without losing any custom elements you may have specified. It's a very good tool for designers who need a technical assist.

Figure 3.8 SiteAssist Professional's wizard steps you through choosing a layout and color design for your site.

Titling Your Page

The first thing you should do with your new page is to add a *title*. The title is the text that appears in the title bar of Web browser windows, at the top of the window (**Figure 3.9**). You'll enter this text in the Dreamweaver document window.

To add a title to your page:

1. If necessary, open the page you want to title.

2. Click in the Title field at the top of the page's document window.

3. Type in the title (**Figure 3.10**).

✔ Tip

■ Don't forget to add the title; it's easy to forget, and when you do forget, it makes it harder for people to find your pages using a search engine. As we wrote this, a quick Google search for "Untitled Document" in the title of pages brought up more than a million hits. Don't be one of them!

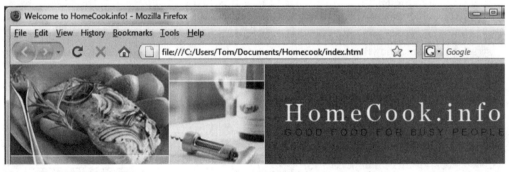

Figure 3.9 The title of an HTML document appears at the top of a Web browser's window.

Figure 3.10 Enter the title in, well, the Title field.

Figure 3.11 Use the Text category of the Insert panel to format your text using HTML markup.

Adding Text to Your Page

In this section, we'll cover adding a bit of text to your page, just enough to get you started. You'll find a much more detailed discussion of working with text in Dreamweaver in Chapter 4. In short, adding text is a lot like typing text in any word processor.

To add text to a page:

1. On the new page, click to set a blinking insertion point. You can press Enter (Return) to move the insertion point down on the page.

2. Type your text.

   The text appears on the page, aligned to the left.

To format the text:

1. In the Insert panel, choose the Text category from the pop-up menu.

   The Text category of the Insert panel appears (**Figure 3.11**).

2. Using the Insert panel and the HTML tab of the Property Inspector, apply any formatting you want, as you would with a word processor.

   See Chapter 4 for much more detail about using the Text category of the Insert panel.

✔ Tip

- This formatting would, of course add HTML markup to you page. You'll probably instead want to use CSS formatting for text. See Chapters 7 and 9 for more information.

Creating Links

To add a hyperlink to a page, you need to select the text you want to turn into a link, then provide the URL for the link. A URL (Uniform Resource Locator) is the Web address that you would type into the Address bar of a Web browser.

You will find much more information about adding links to your pages in Chapter 6. You'll see how to add links to either text or graphics and lots of other linky goodness.

To add a link to a page:

1. Select the text you want to turn into a link (**Figure 3.12**).

In this example, I want to turn the "HomeCook.info" text at the top of the page into a link to the home page of the site, so I've selected that text.

2. Do one of the following:

If you are linking to a page in your site, click the Point to File button in the Property Inspector (**Figure 3.13**), then drag to a file in the Files panel (**Figure 3.14**). When you release the mouse button, the file name appears in the Link field.

or

Figure 3.12 Begin creating a link by selecting the text that you want to turn into the link.

Figure 3.13 Click the Point to File button to begin the linking process...

Link field
Browse for File button
Point to File button

CREATING LINKS

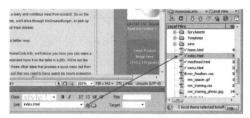

Figure 3.14 ...then drag to point at the file you want to link to in the Files panel. As you drag, Dreamweaver follows your mouse pointer with an arrow to make it clear which file you're pointing at.

Figure 3.15 You can also create a link by clicking the Browse for File button in the Property Inspector, which brings up a Select File dialog.

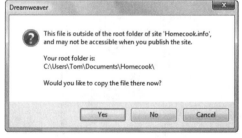

Figure 3.16 If the file you are selecting is outside your local root folder, Dreamweaver offers to copy the file to that folder as part of the linking process.

If you are linking to a file on your hard drive (inside or outside of your local site folder), click the Browse for File button in the Property Inspector. The Select File dialog appears (**Figure 3.15**). Navigate to the file you want to link to, select it, then click OK (Choose). The file name appears in the Link field. If the file is outside of the local root folder, Dreamweaver lets you know and offers to copy the file into the local root folder (**Figure 3.16**).

or

If you are linking to a Web address, click in the Link field in the Property Inspector and type the full URL of the link destination. You must include the http:// portion of the address.

✔ Tips

- You can also copy a URL from the Address bar of a Web browser (or anywhere else) and paste the URL into the Link field.

- You aren't limited to Web links, which begin with http://, of course; you can put any valid URL in the Link field, including links for FTP, email addresses, and more. Again, see Chapter 6 for more information.

*links to Public
Server folder
WEFTEC
AWWA
conferences
attending
links to references
emails*

Adding Images

Much of the visual interest in Web pages is provided by images, and Dreamweaver makes it easy to add images to your pages. For much more information about adding images, sound, or movie files to your pages, see Chapter 5.

To add an image to your page:

1. In your document, click where you want the image to appear.

2. In the Common category of the Insert panel, click the Images button (**Figure 3.17**).

   The Select Image Source dialog appears (**Figure 3.18**).

Figure 3.17 To add an image to your page, click the Images: Image button in the Common category of the Insert panel.

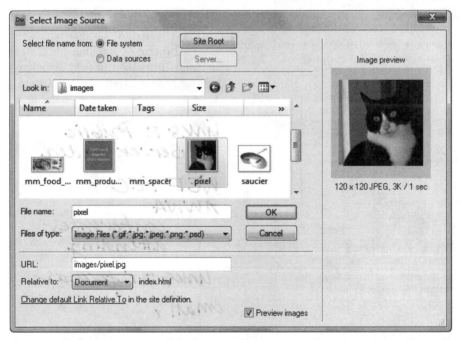

Figure 3.18 The Select Image Source dialog lets you pick an image, and shows you a preview of it as well.

Figure 3.19 Use this dialog to enter the alternate text for an image.

Figure 3.20 The image appears on the page at the insertion point.

3. Navigate to the image file you want, and select it.

Dreamweaver shows you a preview of the image in the Select Image Source dialog.

4. Click OK (Choose).

If the image is not inside the /images directory of your local root folder, Dreamweaver copies the image to that location. Dreamweaver next displays the Image Tag Accessibility Attributes dialog (**Figure 3.19**).

5. (Optional, but strongly recommended) Enter the Alternate text for the image.

Alternate text is text attached to the image for use by screen readers for the visually impaired, or for people who are browsing with images turned off.

6. Click OK.

The image appears in your document (**Figure 3.20**).

✔ Tips

- The Long description field in the Image Tag Accessibility Attributes dialog links to a file that can contain a full description of the image. This option is not often used.

- If you don't want to add alternate text, you can turn the prompt dialog off in the Accessibility category of Dreamweaver's Preferences. But you shouldn't; this is a key attribute to add for the benefit of visually disabled visitors to your site.

ADDING IMAGES

71

Naming and Saving Your Page

After you've built your page, you'll want to name it and save it in your local site folder. After you work on the page, you'll need to save your changes. You should get in the habit of saving often; there's nothing more annoying than lost work due to a power failure or because your computer decides to lock up.

It's important to understand the difference between a page's *title* and its *name*. The *title* appears at the top of the page in a Web browser; the *name* is the file's name, and will be part of the Web address, or URL, of the page. For example, "Welcome to HomeCook. info!" is the page's title, but `index.html` is the page's name.

To save your page for the first time:

1. Choose File > Save, or press Ctrl-S (Cmd-S).

   The Save As dialog appears (**Figure 3.21**).

2. Enter the name for the page.

   Dreamweaver gives the page a default name of Untitled-*x*, where *x* is the number of pages you've created since you launched Dreamweaver. On Windows, the dialog shows the name in the "File name" field without showing the extension; on the Mac, the name appears with the extension, but only the name is selected, ready for replacement with whatever you type (**Figure 3.22**).

   Not all characters are acceptable in a file name; be sure to read the "What's in a Name?" sidebar.

Figure 3.21 Use the Save As dialog to place your new document where you want it inside your local root folder, and also to give it a file name.

Figure 3.22 The Mac version of the Save As dialog shows you the document's extension, and selects the name for you.

3. You should save the file inside your local site folder. If you want the file to be in a particular folder inside your site, navigate to that folder.

4. Click Save.

To save changes you make in your pages:

◆ Choose File > Save, or press Ctrl-S (Cmd-S).

What's in a Name?

Your computer may allow you to enter characters in a file name that aren't acceptable in a URL. For example, on the Mac, it's perfectly okay to use the slash (/) in a file name. But you can't use a slash in a URL (Web servers can't handle a slash in a file name), so you *shouldn't* include slashes. Similarly, you can use spaces in file names on both Windows and Mac, but you cannot have spaces in a URL, so don't use spaces in your file names. Other characters to avoid include #, $, &, and %. We recommend that for safety's sake, you use only letters, numbers, and the underscore character (to substitute for a space). Remember that some people may want to manually type a URL from your site into a browser, so make things easy for them by using relatively short file names. Using all lowercase makes it easier for visitors, too.

Opening a Page

Opening a page is straightforward; you'll usually want to use Dreamweaver's Files panel. You can also use the File menu or the Welcome screen if you like.

To open a page:

1. In the Files panel (**Figure 3.23**), find the page you want to open, and double-click it.

    The page opens.

    or

    Choose File > Open, or press Ctrl-O (Cmd-O).

    The Open dialog appears.

2. Navigate to the file, select it, and click Open.

    The file opens in a new window (or in a new tab, if you already have open windows).

✔ Tips

■ If you want to open a page that you worked on recently, find the page in the Open a Recent Item category in the Welcome screen, and click it.

■ Click the Site Root button in the Open or Save As dialog to jump quickly to the site's root folder.

Figure 3.23 Use the Files panel to find a page and open it.

Figure 3.24 You can see the difference in rendering the same page in different browsers here. Note that Internet Explorer 7 for Windows (top) fails to display the text in the column under the clouds (the text does appear, but incorrectly positioned below the bottom of the window), while Mozilla Firefox (middle) and Safari on the Mac (bottom) have no problem displaying the page.

Previewing in a Browser

The page preview you see in Dreamweaver's Design view is useful, but it's no substitute for previewing your pages in real Web browsers. The reason is simple: the Design view shows one rendering of the HTML page, but Web browsers, which may be based on different rendering software (often called "rendering engines"), may show the same page differently. For example, you'll often see pages that look different in Internet Explorer for Windows, Mozilla Firefox, and Safari on the Mac. That's because each of those browsers uses a different rendering engine, and they each lay out and draw pages differently (**Figure 3.24**). Even the preview you get in Live View isn't the same as the most common Windows browsers.

By default, Dreamweaver makes your computer's default Web browser the default browser for previewing pages, but you can change that if you prefer.

continues on next page

To preview a page in a Web browser:

1. Save your page.

Dreamweaver requires that the page be saved before it can create a preview. If you forget, you'll be asked with a dialog if you want to save. If you click No in this dialog, the preview that appears will be of the last saved version of the page, not necessarily the latest version, so get used to saving before previewing.

2. Press F12 (Opt-F12).

The page opens in the default preview browser.

or

Choose File > Preview in Browser, then choose a browser from the submenu (**Figure 3.25**).

The page opens in the browser you selected.

or

Click the Preview/Debug in Browser button on the Document toolbar (**Figure 3.26**). A pop-up menu appears with the browser choices available on your system.

✔ Tips

- If you're using a Mac laptop, you must press Fn-Opt-F12.

- Depending on which version of Mac OS X you're running, F12 may be assigned by the system to either Exposé or Dashboard. On the Mac, Dreamweaver requires that you use Opt-F12 for the primary browser, and Cmd-F12 for the secondary browser. If you have any Exposé or Dashboard features that use these keys, you can change them to different keys in the Dashboard and Exposé panel of System Preferences.

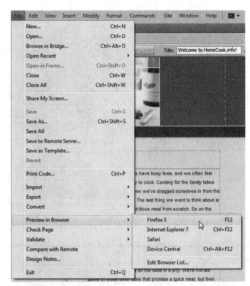

Figure 3.25 Choose the browser you want to use for the preview from the Preview in Browser submenu.

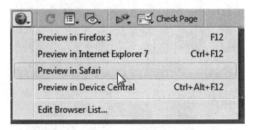

Figure 3.26 You can also choose your preview browser from the Preview/Debug in Browser button on the Document toolbar.

To set the browsers that appear in the Browser list:

1. Choose File > Preview in Browser, then choose Edit Browser List from the submenu.

   The Preview in Browser category of Preferences appears (**Figure 3.27**).

2. Do one or more of the following:

   ▲ To add a browser to the list, click the + button, then fill out the information in the resulting Add Browser dialog.

   ▲ To remove a browser from the list, select the browser and click the – button.

▲ To set a browser as the primary preview browser (this will cause it to open when you press F12 (Opt-F12)), select it and click the Primary browser check box.

▲ To set a browser as the secondary preview browser (this will cause it to open when you press Ctrl-F12 (Cmd-F12)), select it and click the Secondary browser check box.

3. Click OK to close the Preferences dialog.

Figure 3.27 You can choose which browsers on your system appear in the Preview in Browser list, and also set browsers as your primary and secondary preview browsers.

PREVIEWING IN A BROWSER

Setting Page Properties

Information that is contained in the <head> tag concerns the entire page. These *page properties* include information about the appearance of the page, how links should be displayed, the font settings for headings, and the *encoding* to be used, which is the character set a browser should use to render the page.

For example, Dreamweaver defaults to the Unicode (UTF-8) encoding, which can safely represent all characters. Dreamweaver and Web browsers both use the encoding to load the appropriate character set for the page. If you set the encoding to, say, one of the Chinese encodings, Dreamweaver and the Web browser will load the appropriate Chinese character set.

Dreamweaver defines CSS rules for properties that you specify in the Appearance (CSS), Links (CSS), and Headings (CSS) categories of Page Properties. These rules are placed in the <head> section of the page.

To set page properties:

1. Choose Modify > Page Properties, or choose Ctrl-J (Cmd-J).

    The Page Properties dialog opens (**Figure 3.28**).

2. Click the category you want.

    See the following sections for details on each of the categories and their options.

3. Set the options as you like.

4. Click Apply to see the changes on the open document without closing the Page Properties dialog.

    or

    Click OK to save your changes.

Figure 3.28 Use the Appearance (CSS) category of the Page Properties dialog to set the page font and size, text and background colors, background images, and margins using CSS styles.

✔ Tip

■ Note that the available encodings are different on Windows and Mac. This is not a problem for English, but if you will be working in languages other than English, you should make sure that you use an encoding for that language that will work well across platforms, and test your site using browsers on Windows and Mac.

Appearance (CSS)

The Appearance (CSS) category of the Page Properties dialog (Figure 3.28) has the following options that apply CSS styles:

◆ **Page font** specifies the default font family your Web pages will use. Dreamweaver uses the font family you specify unless the font is overridden by a CSS style sheet. You can also set the font to be bold or italic.

◆ **Size** sets the default font size. Dreamweaver uses this font size unless the size is overridden by a CSS style sheet. You can choose an absolute size (such as 9, 10, 12, and so forth) or relative sizes (such as small, medium, large, x-large, and so on). Choosing an absolute size allows you to pick any of the measurement units (pixels, points, in, cm, mm, picas, ems, exs, and %).

◆ **Text color** lets you set the default color for text. Click the color well to bring up a color picker to help you set the color.

◆ **Background color** lets you set the default color for the page background. Click the color well to bring up a color picker to help you set the color.

◆ **Background image** allows you to set an image that will appear behind all the text and images on the page. Click the Browse button to bring up the Select Image Source dialog, navigate to the image, then click OK (Choose). If you set a background image, it overrides the background color.

◆ **Repeat** sets how the background image will be displayed if it doesn't fill the whole page. You can choose repeat to tile the image horizontally and vertically; repeat-x to tile the image horizontally; repeat-y to tile the image vertically; or no-repeat to display the image only once.

◆ **Margins** allows you to set the Left, Right, Top, and Bottom margins of the page. You can use any of the measurement systems as units, as you can with text size.

SETTING PAGE PROPERTIES

Appearance (HTML)

The Appearance (HTML) category of the Page Properties dialog (**Figure 3.29**) has the following options, implemented as HTML markup:

Figure 3.29 The Appearance (HTML) category applies properties to your page using HTML markup.

◆ **Background image** allows you to set an image that will appear behind all the text and images on the page. Click the Browse button to bring up the Select Image Source dialog, navigate to the image, then click OK (Choose). If you set a background image, it overrides the background color.

◆ **Background color** lets you set the default color for the page background. Click the color well to bring up a color picker to help you set the color.

◆ **Text** lets you set the default color for text. Click the color well to bring up a color picker to help you set the color.

◆ **Links** sets the color to apply to link text. Click the color well to bring up a color picker to help you set the color.

◆ **Visited links** sets the color to apply to visited link text. Click the color well to bring up a color picker to help you set the color.

◆ **Active links** sets the color to apply to link text when you click the text. Click the color well to bring up a color picker to help you set the color.

◆ **Margins** allows you to set the Left, Right, Top, and Bottom margins of the page. You can use any of the measurement systems as units.

Figure 3.30 You can control many aspects of how links display with the Page Properties dialog, applied by setting link properties through CSS.

Links (CSS)

You find the following options in the Links category—unsurprisingly all affecting how links are displayed (**Figure 3.30**):

◆ **Link font** specifies the default font family your Web pages use to display links. Dreamweaver uses the font family you specify unless the font is overridden by a CSS style sheet. You can also set the font to be bold or italic.

◆ **Size** sets the default font size for link text. Dreamweaver uses this font size unless the size is overridden by a CSS style sheet. You can choose an absolute size or a relative size. Choosing an absolute size allows you to pick any of the measurement units (pixels, points, in, cm, mm, picas, ems, exs, and %).

◆ **Link color** sets the color to apply to link text. Click the color well to bring up a color picker to help you set the color.

◆ **Visited links** sets the color to apply to visited link text. Click the color well to bring up a color picker to help you set the color.

◆ **Rollover links** sets the color to apply to link text when you place the mouse cursor over the text. Click the color well to bring up a color picker to help you set the color.

◆ **Active links** sets the color to apply to link text when you click the text. Click the color well to bring up a color picker to help you set the color.

◆ **Underline style** sets the way links are underlined. Your choices are Always underline, Never underline, Show underline only on rollover, and Hide underline on rollover.

✔ Tip

■ If your page already has an underline style defined through an external CSS style sheet, the Underline style pop-up menu displays Don't change. You can actually change it; the option is there to tell you that there is already a style defined. If you change the underline style in Page Properties, it overrides the previous underline style definition.

Headings (CSS)

The Headings category (**Figure 3.31**) has the following options for headings:

◆ **Heading font** specifies the default font family used for headings. Dreamweaver uses the font family you specify unless the font is overridden by a CSS style sheet. You can also set the font to be bold or italic.

◆ **Heading 1** through **Heading 6** allows you to set size and color options for each heading size. The size pop-up menus allow you to set absolute sizes (sized with numbers, such as 9, 12, 18, and so on) or relative sizes (such as small, medium, or large), and for absolute sizes, you can choose from any of the available measurement units. Click the color well to bring up a color picker to help you set the heading color.

✔ Tip

■ You'll get more control over the text if you use a CSS style sheet to redefine a Heading style. See Chapter 7 for more information about redefining HTML styles.

Figure 3.31 You can set the default font, size, and color for headings in the Headings (CSS) category.

Figure 3.32 Set the title, document type, and encoding for the page in this dialog.

Title/Encoding

The Title/Encoding category allows you to change the title and some of the more arcane items in a Web page (**Figure 3.32**):

◆ **Title** allows you to change the page title. It's equivalent to the Title field at the top of a document window.

◆ **Document Type (DTD)** allows you to change the doctype of the page. When you make a change here, Dreamweaver changes the page's code (if necessary) to make it compliant with the selected DTD.

◆ **Encoding** sets the encoding used for the page.

◆ **Unicode Normalization Form** and **Include Unicode Signature (BOM)** are only enabled when you use Unicode UTF-8 as the encoding. Choose Help > Dreamweaver to learn more.

✔ Tip

■ If you keep the default Unicode (UTF-8) encoding, you should also make sure that from the Unicode Normalization Form pop-up menu you choose C (Canonical Decomposition, followed by Canonical Composition). The exact meaning of this is mostly of interest to true character set geeks. What you need to know is that the C setting is the one used for Web pages.

Tracing Image

Some people prefer to design their pages in a graphics tool such as Adobe Photoshop or Adobe Fireworks. They can then export that image and bring it into Dreamweaver as a background image. It isn't a background image for the page; rather, it is a guide that you can use as a reference to re-create the same look in Dreamweaver. This guide is called a *tracing image*. The tracing image only appears in Dreamweaver; it doesn't show up when you preview the page in a browser.

The tracing image category only has two options (**Figure 3.33**):

◆ **Tracing image** has a Browse button that, when clicked, brings up the Select Image Source dialog. Navigate to the image, then click OK (Choose).

◆ **Transparency** is a slider that controls the opacity of the tracing image. You can set the image from zero to 100% opacity.

Figure 3.33 A tracing image can be a useful guide for re-creating page designs created in a graphics program.

Defining Meta Tags

Information about the page is contained in a kind of HTML tag called a *meta tag*. Meta tags can include a variety of the page's summary information, including keywords to help search engines index the page, a text description of the page, and links to external documents, such as a style sheet.

When you insert meta information, it appears within the document's <head> tag, inside a <meta> tag:

```
<meta name="keywords" content=
"HomeCook.info, food, wine, cooking,
home cooking, homecook, dining">
```

You can set six categories of meta tags:

◆ **Meta** is a general category that allows you to add any information you want. You must give it a name and specify the content.

◆ **Keywords** adds one or more words to the document for use by search engines to aid them in indexing the page.

◆ **Description** adds a text description of the site, again for use by search engines.

◆ **Refresh** reloads the current document after a specified interval of seconds, or redirects the document to another URL.

◆ **Base** sets the base URL for the page. All of the document-relative paths in the page are considered relative to the base URL. For more information about document-relative links, see Chapter 6.

◆ **Link** adds a link to an external document. It's used most often to define the location for an external CSS style sheet.

DEFINING META TAGS

To add a meta tag:

1. Choose Insert > HTML > Head Tags, then choose the tag you want from the sub-menu (**Figure 3.34**).

   Depending on the kind of tag you chose, the appropriate dialog appears. For example, if you choose Keywords, the Keywords dialog appears (**Figure 3.35**). In this dialog, you need to enter the page's keywords, separated by commas.

2. Fill out the dialog, then click OK.

✔ Tip

■ Don't go overboard with your Keywords or Description. Search engines have long since figured out that lots of keywords or a very long description are attempts to artificially improve search engine rankings, and sites with excessive keywords or descriptions will be screened *out* of search results.

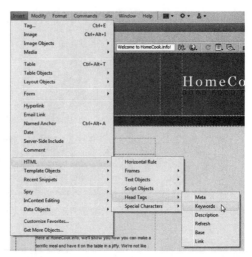

Figure 3.34 Dreamweaver allows you to set many meta tags for your document.

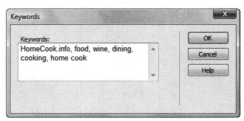

Figure 3.35 Separate Keywords with commas; Dreamweaver turns these keywords into a meta tag for you.

Adding Text To Your Pages

The main message of most Web sites is conveyed by the site's text, and a major part of your job in working with any site will be adding, modifying, and styling that text. Dreamweaver gives you the tools you need to effectively put text on your pages and get your message across.

When you add text, you need to deal with two different aspects of the text: its *structure* and its *presentation*. Structural elements are things like paragraphs, headings, lists, and the like; presentation is how the text looks, including things like the font, font size, text color, and so on. Most sites these days separate the structure and the presentation. Structure is about organizing the content on the page, and presentation is concerned with making the content look good.

In this chapter, we'll concentrate on getting text onto your page and applying structure using headings and lists. We'll also cover using basic HTML text styles to change the look of your text. You'll learn how to more precisely style text and present it using Cascading Style Sheets in Chapter 7.

Adding Text

Most of the text on a Web page is formatted in *blocks*, which are enclosed by beginning and ending HTML tags. For example, the HTML for a line of text with paragraph tags wrapped around it looks like this:

```
<p>This text is wrapped in beginning and
ending paragraph tags.</p>
```

In order for a browser to understand that this is a paragraph, you (or in this case, Dreamweaver) have to make it one by adding the surrounding <p> tags.

Of course, in Dreamweaver's Design view, you won't see the HTML tags. All of the text contained between the opening <p> tag and the closing </p> tag is considered by a Web browser to be within the same paragraph, no matter how much text is between the tags. The <p>...</p> combination is an example of a *container tag*. Virtually all of the structural formatting that you can apply with Dreamweaver is done with container tags.

When you add text to a page with Dreamweaver, the program automatically wraps the text with paragraph tags when you press the Enter (Return) key on your keyboard. You can see this if you switch to Code view, by clicking the Code button at the top of the Dreamweaver editing window, as shown in **Figure 4.1**.

Dreamweaver also has special commands that help you import entire Microsoft Word or Excel documents as Web pages. (See "Using Paste Special," later in this chapter, and Chapter 16 for more information.)

To insert text:

1. In Dreamweaver's Design view, click in the page where you want to add text.

2. Type the text you want.

Figure 4.1 Dreamweaver adds paragraph tags around text when you press the Enter (Return) key.

Selecting Text

Besides selecting text by dragging over it with the mouse cursor, Dreamweaver also gives you some text selection shortcuts in Design view:

◆ Double-click a word to select it.

◆ Move your cursor to the left of a line of text until the cursor changes from an I-beam to an arrow pointing at the text. Then click once to highlight a single line, or drag up or down to select multiple lines.

◆ Triple-click anywhere in a paragraph to select the entire paragraph.

◆ For finer control over selecting individual letters, hold down the Shift key and press the left or right arrow keys to extend the selection one letter at a time.

◆ Ctrl-Shift (Cmd-Shift) plus the left or right arrow key extends the selection one word at a time. Ctrl (Cmd) plus the left or right arrow key moves the cursor one word to the left or right, but doesn't select any text.

◆ Press Ctrl-A (Cmd-A) to Select All (the entire contents of the current document).

Cutting, Copying, and Pasting Text

Just like a word processor, you can cut, copy, and paste text on a page in Dreamweaver, which shares the same menu commands with virtually all standard Windows and Mac word processors and text editors. When pasting text in Design view from one part of a Dreamweaver page to another or between Dreamweaver pages, text formatting is automatically maintained.

Dreamweaver also allows you to paste text and maintain some or all of the text's formatting. This is especially useful when moving text from applications such as Microsoft Word or Excel to a Web page. See "Using Paste Special," later in this chapter.

To cut or copy text:

1. Select the text you want to cut or copy.

2. To cut the text to the Clipboard, choose Edit > Cut, or press Ctrl-X (Cmd-X) on the keyboard.

or

To copy the text to the Clipboard, choose Edit > Copy, or press Ctrl-C (Cmd-C) on the keyboard.

The text is placed on the Clipboard.

✔ Tip

■ When you have text selected, most of the time you can right-click to cut or copy the text using a shortcut menu. You can also right-click to paste text from the shortcut menu. If you have a single button mouse on the Mac, you can Ctrl-click to bring up the shortcut menu.

CUTTING, COPYING, AND PASTING TEXT

To paste plain text:

1. Click to place the insertion point on the page where you want the text to appear.

2. Choose Edit > Paste, or press Ctrl-V (Cmd-V) on the keyboard.

✔ Tips

■ If you copy some HTML source code from another program, such as the Source view of a Web browser, and paste it into a Dreamweaver page in Design view, the HTML appears on the page, with tags and all. That's because while what you've pasted in is HTML markup, Dreamweaver is trying to be smarter than you—it's assuming that markup is what you want to display. If that's not what you want, but rather you want the result of the markup to display in your page, just switch to Code view in Dreamweaver before you paste. The HTML code will paste into the page, and when you switch back to Design view, it will display the proper formatting.

■ Dreamweaver offers Undo and Redo commands in the Edit menu, which can often be very useful for fixing mistakes or repeating operations. You can also use the keyboard shortcuts Ctrl-Z (Cmd-Z) for Undo and Ctrl-Y (Cmd-Y) for Redo.

Figure 4.2 Begin dragging and dropping text by selecting it.

Figure 4.3 When you release the mouse button, the text moves to where you dragged it.

Dragging and Dropping Text

If all you want to do is move some text from one place on a page to another, it's often faster to drag and drop the text.

To drag and drop text:

1. Select the text you want to move (**Figure 4.2**).

2. Move the cursor over the selected text. The cursor changes from an I-beam to an arrow.

3. Click and hold your mouse button over the selected text, and drag it to its new location, releasing the mouse button when the cursor is where you want the text (**Figure 4.3**).

   The text moves to its new home.

✔ Tip

- To duplicate the text, hold down the Ctrl (Option) key while dragging and dropping. A copy of the text appears when you release the mouse button.

Using Paste Special

Dreamweaver's Paste Special command in the Edit menu gives you a variety of options that control the way formatted content is pasted into Dreamweaver's Design view.

You will probably use the Paste Special command most often when pasting in text from Microsoft Word or Excel, in order to maintain the formatting that the text had in those programs (**Figure 4.4**). Text pasted in from Excel can appear in Dreamweaver as a formatted table which saves you a lot of time and effort.

The Paste Special options are:

◆ **Text only** pastes just the text; paragraph marks and all formatting are stripped from the text (**Figure 4.5**).

◆ **Text with structure** pastes the text and maintains the structure (notably paragraphs, tabs, and lists), but eliminates other text formatting (**Figure 4.6**).

◆ **Text with structure plus basic formatting** keeps the text and text structure and retains bold and italic formatting (**Figure 4.7**).

◆ **Text with structure plus full formatting** preserves the text, structure, and styles from the original document (**Figure 4.8**).

Figure 4.4 Paste Special will do a great job of maintaining the formatting from this Microsoft Word document.

Figure 4.5 This is the "Text only" version of the text from Figure 4.4, with paragraph marks and formatting stripped out.

Figure 4.6 With the "Text with structure" option, the text and paragraph marks are there, but there's no character formatting.

Figure 4.7 The "Text with structure plus basic formatting" option maintains bold and italic formatting.

Figure 4.8 The final option, "Text with structure plus full formatting," maintains all the formatting from the Word document.

Figure 4.9 Choose the option that you want from the Paste Special dialog.

To use Paste Special:

1. Select the text you want to cut or copy.

   The text will usually be in a different application than Dreamweaver.

2. Cut or copy the text.

3. Switch to Dreamweaver, and click to set the insertion point where you want the text to appear.

4. Choose Edit > Paste Special, or press Ctrl-Shift-V (Cmd-Shift-V).

   The Paste Special dialog appears (**Figure 4.9**).

5. In the dialog, click the radio button next to the paste option you want.

6. Click OK.

   The text pastes in according to the option you selected.

✔ Tips

- If you use the "Text with structure plus basic formatting" or "Text with structure plus full formatting" choices, you can also paste graphics into Dreamweaver along with the formatted text.

- You can copy and paste graphics from most applications into Dreamweaver, but if you want to paste a graphic along with formatted text, you must use Paste Special.

Applying Headings

After paragraphs, headings are the most important structural element on most Web pages. Headings point your site's visitors to essential information on the page, and they separate sections of the page. Think of headings as being similar to headlines in a newspaper.

Text you enter into Dreamweaver begins with no heading; Dreamweaver refers to this text as None in the Property Inspector. As soon as you press Enter (Return), Dreamweaver wraps the text in paragraph tags, and the text becomes paragraph text.

HTML has six sizes of headings, plus paragraph text, as shown in **Figure 4.10**. These headings don't have a fixed point size, unlike headings in say, Microsoft Word or Adobe InDesign. Instead, they are sized relative to one another and the size of the paragraph text, and the size that the user sees depends on the settings in the user's Web browser. By default, headings are usually displayed in boldface.

You can change the look of headings (their size, font, color, and so forth) using CSS, which we'll cover in Chapter 7.

✔ Tips

- You can only have one size of HTML heading in a particular element. You can work around this limitation with CSS styles.

- Headings are also important because they help search engines find and index content on your pages. Google in particular uses headings in this fashion, so it's a good idea to use headings when they are appropriate to your content.

h1	It doesn't get more important than this.
h2	This is perhaps a bit less important.
h3	This is middling priority.
h4	We'll let you know when you need to pay attention.
h5	Check this out if you really want to.
h6	Hey! Wake up!
paragraph	This is the everyday text that you'll see in most paragraphs.

Figure 4.10 Here are examples of the six Heading sizes, plus Paragraph, which is usually used for body text.

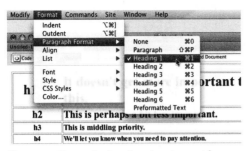

Figure 4.11 Choose the heading size you want from the Paragraph Format submenu.

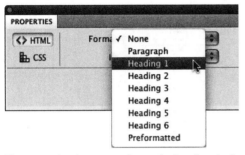

Figure 4.12 Another way to choose the heading size is to use the Format pop-up menu in the HTML mode of the Property Inspector.

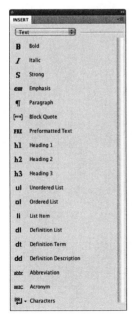

Figure 4.13 The Text category of the Insert panel gives you buttons with many options, including ways to apply three heading sizes.

To apply a heading:

1. Click in the line you want to change.

   Note that you don't have to select text; a heading is a block style, so it affects the entire paragraph the cursor is in.

2. Choose Format > Paragraph Format > Heading x, where x is the heading size you want (**Figure 4.11**).

   or

   Press Ctrl-1 for Heading 1, Ctrl-2 for Heading 2, and so on. On the Mac, press Cmd-1 for Heading 1, Cmd-2 for Heading 2, and so on.

   or

   Choose a heading from the Format pop-up menu in the HTML mode of the Property Inspector (**Figure 4.12**).

   or

   Click one of the heading buttons in the Text category of the Insert panel (**Figure 4.13**).

   There are only buttons for Heading 1, Heading 2, and Heading 3, listed as h1, h2, and h3, respectively.

   The text changes to the heading you selected.

To turn text into paragraph text:

1. Click in the line you want to change.

2. Choose Format > Paragraph Format > Paragraph.

    or

    Choose Paragraph from the Format pop-up menu in the HTML mode of the Property Inspector.

    or

    Press Ctrl-Shift-P (Cmd-Shift-P).

    Dreamweaver changes the text into a paragraph.

To remove heading formatting:

1. Click in the line you want to change.

2. Choose Format > Paragraph Format > None.

    or

    Press Ctrl-0 (Cmd-0). (Those are zeros, not the letter "O".)

    The Format menu of the Property Inspector changes to None, indicating that the text has no heading or paragraph style assigned to it.

APPLYING HEADINGS

Applying Character Formats

Character formatting is styling that you can apply to words and individual characters, rather than to blocks such as paragraphs. This formatting includes changing the font, font size, and font color.

Beginning several versions ago, and continuing through Dreamweaver CS4, the program dispensed with the old method of applying these sorts of character formatting (which was to use the HTML <font> tag), in favor of using CSS styles. This change happened mostly behind the scenes in Code view, so if you have been using Dreamweaver for quite some time, you may not have even noticed the change. Dreamweaver CS4 takes another step towards enforcing the use of CSS for text styling, by requiring you to participate in defining CSS rules for changing fonts, font sizes, and font color.

The reason for the change to CSS is important. Pages styled with CSS are much more flexible than pages that use HTML <font> tags, and they can be maintained more easily. For example, when a site is redesigned, every page that uses <font> tags must be individually changed to match the new design. If you have hundreds or thousands of pages in your site, that's a lot of work. Sites that use CSS to style text only need to change the stylesheet document, and the changes automatically ripple through the whole site. You'll learn more about using CSS to style text (especially setting font properties) in Chapter 7. Some other formatting operations are still performed using HTML markup, and those are the ones we'll explore in this chapter.

Applying HTML Text Styles

The most common text formatting is to make text bold or italicized, and of course Dreamweaver can do that, with either HTML markup or a CSS rule. But it can also apply several other text styles, some of which are for specialized uses, as shown in **Figure 4.14** and **Table 4.1**.

Many of these text styles are meant for displaying programming or script code, so they won't be used at all on many sites. Others, such as Underline and Strikethrough, are deprecated in the HTML 4.01 standard, which means that they are obsolete and may not work in future browsers. Instead, you should use a CSS property. See "Dreamweaver CSS Categories" in Chapter 7.

Bold style	*Variable style*
Italic style	`Sample style`
Underlined style	`Keyboard style`
~~Strikethrough style~~	*Citation style*
Emphasis style	Definition style
Strong style	~~Deleted style~~
`Code style`	Inserted style

Figure 4.14 Dreamweaver offers a number of useful (and not so useful) HTML text styles.

Table 4.1

Text Styles

STYLE	DESCRIPTION
Bold	Makes text boldface.
Italic	Italicizes text.
Underline	Underlines text.
Strikethrough	Text is shown with a line through it.
Teletype	Reminiscent of an old typewriter. Usually shows text in a monospaced font such as Courier.
Emphasis	Italicizes text on screen. Causes screen readers to stress importance in speech.
Strong	Bolds text on screen. Causes screen readers to add additional importance to speech.
Code	Depicts programming code, usually in a monospaced font.
Variable	Marks variables in programming code. Usually displayed as italics.
Sample	Meant to display sample output from a computer program or script. Usually displayed in a monospaced font.
Keyboard	Meant to depict text a user would type on the keyboard. Usually displayed in a monospaced font.
Citation	Used to mark citations and references. Usually displayed as italics.
Definition	Used to mark the first, defining usage of a term in a document. Usually displayed as italics (Safari on the Mac displays this as regular text).
Deleted	Marks deleted text. Shown the same as strikethrough.
Inserted	Marks inserted text. Shown the same as underlined.

To apply an HTML text style:

1. Select the text you want to change.

2. Choose Format > Style, then choose the style you want from the submenu.
   The text's appearance changes.

✔ Tip

■ Actually, by default Dreamweaver does not use the traditional <b> and <i> HTML tags for bold and italic, respectively. Instead it uses <strong> and <em> (for emphasis). The latter tags are preferred as part of best practices, because they are better handled by screen readers used by visually impaired users. If you want to switch Dreamweaver back to using <b> and <i>, choose Edit > Preferences (Dreamweaver > Preferences), and in the General category of the Preferences dialog, deselect "Use <strong> and <em> in place of <b> and <i>."

Using Preformatted Text

Browsers usually ignore invisible formatting that doesn't affect page content, such as tabs, extra spaces, extra line feeds, and the like. If you need to display text exactly as entered, however, you can use the Preformatted paragraph format, which wraps the text in the <pre>...</pre> tags and makes browsers display all of the text characters.

Originally, preformatted text was meant to display tabular data in rows and columns, such as the output of a spreadsheet. In order to make the information line up, browsers display preformatted text in a monospaced font such as Courier (**Figure 4.15**).

Planet	Orbital period (years)	Day (days)	Moons
Mercury	0.241	58.6	none
Venus	0.615	-243	none
Earth	1.00	1.00	1
Mars	1.88	1.03	2
Jupiter	11.86	0.414	63
Saturn	29.46	0.426	49
Uranus	84.01	0.718	27
Neptune	164.79	0.671	13
Pluto	248.5	6.5	1

Figure 4.15 Preformatted text lines up neatly, as with this table.

To apply preformatting:

1. Select the text you want to change.

2. From the Format pop-up menu of the HTML mode of the Property Inspector, choose Preformatted.

   or

   In the Text category of the Insert panel, click the Preformatted Text button (**Figure 4.16**).

   or

   Choose Format > Paragraph Format > Preformatted Text.

   The text changes appearance.

✔ Tip

■ If you want to display tabular data, it often makes more sense to use a table, rather than preformatted text. You get much more control over the table style and spacing of the items in the table, and you can add CSS to style the table's contents if needed. See Chapter 10 for information about using tables.

Figure 4.16 Apply the style with the Preformatted Text button.

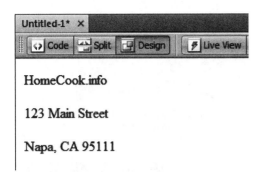

Figure 4.17 Paragraphs have whitespace before and after them, which isn't really appropriate for things like addresses.

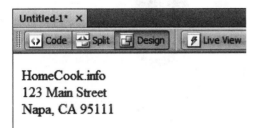

Figure 4.18 After you replace the paragraph tags with line breaks, the address looks better.

HomeCook.info
123 Main Street
Napa, CA 95111

Figure 4.19 With the appropriate preference enabled, you can see the invisible line break characters.

Adding Line Breaks

Just as in a word processor, you press Enter (Return) in Dreamweaver to create a new paragraph. This is fine when you want to actually create a new paragraph, but not so great when you just want to move the cursor down a line, as you might want to do when entering an address. That's because Web browsers (and Dreamweaver) insert a blank line above and below a paragraph, so if you make each line of the address its own paragraph, it looks goofy (**Figure 4.17**).

What you want to do is add a *line break*, which moves the cursor down one line without creating a new paragraph. In the code, Dreamweaver adds the HTML <br /> tag to the end of the line.

To insert a line break:

◆ At the end of the line you want to break, press Shift-Enter (Shift-Return).

or

At the end of the line you want to break, in the Text category of the Insert panel, select Line Break from the Special Characters pop-up menu.

The text changes (**Figure 4.18**).

✔ Tip

■ Line breaks are invisible characters in both Dreamweaver and Web browsers, but you can make them visible in Dreamweaver if you want. Choose Edit > Preferences (Dreamweaver > Preferences), then click the Invisible Elements category. Click the check box next to "Line breaks," then click OK. Dreamweaver then displays line breaks in Design view (**Figure 4.19**).

Indenting Text

You won't indent text in Dreamweaver as you would with a word processor. The most common kind of indenting, indenting the first line in a paragraph, is usually done with a tab in a word processor, but tabs have no effect in HTML. Instead, you can use the `text-indent` CSS style property. See Chapter 7 for more about using CSS.

You can add whitespace to text—and simulate a tab—with non-breaking spaces. See "Inserting Special Characters," later in this chapter.

When you are indenting paragraphs to set them apart from preceding and following paragraphs, Dreamweaver uses the HTML `<blockquote>` tag. This indents both the left and right margins of the block quoted paragraph. You aren't limited to paragraphs; you can block quote any block element, such as headings.

To block quote text:

1. Click in the paragraph or other block element you want to indent.

2. Click the Indent button on the HTML mode of the Property Inspector (**Figure 4.20**).

   or

   In the Text category of the Insert panel, click the Block Quote button.

   or

   Choose Format > Indent or press Ctrl-Alt-] (Cmd-Opt-]).

   The text changes (**Figure 4.21**).

Indent ——— *Outdent*

Figure 4.20 Use the Indent button to apply a block quote to your text.

Shakespeare's Sonnets

Sonnet 18

Perhaps the most famous of all the Bard's sonnets, this is justifiably a favorite amongst poets and lovers.

> Shall I compare thee to a summer's day?
> Thou art more lovely and more temperate:
> Rough winds do shake the darling buds of May,
> And summer's lease hath all too short a date:
> Sometime too hot the eye of heaven shines,
> And often is his gold complexion dimmed,
> And every fair from fair sometime declines,
> By chance, or nature's changing course untrimmed:
> But thy eternal summer shall not fade,
> Nor lose possession of that fair thou ow'st,
> Nor shall death brag thou wander'st in his shade,
> When in eternal lines to time thou grow'st,
> So long as men can breathe, or eyes can see,
> So long lives this, and this gives life to thee.

Let's go through that sonnet line by line, and add commentary that explains and modernizes the language Shakespeare used.

Figure 4.21 The block quote nicely sets off the sonnet from the commentary text.

✔ Tips

- To add more indenting, click the Indent button on the Property Inspector again. This nests the `<blockquote>` tags.

- The CSS `margin` style property is a much more flexible way to indent block elements. See Chapter 7.

To remove block quoting:

1. Click in the paragraph or other block element you want to indent.

2. Click the Outdent button on the Property Inspector.

    or

    Choose Format > Outdent or press Ctrl-Alt-[(Cmd-Opt-[).

    The text changes.

Aligning Text (HTML Method)

Dreamweaver can align text with the left margin, right margin, or center of the page. You can also justify text, which adds space as needed between words so that both the left and right margins are aligned.

The method shown here adds alignment attributes to the HTML markup. You can also use Cascading Style Sheets to align text. See Chapters 7 and 8.

To align text with HTML:

1. Click inside the paragraph you want to align.

2. Choose Format > Align > Left, Center, Right, or Justify (**Figure 4.22**).

   or

   Use one of the keyboard shortcuts listed in **Table 4.2**.

✔ Tip

■ Longtime Dreamweaver users may be thrown a bit by the removal of the alignment buttons from the HTML mode of the Property Inspector. Those buttons have been moved to the CSS mode of the Property Inspector, and Dreamweaver will enforce creating and naming a new style rule if you use the alignment buttons. The program will also alert you if you enter a name for the style rule that is the same as the HTML alignment attributes (left, center, right, or justify). Use different names to prevent possible confusion.

Figure 4.22 Choose a text alignment from the Format menu.

Table 4.2

Alignment Shortcut Keys		
SHORTCUT KEY (WINDOWS)	SHORTCUT KEY (MAC)	WHAT IT DOES
Ctrl-Alt-Shift-L	Cmd-Opt-Shift-L	Left alignment
Ctrl-Alt-Shift-C	Cmd-Opt-Shift-C	Center alignment
Ctrl-Alt-Shift-R	Cmd-Opt-Shift-R	Right alignment
Ctrl-Alt-Shift-J	Cmd-Opt-Shift-J	Full justification

Lucy Kaplansky Discography

1. The Tide (1994)
2. Flesh and Bone (1996)
3. Ten Year Night (1999)
4. Every Single Day (2001)
5. The Red Thread (2004)
6. Over the Hills (2007)

Lucy Kaplansky Discography

1. The Tide (1994)
2. Flesh and Bone (1996)
3. Cry Cry Cry (1998) w/Richard Shindell, Dar Williams
4. Ten Year Night (1999)
5. Every Single Day (2001)
6. The Red Thread (2004)
7. Over the Hills (2007)

Figure 4.23 Numbered lists automatically renumber if you insert a new item between two existing items.

Global Survival Kit

- Metal box
- Survival knife
- Compass
- Fire starter
- Water bag
- Water purification tablets
- Rescue whistle
- Fishing and foraging kit

Figure 4.24 Bulleted lists are single-spaced and indented.

Excerpts from *The Devil's Dictionary*, by Ambrose Bierce
Originally published 1911 (copyright expired)

CHILDHOOD , n.
  The period of human life intermediate between the idiocy of infancy and the folly of youth -- two removes from the sin of manhood and three from the remorse of age.
DAWN , n.
  The time when men of reason go to bed. Certain old men prefer to rise at about that time, taking a cold bath and a long walk with an empty stomach, and otherwise mortifying the flesh.
DELIBERATION , n.
  The act of examining one's bread to determine which side it is buttered on.
NONSENSE , n.
  The objections that are urged against this excellent dictionary.
SCRIBBLER , n.
  A professional writer whose views are antagonistic to one's own.

Figure 4.25 Definition lists have the definitions indented under the definition terms. The definition terms don't have to be all uppercase—they just happen to be in this figure.

Working with Lists

Lists are an easy way to organize content on your Web page. Dreamweaver supports three types of lists:

◆ **Numbered lists or Ordered lists,** for lists with items that need to be in a particular order (**Figure 4.23**). List items are numbered and indented from the left margin. If you add or remove items from the numbered list, it automatically renumbers.

◆ **Bulleted lists or Unordered,** for lists of items in no particular order (**Figure 4.24**).

◆ **Definition lists,** where each item has an indented subitem (**Figure 4.25**).

To create a list:

1. Type the items for your list into the window. After typing each item, press Enter (Return).

2. Select the items in the list.

3. Choose Format > List, then choose Unordered List, Ordered List, or Definition List from the submenu.

   or

   Click either the Unordered List or Ordered List button in the HTML mode of the Property Inspector.

   or

   Click one of three buttons in the Text category of the Insert panel: *ul* for Unordered List, *ol* for Ordered List, or *dl* for Definition List.

   The text changes to the kind of list you chose.

✔ Tips

■ At the end of your list, you can turn off the list function either by pressing Enter (Return) twice or by clicking the appropriate list button in the Property Inspector again.

■ There are three other buttons in the Text category of the Insert panel that you can use to apply list tags to text. The *li* button marks text as a *list item;* the text must be within a bulleted or numbered list. The other two buttons are used for definition lists. The *dt* button marks text as a *definition term,* and the *dd* button marks text as a *definition description.*

■ Because the Text category of the Insert panel was originally designed to help you work in Code view, some of the list buttons will cause the Dreamweaver window to change to Split view, so you can see the code and design panes at the same time. If you want to avoid code altogether, use the Property Inspector or the menu bar to format your lists.

Table 4.3

List-Numbering Options	
LIST NAME	EXAMPLE
Number	1, 2, 3, 4 …
Roman Small	i, ii, iii, iv …
Roman Large	I, II, III, IV …
Alphabet Small	a, b, c, d …
Alphabet Large	A, B, C, D …

Figure 4.26 In the List Properties dialog, you can change the way lists are numbered and bulleted.

Setting List Properties

You can change numbered list and bulleted list properties in Dreamweaver. Choose between five types of numbering, as shown in **Table 4.3**. For bulleted lists, you can choose either a round bullet (the default) or a square bullet. There are no properties to set for a definition list.

To set list properties:

1. Click in the list you want to change to place the insertion point.

2. Choose Format > List > Properties.

   The List Properties dialog appears (**Figure 4.26**).

3. Do one or more of the following:

   ▲ In the List type pop-up menu, select Bulleted List, Numbered List, or Directory List ("definition list" is called "Directory List" in this dialog for some reason).

   ▲ In the Style pop-up menu, select one of the Bulleted List or Numbered List styles.

   ▲ Use the Start count text box to set the value for the first item in the numbered list.

4. Click OK.

✔ Tip

■ You may notice that there is a fourth choice in the List type pop-up menu, called Menu List. That choice creates an unusual type of list that is based on the <menu> tag. That tag was deprecated (that is, recommended that it not be used) when HTML 4.01 was standardized in 1999. We suggest that you avoid the use of the Menu List option.

SETTING LIST PROPERTIES

Nesting Lists

You can indent lists within lists to create *nested lists*. Because nested lists do not have to be of the same type, you can create, for example, a numbered list with an indented bulleted list, and you can have multiple levels of nested lists within one overall list (**Figure 4.27**).

To create a nested list:

1. Click the end of a line within an existing list to place the insertion point.

2. Press Enter (Return).

   Dreamweaver creates another line of the list.

3. Press Tab.

   Dreamweaver creates a new indented sublist of the same type as the parent list. For example, if the parent list is a numbered list, the new sublist will also be a numbered list.

4. (Optional) If you want the sublist to be a different type of list than the parent list, click the Numbered List or Bulleted List button in the HTML mode of the Property Inspector.

5. Type the list item.

6. Press Enter (Return).

   Dreamweaver creates a new sublist item.

7. To return to the original list, use the up or down arrow keys to move the insertion point into one of the items in the original list, or click to place the insertion point where you want it.

Desktop Macs

1. Mac mini
   - 1.83 GHz with Combo Drive
   - 2.0 GHz with SuperDrive
2. iMac (all with SuperDrive)
   - 20 inch, 2.4 GHz
   - 20 inch, 2.66 GHz
   - 24 inch, 2.8 GHz
   - 24 inch, 3.06 GHz
3. Mac Pro
   - One 2.8 GHz Quad-Core Intel Xeon
   - Two 2.8 GHz Quad-Core Intel Xeon
   - Two 3.0 GHz Quad-Core Intel Xeon
   - Two 3.2 GHz Quad-Core Intel Xeon

Figure 4.27 You can nest bulleted lists inside numbered lists.

✔ Tips

- You can also click the Outdent button in the HTML mode of the Property Inspector to merge the sublist back into the main list.

- Use the List Properties dialog to format sublists as well as lists.

- If you try to create a sublist within a list that is in a table by pressing Tab, Dreamweaver jumps to the next cell, rather than indenting and creating a nested list. One workaround is to create the nested list outside of the table, cut it, then paste it in the table cell where you want it to go.

Figure 4.28 Insert unusual characters from the Special Characters pop-up menu in the Text category of the Insert panel.

Figure 4.29 The Insert Other Character dialog provides the rest of the special characters Dreamweaver can insert.

Inserting Special Characters

You can add special characters, such as the Euro, copyright, or trademark symbol, to your page in Dreamweaver without having to remember their bizarre HTML equivalents or odd keyboard combinations. In Dreamweaver, relief is just a menu choice away.

To insert a special character:

1. Click in the page to place the insertion point where you want the special character to appear.

2. In the Text category of the Insert panel, choose the character you want from the Special Characters pop-up menu (**Figure 4.28**).

   or

   Choose Insert > HTML > Special Characters, then choose the special character you want from the submenu.

   or

   If the character you want doesn't appear in the menu, choose Other Characters from the pop-up menu in the Insert panel, or choose Other from the Insert > HTML > Special Characters submenu. The Insert Other Character dialog appears (**Figure 4.29**).

3. Click the character you want to use, then click OK to close the dialog.

   Dreamweaver inserts the special character on your page.

About Non-Breaking Spaces

An oddity about HTML is that it ignores multiple spaces. One of the special characters you can insert is the *non-breaking space*, which is useful for adding multiple consecutive spaces, and occasionally for nudging text and even images. Dreamweaver uses the HTML code for a non-breaking space (which is) between paragraph tags so that blank lines appear in Web browsers, like so:

```
<p> </p>
```

If you want multiple spaces between words, insert one or more non-breaking spaces. The easiest way to do this is to press Ctrl-Shift-Space (Cmd-Shift-Space), but you can also use the Special Characters pop-up menu in the Text category of the Insert panel or the Insert > HTML > Special Characters submenu.

Dreamweaver by default ignores multiple spaces, but you can change this behavior and force the program to insert multiple non-breaking spaces in the code. Choose Edit > Preferences (Dreamweaver > Preferences), choose the General category, and then select the check box next to "Allow multiple consecutive spaces."

Figure 4.30 Dreamweaver lets you insert dates into your pages in a variety of formats.

Adding Automatic Dates

Dreamweaver can insert the current date and time in a variety of formats into your Web page. You can choose whether or not to add the day of the week.

To insert the current date:

1. Click in your page to place the insertion point where you want the date to appear.

2. Choose Insert > Date.

   The Insert Date dialog appears (**Figure 4.30**).

3. Do one or more of the following:

   ▲ If you want the name of the day to appear, use the Day format pop-up menu to set the appearance of the day of the week.

   ▲ Make a selection from the Date format list.

   ▲ If you want the time to appear, choose the 12-hour or 24-hour format from the Time format list.

   ▲ Select Update automatically on save, if you want that to happen. This is very useful if you want visitors to your site to know when the page was last updated.

4. Click OK.

   Dreamweaver inserts the date (and any additional items you chose) into your page.

ADDING AUTOMATIC DATES

Adding Horizontal Rules

A *horizontal rule* is a line that runs across the page, creating a division between parts of the document (**Figure 4.31**). By default, a horizontal rule in Dreamweaver is the width of the page, is 1 pixel high, and has a small drop shadow. You can change these properties if you want.

To insert a horizontal rule:

1. Click in the page to place the insertion point where you want the horizontal rule to appear.

2. Choose Insert > HTML > Horizontal Rule.

A line appears as wide as the page.

To modify a horizontal rule's properties:

1. Click the horizontal rule to select it.

The Property Inspector changes to show the Horizontal Rule properties (**Figure 4.32**).

2. Do one or more of the following:

▲ Type a number in the W (for Width) field, and choose either pixels or % from the pop-up menu. Choosing pixels creates a fixed-width line; choosing % creates a line that expands or contracts depending on the width of the site visitor's browser window.

▲ In the H (for Height) text box, type a number for the horizontal rule. This height is measured in pixels.

▲ From the Align pop-up menu, choose Default, Left, Center, or Right. The Left and Right choices are only going to be useful if the width of the horizontal rule is less than the width of the page.

▲ The Class pop-up menu allows you to apply a CSS style to the horizontal rule.

▲ If you select the Shading check box, the line appears as an outline.

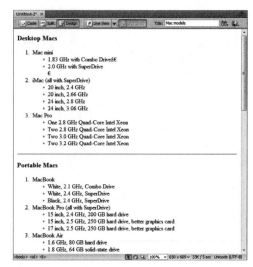

Figure 4.31 This horizontal rule separates two sections of the page.

Figure 4.32 You can change the width and height of a horizontal rule in the Property Inspector.

✔ Tip

■ Horizontal rules are a leftover from the early days of HTML. Use them sparingly, if at all, because they tend to make a page look dated. Instead, use CSS styles to add vertical white space or borders between sections of your document.

Finding and Replacing

Dreamweaver's Find and Replace feature can save you a lot of time, because you can automatically find and change text on a single page, in pages within a folder, on pages you select, or throughout your site. You can choose to change text in Design view, or search and change just in Code view.

Imagine that you have a company's site with dozens of pages devoted to singing the praises of their premier product, the amazing WonderWidget. Then one day you get a call from your client letting you know that because of a trademark dispute, they have to rename the product WonderThing. Rather than opening each page and making one or more changes on each of them, just put Dreamweaver's Find and Replace feature to work, and you'll be done in just a few minutes.

The Find and Replace window

The Find and Replace window, which you open by choosing Edit > Find and Replace, or by pressing Ctrl-F (Cmd-F), will be the tool you use for changing text, as shown in **Figure 4.33**. Let's look at some of the parts of this window.

◆ The **Find in** pop-up menu allows you to tell Dreamweaver the scope of the search. You can choose to find text in the Current Document (the default); Selected Text; Open Documents; in a Folder you select; in Selected Files in Site; or in the Entire Current Local Site.

◆ The **Search** pop-up menu lets you choose what kind of search you want to do. You can choose Text; Text (Advanced), which gives you additional search options; Source Code, which allows you to search in the HTML; or Specific Tag, which searches the contents of HTML tags that you select. The latter two options are covered later in this chapter.

◆ The **Find** field is where you enter the text you wish to find.

◆ The **Replace** field is where you enter the text you want to use to replace the found word.

◆ The **Save Query** button allows you to save searches for later use. This is great for instances where you create complex queries, so you don't have to do all the work to set up the search again.

◆ The **Load Query** button allows you to retrieve a saved search.

◆ The **Search options** let you constrain your searches. "Match case" returns results with the same uppercase and lowercase letters as the text you entered in the Find field. "Match whole word" only finds the text if it matches one or more complete words. "Ignore whitespace" tells Dreamweaver not to pay attention to additional spaces, tabs, and non-breaking spaces. It's on by default, and it's usually best to leave it on. Finally, "Use regular expression" (covered later in this chapter) lets you use wildcard characters to construct extremely complex searches.

Figure 4.33 The Find and Replace dialog provides a lot of power for making quick changes on a single page, or throughout your site.

Cancel currently running search

Reopen Find and Replace with same search items

SEARCH	REFERENCE	VALIDATION	BROWSER COMPATIBILITY	LINK
File			Matched Text	
chap1-1.html			Chapter 1: Getting Acqua	
chap1-1.html			What JavaScript Is	
chap1-1.html			What JavaScript Is	
chap1-1.html			See it run: What JavaScri	
chap1-1.html			...<body bgcolor="#FFFF	
chap1-1.html			...<h1> <script language	
chap10-1.html			Chapter 10: JavaScript ar	
chap10-1.html			...cookie based on a form	

Done. 1753 items found in 1104 documents.

Figure 4.34 The Search tab of the Results panel shows you the file name and matched text when you click the Find All button.

Finding Text with a Simple Search

Simple searches work pretty much the same way that they do in a word processor. Just enter the text you want to find and the text that you want to replace it with, and away you go. Of course, you don't have to replace text; if you want you can just use the Find and Replace dialog to find text in one or more files.

To find text:

1. Choose Edit > Find and Replace, or press Ctrl-F (Cmd-F).

   The Find and Replace dialog appears (Figure 4.33).

2. From the Find in pop-up menu, choose one of the options for the scope of your search.

3. From the Search pop-up menu, choose Text.

4. In the Find field, type the word or phrase that you're looking for.

5. Click the Find Next button.

   Dreamweaver finds and highlights the found text. If the scope of the search included more than one page, Dreamweaver opens the first file the text was found within, and highlights the text. If the text isn't found, you'll get a message to that effect at the bottom of the Find and Replace dialog.

   or

   Click the Find All button.

   Dreamweaver does the search, closes the Find and Replace dialog, and opens the Search tab of the Results panel (**Figure 4.34**).

   continues on next page

FINDING TEXT WITH A SIMPLE SEARCH

6. If you clicked Find All in step 5, double-click one of the search results in the Results panel to open it and highlight the found text.

✔ Tips

- If you select some text before you bring up the Find and Replace dialog, the text automatically appears in the Find field, as long as you selected fewer than 255 characters.

- You can do a quick find on the current page by selecting some text and choosing Edit > Find Selection, or by pressing Shift-F3 (Cmd-Shift-G). Dreamweaver highlights the next occurrence of the text you selected.

- You can click the green triangle button in the Results panel to reopen the Find and Replace dialog with the same search terms.

- If you have a search that's running for a very long time, you can cancel it by clicking the octagonal red Cancel button in the Results panel.

- You can clear the search results in the Results panel by right-clicking in the panel and choosing Clear Results from the resulting shortcut menu.

To find the next result:

◆ Choose Edit > Find Next, or press F3 (Cmd-G).

Dreamweaver finds and highlights the next result of the search, without reopening the Find and Replace dialog.

To find and replace text:

1. Choose Edit > Find and Replace, or press Ctrl-F (Cmd-F).

The Find and Replace dialog appears.

2. From the Find in pop-up menu, choose one of the options for the scope of your search.

3. From the Search pop-up menu, choose Text.

4. In the Find field, type the word or phrase that you're looking for.

5. In the Replace field, type the replacement word or phrase.

6. Click the Find Next button.

When Dreamweaver finds the text, it is highlighted.

7. Click the Replace button.

Dreamweaver replaces the found text with the contents of the Replace field.

or

Click Replace All.

Dreamweaver warns you that you cannot undo changes made in unopened files. Of course, you can undo changes in any open documents by choosing Edit > Undo. If you still want to make the changes, click Yes.

Dreamweaver searches through the entire scope of the search, replacing all occurrences of the found text. When it is done, you'll see a message telling you how many changes it made.

✔ Tips

■ Use a Replace operation to expand abbreviations and save time while you're creating pages. For example, let's say that you're creating a Web site about JavaScript. Rather than typing JavaScript again and again while writing the site, just type "JS," then before you upload the site, do a Find and Replace, changing every occurrence of "JS" to "JavaScript." You can do the same thing with company or people's names, or almost any text that you repeat a lot.

■ Dreamweaver does not update the Search tab of the Results panel when you perform Replace operations.

■ If you get a bunch of search results, but you only want to make replacements in some of those results, you can do that, and save a bunch of time in the process. Rather than opening each page separately and applying the replacement, do it all in one swoop by using the Results panel and the Find and Replace dialog together. First, click the green triangle in the Results panel, which reopens the Find and Replace dialog. In the Results panel, Ctrl-click (Cmd-click) the results where you want to make replacements. Those lines will highlight. Then switch back to the Find and Replace dialog, and click Replace (not Replace All). The files that are modified are marked by a green dot next to their names in the Results panel.

Tag pop-up menu —

Figure 4.35 The Text (Advanced) option allows you to search for text within HTML tags.

Performing Advanced Text Searches

An advanced text search allows you to do a more precise search by looking for text within (or outside of) particular HTML tags. You can further fine-tune the search by specifying particular attributes of the HTML tags.

Perhaps the most common example of why you would want to use such a search lies in the title of your Web pages. Whenever you create a new page in Dreamweaver, the page automatically gets the title "Untitled Document." If you forget to enter titles, you could end up with a bunch of pages on your site with the same "Untitled Document" name (it's easy to do: while writing this section, I found and fixed a page on my personal site that had been titled "Untitled Document" for four years!). A basic search and replace won't help, because "Untitled Document" is within the `<title>` tag of the pages, and a basic search only searches the body of a document. An advanced text search, which combines text and HTML searches, is the solution.

To perform an advanced text search:

1. Choose Edit > Find and Replace, or press Ctrl-F (Cmd-F).

    The Find and Replace dialog appears.

2. From the Find in pop-up menu, choose one of the options for the scope of your search.

3. From the Search pop-up menu, choose Text (Advanced).

    The dialog changes, and adds the option to search tags (**Figure 4.35**).

continues on next page

4. In the Find field, type the word or phrase that you're looking for.

5. Choose either Inside Tag or Not Inside Tag from the pop-up menu next to the + and - buttons.

Inside Tag refers to text that is enclosed within a container tag, such as <p>...</p>.

6. Choose an HTML tag from the Tag pop-up menu.

7. (Optional) If you want to narrow the search further by limiting the search to a particular attribute of the tag you chose in step 6, click the + button. If you do not, skip to step 12.

The attribute line is added to the dialog (**Figure 4.36**).

An example of an attribute would be the width attribute of the <table> tag.

8. (Optional) From the first pop-up menu in the attribute line, choose With Attribute or Without Attribute.

9. (Optional) Choose the attribute you want from the next pop-up menu.

Dreamweaver only shows the attributes for the tag you chose in step 6.

10. (Optional) Set a comparison in the next pop-up menu, choosing from = (equal), < (less than), > (greater than), or != (not equal). These only work if the attribute's value is a numeric amount, such as the size attribute of the <font> tag, i.e., <font size="4">.

Figure 4.36 You can narrow your search further by adding one or more attributes to the tag search.

11. (Optional) In the next field (which is also a pop-up menu), type the value of the attribute. This can be a number or text.

or

Choose [any value] from the pop-up menu. This is useful when you want all tags with a particular attribute, but you don't care what the value of the attribute is.

12. If you want to replace the found text, type the replacement word or phrase in the Replace field.

13. Depending on what you want to do, click Find Next, Find All, Replace, or Replace All.

✔ Tip

■ For more information about the different HTML tags and their attributes, choose Window > Results > Reference, then choose O'Reilly HTML Reference from the Book pop-up menu of the Reference tab of the Results panel.

Finding and Replacing in Source Code

Dreamweaver's ability to find and replace within the HTML source code is extremely powerful. You can look for text within particular tags, and you can even look within particular tags for specific attributes. You can also find text relative to other tags. For example, you can change specified text within a `<table>` tag, and leave everything else alone. If you like, you can even use Find and Replace to replace, delete, or change tags and attributes.

Searching and replacing inside source code is much like regular text searches, except that you'll be working in Code view. When you perform the search, Dreamweaver automatically changes to Code view, so you don't have to do it manually before you start the search.

To find and replace in source code:

1. Choose Edit > Find and Replace, or press Ctrl-F (Cmd-F).
   The Find and Replace dialog appears.

2. From the Find in pop-up menu, choose one of the options for the scope of your search.

3. From the Search pop-up menu, choose Source Code (**Figure 4.37**).

4. In the Find field, type the word or phrase that you're looking for.

5. In the Replace field, type the replacement word or phrase.

6. Depending on what you want to do, click Find Next, Find All, Replace, or Replace All.

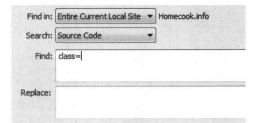

Figure 4.37 Choose Source Code to search the HTML in Code view.

Finding and Replacing with a Specific Tag

A specific tag search lets you find and modify HTML tags. This has many uses; for example, many people are now converting old sites that used <font> tags to CSS. You can use a specific tag search to strip out all those old tags. Or you can change the now-passé <b> and <i> tags to their more modern equivalents, <strong> and <em>.

The key to the specific tag search is the Action menu, which specifies what replacement action Dreamweaver will carry out on the tags found in the search. See **Table 4.4** for a list of the actions available.

Table 4.4

Action Menu Options	
ACTION	DESCRIPTION
Replace Tag & Contents	Replaces the tag and everything within the tag with the contents of the field that appears to the right of the Action pop-up menu when this action is selected. This can be either plain text or HTML.
Replace Contents Only	Replaces the contents of the tag with the contents of the With field.
Remove Tag & Comments	Deletes the tag and all of its contents.
Strip Tag	Removes the tag, but leaves any content within the tag.
Change Tag	Substitutes one tag for another.
Set Attribute	Changes an existing attribute to a new value, or adds a new attribute.
Remove Attribute	Removes an attribute from a tag.
Add Before Start Tag	Inserts text or HTML before the opening tag.
Add After End Tag	Inserts text or HTML after the closing tag.
Add After Start Tag	Inserts text or HTML after the opening tag.
Add Before End Tag	Inserts text or HTML before the closing tag.

To find and replace within a specific tag:

1. Choose Edit > Find and Replace, or press Ctrl-F (Cmd-F).

   The Find and Replace dialog appears.

2. From the Find in pop-up menu, choose one of the options for the scope of your search.

3. From the Search pop-up menu, choose Specific Tag.

   The Find and Replace dialog changes to show the tag functions (**Figure 4.38**).

4. Choose the tag that you want from the tag pop-up menu that appears next to the Search pop-up menu.

   You can either scroll the pop-up menu to find a tag, or you can type the first letter of the tag in the box. Dreamweaver automatically scrolls the list.

5. (Optional) If you want to narrow the search to a particular attribute of the tag that you selected, click the + button, then choose values for that attribute, as discussed previously in this chapter.

   If you want to narrow the search further, you can do so by clicking the + button and adding attributes.

6. Choose from the Action pop-up menu and, depending on the action you chose, set any required values.

7. Depending on what you want to do, click Find Next, Find All, Replace, or Replace All.

Figure 4.38 When you are searching within a specific tag, you can add attributes for that tag, and you can also specify actions that you want to perform on the found tag.

Table 4.5

Regular Expression Special Characters	
CHARACTER	MATCHES
\	Escape character; allows you to search for text containing one of the below special characters by preceding it with the backslash
^	Beginning of text or a line
$	End of text or a line
*	The preceding character zero or more times
+	The preceding character one or more times
?	The preceding character zero or one time
.	Any character except newline
\b	Word boundary (such as a space or carriage return)
\B	Non-word boundary
\d	Any digit 0 through 9 (same as [0-9])
\D	Any non-digit character
\f	Form feed
\n	Line feed
\r	Carriage return
\s	Any single white space character (same as [\f\n\r\t\v])
\S	Any single non-white space character
\t	Tab
\w	Any letter, number, or the underscore (same as [a-zA-Zo-9_])
\W	Any character other than a letter, number, or underscore
[abcde]	A character set that matches any one of the enclosed characters
[^abcde]	A complemented or negated character set; one that does not match any of the enclosed characters
[a-e]	A character set that matches any one in the range of enclosed characters
[\b]	The literal backspace character (different from \b)
{n}	Exactly *n* occurrences of the previous character
{n,}	At least *n* occurrences of the previous character
{n,m}	Between *n* and *m* occurrences of the previous character
()	A grouping, which is also stored for later use
x|y	Either x or y

Using Regular Expressions for Searching

A *regular expression* is a pattern, written using special symbols, which describes one or more text strings. You use regular expressions to match patterns of text, so that Dreamweaver can easily recognize and manipulate that text. Like an arithmetic expression, you create a regular expression by using *operators*, in this case operators that work on text, rather than numbers.

The operators in a regular expression (see **Table 4.5**) are like the wildcard symbols that you may have seen in find and replace features in other programs, such as word processors, except that regular expressions are much more powerful. They can also be complex and difficult to learn and understand, so if Dreamweaver's other finding and replacing methods are sufficient for you, you may not need to bother with regular expressions.

Learning regular expressions is beyond the scope of this book, but we'll show you how to use one in an example. Let's say that you want to find all of the HTML comments throughout your site. You can use this simple regular expression:

`<!--[\w\W]*?-->`

Let's break that expression down. You read a regular expression from left to right. This one begins by matching the beginning characters of the HTML comment, `<!--`. The square brackets indicate a range of characters; for example, [a-z] would match any character in the range from a to z. In this case, the range includes two regular expression operators: \w means "any single letter, number, or the underscore," and \W means "any character other than a letter, number, or underscore." Taken together as a range, [\w\W] means "any range of characters."

continues on next page

The * means "the preceding character (in this case, everything found by the contents of the square brackets) zero or more times" and the ? means "the preceding character zero or one time." Taken together, they match a comment of any length. The regular expression ends by matching the closing characters of an HTML comment, -->.

To search with a regular expression:

1. Choose Edit > Find and Replace, or press Ctrl-F (Cmd-F).

   The Find and Replace dialog appears.

2. From the Find in pop-up menu, choose one of the options for the scope of your search.

3. From the Search pop-up menu, choose any of the options.

   In this case, since we're looking for HTML comments, you should choose Source Code.

4. Enter the regular expression in the Find field (**Figure 4.39**).

5. Select the check box next to "Use regular expression."

   When you choose "Use regular expression," it disables the "Ignore whitespace" search option, because they are mutually exclusive.

6. (Optional) Enter text or a regular expression in the Replace field.

7. Depending on what you want to do, click Find Next, Find All, Replace, or Replace All.

Figure 4.39 You can add regular expressions to both the Find and Replace fields.

✔ Tip

■ There's a lot to say about regular expressions, certainly enough to fill an entire book or twelve. If you're interested in learning more, check out *Mastering Regular Expressions,* by Jeffrey Friedl (2006, O'Reilly & Associates). For a lighter read, try *Teach Yourself Regular Expressions in 10 Minutes* by Ben Forta (2004, Sams). There are also many Web sites that provide regular expression tutorials, which you can find with a Google search.

Figure 4.40 Click Add to Personal in the Check Spelling dialog to add an unknown word to Dreamweaver's personal dictionary.

Checking Spelling

No word processor comes without a spelling checker these days, and Dreamweaver is no different. You can check the spelling on the currently open page and add words to Dreamweaver's spelling checker in a personal dictionary.

To spell-check your page:

1. Choose Commands > Check Spelling, or press Shift-F7 (same on Windows and Mac).

   If Dreamweaver finds a word it believes is spelled incorrectly, the Check Spelling dialog opens (**Figure 4.40**). Otherwise, you'll get a dialog that says "Spelling check completed."

2. Click Add to Personal if the word Dreamweaver found is correct and you want to add it to your personal dictionary so that Dreamweaver doesn't flag it as an error again.

   or

   Click Ignore to tell the spelling checker to ignore this instance of the word, or Ignore All to ignore the word throughout the document.

   or

   Select a replacement from the Suggestions list, or type the replacement in the Change to text box. Then click the Change button, or click Change All to replace the word throughout the document.

3. When the spelling check is finished, click Close.

INCLUDING IMAGES AND MEDIA

5

Image and media files convey an important amount of the message of your Web site. Depending on your site, you may even get most of your message across with pictures and moving media, such as video and animation. Most sites, however, use images to supplement the text, which is the main source of information and interest to your site's visitors.

On the other hand, we've all seen Web sites that suffer from graphic overkill. There's a balancing act between sites that use graphics to enhance the message and those that use images to bludgeon the visitor into submission. Just think of all the sites that you've seen that use images of green text on a red background, for instance, or the sites that are so proud of their "fabulous" graphic look that they relegate the text to microscopic type.

Dreamweaver has many ways to place and modify images, as well as to control how text wraps around images. The program does a great job of adding dynamic media to your pages, such as Flash animations and movies, and also other formats such as QuickTime and Windows Media. In this chapter, we'll cover how you can use Dreamweaver to add graphics and media files to your Web pages. You'll get to use your talents to add images to express and enhance your site's message.

Adding Images

Dreamweaver can place images on your Web page that come from your local hard disk or that are already on your Web site. By default, Dreamweaver CS4 prompts you to add *alternate text* to the image, which is text that is read aloud by screen reader software used by the visually disabled. If you have existing images on your pages that don't have alternate text, it's easy to add. You can, of course, easily delete images from your page.

To add an image to your page:

1. Click to place the insertion point in the document where you want the image to appear.

2. In the Common category of the Insert panel, click the Images button (**Figure 5.1**).

   The Images button is actually a pop-up menu that allows you to add a variety of image types. We'll be talking about these different types later in this chapter.

   or

   Choose Insert > Image, or press Ctrl-Alt-I (Cmd-Opt-I).

   or

   Drag the icon of an image file from the Windows or Macintosh desktop into your document. If you choose this method, skip to Step 5.

   The Select Image Source dialog appears (**Figure 5.2**).

   By default, the dialog will be set to the images folder of your local site folder.

3. In the dialog, navigate to and select the file that you want to insert.

   A preview of the image appears in the Select Image Source dialog, with information below the image including the image's size in pixels, its graphic format, its file size, and the estimated time for the file to download (based on the

Figure 5.1 Begin inserting an image by clicking the Images button in the Insert panel.

Figure 5.2 Navigate to the image you want in the Select Image Source dialog.

Figure 5.3 Dreamweaver lets you know that it will use an absolute file reference, rather than a relative reference to the image file, until you save the document.

Figure 5.4 Enter alternate text for use by screen reader software used by the visually disabled.

Figure 5.5 The image appears in the document.

Figure 5.6 You can set Accessibility settings in Dreamweaver's Preferences dialog.

■ If you click Cancel in the Image Tag Accessibility Attributes dialog, the image appears on your page without alternate text. You can always add alternate text later using the Property Inspector.

Connection Speed pop-up menu in the Status Bar category of Dreamweaver's Preferences).

4. Click OK (Choose).

If you have not already saved the document, Dreamweaver displays an alert letting you know that it can't use a document-relative path, and that it will use an absolute file reference until you save the file (**Figure 5.3**).

5. Click OK to dismiss the alert.

The Image Tag Accessibility Attributes dialog appears (**Figure 5.4**). This is the dialog you use to add alternate text.

6. In the Alternate text text box, type the alternate text you want to use for the image.

7. (Optional) In the Long description text box, add a URL that leads to a page with a detailed description of the image.

8. Click OK.

The image appears on your page (**Figure 5.5**).

✔ Tips

■ In some browsers, an image's alternate text appears when you hover the mouse pointer over the image on the page.

■ The Image Tag Accessibility Attributes dialog only appears if the option for images has been set in the Accessibility category of the Preferences dialog (**Figure 5.6**). Because using alternate text is one of the commonly accepted Web best practices, the option is turned on by default. If you don't want Dreamweaver to prompt you for alternate text every time you insert an image, clear the Images check box in Preferences.

To add alternate text to an existing image on your page:

1. Click on an image to select it.

2. In the Alt text box in the Property Inspector (**Figure 5.7**), type the alternate text, then press Enter (Return).

   Dreamweaver adds the alternate text to the image.

To delete an image:

1. Click on an image to select it.

2. Press Backspace (Delete).

   The image disappears from the page.

✔ Tip

- You can cut, copy, or paste images as you would with text.

Figure 5.7 You can also add alternate text in the Alt field of the Property Inspector.

About Graphic Formats

There are three main still (as opposed to moving) image formats used on the Web: JPEG, GIF, and PNG. If you are not already familiar with these formats, here's a quick rundown, in the order in which they were originally developed:

◆ **GIF,** which stands for Graphics Interchange Format, is a lower-resolution graphics format with only eight bits of color information, which means that a GIF file can only contain up to 256 colors. GIFs are usually used for line drawings, flat cartoons, logos, and the like; in other words, images that don't need thousands or millions of colors (as would, for example, a photograph). There are two nice things about the GIF format. One is that it allows for *transparency*, which means you can set one or more colors in the GIF file to be the same as the background color of the page. This allows for irregularly shaped objects to appear on your page and for them to appear to be other than a rectangular image. The other useful feature of this format is the ability to add simple animation to images. A particular GIF file can contain multiple frames, and the file automatically steps through the frames to produce a rudimentary animation, like a flipbook.

◆ **JPEG,** which stands for Joint Photographic Experts Group, is a format that was developed specifically to handle photographic images. A JPEG file can use 24 bits of color information, which allows it to offer millions of colors. The JPEG format is "lossy," which means that it uses compression to reduce the file size. The look of the image depends on the amount of compression used to record it. High levels of compression will result in noticeable image degradation, because image information is actually being thrown away in order to reduce the file size. However, you can realize a significant reduction in file size at moderate levels of compression, with little or no visible effect, especially at the relatively low resolutions provided on Web pages. Unlike the GIF format, a JPEG file can contain neither transparency nor animation.

◆ **PNG,** or Portable Network Graphics, was created to replace the GIF format with an image format that didn't require a patent license to use (the owner of the GIF patent began enforcing the patent in 1995 and demanding royalty payments from software companies whose software created GIF files; those patents have since expired). PNG also improves upon GIF's 256-color limitation; a PNG file supports millions of colors and much better transparency options (but PNG does not offer animation). PNG files are usually smaller than the same file in GIF format, due to better compression. Adobe Fireworks uses PNG as its native file format, and of course Dreamweaver fully supports the PNG format. Some very old Web browsers (for example, Internet Explorer 3) don't support PNG graphics, but there are so few of these browsers still in use that you generally shouldn't worry about it.

Inserting Images from the Assets Panel

Any images that you've used on your site will be listed in the *Assets panel*, which is a tab in the same panel group as the Files panel. The Assets panel has buttons running down its left side that show you different asset categories (**Figure 5.8**). The first of these categories is Images. When you click the Images button in the panel, you get a list of all of the images in your site. Clicking an item in the list shows you a preview of the image in the Assets panel's preview pane, allowing you to easily browse through the images. You can browse any of the other asset categories in the same fashion.

To insert an image from the Assets panel:

1. Click in your document to set the insertion point where you want the image to appear.

2. If it's not already showing, click the tab for the Assets panel, or choose Window > Assets, or press F11 (Opt-F11).

3. Click the Site radio button at the top of the Assets panel.

   The images in your site appear in the asset list.

4. Click on the image you want to insert.

   A preview of the image appears in the Assets panel's preview pane.

5. Click the Insert button at the bottom of the Assets panel.

   or

   Drag the image from the asset list into the document.

   or

   Right-click the image you want in the asset list, then choose Insert from the resulting shortcut menu.

   The image appears in your document.

Figure 5.8 Choose the image that you want to work with in the Assets panel.

Figure 5.9 Use the Images pop-up menu in the Insert panel to insert an image placeholder.

Figure 5.10 Use the Image Placeholder dialog to specify the placeholder's parameters.

Adding Image Placeholders

When you first work on a page, you'll often be creating pages without all of the finished elements, such as the text and images. That shouldn't stop you from working on the page's design, of course. You can always copy and paste "The quick brown fox…" or similar text as a placeholder for the text that's to come, and Dreamweaver gives you the ability to insert image placeholders, as well. The placeholder lets you allot the space on the page for a future image, allowing you to position and size the placeholder and finish your design before you have all the content. When you are ready to turn the placeholder into the final image, all you have to do is double-click the placeholder.

To insert an image placeholder:

1. Click in your document to set the insertion point where you want the image placeholder to appear.

2. Choose Insert > Image Objects > Image Placeholder.

   or

   In the Common category of the Insert panel, choose Image Placeholder from the Images pop-up menu (**Figure 5.9**).

   The Image Placeholder dialog appears (**Figure 5.10**).

3. Fill out the Width and Height fields for the image placeholder (the units are pixels).

   The Name and Alternate text fields are optional; if you fill them out, the text will appear in the Property Inspector in the Name and Alt text boxes. You cannot use spaces in the Name field.

   continues on next page

The default color for an image placeholder is a light gray; if you want to change that color, click in the color well and choose a new color from the resulting color picker.

4. Click OK.

The new image placeholder appears in your document (**Figure 5.11**).

To replace the placeholder with an image:

1. Double-click the image placeholder.

The Select Image Source dialog appears (Figure 5.2).

2. Select the file that you want to insert.

3. Click OK (Choose).

The image appears on your page.

✔ Tip

■ If you are also responsible for creating the images on your site and you own Adobe Fireworks, when you select an image placeholder you'll see a button in the Property Inspector that has the Fireworks logo and the word Create (**Figure 5.12**). Clicking this button launches Fireworks and creates a new image with the same dimensions as the placeholder. After you finish making the image in Fireworks, save the image in your site's images folder. You are then returned to Dreamweaver. The new image is inserted automatically in your document, replacing the image placeholder.

Figure 5.11 The image placeholder appears in the document, with its name and size (these are cut off if the image isn't big enough, as shown here).

Figure 5.12 Click the Create button in the Property Inspector when an image placeholder is selected to launch Adobe Fireworks so that you can replace the placeholder with a finished graphic.

Figure 5.13 Clockwise from upper left, this shows the effects of the Default, Bottom, Middle, and Top vertical alignments.

Figure 5.14 The horizontal alignments are Left alignment (left) and Right alignment (right).

Image alignment pop-up menu

Figure 5.15 Align images with the image alignment settings in the Property Inspector.

- Make sure that you don't confuse the image alignment settings and the paragraph alignment settings (Left, Middle, and Right) that are in the CSS tab of the Property Inspector. The former apply to just images, and the latter apply to entire paragraphs.

Aligning Images

As with text, images can be aligned to the left, middle, or right side of a page. You also have some control over how text wraps around images.

Unless you've explicitly set up some way of laying out pictures and text (such as using CSS to position page elements, or using an invisible table), images appear *inline*, that is, in the flow of the text on the page. Because images are usually larger than the accompanying text, inline image settings can cause text to wrap in ways you might not expect.

There are four settings in the Property Inspector that you can use for vertical alignment: Default, Bottom, Middle, and Top (**Figure 5.13**). Two settings control horizontal alignment: Left and Right (**Figure 5.14**).

To set image alignment:

1. Click to select the image you want to align.

2. In the Property Inspector, choose the alignment option you want from the Align pop-up menu (**Figure 5.15**).
   The image aligns as you command.

✔ Tips

- The Property Inspector offers you four other alignment options: Baseline, TextTop, Absolute Middle, and Absolute Bottom. These are obsolete properties that don't work in all browsers. Don't use them.

- When you use the Property Inspector to align images, Dreamweaver applies an alignment property to the <img> tag. While that's acceptable, it's not an example of best practices; instead consider using CSS to align images, as described in Chapter 7.

Setting Image Properties

Besides alignment, there are several other properties that you can set for images using the Property Inspector (**Figure 5.16**):

◆ **ID** lets you name the image. This name is used to refer to the image in scripts, and you must enter a name for scripts to be able to manipulate the image, as you might want to do for a rollover. You cannot use spaces or punctuation in an image name.

◆ **W** (for Width) is the width of the image in pixels.

◆ **H** (for Height) is the height of the image in pixels.

◆ **Src** (for Source) shows the path to the image file on your site.

◆ **Link** shows the destination if the image has a link to a URL.

◆ **Alt** shows the alternate text for the image.

◆ **Class** shows the CSS class, if any, that has been applied to the image.

◆ **Edit** includes buttons that allow you to edit the image in an external editor; change image setting, including image file format; and update SmartObjects (more about SmartObjects later in this chapter).

Figure 5.16 You can make a variety of adjustments to an image in the Property Inspector.

SETTING IMAGE PROPERTIES

- **Map** is a field and four tools that allow you to name and add an image map to the image. See "Creating Image Maps" in Chapter 6 for more information.

- **V Space** allows you to put vertical margins, in pixels, above and below the image.

- **H Space** allows you to put horizontal margins, in pixels, to the right and left of the image.

- **Target** specifies the frame or window in which the destination of a link should load. The pop-up menu next to the Target field shows the names of all the frames in the current frameset. There are also four other target possibilities. The _blank target loads the linked file into a new browser window. The _parent target loads the linked file into the parent frameset, the window of the frame that contains the link, or the full browser window. The _self target loads the linked file into the same frame or window as the link. This is the default choice. The _top target loads the linked file into the full browser window and removes all frames.

- **Original** shows the location of the original file (usually a Photoshop file) that is the basis of the selected image. This field shows the path to the source of a SmartObject.

- **Border** allows you to add a colored border, in pixels, around the entire image.

- **Crop**, **Resample**, **Brightness and Contrast**, and **Sharpen** are a group of tools that allows you to make adjustments to the image.

To set image properties:

1. Click to select the image to which you want to apply one or more properties.

2. In the Property Inspector, apply the property you want.

   The property is immediately applied.

✔ Tips

- If you don't want to apply an interactive effect like a rollover to an image, you can leave its ID field blank.

- The pop-up menu next to the Alt field has one choice, <empty>. You can use this attribute for images, such as spacer GIFs, that don't need to be read by screen readers for the visually disabled. Because accessibility guidelines state that all images should have alternate text, it's a good idea to apply this attribute to any images that are literally just taking up space.

- Though you can add white space around images using the V space and H space properties, you'll have more control (and have valid XHTML pages) if you use CSS to provide margins for images.

- You should also use the CSS border properties, rather than the Border option in the Property Inspector. You'll have more control over the kind and color of the border.

SETTING IMAGE PROPERTIES

Edit

Edit Image Settings

Update from Original

Sharpen

Crop

Resample

Brightness/Contrast

Figure 5.17 The Property Inspector gives you access to a variety of image editing tools.

Editing Images

When you're working with images on your site, you'll often want to tweak them to improve their looks. You could use an external image editing program, such as Adobe Photoshop or Adobe Fireworks, to do the job, but it's more convenient to work right in Dreamweaver for simple changes. For extensive modifications, you'll still need an external image editor, however.

The Property Inspector gives you seven buttons that allow you to edit an image (**Figure 5.17**). Two of the buttons, Edit and Update from Original, hand the image off to Photoshop for editing and update the Dreamweaver image when the original Photoshop image changes. We cover using these buttons in "Working with Photoshop," later in this chapter.

Edit Image Settings lets you change the file format and optimization of the image. We'll cover this in more detail in "Optimizing Images," later in this chapter.

The other four buttons let you make quick image adjustments right in Dreamweaver. They are: Crop, which lets you trim away portions of an image; Resample, which adds or subtracts pixels from an image that has been resized (this reduces the image size for better download performance); Brightness and Contrast, which allows you to correct images that are too dark or too light; and Sharpen, which changes the contrast of the edges inside an image, making it appear to be more in focus.

✔ Tips

■ If you select an image and the image editing tools are grayed out, it's probably because you enabled Check In/Check Out for your site, and you need to check out the file for editing. For more about Check In/Check Out, see Chapter 18.

■ To halt the editing process after you begin it and leave the image unchanged, press the Esc key.

141

EDITING IMAGES

To crop an image:

1. Select the image that you want to crop.

2. In the Property Inspector, click the Crop button.

   or

   Choose Modify > Image > Crop.

3. Dreamweaver puts up an alert dialog letting you know that the changes you will be making to the image are permanent, but that you can still use Undo to back away from the changes. Click OK.

   A crop selection box with eight resize handles appears within the image. Parts of the image outside of the crop selection box are dimmed (**Figure 5.18**).

4. Click and drag the crop selection box to move it around the image, and resize the box by dragging any of its selection handles, until you have the portion of the image you want to keep inside the box.

5. To complete the crop, press Enter (Return).

   or

   Double-click inside the crop selection box. Dreamweaver trims the image.

To resize and resample an image:

1. Select the image that you want to change.

2. Using the image's resize handles, make the image larger or smaller.

   or

   Use the W and H text boxes in the Property Inspector to resize the image numerically.

   The image resizes, and the Resample button in the Property Inspector becomes available for use.

Figure 5.18 The part of the image outside the selection rectangle will be cropped out.

Figure 5.19 Drag the sliders in the Brightness/Contrast dialog to change the intensity of the image.

3. In the Property Inspector, click the Resample button.

or

Choose Modify > Image > Resample.

Dreamweaver resamples the image. On many images, the effect is quite subtle.

To adjust the brightness and contrast of an image:

1. Select the image that you want to adjust.

2. In the Property Inspector, click the Brightness and Contrast button.

or

Choose Modify > Image > Brightness/Contrast.

The Brightness/Contrast dialog appears (**Figure 5.19**).

3. If it isn't already checked, select the Preview check box.

This makes adjusting the image a little slower, but it allows you to see the effects of your changes on the image as you make them.

4. Move the Brightness and the Contrast sliders until the picture looks the way you want it.

or

Enter a numeric value in the text boxes next to Brightness and Contrast. The sliders begin in the middle of the range, and the acceptable range for each slider is from -100 to 100.

5. Click OK.

To sharpen an image:

1. Select the image that you want to sharpen.

2. In the Property Inspector, click the Sharpen button.

   or

   Choose Modify > Image > Sharpen.

   The Sharpen dialog appears (**Figure 5.20**).

3. If it isn't already checked, select the Preview check box.

   This makes sharpening the image a bit slower, but it allows you to see the effects of your changes on the image as you make them.

4. Move the Sharpness slider until the picture looks the way you want it.

   or

   Enter a numeric value in the text box next to Sharpness. The slider begins at zero and goes to 10.

5. Click OK.

✔ Tip

■ Use a light hand when using the Sharpen tool. Over-sharpening an image often makes it look unnatural, with edges in the picture that look too prominent, or even oddly outlined (**Figure 5.21**).

Figure 5.20 Sharpening an image often brings out important detail that isn't as noticeable in the unsharpened image.

Figure 5.21 Over-sharpening an image (bottom) can make items in the image look weird.

EDITING IMAGES

Figure 5.22 You can make a variety of changes in the Image Preview dialog, including changing the graphics format.

Figure 5.23 Use the File tab of the Image Preview dialog to scale the image.

Optimizing Images

You can *optimize* images that are in a Dreamweaver document. Optimization means that you can change the image from one format to another (for example, from PNG to JPEG), change the JPEG quality setting, crop the image, and more.

To optimize an image:

1. Select the image you want to optimize.

2. In the Property Inspector, click the Edit Image Settings button (Figure 5.17).

   or

   Choose Modify > Image > Optimize.

   The Image Preview dialog appears, with your image displayed (**Figure 5.22**). The dialog has two tabs on the left (Options and File) and a preview area on the right.

   On the Options tab, you can use the Format pop-up menu to change the file format to GIF, JPEG, or PNG. Depending on the format you choose, the tab will change to show the appropriate settings used to modify the parameters of the selected format.

   The File tab (**Figure 5.23**) allows you to scale the image and select an export area, which changes the shape of the placed image (it's like cropping the image).

continues on next page

OPTIMIZING IMAGES

The preview area (**Figure 5.24**) has information on the current format at the top, with a pop-up menu that lets you pick from six different GIF and JPEG presets. In the middle is the image preview itself, and at the bottom are selection, crop, and zoom tools.

3. Make your adjustments to the image in the Image Preview dialog.

4. Click OK.

The image is saved and updated.

Figure 5.24 The preview area of the Image Preview dialog tells you the image's file format, and gives you tools to make further adjustments and edits.

Working with Photoshop

Dreamweaver has built-in integration with Adobe Photoshop CS3 or later. There are two methods of moving Photoshop images into your Dreamweaver document. In the first, you begin in Photoshop by opening an image and copying all or a portion of the image (a portion can be a selected part of the image, or one or more image layers). Then you switch to Dreamweaver and paste. Dreamweaver asks you how you want to save your image, and then places it on your Web page. Dreamweaver remembers the path to the Photoshop source file and allows you to reopen it for modifications in Photoshop.

In the second method, new to Dreamweaver CS4, you can choose a Photoshop file in the Select Image Source dialog, then place it into Dreamweaver. It is copied and placed into Dreamweaver in JPEG, GIF, or PNG format as a *SmartObject*, which maintains a link to the original Photoshop .psd file. When the .psd file is updated, Dreamweaver recognizes the changes and offers to update the copy in the Dreamweaver document.

The benefit of the SmartObject approach is that you can have a single .psd file that is used in many different pages of your site. When you update the Photoshop file, you can update all the different copies of the file throughout your site at once.

continues on next page

To copy and paste Photoshop images into Dreamweaver:

1. In Photoshop, open the image you want to bring into Dreamweaver.

2. Select the image or part of the image you want to copy.

   You can select one or more layers in your document, or use one of Photoshop's many other selection tools (**Figure 5.25**).

3. If you made a selection from a single layer, choose Edit > Copy.

   or

   If you selected multiple layers, choose Edit > Copy Merged.

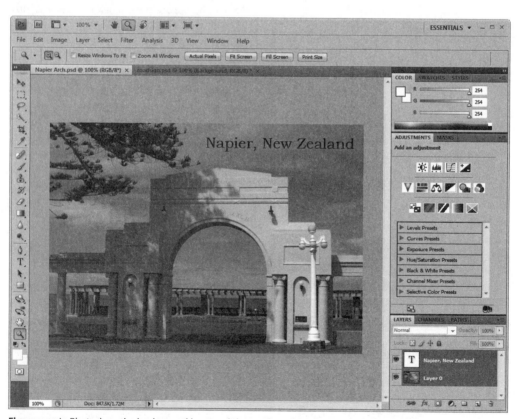

Figure 5.25 In Photoshop, the background layer and the text layer have been selected in the Layers panel.

4. Switch to Dreamweaver.

5. Choose Edit > Paste.

The Image Preview dialog appears (**Figure 5.26**).

6. Make any adjustments you want in the Image Preview dialog:

▲ On the Options tab, you can change the format of the saved image to GIF, Animated GIF, JPEG, or PNG, and make adjustments specific to each file type. For example, if you choose GIF format, you can set one of the colors in the image to be transparent.

▲ On the File tab, you can scale the image by percentage or by absolute size in pixels.

▲ The Animation tab is only active if the image is an Animated GIF. You can set properties for each frame of the animation.

▲ The Saved Settings pop-up menu above the image has several common options for GIF and JPEG formats.

▲ The toolbar below the image allows you to magnify or crop the image.

continues on next page

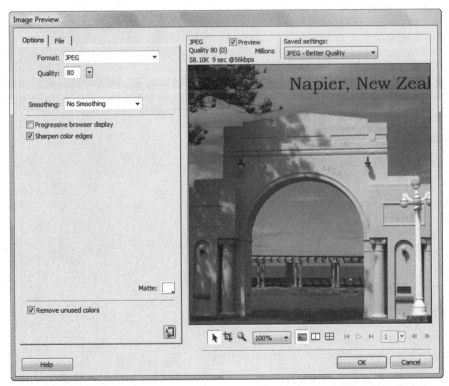

Figure 5.26 In Dreamweaver's Image Preview dialog, you can see that the image contains both the text and background layers from the Photoshop image. You can also make adjustments to the image optimization settings.

WORKING WITH PHOTOSHOP

7. Click OK.

The Save Web Image dialog appears (**Figure 5.27**).

8. Give the image a name, and navigate to where you want to save it (usually inside your site's images folder).

Remember that you can't use spaces in names for images for the Web, and that the only other characters you should use besides letters and numbers are the hyphen and underscore.

On Windows, you need to type the file extension, such as .jpg, .gif, or .png. The Mac adds these for you automatically as part of the name.

9. Click Save.

The Image Description (Alt Text) dialog appears (**Figure 5.28**). Alternate text is used by screen reading programs utilized by the disabled.

10. Enter the description for the image, then click OK.

The image from Photoshop appears on your Web page.

✔ Tips

- This copy-and-paste integration process also works with Fireworks.

- When images are placed and saved in Dreamweaver, they are flattened and lose their layers. If you want to maintain layers, use the SmartObject method to maintain a link to the original .psd.

- Information about the image, such as the optimization settings and the location of the original .psd source file, is saved in a Design Note, regardless of whether you have enabled Design Notes for your site.

Figure 5.27 Give the image a name, and save it in your images directory.

Figure 5.28 Enter a description of the file for screen readers used by the disabled.

To edit copy and pasted images using Photoshop:

1. Select the image in Dreamweaver.

2. Control-double-click (Windows) or Command-double-click (Mac) the image.

   or

   Click the Edit button in the Property Inspector (Figure 5.17).

   Dreamweaver opens the source .psd file in Photoshop.

3. Make your changes to the image in Photoshop and save the file.

4. Select all or part of the image and choose Edit > Copy, or if you selected multiple layers, choose Edit > Copy Merged.

5. Switch to Dreamweaver.

6. Paste the image over the image in the Web page. Dreamweaver optimizes the .psd image on the Clipboard using the original optimization settings, and then replaces the image on the page with the updated version.

WORKING WITH PHOTOSHOP

To place a Photoshop image as a SmartObject:

1. Click to place the insertion point in the document where you want the image to appear.

2. In the Common category of the Insert panel, click the Images button (Figure 5.1).

   or

   Choose Insert > Image, or press Ctrl-Alt-I (Cmd-Opt-I).

   The Select Image Source dialog appears (Figure 5.2).

3. In the dialog, navigate to and select the Photoshop file that you want to insert.

   With Photoshop files, you don't get the usual preview of the image in the Select Image Source dialog.

4. Click OK (Choose).

5. The Image Preview dialog appears (Figure 5.26).

6. Select the file format you want to use, and make any other changes you prefer.

7. Click OK.

   The Save Web Image dialog appears (Figure 5.27).

8. Give the image a name, and navigate to where you want to save it.

9. Click Save.

   The Image Tag Accessibility Attributes dialog appears.

10. Enter the description for the image, then click OK.

    The image from Photoshop appears on your Web page, with a difference; it has a badge in the upper-left corner showing that it is a SmartObject (**Figure 5.29**).

SmartObject badge

Figure 5.29 The road sign has the SmartObject badge in its upper-left corner.

Figure 5.30 It's kind of difficult to tell in black and white, but the bottom arrow in this SmartObject badge has turned red, indicating that the image is out of sync with the original Photoshop file.

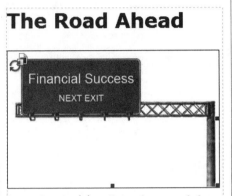

The Road Ahead

Financial Success

NEXT EXIT

Lorem ipsum dolor sit amet, consectetuer adipiscing elit. Praesent aliquam, justo convallis luctus rutrum, erat nulla fermentum diam, at nonummy quam ante ac quam. Maecenas urna purus, fermentum id, molestie in, commodo porttitor, felis. Nam blandit quam ut lacus.

Figure 5.31 After updating, the image shows the changes that had been made to the Photoshop file.

To update a SmartObject:

1. Click to select the image that you want to change.

   If the SmartObject needs updating, the badge will change, with the bottom arrow turning red, indicating that the copy of the image in the Dreamweaver document is out of sync with the original Photoshop file (**Figure 5.30**).

2. Click the Update from Original button in the Property Inspector (Figure 5.17).

   or

   Right-click the image and choose Update from Original from the resulting shortcut menu.

   The image updates to show the changes in the Photoshop document (**Figure 5.31**) and the SmartObject badge shows that it is in sync.

✔ Tips

■ The SmartObject badge only appears in Dreamweaver, not on your published Web pages.

■ You can have multiple SmartObjects on a single page (perhaps in different sizes, or cropped differently) that all link to the same Photoshop file. You can update each SmartObject independently.

■ You can update SmartObjects in the Assets panel by right-clicking them and choosing Update from Original from the resulting shortcut menu. The great thing about this method is that if you have used the SmartObject on multiple Web pages, the image is updated on all pages without you needing to open them.

Adding a Background Image

Most pages use a solid color or no color as their background, but sometimes you may want to use an image as the background of your page. This image will underlie all of the text and other images on your page. Though background images are a bit of a dated look, they can still be used on modern pages, if you use them well.

Figure 5.32 Use the Page Properties dialog to insert a background image.

Dreamweaver creates background images by creating a CSS rule to redefine the <body> tag. You can do this by creating the rule manually (see Chapter 7 for details on how to do that), but it's easier to use the Page Properties dialog.

To add a background image to your page:

1. Open the page to which you want to add the background image.

2. In the Property Inspector, click the Page Properties button.

   or

   Choose Modify > Page Properties, or press Ctrl-J (Cmd-J).

   The Page Properties dialog appears (**Figure 5.32**).

3. In the Appearance (CSS) category of the dialog, click the Browse button next to "Background image."

   The Select Image Source dialog appears.

4. Navigate to and select the image you want to use as the background image, then click OK (Choose).

5. From the Repeat pop-up menu in the Page Properties dialog, choose how you want the image to be repeated on the page (if it is smaller than the page):

▲ **repeat** tiles the image across and down the page, filling the page.

▲ **repeat-x** tiles the image across the top of the page.

▲ **repeat-y** tiles the image down the left edge of the page.

▲ **no-repeat** places the image on the page just once, in the upper-left corner of the page.

6. To see how the image will appear on the page, click Apply.

The background image appears on the page (**Figure 5.33**).

7. Click OK.

✔ Tips

■ Before CSS, designers set background images by adding a background attribute to the <body> tag. If you are asked to work on older sites, one of the renovations you should make is to remove this old attribute and replace it with a CSS rule.

■ Be careful when using tiled background images. As you can see from the figure that showcases our cat, it can make the page very hard to read.

Figure 5.33 The small background image of our cat was repeated endlessly on this page by setting the Repeat field to "repeat."

ADDING A BACKGROUND IMAGE

Adding a Favicon

One of the little touches that will finish off your Web site is if you add a *favicon*, that little icon that appears in the address bar of a browser when your site loads (**Figure 5.34**). A favicon is another way to underscore your site's brand identification, and often represents the logo of the organization that runs the site. Favicons are only 16 by 16 pixels large, and all modern Web browsers support them.

Before you can add a favicon to the index page of your site, you'll need to create one. There are dedicated favicon editing programs available for purchase, but we prefer to use one of the free online tools that converts a JPEG or GIF file into a favicon for you, such as the ones at www.chami.com/html-kit/services/favicon/, or http://tools.dynamicdrive.com/favicon/.

Once you have your favicon file, which must be named favicon.ico, you'll add it to your site's pages in Dreamweaver. You'll do that with the <link> tag, which, while more often used for linking CSS style sheets, works fine for this purpose, too.

To add a favicon to your page:

1. Obtain your favicon.ico file, and move it into your local site folder.

   Because it's an image, it makes sense to us to put the favicon file into the images folder, but you can put it anywhere you want in the local site folder.

2. Open the page to which you want to add the link to the favicon.

Figure 5.34 Here are the favicons for four different sites, as seen in Mozilla Firefox.

Figure 5.35 The Link dialog allows you to add the path to the favicon file.

3. Choose Insert > HTML > Head Tags > Link. The Link dialog appears (**Figure 5.35**).

4. In the Href text box, enter the path to the favicon.ico file.

or

Click the Browse button to open the Select File dialog. Navigate to the favicon.ico file and click OK (Choose).

5. In the Rel text box, type shortcut icon.

6. Click OK, then save the page by choosing File > Save.

After you next synchronize your local site to the remote site, the favicon will show up when you load the page in a Web browser.

✔ Tip

- You must repeat the process of adding the link to the favicon on every page in your site. If your site uses templates, adding the link to a template file automatically adds it to all the pages based on that template. For more about using templates, see Chapter 15.

ADDING A FAVICON

What Happened to FlashPaper?

A FlashPaper document is a Flash file that has been optimized to display printed documents, in a similar manner to the Adobe Acrobat format. FlashPaper was a casualty of Adobe's take-over of Macromedia.

Because the Flash file format is especially efficient, a FlashPaper document is usually smaller, often dramatically so, than the source document. This made FlashPaper superior to PDF for some applications, especially display on the Web.

However, at Adobe, Acrobat and its PDF format are king, so FlashPaper has been discontinued; you can no longer purchase the FlashPaper program, which created the documents. You can see a vestige of Dreamweaver's FlashPaper support, because you can still insert FlashPaper documents by choosing Insert > Media > FlashPaper. We expect even this remainder to go away in future versions of Dreamweaver.

Adding Flash and Shockwave

Because Adobe is the maker of the Flash multimedia format, it should come as no surprise that Dreamweaver makes it easy to add many different varieties of Flash objects to your pages. The two kinds we'll discuss here are *Flash animations* and *Shockwave animations*. A Flash animation is a Flash file that has been optimized for playback on the Web. This kind of file has the .swf extension. You can play this animation in Dreamweaver, or in a Web browser. A Shockwave file is an animation format very similar to a Flash file, but it is created by Adobe Director, rather than Adobe Flash. A Flash file can be displayed by any Web browser that has the free Flash Player; Adobe claims that more than 98% of Internet users have the Flash Player.

Figure 5.36 Add alternate text for the Flash or Shockwave file in the Object Tag Accessibility Attributes dialog.

✔ Tip

■ Files with the .fla extension are Flash document files that can only be opened in the Flash program itself. These sorts of files can't be played in Dreamweaver or Web browsers.

To insert a Flash or Shockwave animation:

1. Click to set the insertion point where you want the Flash or Shockwave animation to appear.

2. Choose Insert > Media > SWF, or press Ctrl-Alt-F (Cmd-Opt-F).

   or

   Choose Insert > Media > Shockwave.

   The Select File dialog appears.

3. Navigate to the file you want, select it, and click OK (Choose).

   The Object Tag Accessibility Attributes dialog appears (**Figure 5.36**).

4. Enter alternate text in the Title field of the dialog.

5. Click OK.

Dreamweaver inserts the animation file into your document as a placeholder.

✔ Tip

■ The Access key and Tab index fields in the Object Tag Accessibility Attributes dialog are used with forms. See the "Labeling Your Fields" sidebar in Chapter 11 for more information.

To play the animation placeholder in Dreamweaver:

1. Select the placeholder.

Selection handles appear at the edges of the placeholder.

2. Click the Live View button at the top of the document window.

or

Click the Play button in the Property Inspector (**Figure 5.37**).

Dreamweaver plays the animation file in the document window.

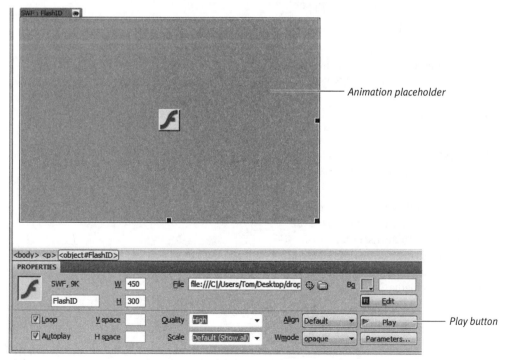

Animation placeholder

Play button

Figure 5.37 Use the Play button in the Property Inspector to preview your animation.

Adding Flash Video

Flash video is a way of showing video on your Web site. Like other video formats, such as QuickTime, Windows Media, Silverlight, and RealVideo, Flash video can show full-motion video in context on your Web page. But one of the big advantages of Flash video is that most browsers already have the Flash plug-in installed, so your video is likely to be viewable by more people.

Before you can put a Flash video file on your Web page, you must, of course, convert your video to the Flash video format, which has the .flv extension. Adobe CS4 includes the Flash Video Encoder, which can convert QuickTime, DV, MPEG, AVI, and Windows Media files into Flash video.

To insert a Flash video file:

1. Click to place the insertion point where you want the Flash video file to appear.

2. Choose Insert > Media > FLV.

   or

   In the Common category of the Insert panel, choose FLV from the Media pop-up menu.

   The Insert FLV dialog appears (**Figure 5.38**).

3. From the Video type pop-up menu, choose either Progressive Download Video or Streaming Video.

   You will most often choose Progressive Download Video, which downloads the Flash video file to the user's hard disk and then plays it. The Streaming Video choice requires extra server-side software (Adobe Flash Media Server).

Figure 5.38 You get a preview of the different media controllers available to you for Flash video directly below the Skin pop-up menu.

Figure 5.39 When you've set all the options in the Insert FLV dialog, a placeholder appears in the document window.

Figure 5.40 When you preview the Flash video in Live View, you can see and hear the video playing.

4. In the URL field, enter the path to the Flash video file. You could also click the Browse button, which brings up the Select File dialog, and allows you to navigate to select the video file.

If the media file is not inside your site folder, Dreamweaver will, as usual, offer to copy it there for you.

5. From the Skin pop-up menu, choose the kind of video controller you want to appear with the video.

As you choose the skin, the dialog shows you a preview of what the video controls look like for that skin.

6. Enter the Width and Height (in pixels) that you want to use to display the video.

or

Click the Detect Size button, which attempts to read the Flash video file and figure out what size it is. Depending on your video, this option sometimes may not work, but it is worth trying.

7. If you want the video to automatically begin playing when the Web page is loaded, select the Auto play check box.

8. If you want playback control to automatically return to the starting position after the video finishes playing, select the Auto rewind check box.

9. Click OK.

A placeholder for the Flash video file appears on your page (**Figure 5.39**). To play the Flash video file inside Dreamweaver, click the Live View button at the top of the document window (**Figure 5.40**).

To edit a Flash video file's properties:

1. Click to select the Flash video file.

2. In the Property Inspector, make the changes you want (**Figure 5.41**).

✔ Tip

■ There are many variables involved in converting one kind of video file to another, and a complete discussion is way beyond the scope of this book. Instead, we suggest that you begin learning more about Flash video on the Adobe Web site at *www.adobe.com/devnet/flash/video.html*.

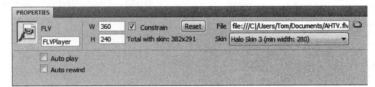

Figure 5.41 Adjust the settings for a Flash video file in the Property Inspector.

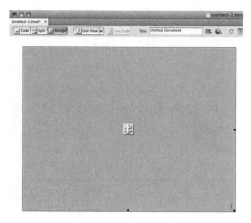

Figure 5.42 Dreamweaver puts a placeholder for the plug-in media file in the document window.

Adding QuickTime and Other Media

Video and audio files, with the exception of the various flavors of Flash media, are handled by Dreamweaver as *plug-in media*. That's because these files need plug-in software to be installed in a Web browser in order to be played. The most common plug-in media are QuickTime, Windows Media, RealAudio or RealVideo, Silverlight, and MP3 audio files.

To add plug-in media files:

1. Click to place the insertion point where you want the media file to appear.

2. Choose Insert > Media > Plugin.

or

In the Common category of the Insert panel, choose Plugin from the Media pop-up menu.

The Select File dialog appears.

3. Navigate to and select the media file you want, then click OK (Choose).

A placeholder for the plug-in file appears on your page (**Figure 5.42**).

To preview your media file:

1. Select the placeholder for the media file.

2. In the Property Inspector, click the Play button.

   This may not work if Dreamweaver can't find the appropriate plug-in on your system. In that case, save the page and preview the file in a Web browser (**Figure 5.43**).

✔ Tip

■ Dreamweaver creates the placeholder file as a small square icon on the page. When you preview the file, that icon will be replaced by the media file controller, which has the playback controls. The small size of the icon won't allow you to use the media controller, so before you preview the file, click the placeholder icon and use its selection handles to make it wide enough so that you can see the entire media controller.

To edit a plug-in file's properties:

1. Click to select the plug-in file.

2. In the Property Inspector, make the changes you want (**Figure 5.44**).

Figure 5.43 You usually need to preview media that uses plug-ins, like this QuickTime movie, in a Web browser.

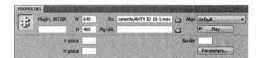

Figure 5.44 You can adjust the settings for a plug-in media file in the Property Inspector.

Working with Links

Links are what make the Web, well, *webby*—the interconnections between pages and sites are a fundamental part of why the Web is different from print. Without links coming in to your site, no one will ever find it. And without links going out from your site, it's a dead end. Dreamweaver makes it easy to add links to your site.

There are a number of different kinds of links: some links are internal to a page, some internal to a site, and some links go to another server altogether. This chapter will cover all of these, along with targets, image links, and email links.

Creating Text Links

If you can drag your mouse from here to there, you can create a link inside Dreamweaver. All you have to do is decide what on the page you want to turn into the link, and where you want that link to point.

Because creating links is such a large part of developing a Web site, there are multiple ways to create links. You can figure out which method works best for you.

To create a text link:

1. Select some text on the page to be the link. **Figure 6.1** shows that the title "HomeCook.info" has been selected.

Figure 6.1 Drag the Point to File icon, and the arrow will follow to the selected link file.

Figure 6.2 You can also select a link file from the Select File dialog.

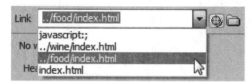

Figure 6.3 Or use this pop-up menu in the Property Inspector.

Figure 6.4 Finally, you can type the link file name in the Hyperlink dialog.

2. In the HTML tab of the Property Inspector, click the Point to File icon immediately to the right of the Link field. An arrow appears and that arrow can be dragged into the Files panel. Drag it to the file you want, and release the mouse.

or

In the Property Inspector, click the Browse for File icon, which looks like a folder, to the right of the Link field. The Select File dialog appears (**Figure 6.2**). Choose the file you want and click OK (Choose).

or

In the Property Inspector, click in the Link text field and type the name of the file you want to link to.

or

In the Property Inspector, click the pop-up menu to the right of the Link text field, and choose from the list of recently used links (**Figure 6.3**).

or

In the Common category of the Insert panel, click the Hyperlink button. The Hyperlink dialog appears (**Figure 6.4**). Type the name of the file to link to, or click the Browse for File icon to select a file. Click OK when you're done.

✔ Tip

■ If you want to remove a link, click inside the text you want to de-link, click the <a> in the tag selector, and then clear the Link text field in the Property Inspector.

CREATING TEXT LINKS

The Different Types of Links

When you create a link from one Web page to another, there are three possible types of links you can add: *absolute*, *document relative*, or *site root relative*. **Figure 6.5** shows the file list from `www.homecook.info`, a fairly typical site, with a number of files inside various folders. **Figure 6.6** shows another way of looking at the same information.

Figure 6.5 Here's a list of folders and files (as seen in the Files panel) from a site of medium complexity.

◆ **Absolute:** The `index.html` file contains a link to `http://www.dori.com/index.html`, which is another site altogether. This is an absolute link. The link starts with the explicit name of a server where the file can be found. It's also correct for the link to just go to either `http://www.dori.com/` or `http://www.dori.com`; in both cases, the link takes you to the default file for that domain (in this case, `index.html`).

◆ **Document Relative:** The `index.html` file also contains a link to the `index.html` file inside the `about` folder. To tell the browser how to navigate from one to the other, the link is `about/index.html`. That link is *relative* to the document it's being called from: the server knows, based on that link, that it needs to find a folder named `about` at the same level as the `index.html` file, and inside that folder, a file named `index.html`.

If `about/index.html` linked back to `index.html`, it would link to `../index.html`. Once again, the server starts looking for the next file at the same level as the current file, and those two periods tell the server to go *up* a level—back to `www.homecook.info`. And from there, it's easy to find the `index.html` file. A file two levels deep would link to the main index page by linking to `../../index.html`. It goes up two levels of folders before looking for a particular file.

Document relative links are especially useful when you're testing on your local machine—the browser can get from one page to another just based on the location of the current document.

The Different Types of Links *continued*

◆ **Site Root Relative:** Another way to reference files within the same site is by referencing them by where they are within the site, that is, relative to the root of the site, not the current document. The root of the site is always identified with a forward slash: /. With a site root relative link, the page at /food/index.html would link to /index.html. You no longer need to tell the server to go up a level or two; instead, you just tell it to start at the root and look for that particular file.

Site root relative links are useful when you're creating site-wide Library items. For instance, the left-hand menu in Figure 6.1 contains links to /about/index.html and /food/index.html. With site root relative links, you know that those links work everywhere on the site, no matter what page contains that menu. Library items are covered in Chapter 15.

Links to external sites must be absolute links. Links within a site can use either document relative or site root relative links or a combination of the two. The kind of link a site uses by default is set in Dreamweaver's preferences (see "Changing Link Relative To").

Figure 6.6 The about, news, food, and recipes folders (or directories) are all contained within the site root folder.

Changing Link Relative To

It's awkwardly named, but it's useful: you can change the *Link Relative To* (that is, whether the link is document relative or site root relative) for either a single file or for the site as a whole. As mentioned in "The Different Types of Links" sidebar, your links can either be document relative or site root relative, or even a mix of those on each page.

To change the "Link Relative To" for a link:

1. In the Property Inspector, click the Browse for File icon. The Select File dialog appears (Figure 6.2).

2. Near the bottom of the dialog, there's a pop-up menu with the label "Relative to." From that pop-up, you can switch between Document and Site Root (**Figure 6.7**), and the URL for the link will change.

3. Click OK to save your changes.

Figure 6.7 Use the Select File dialog to make your link site or document relative.

Figure 6.8 Or you can set the "Links relative to" for the entire site.

To change the "Link Relative To" for a site:

1. In the Property Inspector, click the Browse for File icon. The Select File dialog appears (Figure 6.2).

2. Near the bottom of the dialog, there's a link that says "Change default Link Relative To in the site definition." If you click the link (the part that's blue and underlined), you'll end up at the Advanced tab for the Site Definition for your site, with the Local Info category chosen (**Figure 6.8**). From here, you can choose either radio button next to "Links relative to," where the choices are Document or Site root. This changes the link that you're currently modifying, and the default for future links, but it will not change any other existing links on the page or site.

3. Click OK to save your changes.

✔ Tip

■ You can also follow the directions (found in Chapter 2) for editing the site definition. If you click the Advanced tab and choose the Local Info category, you'll end up in the same place.

Formatting Links

One of the most common uses of CSS is to change the way links are displayed in the browser. Want your links to only be underlined when the cursor is over them? Want the background or text color to change when a visitor clicks? Or maybe you just want something other than your visitor's default colors? That's all CSS, and Dreamweaver can handle that. You'll need to know if your site is going to use internal or external styles (see Chapter 7).

To format links:

1. Click the New CSS Rule button at the bottom of the CSS Styles panel. The New CSS Rule dialog appears.

2. If you want to set a style that will apply to all links (whatever their state), or to set the default appearance for links, in the Selector Type section, choose "Tag (redefines an HTML element)" for the Selector Type, and in the Selector Name section, choose *a*.

   or

   For the Selector Type, choose "Compound (based on your selection)," and for Selector name, choose any option from the pop-up menu: *a:link, a:visited, a:hover,* or *a:active* (**Figure 6.9**). Other CSS rules attached to your document can also appear in this pop-up menu.

   ▲ *a:link* is the default state of the link, seen when none of the other states are in use.

   ▲ *a:visited* is how the link will appear after the link has been clicked and the linked page loaded.

   ▲ *a:hover* is how the link will appear while the visitor's cursor is over the link.

   ▲ *a:active* is how the link will appear while the visitor is clicking that particular link.

Figure 6.9 The New CSS Rule dialog lets you choose which rule you're going to define.

Figure 6.10 When you want a new style sheet, you can create that file here.

Figure 6.11 After you create the rule, define its values here.

Figure 6.12 The CSS Styles panel, after various a rules have been defined. New properties can be set from here, also.

3. For Rule Definition, there are at least two options: (New Style Sheet File) or (This document only). If the current document links to any style sheets, their names are included in the pop-up menu. Choose whichever is appropriate for this site, and click OK.

4. If you chose to create a new style sheet, you'll see the Save Style Sheet File As dialog (**Figure 6.10**). Choose where to save it and what to name it, and click Save. The CSS Rule Definition dialog appears (**Figure 6.11**). You can create the specific rules you want for links either here or directly in the CSS Styles panel (**Figure 6.12**).

✔ Tips

- It is important to set styles for your links, otherwise they are likely to display underlined and blue (unvisited) and purple (visited)—but you can't be sure of that. To have control of the look of your page, set the link styles.

- Figure 6.12 shows some of the most common rules for CSS-formatted links: bold font-weight, and no underline except when the cursor is over the link.

The Style of Links

How to style links has been an ongoing controversy over the years: should a Web designer ever mess with a user's defaults? Should links always be underlined? Should links always, sometimes, or never say, "Click here"?

The answers, as with so much about Web design, depend on who's visiting your site. If you have a traditional e-commerce site geared towards average surfers, you'll probably want to make things as simple and straightforward as possible. If you have a cutting-edge art gallery site that attracts people used to fashion-forward sites, you can be a little more daring. If you aren't sure which way to go, figure out what sites attract visitors like yours, and style your links similarly.

There's one rule that's always true: be consistent across your site. No one should ever have to learn a new navigation style on every page.

Targeting Links

Sometimes you want a link to go to a new window or to an existing window other than the one you're clicking. That's done by giving the link a *target*—which is the name of the window in which you want the new page to load.

Figure 6.13 Set a link's target in the Property Inspector with this pop-up menu.

To give a link a target:

1. Follow the steps above to create a link, and then click the *<a>* in the tag selector.

2. Directly next to Link in the Property Inspector is a text field named Target where the target is entered. Alternatively, you can click the pop-up menu to the right of the field to choose the target.

3. If you're working on a site without frames, you have four choices: _blank, _parent, _self, and _top (sites with frames are different and are covered in Chapter 12). Choose one from the pop-up (**Figure 6.13**), and the target field will show your choice.

   ▲ _blank: Open a new, blank window.

   ▲ _parent: If the current window was opened by a previous link to a blank target (that is, the current window is a newly opened window), open this link in the previous window. If the current window wasn't opened that way, what happens depends on the user's browser—but usually, it just opens in the current window.

   ▲ _self and _top: For non-framed sites, these are both equivalent to not using any target at all.

✔ Tips

- To remove a target, just click in the Target text field in the Property Inspector and erase its content.

- The underscore before the name of a target is there to tell the browser that this is a special type of target and not just the name of another window. You'll learn about named windows in Chapter 12.

Figure 6.14 The Named Anchor dialog lets you create a new anchor on your page.

Adding Named Anchors

Normally, when a new Web page is displayed, it does so showing the very top of a page. Adding an *anchor* to a link allows you to choose to display the page starting at a given point on a page. In order to use an anchor, you'll need to create at least two things: the anchor itself and then the link to that anchor.

To create an anchor:

1. Open your document, and click in the spot in the file where you want the named anchor to be.

2. In the Common category of the Insert panel, click the Named Anchor button, and the Named Anchor dialog appears (**Figure 6.14**).

3. Choose a name for the anchor that will be unique for this page. Remember that this anchor is going to be part of a URL, so it can only contain characters that are valid: no spaces, ampersands, question marks, etc.

continues on next page

ADDING NAMED ANCHORS

4. Click OK. In the spot where you created the new anchor, an anchor icon appears (**Figure 6.15**). If you click that anchor, the tag selector will show the anchor with its name, and the Property Inspector will allow you to modify the name (**Figure 6.16**).

✔ Tips

■ While you do see that anchor on the page in Dreamweaver, it's not going to be there when you or anyone else sees the page in a browser—it's just there for your editing convenience, and it's one of the few ways in which Dreamweaver isn't 100% WYSIWYG. Hate seeing them? From the menu bar, choose View > Visual Aids > Invisible Elements to toggle the visibility of these icons on or off.

■ There are many ways to delete a named anchor. One way is to click to select the anchor icon, and delete it. Or, in the Property Inspector, clear the NamedAnchor Name field. Or, of course, you can do it in Code View.

August 11, 2008

Today, I had a cheese sandwich for lunch.

August 12, 2008

I overslept and was late to work.

Figure 6.15 The part of the page shown here has two anchors: the selected one is blue, and the unselected one is yellow.

Figure 6.16 The Property Inspector for a named anchor.

To link to an anchor on the same page:

◆ Follow the directions from "Creating Text Links" earlier in this chapter, but drag the Point to File icon to the Named Anchor icon on the page. The selected text is now linked to the new anchor.

✔ Tip

■ It's possible that the Point to File icon and the Point to File arrow can end up going to different spots on the page. The one that matters, in this case, is the icon itself, *not* the tip of the arrow.

To link to an anchor on another page:

◆ If you're using Dreamweaver's tabbed interface, you won't be able to see both the link source and the destination at the same time, so you'll have to add the anchor part of the link manually. Follow the directions from "Creating Text Links" earlier in this chapter to link to another file, and when that's complete, click in the Link field in the Property Inspector and add a # followed by the anchor name to the end of the existing link. So if you want to link to the chap07 anchor on the dwvqs.html page, your link would be to dwvqs.html#chap07.

or

If the two files are open in different windows, arrange the windows such that you can see both the link source and the link destination. Then, follow the directions for linking to an anchor on the same page, but drag the Point to File icon to the anchor on the other page.

ADDING NAMED ANCHORS

Adding Links to Graphics

Making a graphic a link isn't all that different from creating a text link. The main difference is that the link and target fields on the Property Inspector are in different areas, so you might not see them at first glance. Additionally, you don't get the handy pop-up menu on the Link field, so you can't just reuse one of the links you've recently made.

To add a link to a graphic:

1. Select the image in the document window.

2. Using the Property Inspector (**Figure 6.17**), click the Point to File icon next to the Link field. An arrow appears, and that arrow can be dragged into the Files panel. Drag it to the file you want, and release the mouse.

✔ Tips

■ As mentioned in "Creating Text Links," there are many ways to create links. Over time, you'll find the one that works best for you.

■ It's very common that images in the top-left corner of a Web page link back to a site's home page; common enough that if you don't do this, your site's visitors may be confused. Unless there's a good reason why you shouldn't do this for a site, set this up as the default.

■ You can make individual parts of an image link to different Web pages. That's done with *image maps*, and they are covered in the next section.

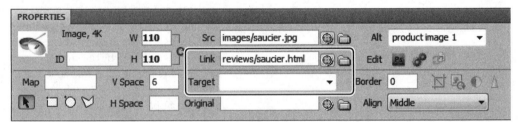

Figure 6.17 For images, the Link and Target fields aren't where you might expect them to be on the Property Inspector.

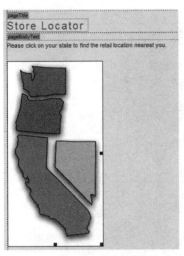

Figure 6.18 We'll turn this map of four Western states into an image map.

Figure 6.19
Both the image
and the image map
have been named in
this figure.

— Polygon

— Circle

— Rectangle

— Selection

Creating Image Maps

It's easy to add a link to an image; just select the image and use the Link text box in the Property Inspector to define the link's destination. But what if you wanted to have different parts of an image link to different pages? You'll need an *image map*. With an image map, you can define areas of the image as *hotspots*, and each hotspot has its own link.

To create an image map:

1. Select the image you want to turn into an image map.

   In this example, we're using a map of Washington, Oregon, California, and Nevada (**Figure 6.18**). We'll add hotspots to each of the states.

2. In the Map text box of the Property Inspector, enter a name for the image map (**Figure 6.19**).

   The name cannot begin with a number and can only contain letters, numbers, and the underscore character.

3. Use the Rectangle, Circle, or Polygon tool to draw a hotspot over part of your image.

   The tool you use depends on the shape of the area that you want to make into a hotspot. For example, we used the Rectangle tool to create the hotspots for Washington and Oregon, and the Polygon tool to create the hotspots for California and Nevada.

   continues on next page

CREATING IMAGE MAPS

Dreamweaver shows the hotspot as a light blue area overlaid on your image (**Figure 6.20**). The blue highlighting won't show up on your Web pages.

4. When a hotspot is selected, the Property Inspector shows properties for the hotspot (**Figure 6.21**). Use the Link field to attach a link to the hotspot.

5. (Optional) Use the Target pop-up menu to target the destination of the link.

   If you need more information about the use of the Target control, see "Targeting Links," earlier in this chapter.

6. Enter the alternate text for the hotspot in the Alt field.

7. Repeat steps 3-6 for each of the other areas on the image you want to turn into hotspots.

✔ Tips

■ To change the properties of a hotspot, use the hotspot selection tool to select the hotspot, then make changes in the Property Inspector.

■ You can resize and reshape hotspots; just select the hotspot with the hotspot selection tool, then click and drag one of the selection handles that appear at the corners of the hotspot.

■ Image maps have somewhat fallen out of favor recently; you see more sites using interactive Flash movies to provide users the benefits of clickable images.

Figure 6.20 Each of the state images has been overlaid with a hotspot.

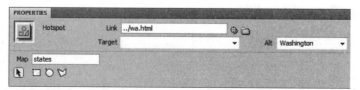

Figure 6.21 Add the link for a hotspot in the Property Inspector.

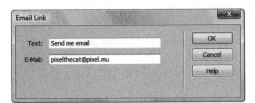

Figure 6.22 The Email Link dialog lets you set both the link (the email address) and the text that will be displayed on the Web page.

Adding Email Links

If you want your site's visitors to be able to contact you, you'll need to add a link that allows people to send you email.

To add an email link:

1. Click the spot on the page where you want to add an email link.

2. In the Common category of the Insert panel, click the Email Link button, and the Email Link dialog appears (**Figure 6.22**).

3. Fill in the text field with the text you want to display in the Web browser, and fill in the E-Mail field with the email address. Click OK when you're done.

✔ Tips

- Dreamweaver doesn't do any kind of error checking to make sure that the email address is in a valid format, so be careful when you're entering it.

- Putting an email address on a Web site can lead to that address getting all kinds of garbage or spam. There are a variety of ways to help protect your email address. The simplest is just to encode it—put it into a format such that the browser can understand it, but a spider sent out by a spammer can't. To learn more about this, search on Google for "email" + "obfuscator." This approach works with some spambots that harvest email links from Web pages, but certainly not all.

STYLING PAGE CONTENT

7

You want your Web site to look inviting, colorful, and organized, right? You need style! With styles, your site doesn't just look good— you get other benefits as well. Compared to older font-tag-based styling, your site is easier to maintain and update, it downloads faster and uses less bandwidth, and it's more accessible to every type of browser. In this chapter you'll get a basic understanding of Cascading Style Sheets, better known as CSS. Then we'll get into the details of how Dreamweaver uses the CSS Styles panel and the CSS Rule definition dialog to give you control over creating and applying styles to your pages.

Understanding CSS

Cascading Style Sheets are all about style, looks, and presentation. CSS properties and rules give you an amazing array of control over foregrounds, backgrounds, colors, fonts, positions, alignments, margins, borders, lists, and other aspects of presentation.

Appendix C contains a list of CSS properties. That list is amazing in its scope, but it can be a little overwhelming as well. Dreamweaver organizes all the properties listed in Appendix C into a couple of manageable interfaces: the CSS Rule definition dialog and the CSS Styles panel. With these two features, you can control every style aspect of every element on your page. From your document's body to its paragraphs, lists, tables, and links, to styling individual words or even individual letters, it's all handled with the CSS Styles panel or the CSS Rule definition dialog.

Content vs. presentation

Content is king, the saying goes, because users seek content when they come to your site. Content is the actual information in the headings, paragraphs, lists, divs, tables, forms, images, blockquotes, links, and other HTML elements you use on a page. With no styling, content looks something like an outline (**Figure 7.1**).

The unstyled content should be useful and informative, even if it doesn't look like much. That's because some users are getting only the text content; for instance, those with screen readers, PDA browsers, cell phone browsers, or text-only browsers. Some of these also get images, but not all, so be careful to never require images on your pages.

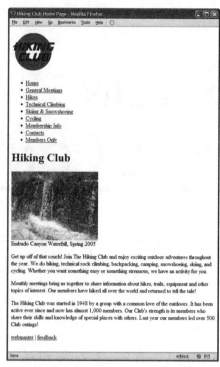

Figure 7.1 A page with no styles shows content and working links, even though it isn't beautifully arranged.

Figure 7.2 Add styles to the same page to determine rules for layout, background, fonts, margins, and other presentation features.

Once you add presentation rules in a style sheet, you have the layout, color scheme, font choice, background, and other "pretties" that make a Web page look good in a standard browser (**Figure 7.2**). The content itself hasn't changed. What has changed is the way the content is presented on the page. With different presentations, that is, different styles, the same content could look entirely different.

The power of CSS derives from the separation of content from presentation. You can make the content look like anything you want simply by changing the way it is styled and presented.

Working with tags

When you look through this chapter, you might be thinking to yourself, "Hey, I bought a WYSIWYG tool so I wouldn't have to learn about HTML tags!" That's understandable—but you'll need to learn at least a little something about HTML tags in order to take full advantage of CSS.

For instance, each paragraph inside your documents should be inside a <p> tag, where <p> stands for paragraph. Makes sense so far, right? Next, in order to apply a style to that paragraph, you apply it to that <p> tag. You're not taking anything out of the paragraph or adding anything to the paragraph itself. It's still a paragraph; but with CSS, you have some say about how that paragraph appears. Each style has instructions that define the style and what it does; these instructions are called *rules*.

You can learn just enough about HTML tags by looking at the tag selector of your Dreamweaver document. If you find you want to know even more, check out Chapter 17, "Editing Code."

Setting CSS Preferences

When you're first learning CSS, you'll want to set your preferences so that Dreamweaver gives you the maximum help:

In the CSS Styles category (**Figure 7.3**), setting the styles to use *shorthand* is optional. Shorthand saves on bandwidth when downloading style sheets since default values are omitted, but it can have problems with some browsers. For the most dependable results, don't use shorthand.

For the "When double-clicking in CSS panel" preference, it's easiest to rely on "Edit using CSS dialog" while you learn about styles. If you find you prefer to edit using the Properties pane in the CSS Styles panel, you can change it later.

Figure 7.3
The CSS Styles Preferences should be set based on how you like to work.

Anatomy of the CSS Styles Panel

The CSS Styles panel was extensively reworked and revised in Dreamweaver 8, so it's worth taking the time to familiarize yourself with it if you're upgrading from an old version. And if you're new to Dreamweaver, take the time now because the CSS Styles panel will become a good friend.

Figure 7.4 shows the CSS Styles panel in All mode, with the All Rules and Properties panes displayed. The Properties pane is in Category view.

Figure 7.5 shows the CSS Styles panel in Current mode, with the Summary, Rules, and Properties panes displayed. The Properties pane is in Set view.

Anatomy of the CSS Styles Panel *continued*

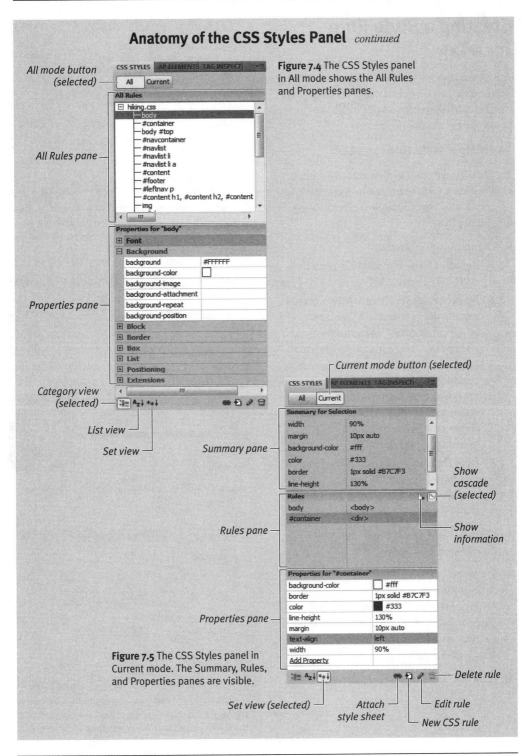

All mode button (selected)

All Rules pane

Properties pane

Category view (selected)

List view

Set view

Figure 7.4 The CSS Styles panel in All mode shows the All Rules and Properties panes.

Current mode button (selected)

Summary pane

Show cascade (selected)

Rules pane

Show information

Properties pane

Figure 7.5 The CSS Styles panel in Current mode. The Summary, Rules, and Properties panes are visible.

Set view (selected)

Attach style sheet

Delete rule

Edit rule

New CSS rule

ANATOMY OF THE CSS STYLES PANEL

Creating a Style Rule for a Tag

A style rule begins with a *selector*. A selector can be a tag, an `id`, or a `class`. Everything you do to create new styles, apply styles, and edit styles starts with creating a rule.

To create a style rule for a tag:

1. With a page open in Dreamweaver, click the New CSS Rule button in the CSS Styles panel. The New CSS Rule dialog appears (**Figure 7.6**).

2. Complete the following:
   - ▲ **Selector Type:** Choose Tag (redefines an HTML element).
   - ▲ **Selector Name:** Dreamweaver makes its best guess (based on your current selection or cursor placement when you clicked the New CSS Rule button) as to what tag you wanted this style to apply to. That tag automatically appears in the Selector Name field. If that tag isn't the one you wanted, choose the correct tag using the pop-up menu (**Figure 7.7**).
   - ▲ **Rule Definition:** Select "This document only" to add the style to just the document you have open. We'll cover the other options available here later.

3. Click OK, and the CSS Rule definition dialog appears (**Figure 7.8**).

4. Set properties in the eight categories as desired. Which category contains which field is covered in "Dreamweaver CSS Categories," next. If you want to see how something looks without dismissing the dialog, click Apply.

5. Click OK, and the new rule will take effect.

Figure 7.6 If a tag is selected in the document, it may automatically appear in the Selector Name field in the New CSS Rule dialog.

Figure 7.7 Any tag can be styled—just select the one you want.

Figure 7.8 Font rules are set in the Type category and the colors picked here are foreground (text) colors.

✔ Tips

- New rules can also be created by selecting text in the document window and choosing Format > CSS Styles > New.

- There's a lot more to the New CSS Rule dialog, but don't fret; we'll cover its other options later in this chapter.

- Not familiar with classes and ids? What you'll need to know is covered in the sidebar "Choosing Between Classes and IDs" later in this chapter.

- This example creates an *internal* style: one where the style information is included inside the Web page itself. Internal styles are useful for testing, but in the long run, you'll want to make all your styles *external*, that is, in their own file. We'll cover that in Chapter 9, "Managing Styles."

Choosing Between Divs and Spans

Divs and *spans* are generic containers. Div is short for *division*. A div is meant to hold a section of a page that you use and style as a block. Use divs to organize content into meaningful containers. You might structure your page with a div for the masthead, a div for the navigation, a div for the content, and a div for the footer. The way you choose to position the divs creates your layout. Divs for smaller blocks of content can be nested inside other divs. In **Figure 7.9**, for example, the highlighted div #photofeature is inside the div #content, which is inside the div #container.

Span elements are for inline use. A span, for example, can enclose a letter, word, or phrase. With a style rule attached to the span, you achieve a distinctive presentation for an inline element.

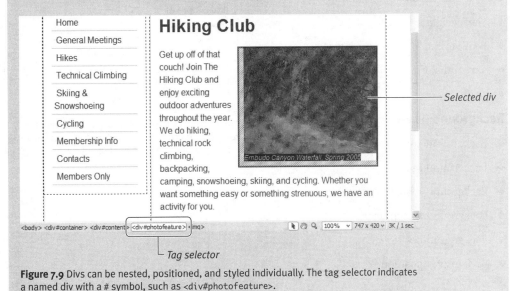

Selected div

Tag selector

Figure 7.9 Divs can be nested, positioned, and styled individually. The tag selector indicates a named div with a # symbol, such as <div#photofeature>.

CREATING A STYLE RULE FOR A TAG

Dreamweaver CSS Categories

Dreamweaver uses the CSS Rule definition dialog to break down CSS into various categories. Below, you'll find each of the categories in the CSS Rule definition dialog, along with what you can find in that category. Each item in the dialog is named according to its CSS property value, which is a change in Dreamweaver CS4. For example, in the Type category, the Font-family property was called Font in previous versions. By using the actual CSS name, it helps you learn and understand the CSS property names. If you want more details about valid values for each field, check out Appendix C.

Type (Figure 7.10)

◆ Font-family

◆ Font-size

◆ Font-style

◆ Line-height

◆ Text-decoration

◆ Font-weight

◆ Font-variant

◆ Text-transform

◆ Color

Background (Figure 7.11)

◆ Background-color

◆ Background-image

◆ Background-repeat

◆ Background-attachment

◆ Background-position (X)

◆ Background-position (Y)

Figure 7.10 In the Type category, you can set the most common styling properties to text.

Figure 7.11 Always give a page a background color, even if you're using a background image.

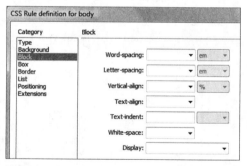

Figure 7.12 Set rules for spacing and alignment of text in the Block category. Text indent affects first line only—yes, you can indent paragraphs with CSS!

Figure 7.13 Set rules for width and height in the Box category. Margin and padding are both transparent, which means that a background shows through either.

Figure 7.14 Set rules for borders in the Border category. Uncheck "Same for all" to style borders individually.

Figure 7.15 Set rules for list type and position in the List category. If you want an image instead of a standard bullet, specify it here.

Block (Figure 7.12)

◆ Word-spacing

◆ Letter-spacing

◆ Vertical-align

◆ Text-align

◆ Text-indent

◆ White-space

◆ Display

Box (Figure 7.13)

◆ Width

◆ Height

◆ Float

◆ Clear

◆ Padding (Same for all, Top, Right, Bottom, Left)

◆ Margin (Same for all, Top, Right, Bottom, Left)

Border (Figure 7.14)

◆ Style (Same for all, Top, Right, Bottom, Left)

◆ Width (Same for all, Top, Right, Bottom, Left)

◆ Color (Same for all, Top, Right, Bottom, Left)

List (Figure 7.15)

◆ List-style-type

◆ List-style-image

◆ List-style-Position

DREAMWEAVER CSS CATEGORIES

Positioning (Figure 7.16)

◆ Position

◆ Width

◆ Height

◆ Visibility

◆ Z-Index

◆ Overflow

◆ Placement (Top, Right, Bottom, Left)

◆ Clip (Top, Right, Bottom, Left)

Extensions (Figure 7.17)

◆ Page-break-before

◆ Page-break-after

◆ Cursor visual effect

◆ Filter visual effect

✔ Tips

■ Page break properties are used in style sheets for print.

■ The eight categories of style definitions in the CSS Rule definition dialog cover nearly every CSS property included in Appendix C. Even more impressive is that you can apply any of the properties in any of the eight categories to *any element* in your document. Backgrounds, for example, can be used in the body element, but can also be used with div, class, table, blockquote, span, acronym, quote, form, paragraphs, or any other element.

Figure 7.16 Set position in the Positioning category. The Z-Index refers to the stacking order when more than one layer occupies the same position. Clip refers to material that might overflow the size set for width and height.

Figure 7.17 Set extensions in the Extensions category. Internet Explorer for Windows is the only browser that supports the Filter extensions.

Figure 7.18 A class selector name is preceded by a period when creating a new style.

Creating a Custom Class

Redefining the style for a tag gives you considerable control, as HTML has a tag for nearly any type of text you need to format. And yet, there are times when you want to create a style rule for something that doesn't already have a logical tag as a label. You can do that with a `class`. You get to create a custom name for the style when you create a class.

To create a class:

1. With a page open in Dreamweaver, click the New CSS Rule button in the CSS Styles panel. The New CSS Rule dialog appears (**Figure 7.18**).

2. Set the Selector Type to Class (can apply to any HTML element), and set the Selector Name to a name of your own choosing, preceded by a period (.). This is your new `class` name.

3. Click OK, and the CSS Rule definition dialog appears.

4. When you've completed filling out the CSS Rule definition dialog, click OK to accept your changes.

✔ Tips

■ Don't create classes to describe text when there are already logical tags that do the job. For example, don't create a class to make text big and bold and use it as a heading. HTML already provides six heading tags (h1, h2, h3, h4, h5, and h6). Simply redefine one of the existing heading tags to suit your purpose. Remember, you want to use HTML to create a logical structure for your content, and CSS to style the structured content.

■ Pick a `class` name that will serve you over time. A name that describes a purpose rather than a particular property works best. For example, if you wanted to highlight certain vocabulary words in red, you could name a class either .red or .vocab. If you redesign the site later and change the color scheme, the name .red might not make sense any longer, but .vocab would still have meaning.

Choosing Between Classes and IDs

You can identify a particular element on a page by assigning it a name. Named elements can then be targeted with CSS rules. The two available methods for assigning names in CSS are with *classes* and *ids*.

A class is reusable. Many different elements on a page can be assigned to the same class. For example, in a blog you might create a class style called blogentry and assign it over and over again to every blog entry. Or there might be several vocabulary words on a page assigned to the class vocab.

An id, on the other hand, can only be used once per page. Since ids are unique, they are used for all sorts of things in addition to CSS rules, such as JavaScripts and link destinations. IDs are very useful in CSS when assigned to divs. Giving a div a named id enables you to write CSS rules for a specific block of content with regard to its position, background, margins, and other properties.

In the CSS Styles panel, you see the name of each id or class style rule you add to your style sheet (**Figure 7.19**). In the style sheet a hash or pound sign (#) precedes an id selector. A period (.) precedes a class selector.

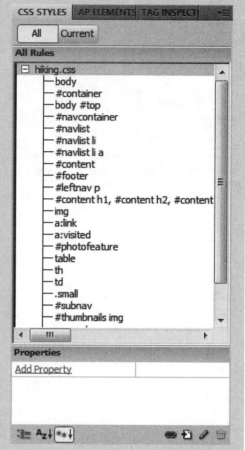

Figure 7.19 This complete style sheet contains ids (#navlist), restyled table cell tags (td), classes (.small), and pseudo-class selectors (a:visited).

Figure 7.20 The pseudo-class selectors are available from a pop-up menu for Compound selector types.

Figure 7.21 A selector based on an id must begin with a pound sign (#).

Creating Compound Selectors

Elements in HTML can nest. Inside the body might be a div named content, with a div named newitem nested inside that. Each of these nested elements exists in a parent-child relationship that allows CSS properties to be inherited. The child elements are *descendants* of the parent elements and inherit properties from them.

Descendant elements can be pinpointed precisely to create extremely selective selectors. Take the lowly list item, or li. If you redefine the li tag, you style every list item anywhere in the body. However, if you have a div named content, and a list item li within that, you can write a style for the selector #content li. Instead of styling every li anywhere in the document, it will only style each li *inside* the content div.

Dreamweaver calls *contextual* selectors like this *compound*. There's more about compound selectors in the "Compound Terminology" sidebar, later in this chapter.

To create a compound style:

1. With a page open in Dreamweaver, click the New CSS Rule button in the CSS Styles panel. The New CSS Rule dialog appears (**Figure 7.20**).

2. Set Selector Type to Compound (based on your selection). For Selector Name, one of the pseudo-class selectors may appear in the dialog by default. Select a pseudo-class selector from the pop-up menu or type a selector of your own choosing in this field by doing one of the following:

   Type a pound sign (#) and the id name to style a named section of the page—usually a div (**Figure 7.21**).

   or

continues on next page

Type a pound sign (#), the id name, and a space before the pseudo-class selector to style only those navigation links in a particular named section of the page (**Figure 7.22**).

or

Type a pound sign (#), the id name, a space, and an HTML tag to style an element found only in the named section of the page (**Figure 7.23**).

or

Type a group of selectors, separated by a comma and a space, to assign the same style properties to every selector in the group with a single rule (**Figure 7.24**).

If possible, Dreamweaver will parse your selectors and give you an explanation of them in the dialog (Figure 7.21 and Figure 7.23).

3. Click OK, and the CSS Rule definition dialog appears.

4. When you've completed filling out the CSS Rule definition dialog, click OK to accept your changes.

Figure 7.22 Type in the Selector Name field to create selectors that fit your document.

Figure 7.23 A contextual or compound selector lets rules apply only to tags within certain named divs.

Figure 7.24 Every tag in this group list of selectors will follow the same style rule.

Figure 7.25 Dreamweaver politely suggests that you create a new rule for a new div as soon as you insert it in your document.

✔ Tips

- Rules for link pseudo-classes won't work reliably with the cascade unless you define them in the following order: a:link, a:visited, a:hover, a:active. A way to remember the L-V-H-A order is the memory device LoVeHAte.

- If you use the Insert Div Tag button in the Insert panel (found in both the Common and Layout categories) to insert a div, Dreamweaver offers you the chance to create a new advanced style for the div immediately (**Figure 7.25**). Click the New CSS Rule button in the Insert Div Tag dialog to define properties for the new div.

Compound Terminology

Compound selectors are extremely powerful, so specific vocabulary exists to describe them.

Pseudo-classes are so named because pseudo-states don't actually exist in the document. The user must do something to create the pseudo-class, such as visit a link, hover over a link, or even hover over a visited link.

Comma-separated lists of selectors (p, td, li) are called *group* selectors.

Selectors such as #nav li or #content p are known as *contextual* selectors (or *descendant* selectors). These selectors are the workhorses of CSS because they allow you to write specific rules for text based on the element in context (or the element from which it descends). The selector #content p styles only the p elements in the #content div. The selector #footer p styles only the p elements in the #footer div. So while you may have paragraphs in your content area and paragraphs in your footer area, there is no reason why they have to share the same presentation rules.

Working with the CSS Styles Panel

The CSS Styles panel (Window > CSS Styles) shows all the styles affecting a document or a selected style. You can apply, modify, delete, and do other style-related tasks right in the CSS Styles panel without having to open the CSS Rule definition dialog. If you need an overview of what's where in the panel, look back at the "Anatomy of the CSS Styles Panel" sidebar, earlier in this chapter.

To work in All mode:

1. In your document, click All at the top of the CSS Styles panel (**Figure 7.26**). All the styles affecting the document appear: any linked or imported external style sheets as well as any styles in only the open document. An external style sheet is indicated by a file name, for example, hiking.css. Styles internal to this document only are in the <style> category.

   Click the plus (+) (Windows) or the disclosure triangle (Mac) to expand a category if it isn't already expanded.

Figure 7.26 When you're in All mode in the CSS Styles panel, any external style sheets are listed by file name, while internal styles are shown in <style>.

2. Examine the rules for individual styles by highlighting a specific style and doing one of the following:

Click the Show category view icon at the lower left of the CSS Styles panel. Properties for the selector appear in categories in the Properties pane at the bottom (**Figure 7.27**). Click the plus (+) or the disclosure triangle (Mac) to expand any category.

or

Click the Show list view icon at the lower left of the CSS Styles panel. Properties for the selector appear as a list in the Properties pane at the bottom (**Figure 7.28**).

or

continues on next page

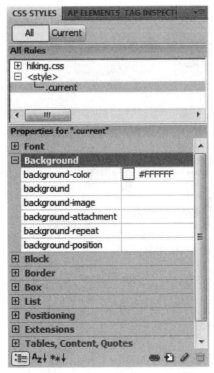

Figure 7.27 Expand a style sheet name to see all the style rules. The Category view of the Properties pane shows categories, which must be expanded to examine properties.

Figure 7.28 Pick a specific style from the list and its properties are shown in the Properties pane. In List view, the Properties pane shows a list of all the properties for a selected style.

WORKING WITH THE CSS STYLES PANEL

Click the "Show only set properties" icon at the lower left of the CSS Styles panel. Set properties for the selector appear in the Properties pane (**Figure 7.29**).

3. To add a new property directly in the CSS Styles panel, click the icon for "Show only set properties", and then click Add Property. An editable field appears with a pop-up menu listing every possible property (**Figure 7.30**).

4. To modify a property, click on the property value. An editable field appears (**Figure 7.31**). Type any change and press Return (Enter).

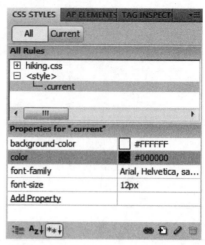

Figure 7.29 In Show only set properties view, the Properties pane eliminates everything from view except the set properties for the selected style.

Figure 7.30 To set a new property while in the Properties pane, choose from the list.

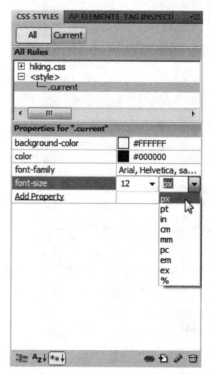

Figure 7.31 Any property value is editable in the Properties pane.

Tag selector

Figure 7.32 Elements you want to style can be selected in the document window with the tag selector.

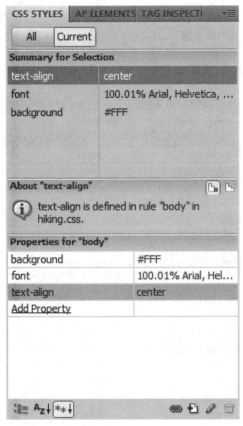

Figure 7.33 Current mode focuses on only the currently selected style.

To work in Current mode:

1. In your document, do one of the following:

   Place the cursor in an element in the document window.

   or

   Select an element using the tag selector at the lower left of the document window (**Figure 7.32**).

2. Click Current at the top of the CSS Styles panel (**Figure 7.33**). The Summary for Selection pane appears.

   continues on next page

3. In the middle pane, you can choose whether to show information about the selected property (About, Figure 7.33), or show the cascade of rules for the selected tag (Rules, **Figure 7.34**). Click on a property highlighted in the Summary for Selection list, and then choose either the About or Rules button on the right.

At the bottom, the Properties list shows the properties and their values.

4. If properties for the selected element were overridden by rules for other selectors, Dreamweaver indicates this with a strike-through of the property name (**Figure 7.35**). Use the mouse to hover over the property showing a strikethrough and a pop-up tip appears explaining why this property is not applied.

✔ Tips

■ Verify how styles are implemented on your pages by previewing them in a variety of browsers, as well as Dreamweaver's Live View. More than one style rule can affect a particular page element. Sometimes the style rules conflict and you get unexpected results.

■ When things don't look as expected in the browser, troubleshoot style rules using Current mode in the CSS Styles panel. The Properties pane provides valuable help to spot style conflicts.

■ Inheritance information in the About pane of the CSS Styles panel in Current mode is also useful when troubleshooting conflicting style rules.

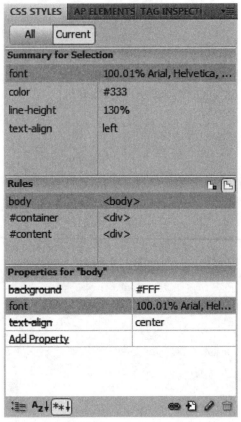

Figure 7.34 You can see information about the selected property or see the cascade of rules that apply to the selected tag.

Properties for "#container"		
~~background-color~~	☐	#fff
~~border~~	1px solid #B7C7F3	
color	■ #333	
line-height	130%	
~~margin~~	10px auto	
text-align	left	
~~width~~	90%	
Add Property		

Figure 7.35 In Current mode, you can see inherited styles affecting a selector. The style is shown with a strikethrough if it doesn't apply to the current selection.

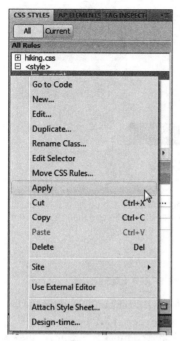

Figure 7.36 Use the contextual menu to apply a class style rule.

Applying Styles

Most styles take effect immediately in the current document and in any other documents linked to an external style sheet. If you redefine a tag, for example, h3, then any time you use the h3 tag, the style is applied. Pseudo-class selectors such as a:link also are immediately applied to the selected elements in any linked documents.

Other styles are different—your document doesn't use them until you add them to an element. For instance, after you create a style rule for a class, you must then apply that class to text in the document, and the same goes for ids.

To apply a style to a class:

1. In a document, select the text to which you want to apply the style.

   or

   Place the cursor anywhere in a paragraph to apply the class to the entire paragraph.

   or

   Select a tag with the tag selector at the lower left of the document window.

2. Do one of the following:

   In the CSS Styles panel, select All mode, then right-click the name of the style you want to apply, and choose Apply from the contextual menu (**Figure 7.36**).

   or

   In the HTML tab of the Property Inspector, choose the style you want to apply from the Class pop-up menu (**Figure 7.37**).

   or

continues on next page

Figure 7.37 Use the Class pop-up menu on the Property Inspector to apply a class style rule.

APPLYING STYLES

In the document, right-click the selected text, then in the contextual menu, choose CSS Styles and then the style you want to apply.

or

Choose Format > CSS Styles, and in the submenu choose the style you want to apply (**Figure 7.38**).

Figure 7.38 Another way to apply a class style rule is to choose Format > CSS Styles and then choose from the submenu.

APPLYING STYLES

External, Internal, and Inline: Look Ma, It's the Cascade

Styles can be *external*, *internal*, or *inline*. An external style resides in a separate style sheet file, one with a name that usually ends in .css. An internal style lives inside each individual Web page that needs it, located within style tags inside the document's head. And finally, there are inline styles; they live within the HTML tags themselves, and only apply to whatever's inside that tag.

Style rules *cascade*. This means that while multiple styles can cover a particular element, there are rules to determine which style takes precedence. The order of the cascade is first external, then internal (meaning in the document head), and then inline. When style rules conflict, the laws of the cascade determine how the conflict is settled.

In general, the closer a rule is to the element getting styled, the more power the rule has in the battle of conflicting style rules. The whole idea is a lot easier to understand with a specific example.

Let's look at the selector p. Suppose in your external style sheet you redefined p to be black, Arial, and 100% in size. Every p element in your document will be black, Arial, and 100%. No conflict there.

Into your conflict-free life comes a need to have *just one document* that uses your attached external style sheet to display paragraphs that are black, Arial, and 90% in size. You know how to create a style for just one document, and you write an internal style making the p 90%. Now you have a conflict. Is a p element going to follow the rule in the external style or the rule in the internal style? The cascade goes from external to internal, so the internal rule is closer and has the power to overrule the external rule in this conflict. Conflict solved. Any p element in this one document will be 90% in size.

But you want one paragraph to be red, not black. So you write a class rule and apply it inline to the paragraph. Now you have an inline style and a new conflict. The cascade goes from external to internal to inline, so the inline style has the power to overrule both the external rule and the internal rule. Conflict solved. Any p element in this one class will be red.

Selected tag uses a class ┘

Figure 7.39 It's easy to identify elements with classes applied in the tag selector bar. The element has a period in the name, for example <p.current>.

Figure 7.40 Removing a class is as simple as choosing None from the CSS Styles submenu.

To remove a style from a class:

1. Select the text to which the class was applied. The tag selector in the lower left of the document indicates the presence of a class with a period; for example, <p.current> means that the class current has been applied to this <p> tag (**Figure 7.39**).

2. Do one of the following:

   In the Property Inspector, choose None from the Class pop-up menu.

   or

   In the document, right-click the selected text. In the contextual menu, choose CSS Styles and then None (**Figure 7.40**).

   or

   Choose Format > CSS Styles, and in the submenu choose None.

3. The class is no longer applied to the selected text. However, the style is still available in the style sheet.

To apply a style to an id:

1. In a document, select the text or tag to which you want to add an id.

2. Do one of the following:

    In the CSS Styles panel, select All mode, then right-click the name of the style you want to apply, and select Apply from the contextual menu (Figure 7.36).

    or

    Right-click the element in the tag selector, and choose Set ID from the contextual menu, and choose an ID from the sub-menu (**Figure 7.41**).

    or

    If the selected element is a div, use the Property Inspector to choose an id to apply from the pop-up menu (**Figure 7.42**).

3. Check the tag selector to verify that the id has been applied by looking for the name of the tag followed by a # followed by the name of the id.

✔ Tips

- When you remove a class from the selected text, it's still available to be applied elsewhere. Removing the class from the tag doesn't remove the rule itself from your page.

- If you select some text that isn't inside a container (a paragraph or div, for example), and apply a style, Dreamweaver wraps a new span tag around that text and applies the new style to the span.

- If the pop-up menu in the Property Inspector doesn't show the id you want, it may be because that id is used else-where on the page. An id must be unique on the page, so if you want to move it from one place to another, remove it from the first place before attempting to apply it to the second.

Figure 7.41 Even the tag selector has a contextual menu, giving you an easy way to add an id.

Figure 7.42 The Property Inspector can be used to add an id, but only for divs.

APPLYING STYLES

Creating Styles with the Property Inspector

For users who are upgrading from an older version of Dreamweaver, it's the most natural thing in the world to use the Property Inspector to create styles. You can still style text with the Property Inspector, but there are a few things to keep in mind.

The old way of using Dreamweaver added dozens, perhaps hundreds, of font tags to a page with the Property Inspector. Getting rid of all those bandwidth-eating font tags is a good thing. Beginning with Dreamweaver CS4, you can only apply two HTML styling tags with the Property Inspector: <strong> and <em>. All other style choices create CSS styles, and you're prompted to create a new CSS rule when you try to style text.

The other big change in Dreamweaver CS4 is that the Property Inspector has been split into two tabs: HTML (**Figure 7.43**) and CSS (**Figure 7.44**). In the HTML tab, you can apply HTML attributes, such as headings, lists, and indenting. You can also apply CSS classes and ids. In the CSS tab, you can create CSS rules, apply font families, change fonts size and color, and align text.

continues on next page

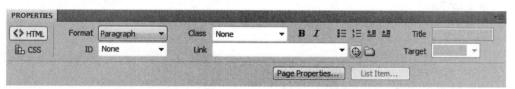

Figure 7.43 The HTML tab of the Property Inspector allows you to apply HTML tags.

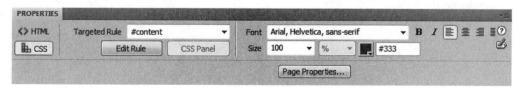

Figure 7.44 The CSS tab of the Property Inspector allows you to apply CSS styles.

To create styles with the Property Inspector:

1. Open a new, blank document, or a document with content but with no styles yet applied.

2. Click the Page Properties button on either tab of the Property Inspector. The Page Properties dialog appears (**Figure 7.45**).

   This dialog applies styles and properties that will affect the entire page, and the styles will be written as an internal style sheet. You can move the styles to an external sheet later, if needed; see "Moving Internal Styles to External," in Chapter 9.

3. The Page Properties dialog contains six categories. You can set properties as desired in the following:

   Appearance (CSS): Set appearance properties for the body, including page font, size, text color, background color, and background image. If you use a background image, you should also set how it repeats. Margins are set individually for top, right, bottom, and left.

   Appearance (HTML): Sets HTML appearance properties for the page, including background image, text colors, link colors, and margins. We recommend that you set these with CSS styles instead (**Figure 7.46**).

   Links (CSS): Set the font and size, colors for unvisited, visited, rollover, and active links, and select underline style from the pop-up menu (**Figure 7.47**).

   Headings (CSS): Set a heading font, and choose a size and color for each heading (**Figure 7.48**).

Figure 7.45 Page Properties for Appearance determine backgrounds, fonts, colors, and margins, using CSS.

Figure 7.46 You can set HTML page properties in the Appearance (HTML) category.

Figure 7.47 Page Properties for Links set up fonts, colors, and sizes for links.

Figure 7.48 Page Properties for Headings set up fonts, colors, and sizes for headings.

Figure 7.49 Page Properties for Title/Encoding determine title, document type, and language encoding.

Figure 7.50 Page Properties for Tracing Image allows you to set an image to trace over when designing your page.

Figure 7.51 The Targeted Rule pop-up menu on the Property Inspector lists available class rules. Choose a class from this menu to apply it.

Title/Encoding: Type a page title. Choose the Document Type (DTD) from the pop-up menu. Leave Encoding and Unicode Normalization Form alone unless you know what you're doing and are creating pages in multiple languages (**Figure 7.49**).

Tracing Image: Browse to locate the tracing image and set the degree of transparency (**Figure 7.50**). We discuss tracing images in Chapter 3, "Building Your First Page."

4. Click Apply to see how your changes look, and then OK to accept your changes.

✔ Tips

■ The styles and properties you set are stored internally in this document only. You can inspect them in Code view. The Document Type appears in the first line of code. The language encoding appears in a `meta` element in the `head`. The styles are enclosed in a `style` element in the `head`. If you set a tracing image, it appears in Design view.

■ Names in the Page Properties dialog are not always standard CSS selector or property names. For example, in the Links category, Rollover links correspond to the CSS pseudo-class selector `a:hover` and Underline style corresponds to the CSS property `text-decoration`.

To create classes or inline styles with the Property Inspector:

1. Open a document and select the text or tag to be styled.

On the CSS tab of the Property Inspector, <New CSS Rule> is automatically selected in the Targeted Rule pop-up menu (**Figure 7.51**).

continues on next page

CREATING STYLES WITH THE PROPERTY INSPECTOR

If you look in the menu, there are other styles you can apply; the Cascade section lists styles available in external sheet(s), the New Rule section allows you to create a new CSS rule or a new inline style, and the Apply Class section allows you to apply existing classes.

or

In the Targeted Rule pop-up menu, choose <New Inline Style>.

2. Set new values for any or all of the following: Font, Size, and Color. For color, use the Color Picker to choose a color for the selected text.

   If you are creating a new inline style, the style is created in the document, and the style is applied to the selection. You're done.

   or

   If you're creating a new CSS style, the New CSS Rule dialog appears (**Figure 7.52**).

   (Optional) Instead of applying values in the Property Inspector, you can click the Edit Rule button on the CSS tab of the Property Inspector.

3. Choose the Selector Type, enter the Selector Name, and choose where you want the new style to reside with the Rule Definition pop-up menu.

4. Click OK. If you formatted the selection with the controls in the Property Inspector in step 2, the style is applied. If you used the Edit Rule button, the CSS Rule definition dialog appears. Set the style properties you need in this dialog, then click OK.

   Dreamweaver creates the `class` with a generic name, and the new `class` appears in the Targeted Rule pop-up menu on the Property Inspector. The `class` is applied with a `span` tag to inline text. If the selected text is a complete element, such as a paragraph, the `class` is applied to the element's tag.

Figure 7.52 The New CSS Rule dialog appears to help you specify the location for your new rule.

Figure 7.53 Right-click any style to reveal the Edit menu choices.

Figure 7.54 Edit any property value directly in the Properties pane.

Modifying a Style

Changing a style is quick and easy. You're already familiar with the CSS Rule definition dialog and the CSS Styles panel, and you can modify styles using either one.

To modify a style with the CSS Rule definition dialog:

1. Open a document. In the CSS Styles panel, click All mode, choose a style, and then do either of the following:

   Right-click the style name and choose Edit from the contextual menu (**Figure 7.53**).

   or

   Click the Edit Rule button at the lower right of the CSS Styles panel (Figure 7.5).

2. The CSS Rule definition dialog appears. Make changes as desired.

3. Click OK to accept your changes.

To modify a style with the CSS Styles panel:

1. Open a document. In the CSS Styles panel, choose a style in either All or Current mode. Properties for the selected style appear in the Properties pane.

2. Click a value in the Properties pane. An editable field appears (**Figure 7.54**).

3. Change as desired, and press Enter (Return) to complete your changes.

Working with Font Groups

Font groups determine which fonts a browser displays on your Web page. A browser uses the first font in the group that is installed on the user's system. If none of the fonts in the group are installed, the browser displays the text as specified by the user's browser preferences.

To modify a font group:

1. Open a document in Dreamweaver.

2. Choose Format > Font > Edit Font List.

or

Choose Edit Font List from the Font pop-up menu in the Property Inspector.

The Edit Font List dialog appears (**Figure 7.55**) and displays three categories of information:

▲ **Font list:** Displays current font groups.

▲ **Chosen fonts:** Displays fonts in the chosen group.

▲ **Available fonts:** Displays all the fonts available on your system. The font selected is displayed in the text field below.

3. Do any of the following:

▲ To add or remove fonts from a font group, select the font and click the arrows buttons between the Chosen fonts list and the Available fonts list.

▲ To add or remove a font group, select it and click the Plus or Minus button at the top left of the dialog.

Figure 7.55 Use the Edit Font List dialog to create, modify, or remove font groups.

▲ To add the name of a font that is not installed on your system, type the font name in the text field below the Available fonts list and click the left-facing arrow button to add it to the group.

▲ To move a font group up or down in the list, select it from the Font list box and then click the arrow buttons at the top right of the dialog.

4. Click OK to accept your changes.

✔ Tips

■ To avoid surprises, it's good practice to stick with the commonly available fonts for most text. If you really need to use a fancy, decorative font for short bits of text, you may be better off making an image of the text and placing it as a graphic.

■ We would love to add something here like, "You can be assured that people with *this* browser and *this* operating system will have *these* fonts"—but we can't. New browser versions get shipped that don't include the same fonts the older versions did. The same goes for operating systems. And then, of course, people can always delete or disable their existing fonts. The font groups that ship with Dreamweaver, as a general rule, are very likely to be dependable. And of course, always end your font list with either serif or sans-serif for best results.

Fonts and Operating Systems

Not all computer systems have the same fonts. For example, a common sans-serif font on Windows systems is Arial. A similar sans-serif font on Macintosh systems is Helvetica. Many Linux systems have Helvetica, but not all. All these systems have some default sans-serif font, however.

When choosing font groups, select fonts that share similar characteristics and try to cover all the bases in terms of operating systems. Then add either the generic serif or sans-serif choice at the end, just in case none of your preferred choices are available.

Why add a font you don't even have to your font group? One reason is that you expect a lot of your viewers to have a particular font (even though you don't have it). For example, if you are developing pages for a corporate client for use in their intranet, your client may ask for a particular font that they know is installed on all of the company's machines.

Working with Font Groups

Working with Related Files

The vast majority of Web pages you see these days aren't standalone HTML files. Rather, they are HTML files with links to other, related files, including CSS style sheets; external JavaScript files; server-side include (SSI) files; and sometimes even XML and other HTML files.

In previous versions of Dreamweaver, it was sometimes difficult to find and get to these related files when you were working on a page. You would have to check the page's source code in Code view, or fiddle around in the CSS Styles panel to track down the name of the external style sheets.

In Dreamweaver CS4, the new Related Files bar (**Figure 7.56**) at the top of the document window gives you quick, one-click access to related files.

Related Files

Figure 7.56 The Related Files bar lets you quickly jump to CSS and script files.

To use Related Files:

1. Open a document that uses external files.

   The names of the files appear in the Related Files bar. At the left side of the bar, you will always see Source Code, so that you can easily display the source code for the current document after you have opened a related file.

2. Click on the name of one of the related files in the Related Files bar.

   Dreamweaver switches to Split view, with the document in the Design view pane, and the related file in the Code view pane (**Figure 7.57**).

3. View or edit code in the Code view pane.

Figure 7.57 When you click the name of a style sheet in the Related Files bar, you end up in Split view, ready to edit the style sheet.

✔ Tips

■ The Related Files feature is enabled by default, but you can turn it off in the General category of Dreamweaver's Preferences.

■ You can also access related files by choosing View > Related Files, then choosing the file you want from the submenu (**Figure 7.58**).

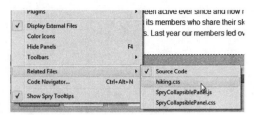

Figure 7.58 You can also see the Related Files in the View menu.

■ Dreamweaver will show all linked CSS files in the Related Files bar, even if the CSS files are linked to one another, rather than to the current document. In other words, the Related Files bar will show all of the style sheets in the cascade. However, it will only show other types of files, such as script files, that are directly linked to the current document.

■ Related Files are especially useful when working with the Code Navigator feature (see the next section) and with Dreamweaver's Live View mode.

■ If you open a frameset file, Dreamweaver does not list the other HTML pages that make up the frameset in the Related Files bar.

Code Navigator indicator

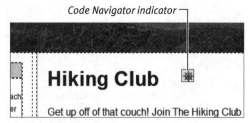

Figure 7.59 Click the Code Navigator indicator to open the Code Navigator window.

Figure 7.60 The Code Navigator window shows the different style sheets associated with the element you selected, and also shows which particular rules affect the element.

Using the Code Navigator

One of the challenges of working with modern sites is that sometimes it can be difficult to figure out which of the linked style sheets or script files is actually being applied to a given element on your page. Sure, you can use the Property Inspector or the CSS Styles panel to get the name of the style that is applied to the element, but that style could be being modified by another style sheet elsewhere in the cascade. What you need is a tool that shows all of the style sheets and scripts that are affecting your selection, then allows you to easily make changes to those styles and scripts. That's what the Code Navigator, new to Dreamweaver CS4, does.

To use the Code Navigator:

1. Point at the element on your page that you want to inspect, then Alt-click (Cmd-Opt-click).

   or

   Press Ctrl-Alt-N (Cmd-Opt-N).

   or

   Right-click the selection or a tag in the Tag Selector, then choose Code Navigator from the contextual menu.

   or

   Choose View > Code Navigator.

   or

   Click the Code Navigator indicator that appears near where you last clicked in the document when Dreamweaver has been idle for a few seconds (**Figure 7.59**).

   The Code Navigator window appears (**Figure 7.60**), showing you the script and CSS files associated with the selection. For CSS styles, indented under the name of each style sheet, the Code Navigator shows the names of the CSS rules that apply to the selection.

continues on next page

USING THE CODE NAVIGATOR

217

2. To jump directly to a particular rule, click its name in the Code Navigator window.

The Dreamweaver window changes to Split view, and places the insertion point in the Code view pane, ready to edit the style rule you chose.

or

To view the properties defined in each of the rules shown in the Code Navigator, hover the cursor over a rule's name. After a moment, a tool tip appears showing you the properties (**Figure 7.61**).

3. If you ended up in the Code View pane in step two, edit the style rule. If all you wanted to do was view the rules and properties for the selection, press Esc or click elsewhere in the document to dismiss the Code Navigator window.

✔ Tips

■ You can also invoke the Code Navigator in Code view by placing the insertion point inside a <script> or <link> tag, or inside a text block that is being styled by CSS, and clicking the Code Navigator button on the Coding toolbar. See Chapter 17 for more information about working in Code view.

■ The Code Navigator indicator (Figure 7.59) is actually pretty annoying, because it pops up whenever you pause your work. You can (and probably will) turn the indicator off by checking the "Disable <Code Navigator symbol> indicator" check box at the bottom of the Code Navigator window.

Figure 7.61 Hovering over a CSS rule reveals the rule's properties.

POSITIONING PAGE CONTENT

8

In Chapter 7, you saw how to use CSS (Cascading Style Sheets) to style text. There's a whole lot more that CSS can do besides make your words look pretty—style sheets can also be used to lay out elements on your page.

This chapter covers the how-tos of positioning and how to use Dreamweaver's layout tools in a way that suits your work style. You'll also get a look at some of the great features in Dreamweaver that help you use CSS for layout and positioning elements. We'll wrap it all up with a historical overview of how older versions of Dreamweaver used to recommend that you position elements on your page and why those approaches just aren't the right choices any longer.

CSS Layout Basics

When CSS first started becoming popular (that is, when enough browsers supported it consistently), its primary use was for styling text, and Web designers were thrilled to say goodbye to the font tag. Besides styling text, it's also possible to use CSS to define how your page is laid out, and thankfully, modern browsers now have sufficient market share that CSS layout has become the standard.

The box model

When you're talking about positioning elements with CSS, you immediately run into the term *the box model*. Here's a quick overview of what you'll need to know to be able to use CSS for positioning.

When working with CSS and layout, you're creating boxes (almost always done by adding a div) and positioning them on your pages. Each box contains several elements (**Figure 8.1**): its margin, border, padding, and content. Using CSS, you can set rules for each element. Additionally, you can (for example) set different rules for the top, right, bottom, and left sides of an element.

Let's say that you want to put a line above and below your text. You can set the border around your text (that is, to the tag that contains your text) to 1px black solid just for the top and bottom. If you don't set the other sides, they'll be set to 0 by default.

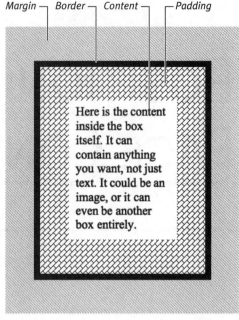

Margin — Border — Content — Padding

Here is the content inside the box itself. It can contain anything you want, not just text. It could be an image, or it can even be another box entirely.

Figure 8.1 The CSS box model, broken down into parts.

Figure 8.2 An example of an absolutely positioned box with set width.

Positioning your boxes

When you've created boxes on your page, you'll want to place them. In order to do that, you need to understand two new concepts: *position* and *float*.

The position of a box can be *static*, *relative*, *inherit*, *absolute*, or *fixed* (**Figure 8.2**).

◆ **Static:** The simplest position is static; it just means that the box ends up wherever it would normally end up, all on its own. Any left or top offsets you give it are ignored.

◆ **Relative:** The next simplest is relative, which is just like static except that you can set its left and top positions.

◆ **Inherit:** Inherit is used when you want a box to automatically inherit the properties of its parent (that is, its container). Wherever that box happens to be, it just takes on the position rules based on its container.

◆ **Absolute:** Absolute and fixed are similar, in that you can specify exactly where on your page you want the box to appear. The difference between the two involves their frame of reference: an absolutely positioned box is positioned in reference to its container. If you have an absolutely positioned box placed 100 pixels from the top of a page, and another absolutely positioned box inside that box that is also set to be 100 pixels down, the interior box will be 200 pixels down, not 100—because its frame of reference is to the box that it's inside.

◆ **Fixed:** Fixed positioning, on the other hand, is based on the page itself. If you set a box to be fixed at 100 pixels down, it will always be there, even if you scroll the page. When you scroll, that box will move down with you so that it's always 100 pixels down from the top of the visible page.

Floating your boxes

Alternatively, a box can be set to float, such that its contents stick to one side or the other of its containing element (**Figure 8.3**). The values for float are *left*, *right*, *none*, and *inherit*.

◆ **Left:** A box that is floated to the left causes everything else on the page (everything that isn't explicitly told to be somewhere else, that is) to wrap around it to the right.

◆ **Right:** Just like left, a box floated to the right causes everything else to wrap around it on the left.

◆ **None:** This is the default, but it's sometimes useful to be able to explicitly tell a box, no, don't float (usually when trying to work around browser bugs).

◆ **Inherit:** If you do want a box to inherit the float value of its container, just say so explicitly by setting float to inherit.

✔ Tips

■ What's described here is how browsers are supposed to handle positioning and floating boxes, and all of the browsers released in the last few years handle it well. Older browsers may have varying degrees of difficulty with these concepts. As always, we recommend testing your site in as many browsers (and versions and platforms) as possible.

■ This is just a quick and dirty definition. Many pages (and some entire books) have been written on the intricacies of the box model.

Hiking Club

Get up off of that couch! Join The Hiking Club and enjoy exciting outdoor adventures throughout the year. We do hiking, technical rock climbing, backpacking, camping, snowshoeing, skiing, and cycling. Whether you want something easy or something strenuous, we have an activity for you.

Embudo Canyon Waterfall, Spring 2005

Monthly meetings bring us together to share information about hikes, trails, equipment and other topics of interest. Our members have hiked all over the world and returned to tell the tale!

The Hiking Club was started in 1948 by a group with a common love of the outdoors. It has been active ever since and now has almost 1,000 members. Our Club's strength is its members who share their skills and knowledge of

Figure 8.3 This graphic and its caption are both floated to the right.

Figure 8.4 The familiar New Document dialog contains handy CSS-based page designs to get you started. Look at the Preview column to decide which of the designs you want to use as the basis for your page.

Figure 8.5 Here's your new page, ready to take your content.

Using the Included Layouts

Initially, you might think that it's difficult to get started using CSS for positioning, but thankfully, Dreamweaver has included something to make getting started easy as can be: using Dreamweaver's included CSS layouts. These files are flexible, professionally developed templates that are available to use as a starting point.

To use the included layouts:

1. From Dreamweaver's menu, choose File > New. The New Document dialog appears (**Figure 8.4**).

2. If it wasn't chosen by default, select the category "Blank Page" and the Page Type "HTML," and 32 designs will be listed in the center column. Choose any of these to see a preview in the right column. Directly below the preview is a short description of the design.

3. If you see a design you like, click Create. A new untitled Dreamweaver document opens in the chosen design (**Figure 8.5**). You now have a template for your site that's entirely CSS-based. You can modify both the page content and its styles.

4. Save the new layout by choosing File > Save, or by pressing Ctrl-S (Cmd-S).

✔ Tip

- Even if none of the included design files suit your taste, take a look at them and check out how they work. They're a good way to learn how to use CSS to position elements on a page.

Laying Out Your Page

Here's where things get interesting: now that we've got the theory, it's time to put it into practice. With the included CSS styles, it's straightforward.

Before you start laying out your page, you need to think about what you want on that page and where you want it to go. As discussed back in Chapter 2, the best way to do that is with pencil and paper. That should tell you what styles you'll need: for instance, a header, footer, content area, and navigation area. Once you have a design in mind, look through the included CSS layouts to see which HTML page best fits your idea (**Figure 8.6**).

Now you're ready to start. In this case, we'll start with the 2-column hybrid layout, with a left sidebar, header, and footer (**Figure 8.7**). The *hybrid* part of the name means that the left-hand sidebar is a fixed size, but the rest of the page can expand/shrink to fit the width of the browser.

Figure 8.6 You'll want to have a plan before you start laying out your page, and here's our planned design.

Figure 8.7 Start by selecting a new blank page with a new layout.

Figure 8.8 This page doesn't just contain dummy text—it also contains some helpful tips in the sidebar.

Figure 8.9 Start your new page off by changing the styles for the body tag.

To lay out your page:

1. Choose the 2-column hybrid layout, and Dreamweaver gives you a bare-bones page to start (**Figure 8.8**).

2. Almost all of the work will be done in the CSS Styles pane of the CSS panel (**Figure 8.9**). Here, the body styles are all fine except for the background—we want it to be white instead of the default gray, so we've changed its value to #FFFFFF.

continues on next page

3. Next is the #container—that's the one large div that contains everything on the page. We change the border from 1 pixel solid black to 1 pixel solid light blue, the margins from 0 pixels at the top and bottom to ten pixels, and the width from 80% to 90%. Finally we add two new properties by clicking the "Add Property" link near the bottom: color, which we set to black and line height, which is set to 130% (**Figure 8.10**).

4. There are two parts to the page header: the background graphic and the foreground logo. We delete the gray background color property from the #header style and replace it with background-image (set to our background image), background-position (set to right center), and background-repeat (set to no-repeat). We also add a light solid gray bottom border (with the border-bottom-color, border-bottom-style, and border-bottom-width properties), and change the padding value slightly (**Figure 8.11**).

Figure 8.10 Next, change the styles for the div named container.

Figure 8.11 Once you've set up the header, you're a long way towards having your Web page just the way you want it.

Figure 8.12 Here's what the header should end up looking like with both the background image and the foreground image (selected so you can see it better).

5. Drag the logo over from the Assets panel (**Figure 8.12**). HTML defaults to putting it on the far left of the div, so it doesn't need any positioning changes to be in the right place for this example. Your page should now look something like **Figure 8.13**.

6. Next up is the navigation sidebar, which Dreamweaver has cleverly named `sidebar1`. Use the tag selector to select `div#sidebar1`. We don't want the gray background color that came with the sample layout, and since the default is to just let the underlying color through, the background color can be deleted. The same goes for the padding (**Figure 8.14**).

continues on next page

Figure 8.13 And here's what our page looks like so far. Next up: the sidebar.

Figure 8.14 Change the sidebar to match our desired design.

LAYING OUT YOUR PAGE

7. Now it's time to add three new rules to handle the navigation in the sidebar: one for the ul, one for the li, and one for the a tags; respectively, an unordered list, each individual list element, and the links themselves. Select the .twoColElsLtHdr #sidebar1 rule in the CSS Styles panel. You should recall from Chapter 7 that rules are added by clicking the New CSS rule button at the bottom of the CSS panel. When you click that button, the New CSS Rule dialog appears (**Figure 8.15**).

8. In the dialog, the Selector Type will automatically be set to Compound, which is fine. You need to change the Selector Name to reflect the rule you are creating; specifically, you need to add the ul tag to the end of the selector. You also don't need the #container part of the selector (it's implied, because everything on the page is inside the container div), so you can eliminate it. You need to apply the selector to the ul tag, so type ul at the end of the Selector Name, with the result shown in **Figure 8.16**. Click OK, and the CSS Rule definition dialog appears (**Figure 8.17**).

9. Set the ul tags to have the list-style-Position outside, with a padding of 1em (you'll find the padding setting in the Box category of the dialog).

Figure 8.15 The New CSS Rule dialog is where you can change the selector name to apply to the tag we want to style.

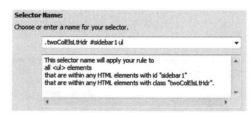

Figure 8.16 We've added the ul tag to the end of the Selector Name.

Figure 8.17 In the CSS Rule definition dialog, set the style properties you want.

Properties for ".twoColElsLtHdr #sidebar1 ul"	
list-style-position	outside
padding	1em
Add Property	

Properties for ".twoColElsLtHdr #sidebar1 li"	
border-bottom-color	B7C7F3
border-bottom-style	solid
border-bottom-width	1px
list-style	none
Add Property	

Properties for ".twoColElsLtHdr #sidebar1 a"	
color	#000000
text-decoration	none
Add Property	

Figure 8.18 This figure shows the properties for the three new rules. First is the unordered lists with the sidebar (top), next, the second new rule applies to all list elements within the sidebar (middle), and finally, the last new sidebar rule applies to all links within list elements.

10. Repeat steps 7 through 9 to create two more rules, one for the li tags and one for the a tags.

    Set the li tags to have a bottom border of light blue and no list-style, and the a tags are set to always be black but never be underlined. **Figure 8.18** shows the properties for the three rules.

11. Select the text in the sidebar, type over it with a list of navigation choices, then select the list and click the Unordered List button on the HTML tab of the Property Inspector.

12. Next up is the main content area, and as you might guess, Dreamweaver has called it mainContent. It needs to be more complex than the default, so set the left-hand border to be light blue, the left-hand margin to be 12em, the max-width to be 36em, and the padding to be 1em (**Figure 8.19**). Then delete the margin property that came with the default.

continues on next page

Figure 8.19 The mainContent div contains the main page content.

LAYING OUT YOUR PAGE

13. We have to add one div to the default layout to handle the photo and its caption. Add a div to the page by clicking the Insert Div Tag button in the Common category of the Insert panel. The Insert Div Tag dialog appears (**Figure 8.20**). Set the ID to photofeature, and click the New CSS Rule button. The New CSS Rule dialog appears (**Figure 8.21**). The Selector Type will be ID and the Selector Name will be #photofeature. Click OK and the CSS Rule definition dialog will appear.

14. In the dialog, set the color, the line-height, font-size and font-style, and the left and bottom padding. Also, set the div to float to the right. Use the values in **Figure 8.22**.

Click OK to dismiss the CSS Rule definition dialog, then click OK again to dismiss the Insert Div Tag dialog.

Figure 8.20 The Insert Div Tag dialog lets you choose whether or not to create a new CSS rule at the same time.

Figure 8.21 If you clicked the New CSS Rule button, you get the New CSS Rule dialog. Here, you can tell Dreamweaver what you want your new rule to apply to.

Properties for "#photofeature"	
color	211A4C
float	right
font-size	0.8em
font-style	italic
line-height	1em
padding-bottom	0.8em
padding-left	0.8em
Add Property	

Figure 8.22 Now set up the properties for photofeature, and the image and its caption will display just the way they should.

Figure 8.23 The content and caption have been added here, and they're doing just what they've been told to do.

15. Drag an image from the Assets panel to the photofeature div, and add a caption. The result should now be similar to **Figure 8.23**.

16. There's only one last bit to go: the footer (**Figure 8.24**). We want our footer to be more prominent than it is in the default, so we'll add a background color, a top border, and change the padding.

17. All that's left is to add your text in the mainContent div, and add your navigation links to the sidebar, and your page is done (**Figure 8.25**).

Properties for ".twoColElsLtHdr #footer"	
background-color	#B7C7F3
border-top	1px solid gray
color	#333
font-size	0.8em
margin	0
padding	0.5em
Add Property	

Figure 8.24 Here are the footer properties. The footer is not fixed in a particular place, so the page can be a variable length.

Figure 8.25 Here's our final page.

✔ Tips

- Dreamweaver automatically adds the text 'Content for id "idName" Goes Here' whenever you create a new div. You'll want to delete that, but don't do it immediately. It can be hard to click inside an empty div, so leave that text there until you've added something inside.

- If you're wondering why mainContent has a left margin of 12em (Figure 8.19), it's because the sidebar has a width of 12em (Figure 8.14). That left margin keeps the main content area from overlapping the sidebar.

- Don't forget that you can inspect any element on the page by Alt-clicking (Option-clicking) to pop-up the Code Navigator (as in **Figure 8.26**), giving you information about that element. In this case, you can see that it's a div named footer. The tip also shows the values (if any) of float, position, top, right, bottom, left, width, height, and overflow. See Chapter 7 for more about using the Code Navigator.

- You don't really need to know that white is #FFF—you can just select the color you want from the color well in the panel.

- Don't forget to add a title to your page in the Title field of the document toolbar.

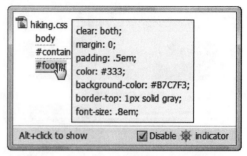

Figure 8.26 Hovering over a style in the Code Navigator gives you useful information about that element.

Figure 8.27 Here's the visual aids menu in the document toolbar and your choices.

Figure 8.28 Or, you can get to it via the menu bar.

Figure 8.29 CSS Layout Backgrounds are gaudy but useful.

Using the Visual Aids

Laying out pages with CSS can be frustrating because it can sometimes be difficult to tell which elements are where and why. Thankfully, Dreamweaver has a few handy features that make creating CSS-based layouts much simpler. Dreamweaver refers to these as *Visual Aids*.

Figure 8.25 shows our example CSS-based page with all visual aids turned off. It's fine, but if we had a problem, it would be difficult to tell where each div begins and ends. That's where the visual aids shine.

The visual aids can be found on the right side of the Document toolbar. Although it looks like a button, that little downward facing arrow means that it's actually a pop-up menu. If you click it, you'll get the options seen in **Figure 8.27**. Or, you can choose View > Visual Aids, and then select any of the submenu options (**Figure 8.28**).

To turn each visual aid on or off, choose it from the menu to toggle its checkmark, or you can choose Hide All (Ctrl-Shift-I or Cmd-Shift-I) to turn them all off temporarily. For day-to-day use, we recommend keeping CSS Layout Backgrounds turned off, and CSS Layout Box Model and CSS Layout Outlines on.

Here's a rundown of the CSS-related items in these menus:

◆ **CSS Layout Backgrounds:** Put on your sunglasses and turn on CSS Layout Backgrounds (**Figure 8.29**). With this aid, Dreamweaver assigns a different background color for every layout block. If you've already set a background color, that will go away, as will background images—note that while you can see the header logo, you can't see the header background graphic.

continues on next page

Dreamweaver's documentation describes the color choices as "visually distinctive," but we prefer to not beat around the bush: we just call them loud and bright. Sorry, but there's no way to change the color choices. On the other hand, the garishness makes it very clear which div is which.

◆ **CSS Layout Box Model:** You've seen the Layout Box Model aid (**Figure 8.30**) used previously in this chapter. When enabled, it shows just the selected element, including its margin, borders, and padding. If you recall from Figure 8.19, the mainContent div had a 1 pixel solid light blue left border, a 12em left margin, and a padding of 1em. When this visual aid is enabled, each of these is shown visually and uniquely on the document along with the dimensions of the div.

◆ **CSS Layout Outlines:** The CSS Layout Outlines option simply puts a dashed line around the border of each layout block (**Figure 8.31**). It can be tricky to see what your borders are set to when this is on, and you should also keep in mind that the dashed line includes the padding but excludes the margins.

Figure 8.30 The CSS Layout Box Model shows you the exact limits of the currently selected element.

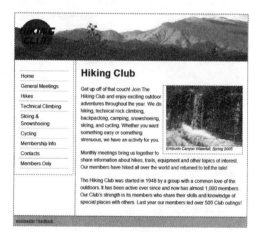

Figure 8.31 CSS Layout Outlines give you a subtle way of telling your elements apart.

Using Design-Time Style Sheets

It's common when working with CSS-based layouts to want something to display in a particular way while you're designing—but *only* while you're designing, that is, during *design time*. You can tell Dreamweaver to use certain style sheets only at design time, and even to turn off certain style sheets only at design time.

As with the previous visual aids, you wouldn't want your real Web site to look like that, but it's handy while trying to do those last few tweaks or track down a problem. If you want something that Dreamweaver's built-in visual aids don't provide, Design-time style sheets allow you to create your own.

continues on next page

CSS Layout Blocks

Dreamweaver uses what it refers to as *CSS layout blocks*, which are one of the following:

- A div without display:inline.
- An element with display:block.
- An element with position:absolute.
- An element with position:relative.

CSS layout blocks are used by the visual aids and design-time style sheets to help designers understand how the parts of a CSS-based layout work together on your page.

For instance, say you have a design-time style sheet that assigns position:relative to all of your links (that is, to all a tags). When you then turn on CSS Layout Backgrounds, all of your links will be their own bright color, allowing you to easily pick them out.

To show a Design-time style sheet:

1. Create and save a new style sheet containing the style rules that should display only inside Dreamweaver. **Figure 8.32** shows an example that contains two simple rules: p is set to `display:block` and h1 gets a background color of `orange`. See the "CSS Layout Blocks" sidebar for an explanation of why you'd want to modify the p tag.

2. To choose a Design-time style sheet, either choose Format > CSS Styles > Design-time (**Figure 8.33**), or right-click inside the CSS Styles panel and choose Design-time from the contextual menu (**Figure 8.34**). The Design-Time Style Sheets dialog appears (**Figure 8.35**).

Figure 8.32 This very simple style sheet gives us extra information in Dreamweaver.

Figure 8.33 Design-time style sheets can be chosen from the Format menu.

Figure 8.34 Or they can be chosen from the CSS panel.

Figure 8.35 But either way, you end up at the Design Time Style Sheets dialog.

Figure 8.36 The Select File dialog lets you choose your Design-time style sheet.

Figure 8.37 Now the h1 is all lit up.

Figure 8.38 Paragraphs are delineated when the background visual aid is used.

3. To add a style sheet that shows only at design time, click the upper plus button. The Select File dialog appears (**Figure 8.36**). Navigate to your new style sheet, choose it, and click OK.

4. Back in the Design-Time Style Sheets dialog, your new style sheet is now listed next to Show only at design time. If it's correct, click OK.

5. The Web page now appears with some slight changes (**Figure 8.37**): the h1 title now has an orange background, and paragraphs can now be identified using the CSS Layout Box Model visual aid. If we use the CSS Layout Backgrounds visual aid (**Figure 8.38**), paragraphs are now clearly distinct from other elements on the page.

To hide a style sheet at design time:

◆ Follow steps 2 through 4 from "To show a Design-time style sheet" earlier, but click the lower plus button instead. Select a style sheet to hide, and click OK.

In **Figure 8.39**, the main style sheet for the page has been hidden. This allows you to see the page without the effect of styles, or to see the page with some styles but not others. This can be a big help when trying to track down CSS-related issues.

To remove a Design-time style sheet:

1. Bring up the Design-Time Style Sheets dialog as described earlier. Select the style sheet to remove and click the minus button above the style sheet name in either box of the dialog. If you have multiple style sheets to remove, continue to delete them in this way.

2. Click OK, and your Web page displays closer to the way it will appear on the Web.

✔ Tips

■ Design-time style sheets are an extremely powerful tool when used in conjunction with Dreamweaver's CSS Layout Blocks.

■ Despite how it looks, your document is not actually being changed, only the way the page is displayed. Design-time style sheets are not really added to or removed from your Web page: Dreamweaver handles it all internally.

■ Don't forget that you also have the Style Rendering toolbar (covered in Chapter 1), which you can use to display your page as it would appear with print style sheets, handheld style sheets, projection style sheets, and so on. You can also use the Style Rendering toolbar to turn off the display of style sheets altogether.

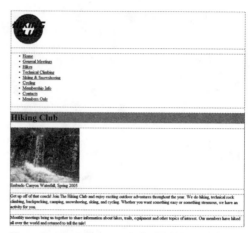

Figure 8.39 Style sheets can also be hidden, as seen on this plain page.

■ It's worth noting that when you remove Design-Time Style Sheets from your document, you're not actually deleting the style sheet itself—you're just removing the relationship between your page and the style sheet.

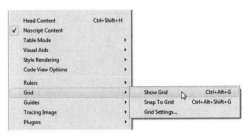

Figure 8.40 You can get to all the grid options from the menu...

Figure 8.41 ...and you can turn them on or off from the View Options menu.

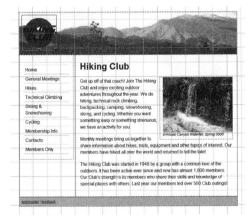

Figure 8.42 Here's our usual page with the grid visible.

Using the Grid

If you want items on a page to line up, a handy way to do it is to use the grid—a feature you may well be familiar with from other applications such as Photoshop. If you're used to it elsewhere, it's easy; if you're not, here's a quick overview.

The grid overlays graph-paper–like lines on your Web page, making it easy to see if elements on the page are horizontally or vertically aligned. Nothing on your page is actually changed, and the lines are only visible inside Dreamweaver. If you choose to have elements on your page *snap to the grid*, whenever you move an element close to a grid line, it will "jump" (or snap) to match up with it. This way, you know for sure that your elements are perfectly aligned.

To turn the grid on or off:

◆ To toggle the grid display, choose View > Grid > Show Grid (**Figure 8.40**), or click the View Options menu button on the Document toolbar (**Figure 8.41**) and choose Grid, or press Ctrl-Alt-G (Cmd-Option-G). Your document displays the grid if it wasn't already displayed (**Figure 8.42**), and vice versa.

To change the grid settings:

1. Choose View > Grid > Grid Settings (Figure 8.40). The Grid Settings dialog appears (**Figure 8.43**).

2. From this dialog, you can change the color, spacing, and whether the grid displays as lines or dots. You can also use this as a way to set the Show grid and Snap to Grid options at the same time. If you want to check how a setting looks, click Apply. When you like your results, click OK, and if the grid is set to show, your document appears with your chosen grid style. If the grid is not set to show, the settings will still be changed, and will display their new values the next time you show the grid.

To make elements snap to the grid:

1. Choose View > Grid > Snap To Grid (Figure 8.40), or check the Snap to grid check box in the Grid Settings dialog (Figure 8.43), or press Ctrl-Alt-Shift-G (Cmd-Option-Shift-G).

2. Move an absolutely positioned page element. It snaps to line up with the grid if you move the element within a few pixels of a grid line.

Figure 8.43 If you don't like the grid defaults, the settings can be changed.

Figure 8.44 You can turn rulers on and off in the View menu.

Figure 8.45 As you could with the grid, you can get to many guide options in the View menu.

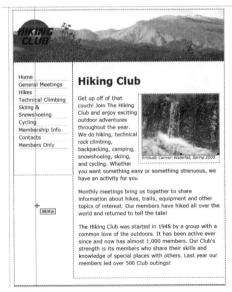

Figure 8.46 By default, guides are measured in pixels.

Using Rulers and Guides

Rulers and guides are tools commonly found in other design applications. Dreamweaver has both horizontal and vertical rulers, and it can use pixels, inches, or centimeters as units.

Guides can do almost everything grids can, and a whole lot more. For instance, guides can be locked into place, guides can be set to percentages of the page, and not only can elements snap to guides, but guides can be set to snap to elements.

To turn rulers on or off:

◆ To toggle the display of rulers, choose View > Rulers > Show (**Figure 8.44**), or click the View Options menu button on the Document toolbar and choose Rulers, or press Ctrl-Alt-R (Cmd-Opt-R). You can also choose the ruler units in this menu.

To turn guides on or off:

◆ To toggle the display of guides, choose View > Guides > Show Guides (**Figure 8.45**), or click the View Options menu button on the Document toolbar and choose Guides, or press Ctrl-; (Cmd-;).

To add a guide to your page:

1. Click the cursor in either the horizontal or vertical ruler, and drag into the document. The guide appears along with a tip that displays the number of pixels that the guide is currently away from the edge of the document (**Figure 8.46**).

2. When the guide is where you want it, release the mouse. The line remains, but the tip goes away.

To edit guide settings:

1. Choose View > Guides > Edit Guides, and the Guides dialog appears (**Figure 8.47**).

2. From here, you can set:
    ▲ The guide and distance colors.
    ▲ Whether guides should show.
    ▲ Whether elements should snap to guides, guides snap to elements, both, or neither.
    ▲ Whether guides are locked.

    You can also use it to clear all the current guides by clicking the Clear All button.

3. When your changes are complete, click OK.

✔ Tips

■ To move a guide, move the mouse over the guide. When the cursor changes, click the guide and drag it to its new location.

■ To remove a guide from your page, move the guide off the document. Mac users will see a little "puff of smoke" animation —sorry, Windows users! You can also remove all the guides at once (without the animated effect) by choosing View > Guides > Clear Guides or by clicking Clear All in the Guides dialog (Figure 8.47).

■ To inspect the current position of a guide, hover the cursor over the guide, and a tip showing the position appears.

■ To position a guide based on the percentage distance of the document rather than pixels, hold down the Shift key while moving the guide (**Figure 8.48**). The tip displays the current location in both pixels and percentages when you're moving it and also when you check the guide's position later.

Figure 8.47 Use the Guides dialog to change any of its settings.

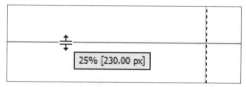

Figure 8.48 If you want a percentage instead of pixels, hold down the Shift key.

Figure 8.49 Holding down the Ctrl (Cmd) key gives you the distance between the document edge and the guide.

Figure 8.50 Double-click a guide to get to the Move Guide dialog.

■ To see how far a guide is from the sides of your document, hold down the Ctrl (Cmd) key. Lines appear showing the distance in pixels (and percentage, if set in the previous tip) to the edges of the document (**Figure 8.49**). If you have multiple guides on your page, the distance shown will be from guide to guide or from guide to edge.

■ Guides can be locked on your page so that they can't be moved. To do this, choose View > Guides > Lock Guides or use the Guides dialog (Figure 8.47). It's a toggle, so just do it again to unlock your guides.

■ Rulers have to be visible for you to add guides, but you can view, move, and delete guides even when the rulers are hidden.

■ Guides can be used to simulate dimensions of standard browsers. Choose View > Guides and pick one of the standard sizes from the bottom of the menu (Figure 8.45). This creates both vertical and horizontal guides on your page. Be careful, though, as you can still move them accidentally, and then they aren't much use at giving you your dimension hints. This is the one exception to the previous tip: you can create guides with this method even when the ruler is hidden.

■ As with the grid, you can choose to snap elements to your guides—but you can also choose to snap guides to your elements. Choose either View > Guides > Snap To Guides, View > Guides > Guides Snap To Elements, or even both (Figure 8.45). Or, you can set them in the Guides dialog (Figure 8.47).

■ If you double-click a guide, the Move Guide dialog appears (**Figure 8.50**). Use this dialog to set the guide to a precise position in pixels, inches, centimeters, or percentages.

Zooming In On Your Page

Yes, it's another feature borrowed from standard design applications, just like the grid and guides. The Zoom feature lets you design your pages more precisely. And as with the grid and guides, you'll need to be in Design view to use it.

To zoom into your page:

◆ Select the Zoom tool from the status bar at the bottom right of your document (**Figure 8.51**), and your cursor changes to a magnifying glass with a plus. While in zoom mode, you can do either of two things:

▲ Click and drag to draw a box over the area you want to zoom in on. That rectangle expands to take up the entire document window (**Figure 8.52**).

▲ Click the spot on the page you want to magnify. Continue to click it until you get the magnification level you want.

or

Press Ctrl-= (Cmd-=) until you've reached the level you want.

or

Select a magnification level from the Zoom pop-up menu in the status bar.

or

Type your desired magnification level into the Zoom text box in the status bar.

or

Select View > Magnification and pick a magnification level (**Figure 8.53**).

or

Select an element on the page, and then choose View > Fit Selection (Figure 8.53).

or

Select an element on the page, and then choose Fit Selection from the Zoom pop-up menu in the status bar.

Figure 8.51 The magnification tools in the Status bar are especially useful when making detailed changes to your pages.

Figure 8.52 You can zoom in on a particular part of the screen.

Figure 8.53 You can also get to the magnification levels from the menu.

To zoom out from your page:

◆ Select the Zoom tool from the status bar at the bottom right of your document. Press Alt (Option) and the cursor changes to a magnifying glass and a minus. Click on the page to zoom out.

or

Press Ctrl- (minus key) (Cmd- (minus key)) until you've reached the level you want.

or

Select View > Magnification and pick a magnification level.

or

Choose View > Fit All or View > Fit Width (Figure 8.53).

or

Choose Fit All or Fit Width from the Zoom pop-up menu in the status bar.

✔ Tips

■ To edit your page in Zoom mode, select the pointer in the status bar and click inside the page.

■ To pan your page after you've zoomed in, select the hand icon in the status bar, and then drag the page to move around.

Setting Page Dimensions

It's handy to be able to easily set guides to show the dimensions of common browsers, but it's not quite the same as seeing how your design actually appears in a window of that size. That's where setting page dimensions comes in.

To resize the window to a preset size:

◆ Click the Window Size pop-up menu in the status bar, and select one of the listed sizes (**Figure 8.54**). Your document window resets itself to that size.

To edit the preset window sizes:

1. Click the Window Size pop-up menu in the status bar, and select Edit Sizes. The Status Bar preferences pane appears (**Figure 8.55**).

   or

   Open Dreamweaver's preferences and select the Status Bar category.

2. Click in any of the fields and write over the current value to replace it. To add a value, click in the first unfilled line (**Figure 8.56**). To delete a value, clear the entire line by deleting the contents of each field.

Figure 8.54 Dreamweaver comes with preset window sizes for the most commonly used monitors.

```
592w

536 x 196   (640 x 480, Default)
600 x 300   (640 x 480, Maximized)
760 x 420   (800 x 600, Maximized)
795 x 470   (832 x 624, Maximized)
955 x 600   (1024 x 768, Maximized)

Edit Sizes...
```

Figure 8.55 You can view or edit the window sizes in the Status Bar category of Dreamweaver's Preferences.

Figure 8.56 New sizes can be added just by clicking in the first unused line and typing the appropriate dimensions.

Window sizes:	Width	Height	Description
	592		
	536	196	(640 x 480, Default)
	600	300	(640 x 480, Maximized)
	760	420	(800 x 600, Maximized)
	795	470	(832 x 624, Maximized)
	955	600	(1024 x 768, Maximized)
	1280	800	MacBook screen size

SETTING PAGE DIMENSIONS

592w
536 x 196 (640 x 480, Default)
600 x 300 (640 x 480, Maximized)
760 x 420 (800 x 600, Maximized)
795 x 470 (832 x 624, Maximized)
955 x 600 (1024 x 768, Maximized)
1280 x 800 MacBook screen size
Edit Sizes...

Figure 8.57 And here's our new window size.

3. Click OK to accept. The new size now appears in the Window Size pop-up menu (**Figure 8.57**).

✔ Tips

■ You can resize the window to a fixed width (leaving the height alone) by entering only a width value. To make the window resize to a fixed height, enter only the height.

■ You can't resize a document on Windows if it's maximized.

■ While it looks like you can sort the values in the Status Bar preferences, you actually can't.

■ Sadly, if you enter a new window size, it doesn't get added as a new possible value for creating guides—it's only for resizing.

■ While you're in the Status Bar preferences, take the chance to reset the Connection speed if it's not appropriate for you or your audience. That number is what Dreamweaver uses to calculate page download time, which is shown on the far-right end of the status bar.

SETTING PAGE DIMENSIONS

Old Time Dreamweaver

Once upon a time, it was difficult to make a Web page look just the way you wanted it to look because browsers had very little support for layout. Dreamweaver worked hard to make positioning possible despite the poor browser support, and the primary way Dreamweaver did this was with what it called *layers*. The remainder of this chapter covers them.

It's important to note that Dreamweaver's layers are not the same thing as the HTML layer tag. The layer tag was implemented in Netscape 4 and only Netscape 4. Neither earlier versions of Netscape, nor later versions of Netscape, nor any other browser ever included it—so don't even bother with it.

Given the capabilities of Dreamweaver, and the browsers that are now commonly used, Dreamweaver's layers are in the same shape as that of the HTML layer tag: obsolete, and not for use going forward. However, you may encounter older sites that were set up with layers, so it's worth learning a little about how they work.

Don't Do It!

We might be coming off a little heavy-handed here, but it's from experience: don't use AP Elements. Just don't. If you have a site that uses AP Elements, it's worth taking the time to carefully convert it to use block positioning layout, divs, and CSS.

AP Elements themselves, along with converting AP Elements to tables and vice versa, are remnants of an older, sadder time. Dreamweaver leaves them in for historical reasons, but if you're just starting out, they're the wrong way to go.

Figure 8.58 When drawn, AP Elements look like a simple box on the screen.

Figure 8.59 When you select an AP Element, it has selection and resize handles.

Figure 8.60 Hovering over an AP Element gives you the div's name, size, and position.

Layers are now AP Elements

If Dreamweaver CS4 is the first version of Dreamweaver you've ever used, or if you never bothered with layers in the first place, you can skip this. For everyone else, though, you may be wondering: what happened to all my layer commands? The answer is, they were renamed AP (absolutely positioned) Elements. We'll use both terms in this section.

You can create an AP Element by going to the Layout tab of the Insert Bar, clicking the Draw AP Div button, and then drawing a box in the document window (**Figure 8.58**). Each box you draw is absolutely positioned on your Web page, with a fixed height and width and a fixed position from the top and left edges of the page.

The divs can be selected, moved, and resized by clicking the border of a layer. Once an AP Element is selected, you can see its selection handle and resize handles (**Figure 8.59**).

Once you've added your AP Elements to your page, they can be used in the same way divs were described earlier—you can add text, images, or whatever you'd like to your AP Elements.

Styles for AP Elements are internal, and each layer has a separate set of rules of its own— usually with meaningful names like apDiv1 and apDiv2. If you want to see which AP Element you're working on, move the cursor over the div and a tip appears giving the id, size, and position of that div (**Figure 8.60**).

AP Elements can overlap other AP Elements if you define them to do so (**Figure 8.61**). If you don't want them to overlap, you can check the Prevent overlaps box in the AP Elements tab of the CSS panel (**Figure 8.62**). That panel also contains the visibility indicator: a blank space, or an open or closed eye, on the left side of the panel. If the eye is open, that AP Element is visible. If the eye is closed, that AP Element is hidden. If the column is blank, the AP Element inherits its parent's visibility (AP Elements that have the document as their parent will be visible). The right column of the table is the *Z-index* of the AP Element. The Z-index indicates the stacking order of the elements. For example, an element with a Z-index of 2 will display over an element with a Z-index of 1 anywhere they overlap. Wherever two AP Elements overlap, the one with the higher Z-index displays. The numbers don't have to be sequential; for instance, if you want something to always display, give it a huge Z-index such as 5000.

Converting AP Divs to tables

You could use AP Elements just like divs, and given that the AP Elements tool actually creates divs, that would be somewhat equivalent. But the real point of AP Elements was to be able to lay out pages visually in the days before divs had widespread browser support. So, that was the next step: converting AP Elements to tables. This is where things get ugly fast.

To convert an AP Divs-based page to tables:

1. Choose Modify > Convert > AP Divs to Table (**Figure 8.63**). The Convert AP Divs to Table dialog appears (**Figure 8.64**).

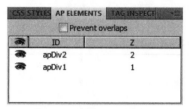

Figure 8.61 AP Elements can be overlapped, and you can tell Dreamweaver which goes on top.

Figure 8.62 The AP Elements tab of the CSS panel lets you show and hide divs as well as set the Z-index.

Figure 8.63 Converting AP Divs to tables is found under the Modify menu.

Figure 8.64 The Convert AP Divs to Table dialog lets you set several options, and Dreamweaver obeys some of them.

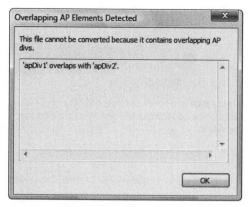

Figure 8.65 Whether you care or not, Dreamweaver won't let you convert your AP Elements to a table if there are any overlaps.

Figure 8.66 Here's our simple page before the conversion.

2. The Convert AP Divs to Table dialog gives you a number of choices:

▲ Whether you want your new table to be as close as possible to the original, or as small as possible, which collapses empty cells. If you choose the latter, you have the option of choosing how small cells must be before they're collapsed.

▲ You can choose if you want to use transparent GIFs. If you do this, the bottom row of your table consists of spacer GIFs, forcing your new table into strictly sized columns.

▲ You can choose if you want your new table to be centered on the page.

▲ You're given a choice of whether or not you want to prevent AP Div overlaps, but it doesn't matter what you pick; Dreamweaver doesn't care. If you turn this option off and turn off the Prevent overlaps choice on the AP Elements tab of the CSS panel, and then try to convert a page that contains overlapping AP Elements, you'll still get **Figure 8.65**, which tells you that you can't convert this page. If that's your situation, move your divs until they no longer overlap (**Figure 8.66**).

▲ You're given a choice of whether or not you want the AP Elements tab of the CSS panel to show after the conversion. If you turn this on, the AP Elements tab and CSS panel will be open when the conversion is done. If you turn it off, and the AP Elements tab was previously open, the CSS panel group collapses. If you turn it off and the AP Elements tab isn't currently open, nothing happens.

▲ You also have a choice of showing the grid, and of whether you want to snap your new table cells to that grid. You can choose one, both, or neither.

continues on next page

OLD TIME DREAMWEAVER

3. Click OK to accept, and your page will be re-created in tables (**Figure 8.67**). Except...it doesn't really work correctly. For instance:

▲ In the original layered version, the right-hand layer had 30 pixels of padding and the text was white. In the new tables version, all of that is gone. However, the colored backgrounds of both remain.

▲ If you look at the source code, the rules that were created for the two AP Elements still exist, even though they aren't used any more.

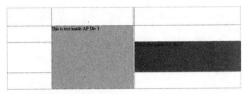

Figure 8.67 And here's our page after the conversion, not looking quite the same—the fonts and padding were lost.

✔ Tips

■ You can't convert just some of the AP Elements on a page. The conversion process converts all AP Elements on the page.

■ We're not sure why anyone would want to check the Show AP Elements panel box. After all, once you've converted from AP Elements to tables, the AP Elements tab is of no further use to you!

■ There really is no excuse to create new pages with this method: you can start and end with tables if that's what works for your site, or you can start and end with divs, but there is no reason to start with AP Elements and end with tables.

Figure 8.68 You can also convert tables to AP Divs, although you shouldn't.

Converting tables to AP Divs

Okay, you're convinced—tables aren't the way to do layout any more, and you want to convert all your pages to CSS and divs. Great!

And then you remember that back in Figure 8.63 there was another option: Modify > Convert > Tables to AP Divs. Well, this is going to be easy, you think: after all, AP Divs are just a sort of div, right? Not so fast there.

To convert tables to AP Divs:

1. Choose Modify > Convert > Tables to AP Divs (Figure 8.63). The Convert Tables to AP Divs dialog appears (**Figure 8.68**).

2. The Convert Tables to AP Divs dialog is similar to the Convert AP Divs to Table dialog, but it has considerably fewer options:

   ▲ You can choose to check Prevent overlaps, but whether or not you check this, none will be created.

   ▲ The Show AP Elements panel choice makes considerably more sense here than it did going the other way around.

   ▲ And again, you can choose to take this opportunity to Show grid and Snap to grid.

continues on next page

OLD TIME DREAMWEAVER

3. Click OK when you're ready to see the mess that ensues. For instance, the HomeCook site (**Figure 8.69**) looks fine in tables; after its conversion to AP Elements (**Figure 8.70**), it appears rather odd:

▲ The HomeCook text in the header has moved up to the top of the screen, while the tagline below it has stayed in place.

▲ All the font styles have been lost.

▲ Font colors have been lost in some places but retained in others.

▲ The bullet points next to the navigation items are gone, and the navigation no longer goes all the way over to the left margin.

▲ The colored vertical bar on the right side that contains reviews now has varying widths.

And so on. The new version also contains 22 divs, each of which has its own style rule including fixed size and position on the page.

✔ Tip

■ If you have a page that contains both tables and other elements, converting that page to AP Elements moves everything (not just the tables!) into AP Elements.

Figure 8.69 Here's a straightforward page designed with tables.

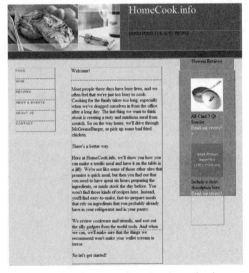

Figure 8.70 But that page doesn't quite make the transition to AP Elements very well.

MANAGING STYLES

The two previous chapters have covered CSS and how it works with your Web pages. After you've gotten the hang of CSS, though, you'll find that you're spending too much time trying to keep track of where your styles are (inline? internal? external?) and in what order they apply to your site. Or maybe it'll be that you're testing styles, but don't want to change your entire site yet.

No matter what your particular issue, Dreamweaver has made it simple and straightforward to manage moving, duplicating, and deleting styles.

Renaming Styles

The names Dreamweaver assigns to styles for you aren't particularly helpful or meaningful. It's a good idea to give styles a descriptive name of your choosing. You may also need to rename a style because your site has changed.

To rename a style for a class:

1. In the HTML tab of the Property Inspector, choose Rename from the Class pop-up menu (**Figure 9.1**). The Rename Style dialog appears (**Figure 9.2**).

    or

    In the CSS Styles panel, find and select the rule you want to rename (**Figure 9.3**). Right-click on the rule name and select "Rename Class" from the contextual menu (**Figure 9.4**). The Rename Class dialog appears (**Figure 9.5**).

2. If the class you want to rename isn't already selected, use the pop-up menu to choose it. Type a name in the New name field, and click OK.

3. If the style you chose is used in multiple places or it's in an external style sheet that can affect multiple pages, you'll be prompted as to whether you want to make this change everywhere (**Figure 9.6**). If you want this (you usually will), click Yes.

    If you click Yes, the Find and Replace dialog appears, with the parameters you need to search for and replace already filled in, and with the scope of the search set for your entire site. See Chapter 4, "Finding and Replacing with a Specific Tag," to learn more about using this dialog. If you click No, the Find and Replace dialog does not appear, and you will need to make any updates manually.

✔ Tip

- The two dialogs have different names, but they do identical things.

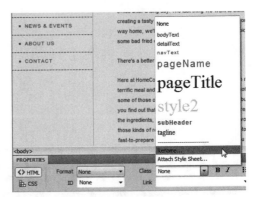

Figure 9.1 Choose Rename from the Class pop-up menu to give a style a new name.

Figure 9.2 Type the new name in the field to rename your style.

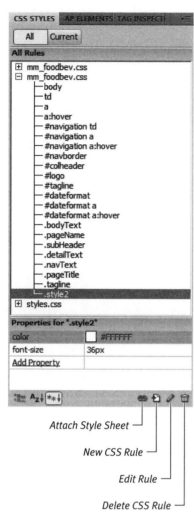

Attach Style Sheet ⎯⎯

New CSS Rule ⎯⎯

Edit Rule ⎯⎯

Delete CSS Rule ⎯⎯

Figure 9.3 You can also rename styles from the CSS Styles panel.

Figure 9.4 In the CSS Styles panel, choose your style, right-click, and choose Rename Class.

Figure 9.5 They may have different names, but the Rename Style dialog and the Rename Class dialog do the same thing.

Figure 9.6 If you want, Dreamweaver will update the name everywhere in your site after you rename a style.

Deleting Styles

When you delete a style from a style sheet, the formatting of any element using that style immediately changes.

To delete a style:

1. Open a document, and in the CSS Styles panel, choose the style name to delete.

2. Click the Delete CSS Rule button in the lower right of the panel. Note that you don't have to click OK or accept anything—it just disappears immediately.

✔ Tip

■ Even though you've deleted the style, any references to it will still exist in the document. That is, classes and ids aren't removed from your pages when you delete rules that apply to those classes and ids.

Show cascade

Show information

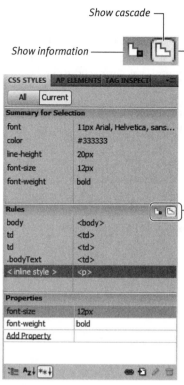

Figure 9.7 To turn an inline style into a rule, first find the <inline style> rule in the CSS Styles panel.

Figure 9.8 To convert the style to a rule, right-click, and choose Convert to Rule.

Creating Rules From Inline Styles

Inline styles (first covered back in Chapter 7) are a handy way to test properties to see if using a particular bit of CSS does what you want it to do. However, remember that the main power of CSS is being able to apply it in many places in a document and many documents in a site—and if you're only applying it to a single tag, you're missing out on all that power. So while inline styles are great for quick tests, once your CSS has passed the test, it's time to turn it into a rule.

To create a rule from an inline style:

1. In your document, click anywhere within the area where the inline style is applied. In the CSS Styles panel, make sure that you're in Current mode, and that the Rules pane is visible by clicking the Show cascade button. You should see a rule called <inline style> (**Figure 9.7**).

2. Right-click on the <inline style> rule and choose "Convert to Rule" from the menu (**Figure 9.8**). The Convert Inline CSS dialog appears (**Figure 9.9**).

continues on next page

Figure 9.9 The Convert Inline CSS dialog lets you set all the options for your new rule.

3. The first choice in that dialog is what type of rule you want to end up with (**Figure 9.10**):

- ▲ A new CSS class, where you get to choose the class name.

- ▲ A rule that applies to all tags of the given type; that is, if the inline style is applied to a <p> (paragraph) tag, you can apply that style to all paragraphs.

- ▲ A new CSS selector, where the default is a rule based on the location of the inline style.

The last two are context-sensitive, so your defaults change depending on your inline style selection.

4. Next, you have a choice of creating the new rule in an external style sheet, or in the head of the current document. Any currently linked external style sheets will be in the pop-up. If you don't have any external style sheets, put the new rule into the head of the current document (you'll see how to move the internal rule to an external stylesheet later in the chapter). Choose one of the options, click OK, and your new rule will be created.

✔ Tips

- ■ It's possible for the Rules pane to show more than one style named <inline style>, so be careful that you're choosing the correct one.

- ■ You can't create a new external style sheet from the Convert Inline CSS dialog. If you want your new rule to be in a new external style sheet, you can either:

  - ▲ Follow the above steps to create a new internal rule, then follow the steps in "Moving Internal Styles to External," later in this chapter.

  or

  - ▲ Follow the steps in the next task, "Creating a New External Style Sheet," and then use the steps in this task to put the new rule into that style sheet.

Figure 9.10 You can make a new class, a new selector, or a new rule that applies to all instances of a certain tag.

Creating a New External Style Sheet

Up to now, we've covered how to create internal styles, but we also mentioned that internal styles may not always be the right choice. Here's how to create a new external style sheet, either from scratch or using one of the many sample files that are included in Dreamweaver as a starting point.

To create a new external style sheet based on a sample file:

1. From Dreamweaver's menu, choose File > New. The New Document dialog appears.

2. If it wasn't chosen by default, select the category Page from Sample. Under Sample Folder, select CSS Style Sheet to display a long list of style sheets in the center column (**Figure 9.11**). Choose any of them to see a preview and description in the right column.

3. If you see a design you like, click Create. A new untitled style sheet document opens in Code view that contains the rules defined in the style sheet you selected. Save this file with a name that ends in .css.

Figure 9.11 Dreamweaver comes with plenty of CSS designs for you to use as starting points.

To create a new external style sheet from scratch:

1. Choose File > New. The New Document dialog appears (Figure 9.11).

2. In the New Document dialog, select Blank Page for the Category, CSS for the page type, and click Create. A new blank style sheet opens in Code view (**Figure 9.12**). Save this file with a name that ends in .css.

   or

1. With a document open, click the Insert Div Tag button in the Common or Layout category of the Insert panel, and the Insert Div Tag dialog displays. Click New CSS Rule, and the New CSS Rule dialog opens (**Figure 9.13**).

Figure 9.12 A blank CSS document, ready for you to add your rules.

Figure 9.13 Use the Insert Div Tag dialog to open the New CSS Rule dialog.

Figure 9.14 If you said you wanted a new style sheet file, here's where it's actually created.

Figure 9.15 Now that you've created a new style sheet file, you need to add rules to it.

Figure 9.16 The new style sheet appears in the Related Files at the top of the document window. In this case, the headerStyles.css file has an asterisk after its name, indicating that it needs to be saved.

2. Enter any class, tag, id, or pseudo-class selector that you'd like in your new CSS file. Set the Rule Definition pop-up menu to "(New Style Sheet File)" and click OK. The Save Style Sheet File As dialog appears (**Figure 9.14**).

3. Choose a file name that ends in .css, and click Save. The CSS Rule Definition dialog appears (**Figure 9.15**). Add the rules you want (as described in Chapter 7), click OK, and you'll be back at the Insert Div Tag dialog, with your new style sheet (including any rules you set) available as a Related File in the bar at the top of the current document (**Figure 9.16**).

4. (Optional) If you created a new style sheet using the Insert Div Tag dialog, and you don't actually want to insert a new div, click Cancel to dismiss the dialog.

✔ Tip

■ If you've created a new style sheet using the Insert Div Tag dialog, your new style sheet is automatically attached to your document. If you created the new style sheet any other way, you'll have to attach it manually. That's covered in "Attaching a Style Sheet," later in this chapter.

Moving Internal Styles to External

There are a number of reasons why your pages might have internal styles instead of using an external style sheet: possibly they're from an older site (when that was more common), or possibly you used internal styles to test your layout. But now your internal style sheet is ready to live on its own, so your styles need to come out of your Web page and into a stand-alone file, because external style sheets are much easier to maintain and a single sheet can apply to many different HTML pages in your site.

To move styles:

1. Open the Web page that contains the style (or styles) you want to move. In the CSS Styles panel, make sure that you're in All mode. Select the rules that you want to move, right-click, and choose Move CSS Rules from the contextual menu. The Move To External Style Sheet dialog appears (**Figure 9.17**).

2. If you are moving the rules to an existing external stylesheet (the default), choose it from the pop-up menu and click OK. If the sheet you want isn't listed, click Browse, find the sheet in the resulting Find Style Sheet File dialog, and click OK.

   or

   If you want to move the rules to a new stylesheet, click "A new style sheet" and click OK. You should be prompted with the correct place to save your file. Come up with a good name (ending in .css) and click Save.

   Your rules will be moved to the style sheet, and the style sheet will be attached to the current page (if that's not already the case).

Figure 9.17 To move a rule to an external style sheet, bring up the Move To External Style Sheet dialog.

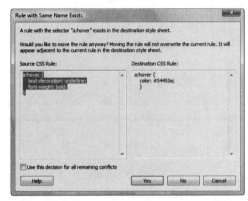

Figure 9.18 If you're moving a rule that might cause a collision, Dreamweaver warns you about the problem.

✔ Tips

- When you moved internal styles to external in versions of Dreamweaver prior to CS3, the styles were only copied, not moved. You no longer have to manually attach the style sheet and then delete the styles from the current document, as Dreamweaver does it all for you.

- If your external style sheet already contains any rules with the same name as the rules you're moving, Dreamweaver displays a dialog like the one in **Figure 9.18**. You can choose if you want both rules in the style sheet or just the previous version.

Figure 9.19 There are at least two ways to attach a style sheet from the CSS Styles panel.

Attaching a Style Sheet

It doesn't do you any good to create a style sheet if your Web pages don't know about it. In order for a Web page to use an external style sheet, that style sheet has to be *attached* to the Web page.

To attach a style sheet:

1. Click the Attach Style Sheet icon at the bottom of the CSS Styles panel (Figure 9.3).

   or

   Right-click in the CSS Styles panel and choose Attach Style Sheet (**Figure 9.19**).

   or

   From the HTML tab of the Property Inspector, choose Attach Style Sheet from the Class pop-up menu (Figure 9.1).

2. The Attach External Style Sheet dialog appears (**Figure 9.20**). Click the Browse button to bring up the Select Style Sheet File dialog (**Figure 9.21**). Navigate to an existing style sheet, select it, and click OK.

   continues on next page

Figure 9.20 Choose which style sheet you want to attach to your Web page, and how you want to attach it.

Figure 9.21 Choose which style sheet file to attach by browsing for it.

ATTACHING A STYLE SHEET

3. Back in the Attach External Style Sheet dialog, select Add as Link if it isn't already chosen, and click OK to attach the style sheet. If your style sheet includes any rules that affect the active document, you'll see those changes reflected immediately.

✔ Tips

■ Take a look at the All Rules pane of the CSS Styles panel. Notice that your style sheet is now included, and all of its properties can be viewed.

■ You're offered a choice of using *link* or *import* to attach your style sheet. Each has its advantages: link works in more browsers, for instance, while import allows you to nest style sheets (i.e., you can attach a style sheet using import, and then that style sheet can include an import of another style sheet, and so on).

■ You can use both link and import in the same document. That's a handy way to use two style sheets, where the link attaches a bare-bones style sheet and the import attaches a more complex style sheet that very old browsers (such as Netscape 4.x) can't handle.

■ When attaching a style sheet, you're also offered a choice of Media in the Attach External Style Sheet dialog. Those choices include all, aural, braille, handheld, print, projection, screen, tty, and tv (**Figure 9.22**). It's also acceptable to use no media type at all; in that case, the style sheet applies to all media types. And finally, you can also enter in a list of media types (comma-separated) if you want your style sheet to apply to some media types but not others.

■ If you set the media type for your style sheet, you can test it by choosing View > Style Rendering and picking which media type to view. When you do this, though, remember that few browsers offer full support for media types.

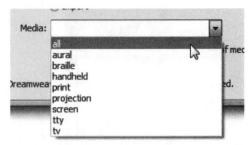

Figure 9.22 Media options are set here. For instance, if you want your style sheet to only apply when the page is printed, choose the print media type.

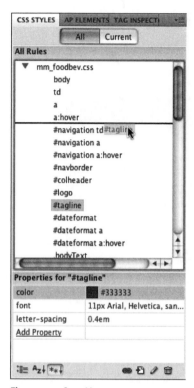

Figure 9.23 On a Mac, you can see which style you're dragging while it's being dragged.

Drag-and-Drop Styles

If you've found all the methods so far for dealing with style management to be somewhat complicated, then here's what you've been wishing you can do: drag and drop styles.

Moving styles inside a document

As mentioned back in Chapter 7 in the sidebar "External, Internal, and Inline: Look Ma, It's the Cascade," where style rules are physically located determines which rules take precedence when there's a conflict. If you have two rules that conflict inside a document (either a Web page or a style sheet) and you want the one that's currently being overridden to dominate, all you have to do is drag that rule below the other.

To move a style inside a document:

1. Open the Web page or style sheet that contains the style (or styles) you want to move. In the CSS Styles panel, make sure that you're in All mode, select the rules that you want to move, and drag them to their new location (**Figure 9.23**). A blue line (a black line on the Mac) appears showing where the rules will be relocated.

   On the Mac, a ghostly version of the style name moves with the cursor. On Windows, a small document icon appears instead.

2. When you're happy with the new location, release the mouse, and Dreamweaver moves the rules for you.

Moving styles from one document to another

Not only can you move styles inside a document, but you can also move them from document to document—whether the documents are style sheets or Web pages.

To move a style from one document to another:

1. Open a Web page that either links to two style sheets, or one that contains the style (or styles) and also links to an external style sheet. In the CSS Styles panel, make sure that you're in All mode and that both files are displayed (if no external style sheet is displayed, follow the directions in "Attaching a Style Sheet"). Select the rules that you want to move, and drag them to their new location (**Figure 9.24**). A line appears showing where the rules will be relocated.

2. When you're happy with the new location, release the mouse, and Dreamweaver moves the rules for you.

✔ Tips

- If you want to copy a style rule (that is, you want it to end up in both the original document *and* the target document), hold down the Control (Option) key while dragging the rules.

- If you're moving a style rule into a document that already contains a rule with that name, you'll get a warning dialog like the one in Figure 9.18.

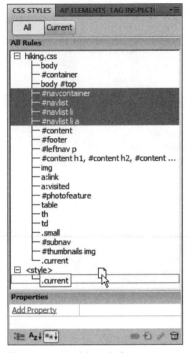

Figure 9.24 On either platform, you can drag multiple style rules at one time.

DRAG-AND-DROP STYLES

The CSS Advisor

Got a CSS problem that's stumping you? Maybe your site works fine in 55 different browser/platform/version configurations—but not the one that your boss cares about most? If that's your situation, Adobe has heard your pain, which is why they've created the CSS Advisor Web site (**Figure 9.25**).

The CSS Advisor (found at `http://www.adobe.com/go/cssadvisor`) contains a community-created database of known CSS-related problems and their solutions. You can search by tags, browser, or CSS property. When you find your problem, you can then see how other people were able to solve it.

If your particular issue isn't covered yet, the CSS community guidelines (at `http://www.adobe.com/communities/guidelines/usingcssadvisor.html`) give some pointers to other online resources where you might be able to get help. If you're successful elsewhere (or you're able to figure it out for yourself), you can go back to the CSS Advisor site and add your problem and its workaround—that's the community-created part of the site.

If you don't think that you're enough of a CSS wiz to be able to offer solutions to the world, you can still contribute to the Advisor community. Log in, and you can rate and offer feedback on existing explanations.

However, it's not a site for posting problems and hoping that other people will help you out. Adobe may delete your contribution if you put up a problem without a corresponding fix.

Figure 9.25 Adobe's CSS Advisor Web site provides help to solve your CSS issues.

10

INSERTING TABLES

You will often use tables on Web pages to present tabular information—that is, data best presented in the form of rows and columns. You can also use tables for layout—that is, to align text and images on the page—but as you'll see later in the chapter, in most cases you should be using CSS for layout instead.

In this chapter, you'll learn how to create and format tables, ensure that tables and their content look the way you intend, work with Dreamweaver's many table tools, and save time when you're using tables.

Moving Away from Tables for Layout

One of the most widespread uses for a table is as a layout device (sometimes called *layout tables*). You can create tables on your page, then use the table cells to contain the text and images on the page. Because you have good control over the size of the cells and the position of their boundaries, you can line up and lay out elements on the page with precision, though it often requires some extremely complex tables. By hiding the borders of the table cells, the site visitor doesn't notice the tables. This, up until the last several years, is how most nicely designed Web pages you've seen were created.

However, there are many problems with using tables for layout. First of all, the table has nothing to do with the *content* of the page (the information your visitor sees); all it does is affect the *presentation* of the content. One of the biggest benefits of CSS is that it *separates* content from presentation. As a result, you can completely redesign CSS-based sites largely by changing one file, the style sheet. If your presentation is mixed with your content, as it is with a table-based layout, it makes site redesigns difficult and expensive. Similarly, tables make it difficult to maintain visual consistency throughout a site (because the layout tables on different pages may not be the same).

So that's what is wrong with tables from the standpoint of the Web designer, but there are problems for the site visitor, too. Tables make the size of an HTML page unnecessarily large (costing you extra bandwidth charges), and site visitors must download the layout tables on every page they visit in the site (ditto). Pages load more slowly than with a CSS-based layout, and slow page loads drive visitors away. Table-based pages are also much more difficult to read by users with disabilities and by visitors using cell phones and PDAs.

Tables were necessary for good-looking Web sites back in 1997, because the Web browsers of the day had many limitations, not the least of which was that none of them supported the then-emerging CSS standards for layout. But all modern browsers have reasonably good support for using CSS for layout (though ironically, a still-popular browser as of this writing, Microsoft Internet Explorer 6 for Windows, lags well behind other browsers such as Internet Explorer 7 and 8, Mozilla Firefox, Apple Safari, and Opera). The vast majority of users of the Web now use Web browsers that can handle CSS-based layouts just fine.

As a result, you can (and should!) use Dreamweaver to build great-looking, CSS-based sites that are faster to load, accessible for everyone, and easier for you to redesign and maintain. To learn more about laying out your pages with CSS, see Chapter 8.

Because table-based layout has been so pervasive for most of a decade, Dreamweaver can still be used to create page layouts with tables. But Dreamweaver CS4 removed a set of tools, called Table Layout Mode, that made it easier to use tables for layout. Adobe is clearly pointing its users towards CSS for layout.

By the way, even with sites that use tables for layout, you can still use CSS to style the text inside the tables. Some CSS markup is devoted to styling text, and some is devoted to positioning elements on the page. You can use the styling kind of CSS to make your text look good, even inside a table. You just shouldn't mix the positioning elements of CSS with tables; choose one method or the other for positioning elements on your pages.

By using CSS for layout, tables can go back to what they were originally intended to do, namely, to display tabular information that lines up in neat rows and columns. Think of a baseball box score, or a timetable showing a bus schedule—both perfect candidates for tables.

Creating a Table

Tables typically consist of one or more rows and one or more columns. Each rectangular area at the intersection of a row and column is called a *cell*. Cells contain the page's text or images, and items within a cell can't extend past the cell's boundaries.

You can insert a table anywhere on a page, even within another table (this is called *nesting* a table). By default, Dreamweaver creates tables with three rows and three columns, but you can easily change that format during the process of inserting the table. After you do make changes, Dreamweaver remembers them and uses them as the defaults for the next table you create.

To add a table to your page:

1. Place the insertion point where you want the table to appear.

2. In the Layout category of the Insert panel, click the Table button (**Figure 10.1**).

   or

   Choose Insert > Table, or press Ctrl-Alt-T (Cmd-Opt-T).

   The Table dialog appears (**Figure 10.2**).

3. Enter the number of rows you want in the table, and press Tab.

4. Enter the number of columns you want in the table, and press Tab.

Figure 10.1 You'll use the Layout category of the Insert panel to add tables to your pages.

Figure 10.2 The Table dialog lets you get started building a table.

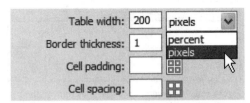

Figure 10.3 You can set the width of your table either in pixels or as a percentage of the browser page width.

5. In the Table width text box, enter a number that will either be in pixels or a percentage of the page width, then choose the units from the pop-up menu to the right of the text box (**Figure 10.3**).

6. Set one or more (or none) of the following (see the "Anatomy of a Table" sidebar for explanations of the settings):

▲ Enter a figure in the Border thickness text box to set the size of the border, in pixels, that will be displayed between cells.

▲ Enter a figure in the Cell padding text box to set the amount of space, in pixels, between the content in the cells and the cell border.

▲ Enter a figure in the Cell spacing text box to set the number of pixels of space between cells.

7. In the Header section, choose the kind of header you want: None, Left, Top, or Both. The icons for the headers tell you what each choice looks like.

8. (Optional, but recommended.) In the Accessibility section, enter a caption for the table. Caption text appears in all browsers. If you enter text in the Summary text box, that text appears only in screen readers for the visually disabled.

continues on next page

CREATING A TABLE

9. Click OK.

The table appears in your page (**Figure 10.4**). When a table is selected, as in the figure, or when the insertion point is in a table cell, Dreamweaver shows green dimension lines above the table. The top line shows the width of the table in pixels. Each column also has a dimension line, which shows the width of the column in pixels if you have set a fixed width for the column. Columns with widths relative to the table width show dimension lines (so you can easily see each column) without pixel values. These dimension lines appear only in Dreamweaver's Design view, not in a Web browser.

✔ Tips

- To insert a table within a table, place the insertion point inside a cell of an existing table, then choose either of the methods in step 2. The new table appears inside the first table (**Figure 10.5**).

- You don't have to get the number of rows and columns right the first time; you can always add or subtract them later. See the sections "Adding Rows and Columns" and "Deleting Table Elements" later in this chapter.

- If you don't want to see the dimension lines above tables, you can turn them off by choosing View > Visual Aids > Table Widths, which removes the checkmark from the menu item.

Figure 10.4 The green dimension lines tell you the width of the table in pixels. The dimension lines above each column do not show pixel widths in this figure because the columns are set to be a percentage of the table width.

Figure 10.5 You can nest a second table inside any cell of an existing table.

- Captions are actually part of the table. When you move the table, the caption moves with it. Table captions appear above the table by default, but you can change that in the code. Switch to Code view, then find the table's `<caption>` tag. Click inside the tag to put the insertion point after the word, then press the Space bar. A pop-up menu appears with the `<caption>` tag's possible attributes. Choose `align` (which inserts `align=""` into the code and gives you another pop-up menu with the alignment values), then choose one of the five possible alignments (`bottom`, `center`, `left`, `right`, `top`) from the pop-up menu.

- To edit a caption, select it and type over the existing text. To change the horizontal alignment of the caption in relation to the table, place the insertion point in the caption, then right-click and pick one of the choices (Left, Center, Right, or Justify) from the Align submenu in the resulting shortcut menu.

CREATING A TABLE

Anatomy of a Table

Besides rows and columns, tables have several other attributes that affect how they look. You'll find controls for these items in the Property Inspector when you select a table.

Border thickness is the width of the border around the table, in pixels (**Figure 10.6**). Dreamweaver sets it to one pixel by default, which results in a thin border. If the border thickness is set to a nonzero amount, you will also see a border between table cells. You'll often see the border thickness set to zero on pages that are using tables for page layout and the designer doesn't want you to see borders. Borders with zero thickness appear in Design view with dotted borders.

Cell padding is the amount of space, in pixels, between a cell's borders and its content (**Figure 10.7**). Use this setting to give cell content more breathing room within cells. If you don't specify a number here, most browsers use a default value of one pixel.

Cell spacing is the amount of space between each table cell, also measured in pixels (**Figure 10.8**). If you don't specify a number here, most browsers use a default value of two pixels. Wide cell spacing gives the table a look that is very 1996, so use this setting with care.

The following table attributes can't be set in the Property Inspector, but can be changed in Code view:

Table header tags part of the table as a header. The header is formatted as bold and centered, but more important, it has the `<th>` HTML tag, which allows screen readers used by visually disabled users to correctly read the table. It's better to use a table header tag in Dreamweaver than to manually make cells bold and centered.

Border color is the color of the border around the table and between the table's cells. This gives a dated look, so use with care.

Sales Territory	1st Quarter	2nd Quarter
North	$2,700	$2,850
East	$3,700	$4,200
South	$2,200	$2,100
West	$2,900	$3,200

Sales Territory	1st Quarter	2nd Quarter
North	$2,700	$2,850
East	$3,700	$4,200
South	$2,200	$2,100
West	$2,900	$3,200

Sales Territory	1st Quarter	2nd Quarter
North	$2,700	$2,850
East	$3,700	$4,200
South	$2,200	$2,100
West	$2,900	$3,200

Figure 10.6 The same table with a border thickness of zero pixels (top), one pixel (middle), and 10 pixels (bottom). Cell padding and cell spacing are set to zero.

Sales Territory	1st Quarter	2nd Quarter
North	$2,700	$2,850
East	$3,700	$4,200
South	$2,200	$2,100
West	$2,900	$3,200

Figure 10.7 Cell padding has been set to 5 pixels, which gives more whitespace around the table contents.

Sales Territory	1st Quarter	2nd Quarter
North	$2,700	$2,850
East	$3,700	$4,200
South	$2,200	$2,100
West	$2,900	$3,200

Figure 10.8 Cell spacing of 5 pixels creates a wide border between cells—a dated look.

Figure 10.9 You can tell this table is selected because it has a thick border around its edges with resize handles.

Figure 10.10 When you move the cursor to the left edge of a table and the pointer changes to an arrow, you can click to select the whole row.

Selecting Table Elements

To work effectively with a table, you'll need to know how to select its elements. You can select an entire table; one or more rows and columns; an individual cell or multiple cells; and nonadjacent cells, rows, or columns.

To select the entire table:

◆ Click the table's upper-left corner.

or

Click the bottom or the right edge of the table.

or

Click in the table, and then choose Modify > Table > Select Table.

A border with resize handles appears around the table (**Figure 10.9**). Dimension lines also appear.

✔ Tip

■ Clicking any interior cell border also selects the entire table.

To select an entire row:

1. Place the pointer at the left edge of a row.

The pointer becomes an arrow.

2. Click to select the entire row (**Figure 10.10**).

You can click and drag to select multiple rows.

The cell borders for the selected row highlight.

To select an entire column:

1. Place the pointer at the top edge of a column.

The pointer becomes an arrow.

2. Click to select the entire column (**Figure 10.11**).

You can click and drag to select multiple columns.

or

Click the triangle in the dimension line above any column to display a pop-up menu, then choose Select Column (**Figure 10.12**).

The cell borders for the selected column highlight.

To select a single cell:

◆ Click and drag in the cell.

or

Click in the cell, then choose Edit > Select All, or press Ctrl-A (Cmd-A).

or

If the cell is empty, triple-click inside the cell.

The cell highlights to show it has been selected.

To select multiple adjacent cells:

◆ Click in the first cell you want to select, and drag to the last cell.

or

Click in the first cell you want to select, hold down Shift, and then click in the last cell. All the cells in between will also be selected. You can also Shift-click in this manner to select rows or columns.

To select nonadjacent cells:

◆ Ctrl-click (Cmd-click) in the first cell, hold down Ctrl (Cmd), and then click the other cells you want to select (**Figure 10.13**). You can also Ctrl-click (Cmd-click) to select nonadjacent rows or columns.

Figure 10.11 The pointer also changes to an arrow above columns. Click to select the column.

Figure 10.12 If you prefer, you can use the pop-up column menu to select the column.

Figure 10.13 By Ctrl-clicking (Cmd-clicking), you can select nonadjacent cells.

Sales Territory	Q1	Q2	Q3	Q4
North	$2,700	$2,850		
East	$3,700	$4,200		
South	$2,200	$2,100		
West	$2,900	$3,200		

Figure 10.14 If you wanted to select the cells under Q3 or Q4, it could be difficult to do so because they are so small.

Figure 10.15 Click the Expanded button in the Layout category of the Insert panel to enter Expanded Tables mode.

Figure 10.16 Expanded Tables mode makes all the tables in the document bigger, so you can select table elements easier. Note the indicator bar at the top of the document window that tells you that you're in a special mode.

Using Expanded Tables Mode for Selecting

When you're selecting tables and table elements, it can sometimes be difficult to select the particular part you're after, especially if some of the table cells are narrow horizontally or vertically (**Figure 10.14**). To make things easier on you, Dreamweaver offers *Expanded Tables mode*, which temporarily adds a border (if there is none) and increases the cell padding and cell spacing. These changes aren't permanent, and don't show up in a Web browser.

To enter Expanded Tables mode:

1. Choose View > Table Mode > Expanded Tables Mode.

   or

   In the Layout category of the Insert panel, click the Expanded button (**Figure 10.15**).

   or

   Press Alt-F6 (Opt-F6).

   The Design view switches to Expanded Tables mode (**Figure 10.16**), changing the appearance of all the tables in the document.

   An indicator bar appears at the top of the document window to let you know you're in the Expanded Tables mode.

2. Select and edit table elements as you like.

✔ Tip

■ Remember that Expanded Tables mode is not a WYSIWYG (What You See Is What You Get) view, as is the standard Design view. Always switch out of Expanded Tables mode before you do any serious page layout or formatting.

To exit Expanded Tables mode:

◆ Choose View > Table Mode > Expanded Tables Mode.

or

In the Layout category of the Insert panel, click the Standard button.

or

Click the [exit] link in the Expanded Tables mode indicator bar at the top of the document window.

or

Press Alt-F6 (Opt-F6).

Insert rows buttons

Insert columns buttons

Figure 10.17 You'll use the Layout category of the Insert panel to make changes to tables.

Sales Territory	Q1	Q2	Q3	Q4
North	$2,700	$2,850		
East	$3,700	$4,200		
South	$2,200	$2,100		
West	$2,900	$3,200		

Figure 10.18 A new row has appeared in the middle of this table.

Adding Rows and Columns

You may find you need to add additional content to your table. Dreamweaver allows you to add rows or columns to your table, either singly or in multiples.

To insert a single row in a table:

1. Place the insertion point in a table cell.

2. In the Layout category of the Insert panel, click either the Insert Row Above or Insert Row Below button (**Figure 10.17**). A new row appears above or below the row where the insertion point is.

   or

   Choose Insert > Table Objects > Insert Row Above or press Ctrl-M (Cmd-M).

   or

   Choose Insert > Table Objects > Insert Row Below.

   or

   Right-click in the cell, and choose Table > Insert Row from the shortcut menu. This adds a row above the row where the insertion point is.

   The row appears in your table (**Figure 10.18**).

✔ Tip

■ If the insertion point is in the last cell of the table, pressing Tab adds a row to the bottom of the table.

To insert a single column in a table:

1. Place the insertion point in a table cell.

2. In the Layout category of the Insert panel, click either the Insert Column to the Left or Insert Column to the Right button. A new column appears to the left or right of the column where the insertion point is.

   or

   Choose Insert > Table Objects > Insert Column to the Left.

   or

   Choose Insert > Table Objects > Insert Column to the Right.

   or

   Right-click in the cell, and from the resulting shortcut menu choose Table > Insert Column. This adds a column to the left of the column where the insertion point is.

   The column appears in your table.

Figure 10.19 Use the Insert Rows or Columns dialog to add multiple rows or columns to a table in one operation.

To insert multiple rows or columns into a table:

1. Place the insertion point in a table cell.

2. Right-click, and then choose Table > Insert Rows or Columns from the shortcut menu.

   or

   Choose Modify > Table > Insert Rows or Columns.

   The Insert Rows or Columns dialog appears (**Figure 10.19**).

3. Select either the Rows or Columns radio button.

4. Enter the number of rows or columns you want to add. You can either type a number into the text box, or use the arrow buttons next to the text box to increase or decrease the number.

5. Next to Where, click the appropriate button to select the location of the new rows or columns.

6. Click OK.

   The rows or columns appear in your table.

Merging and Splitting Cells

Dreamweaver lets you combine two or more adjacent cells into one larger cell (called *merging*), or split a single cell into two or more cells.

To merge cells:

1. Select the cells you want to merge.

2. Choose Modify > Table > Merge Cells, or press Ctrl-Alt-M (Cmd-Opt-M).

   or

   Right-click, and then choose Table > Merge Cells from the shortcut menu.

   The cells merge (**Figure 10.20**).

✔ Tip

■ You can merge an entire row or column into one cell.

To split cells:

1. Place the insertion point in the cell you want to split into two or more cells.

2. Choose Modify > Table > Split Cell, or press Ctrl-Alt-S (Cmd-Opt-S).

   or

   Right-click, and then choose Table > Split Cell from the shortcut menu.

   The Split Cell dialog appears (**Figure 10.21**).

3. Choose whether to split the cell into rows or columns.

4. Enter the number of new rows or columns for the split.

5. Click OK.

   The cell divides into two or more cells (**Figure 10.22**).

✔ Tip

■ Even if you select multiple cells, Dreamweaver can split only one cell at a time.

Figure 10.20 The four cells at the left edge of this table (top) have been merged into one cell (bottom).

Figure 10.21 You can use the Split Cell dialog to divide cells into multiple rows or columns.

Figure 10.22 In this example, the center cell has been split into four cells.

MERGING AND SPLITTING CELLS

Figure 10.23 Use the Property Inspector to change the width of a table numerically.

Resizing Table Elements

You can resize tables horizontally or vertically, and also make columns wider and rows taller. You can specify the width of tables numerically, and numerically specify the width and height of rows and columns.

To resize an entire table:

1. Click the bottom or the right edge of the table. The table will be selected, and a border with resize handles appears around it.

2. Drag one of the resize handles. To widen the table, drag the handle on the right edge of the table; to make the table taller, drag the handle on the bottom edge of the table; and to make the table grow in both directions simultaneously, drag the handle at the bottom-right corner of the table. Holding down the Shift key as you drag maintains the proportions of the table.

To resize a table numerically:

1. Click the bottom or the right edge of the table to select it.

2. In the Property Inspector, enter a number in the W (for width) field (**Figure 10.23**). In the pop-up menu next to the field, choose either %, which makes the table width a percentage of the overall width of the page, or pixels, to set an absolute size for the table width.

3. Press the Tab key or click in the document window to apply your changes.

RESIZING TABLE ELEMENTS

To resize columns:

1. Select the column you want to resize.

2. Drag the column's right border to make the column wider.

   or

   In the Property Inspector, type a number in the W (for width) field (**Figure 10.24**). The width unit is in pixels. Alternatively, in the document window, click the triangle in the dimension line above the column and choose Clear Column Width from the resulting pop-up menu; this makes the column resize to fit the contents.

To resize rows:

1. Select the row you want to resize.

2. Drag the bottom border of the row to make the row taller.

   or

   In the Property Inspector, type a number in the H (for height) field (**Figure 10.25**). The height unit is in pixels.

✔ Tips

- If you set a width in percentage for a table, the table resizes based on the width of the user's browser window. This may really change the look of your table. Be sure to preview the page in a Web browser and resize the browser window to see the effect.

- Tables always stretch to fit the content inside the table.

- Text inside cells usually wraps to fit the width of the cell. To force the cell to expand to the width of the text, you can turn off text wrapping on a cell-by-cell basis. Click in the cell, and then in the Property Inspector, click the "No wrap" check box.

Figure 10.24 When you select a column, the Property Inspector changes and you can numerically set the column's width.

Figure 10.25 Selecting a row allows you to numerically set the row's height.

- Don't be misled into thinking you have ultimate control over row height and column width, and therefore control over what your site visitor sees. Different browsers display content differently, and short of previewing your site with every browser ever made on every computer platform, there's no way to be absolutely certain that your site visitor will see exactly what you intended.

- Older versions of Dreamweaver had a H (Height) field in the Property Inspector for the entire table. That is an invalid property for current HTML, so the field was removed in Dreamweaver CS3.

Clearing and Converting Table Values

When you have a table selected, there are four buttons in the Property Inspector that can be very handy and save you a bunch of time (**Figure 10.26**). These buttons clear the width and height values for the table, or convert table units from percent to pixels or vice versa.

Clear Column Widths and Clear Row Heights are great for collapsing a table to fit its contents. Convert Table Widths to Pixels lets you change widths from relative to fixed measurements. Convert Table Widths to Percent does the opposite, converting a fixed size table to a relative one.

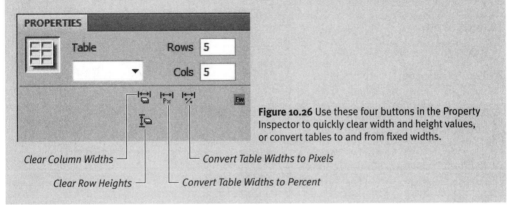

Figure 10.26 Use these four buttons in the Property Inspector to quickly clear width and height values, or convert tables to and from fixed widths.

Clear Column Widths

Clear Row Heights

Convert Table Widths to Pixels

Convert Table Widths to Percent

Deleting Table Elements

If you want to remove tables, rows, or columns, you can make short work of the task.

To delete a table:

1. Select the table by clicking its right or bottom edge. A border with resize handles appears around the table.

2. Press Backspace (Delete).

To delete rows:

1. Select one or more rows.

2. Press Backspace (Delete).

    or

    Choose Modify > Table > Delete Row, or press Ctrl-Shift-M (Cmd-Shift-M).

    or

    Right-click the row, and then choose Table > Delete Row from the shortcut menu.

    The row disappears from the table.

To delete columns:

1. Select one or more columns.

2. Press Backspace (Delete).

    or

    Choose Modify > Table > Delete Column or press Ctrl-Shift-minus key (Cmd-Shift-minus key).

    or

    Right-click the row, and then choose Table > Delete Column from the shortcut menu.

    The columns disappear from the table.

The quick brown fox jumps over the lazy dog. The quick brown fox jumps over the lazy dog. The quick brown fox jumps over the lazy dog. The quick brown fox jumps over the lazy dog. The quick brown fox jumps over the lazy dog. The quick brown fox jumps over the lazy dog.
The quick brown fox jumps over the lazy dog. The quick brown fox jumps over the lazy dog. The quick brown fox jumps over the lazy dog. The quick brown fox jumps over the lazy dog. The quick brown fox jumps over the lazy dog. The quick brown fox jumps over the lazy dog.

Sales Territory	Q1	Q2	Q3	Q4
North	$2,700	$2,850	$2,800	$2,975
East	$3,700	$4,200	$4,000	$4,750
South	$2,200	$2,100	$2,300	$2,350
West	$2,900	$3,200	$3,800	$5,100

The quick brown fox jumps over the lazy dog. The quick brown fox jumps over the lazy dog. The quick brown fox jumps over the lazy dog. The quick brown fox jumps over the lazy dog.
The quick brown fox jumps over the lazy dog. The quick brown fox jumps over the lazy dog. The quick brown fox jumps over the lazy dog. The quick

The quick brown fox jumps over the lazy dog. The quick brown fox jumps over the lazy dog. The quick brown fox jumps over the lazy dog. The quick brown fox jumps over the lazy dog. The quick brown fox jumps over the lazy dog.
The quick brown fox jumps over the lazy dog. The quick brown fox jumps over the lazy dog. The quick brown fox jumps over the lazy dog. The quick brown fox jumps over the lazy dog. The quick brown fox jumps over the lazy dog.

Sales Territory	Q1	Q2	Q3	Q4
North	$2,700	$2,850	$2,800	$2,975
East	$3,700	$4,200	$4,000	$4,750
South	$2,200	$2,100	$2,300	$2,350
West	$2,900	$3,200	$3,800	$5,100

The quick brown fox jumps over the lazy dog. The quick brown fox jumps over the lazy dog. The quick brown fox jumps over the lazy dog. The quick brown fox jumps over the lazy dog. The quick brown fox jumps over the lazy dog. The quick brown fox jumps over the lazy dog. The quick brown fox jumps over the lazy dog. The quick brown fox jumps over the lazy dog. The quick brown fox jumps over the lazy dog.
The quick brown fox jumps over the lazy dog. The quick brown fox jumps over the lazy dog. The quick brown fox jumps over the lazy dog. The quick brown fox jumps over the lazy dog. The quick brown fox jumps over the lazy dog.

The quick brown fox jumps over the lazy dog. The quick brown fox jumps over the lazy dog. The quick brown fox jumps over the lazy dog. The quick brown fox jumps over the lazy dog. The quick brown fox jumps over the lazy dog.
The quick brown fox jumps over the lazy dog. The quick brown fox jumps over the lazy dog. The quick brown fox jumps over the lazy dog. The quick brown fox jumps over the lazy dog. The quick brown fox jumps over the lazy dog.

Sales Territory	Q1	Q2	Q3	Q4
North	$2,700	$2,850	$2,800	$2,975
East	$3,700	$4,200	$4,000	$4,750
South	$2,200	$2,100	$2,300	$2,350
West	$2,900	$3,200	$3,800	$5,100

The quick brown fox jumps over the lazy dog. The quick brown fox jumps over the lazy dog. The quick brown fox jumps over the lazy dog. The quick brown fox jumps over the lazy dog.
The quick brown fox jumps over the lazy dog. The quick brown fox jumps over the lazy dog. The quick brown fox jumps over the lazy dog. The quick

The quick brown fox jumps over the lazy dog. The quick brown fox jumps over the lazy dog. The quick brown fox jumps over the lazy dog. The quick brown fox jumps over the lazy dog. The quick brown fox jumps over the lazy dog.
The quick brown fox jumps over the lazy dog. The quick brown fox jumps over the lazy dog. The quick brown fox jumps over the lazy dog. The quick brown fox jumps over the lazy dog. The quick brown fox jumps over the lazy dog.

The quick brown fox jumps over the lazy dog. The quick brown fox jumps over the lazy dog. The quick brown fox jumps over the lazy dog. The quick brown fox jumps over the lazy dog. The quick brown fox jumps over the lazy dog.

Sales Territory	Q1	Q2	Q3	Q4
North	$2,700	$2,850	$2,800	$2,975
East	$3,700	$4,200	$4,000	$4,750
South	$2,200	$2,100	$2,300	$2,350
West	$2,900	$3,200	$3,800	$5,100

The quick brown fox jumps over the lazy dog. The quick brown fox jumps over the lazy dog. The quick brown fox jumps over the lazy dog.
The quick brown fox jumps over the lazy dog. The quick brown fox jumps over the lazy dog. The quick brown fox jumps over the lazy dog. The quick brown fox jumps over the lazy dog. The quick brown fox jumps over the lazy dog.
The quick brown fox jumps over the lazy dog. The quick brown fox jumps over the lazy dog. The quick brown fox jumps over the lazy dog. The quick brown fox jumps over the lazy dog. The quick brown fox jumps over the lazy dog.

Figure 10.27 The effects of different types of table alignment. From top to bottom: Default, Left, Center, and Right alignments.

Specifying Table Alignment

When you have a table and text together, you can set the alignment of the table, in some cases wrapping the text around the table (**Figure 10.27**). You can choose from four different alignments:

◆ **Default** uses the browser default alignment for tables (usually it places the table to the left side of the page). This setting prevents text from wrapping around the table to the right.

◆ **Left** places the table to the left side of the page, and allows text to wrap around the right side of the table.

◆ **Center** centers the table on the page, with no text wrapping.

◆ **Right** places the table to the right side of the page, and allows text to wrap around the left side of the table.

You can use the Property Inspector to set table alignment. This applies HTML attributes to the `<table>` tag, which is acceptable, but not really compliant with best practices. Instead, you should specify table alignment with a CSS style. See Chapter 7 for more information.

To set table alignment:

1. Select the table you want to align.

2. In the Property Inspector, choose the alignment you want from the Align pop-up menu.

   The table moves to the alignment you selected.

Setting Cell Properties

Alignment of the text or images inside of a cell requires using the Property Inspector to set *cell properties* for each cell. You can use these alignment cell properties to set both the horizontal and vertical alignments. You can also set cell properties for the background color of the cell, and set the color of the cell border.

To set cell alignment:

1. Place the insertion point in the cell you want to format.

2. In the Property Inspector, from the "Horz" pop-up menu choose Default, Left, Center, or Right (**Figure 10.28**).

   The Default choice usually gives the same visual result as Left (**Figure 10.29**).

Figure 10.28 Use the Property Inspector to set horizontal and vertical alignment for cell contents.

Figure 10.29 Horizontal text alignment within a cell. From top to bottom: Left, Center, and Right text alignment.

In December, 2007, NASA's Hubble Space Telescope took this close-up of the red planet Mars when it was just 55 million miles away. This color image was assembled from a series of exposures taken within 36 hours of the Mars closest approach with Hubble's Wide Field and Planetary Camera 2.

In December, 2007, NASA's Hubble Space Telescope took this close-up of the red planet Mars when it was just 55 million miles away. This color image was assembled from a series of exposures taken within 36 hours of the Mars closest approach with Hubble's Wide Field and Planetary Camera 2.

In December, 2007, NASA's Hubble Space Telescope took this close-up of the red planet Mars when it was just 55 million miles away. This color image was assembled from a series of exposures taken within 36 hours of the Mars closest approach with Hubble's Wide Field and Planetary Camera 2.

Figure 10.30 Vertical text alignment within a cell. From top to bottom: Top, Middle, and Bottom alignment.

3. From the "Vert" pop-up menu choose Default, Top, Middle, Bottom, or Baseline.

The Default choice usually gives the same visual result as Middle. Baseline sets the cell alignment to match the baseline of the text within the cell, and is usually used to align images and text that are inside the same cell. Baseline usually gives the same visual result as Bottom (**Figure 10.30**).

To set a cell background color:

1. Place the insertion point in the cell you want to format.

2. In the Property Inspector, click the color well next to Bg to bring up the color picker and select the cell's background color.

The cell's background color changes.

Sorting Table Content

It's not uncommon to enter data into a table, then add more data, and then want to sort the whole thing. You asked for it, Dreamweaver can do it. The program sorts by the content of any column in your table, either numerically or alphabetically, in ascending or descending order, and it can sort on two successive criteria.

There are some limitations to Dreamweaver's sorting abilities. You cannot sort merged cells, and Dreamweaver doesn't have the ability to sort part of a table, so you can't, for example, have the program ignore the merged cells you used for your table's title (though you can have the program include or ignore header rows). Dreamweaver displays an error message if you try to sort a table containing merged cells.

Another problem is that the sorting algorithm Dreamweaver uses isn't terribly smart. For example, you can sort numerically, but Dreamweaver doesn't understand dates in tables, so you're liable to get sorts like this:

3/19/99

3/25/77

3/3/02

Dreamweaver sorted the dates numerically, reading left to right, which resulted in an incorrect sort.

Despite these restrictions, table sorting in Dreamweaver is useful—you just have to be aware of the limitations.

Figure 10.31 The Sort Table dialog lets you sort the contents of your table either alphabetically or numerically.

To sort a table:

1. Place the insertion point in any cell of the table you want to sort.

2. Choose Commands > Sort Table.
   The Sort Table dialog appears (**Figure 10.31**).

3. From the Sort by pop-up menu choose the column you want to use to sort the table.

4. In the Order pop-up menu on the left, choose whether to sort the column alphabetically or numerically.

5. In the Order pop-up menu on the right, choose whether to sort the column in ascending or descending order.

6. If you want to sort on a second set of criteria repeat steps 3 through 5 and use the Then by set of pop-up menus.

7. Make any selections from the Options list. By default, the "Sort includes the first row" option is not selected. This is because the first row of a table is frequently a header row. If your table doesn't seem to be sorting properly, check this option.

8. Click OK.
   Dreamweaver sorts your table according to the criteria you selected.

✔ Tips

- Dreamweaver can't sort on rows, just columns.

- If you want a merged row at the top of your table, do the sort first, and then merge the cells.

- Be careful when you're sorting numbers. If you accidentally leave the sort on Alphabetically, you'll get an alphanumeric sort (1, 10, 2, 20, 3, 30) instead of a numeric sort (1, 2, 3, 10, 20, 30).

Formatting Tables

You can apply a CSS style to an entire table (which can change the look of the table), or you can apply a CSS style to selected table cells, which can change the look of the table contents.

When you use a CSS style to format a table, the table's look is defined by instructions in a CSS style sheet. You can choose to have the table style apply to all tables in your document (if you use the style sheet to redefine the <table> tag), or you can create a custom CSS class for a particular kind of table you want to use, and apply the style to the table with the Property Inspector.

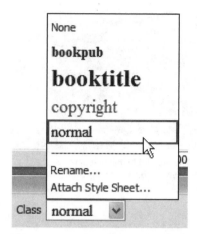

Figure 10.32 Apply a CSS style to a table in the Property Inspector.

To apply a CSS style to a table:

1. Select the table or table cells you want to format.

2. In the Property Inspector, choose the style you want from the Class pop-up menu (**Figure 10.32**).

   The selection takes on the formatting from the CSS style you chose.

✔ Tip

■ You can create, format, and save an empty table for later use. Just create and format the table, select it, then save it as a snippet. See Chapter 15 for more about creating snippets.

Figure 10.33 Tabular data to be imported into Dreamweaver often starts out as a Microsoft Excel worksheet.

Importing and Exporting Tabular Data

Because tables are best used for tabular data, it stands to reason that Dreamweaver has an easy way to import such data (from database programs or Microsoft Excel, for example) and turn it into a table. This data needs to be in the form of a *delimited text file*, that is, a file that includes the data, separated by some character, such as a tab, a comma, or another delimiter.

To explain how a delimited file works, imagine that you have some data that would be displayed well in a table, such as baseball standings. Each row of the table with the standings contains information on a team, and the different columns of the table contain the team's name, number of wins, number of losses, and winning percentage, as in the example (shown in Excel) in **Figure 10.33**. To use this Excel data in Dreamweaver, you first need to export the data out of Excel as a delimited file, which is easy; you simply save a copy of the file in the "Text (Tab delimited)" format. This saves the data in the Excel worksheet as a plain text file. Each column of data is separated by a tab character, and each row of the data ends with a return character. Dreamweaver can then read in this delimited text file and convert it into a table.

Dreamweaver can also do the reverse trick of turning the data in a table into a delimited text file. This allows you to export table data to Excel or a database program for further processing, or you can take a table on a Web page and move it to a word processor or page layout program such as Adobe InDesign.

continues on next page

To import tabular data into a table:

1. Place the insertion point where you want the table to appear.

2. Choose File > Import > Tabular Data.

   or

   Choose Insert > Table Objects > Import Tabular Data.

   The Import Tabular Data dialog appears (**Figure 10.34**).

3. Click the Browse button to select the delimited data file.

   The Open dialog appears.

4. Navigate to the data file, select it in the Open dialog, then click Open.

   The name of the data file appears in the Import Tabular Data dialog's Data file text box.

5. From the Delimiter pop-up menu, choose the delimiter character used in the data file.

   Your choices in this pop-up menu are Tab, Comma, Semicolon, Colon, and Other. If the data file uses an unusual delimiter character, choose Other and type that character into the text box next to the Delimiter pop-up menu.

6. In the Table width section, choose Fit to data if you want the table width to be just as wide as the data, or Set to if you want the table to be a fixed width. If you choose the latter option, enter a number in the text box and choose the units from the pop-up menu (either percent or pixels).

Figure 10.34 Use the Import Tabular Data dialog to select the delimited text file and format the table you are about to create.

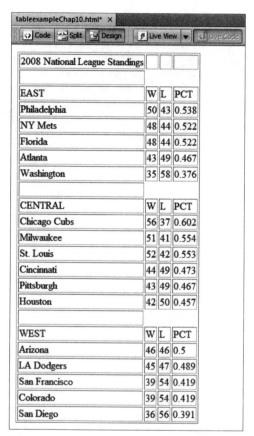

Figure 10.35 The unformatted table, built from the imported data, appears in your document.

7. You can enter values for cell padding, cell spacing, and the table border. You can also choose to format the text in the top row of the table (which is usually a header of some sort). Your choices are no formatting, bold, italic, or bold italic.

8. Click OK.

Dreamweaver reads the delimited text file and inserts it into your page as an unformatted table (**Figure 10.35**).

✔ Tips

■ If you only want to export a portion of a table (for example, the top ten rows), select those rows, copy them, then paste them into a different part of the document, where they will create a new table. Export the new table as a delimited text file, then delete the new table.

■ If the table imports incorrectly, chances are that the data file uses a delimiter different from the one you chose in step 5. You have to delete the incorrect table and import it again with the correct setting.

■ If you are importing tabular data from Word or Excel, consider copying and pasting the data using Edit > Paste Special. Dreamweaver understands Office program formatting and you'll save time, because you won't have to reformat in Dreamweaver. See Chapter 4 for more about using Paste Special.

To export a Dreamweaver table's data to a delimited file:

1. Place the insertion point in any cell of the table.

2. Choose File > Export > Table.

   The Export Table dialog appears (**Figure 10.36**).

3. From the Delimiter pop-up menu, choose the delimiter character you want to use in the exported text file. Your choices are Tab, Space, Comma, Semicolon, or Colon.

4. From the Line breaks pop-up menu, choose the operating system that is the destination for the text file. Your choices are Windows, Mac, or UNIX.

   The reason for this option is that each of the platforms has a different way of indicating the end of a line of text.

5. Click Export.

   The Export Table As dialog appears.

6. Give the file a name, navigate to where you want to save it, and click Save.

   Dreamweaver saves the table data as a delimited text file.

Figure 10.36 Use the Export Table dialog to save the data from a Dreamweaver table as a delimited text file.

USING
FORMS AND FIELDS

INSERT

Forms ▼

- ☐ Form
- ☐ Text Field
- ☐ Hidden Field
- ☐ Textarea
- ☑ Checkbox
- ☷ Checkbox Group
- ◉ Radio Button
- ☷ Radio Group
- ☷ List/Menu
- ↗ Jump Menu
- ☐ Image Field
- ☐ File Field
- ☐ Button
- abc Label
- ☐ Fieldset
- ☐ Spry Validation Text Field
- ☐ Spry Validation Textarea
- ☑ Spry Validation Checkbox
- ☐ Spry Validation Select
- ☐ Spry Validation Password
- ☐ Spry Validation Confirm
- ☐ Spry Validation Radio Group

Figure 11.1 The Forms category of the Insert panel contains all the items you might want to add to your form.

A lot of Web sites exist just to provide information and entertainment to site visitors. But if you want your site to get information back from your visitors, you'll need some way to let them interact with you and your site. To do that, you'll need to add a form.

A form contains fields, and those fields can be anything from a simple check box to a group of radio buttons, or a single or multi-line text entry area. And of course, you'll want some sort of "OK" or "Submit" button so that your visitors know how to send you their completed form. Look at the Forms category of the Insert panel (**Figure 11.1**), and you'll see that it contains everything you need to add any kind of form and field to your site.

Adding a Form to a Page

You could start creating a page by throwing fields onto it, but when your visitor clicks Submit, the browser won't know what to do with the data. That's where you need a form—it tells the browser that all this information is part of one package, and it tells the browser what it should do with all of the information that it has gathered.

To add a form to a page:

1. Choose where on your Web page you want your form, and click the Form button on the Insert panel. A red box appears on your page (**Figure 11.2**).

    The red box is the form area, and behind the scenes in the code, Dreamweaver has added a `<form>...</form>` container tag.

2. If that box isn't automatically selected, select it, and you'll see the options you can change for your new form in the Property Inspector (**Figure 11.3**). The ones that apply solely to forms are:

    ▲ **Form ID:** If you're going to be doing any JavaScript validation of your form, it's a requirement to give it a name. In addition, some CGIs (which stands for Common Gateway Interface and is the program that runs on the server that interprets the data sent by your form) need their associated forms to have a particular name.

    ▲ **Action:** This is the program on the Web server that is executed when the form is submitted. You'll need to get the name of this from your system administrator or hosting provider. It's also commonly referred to as a System CGI.

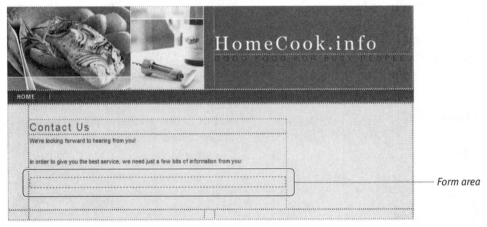

Figure 11.2 A form looks bare until you add the form fields.

Figure 11.3 The Property Inspector is where you set a form's name, action, and method.

▲ **Method:** The most common options are GET and POST. POST passes the form data as part of the header of the request to the server. GET passes the data as part of the URL of the request to the server. Because of this, and because GET has a length limitation, POST is what you'll usually want.

▲ **Enctype:** This field describes the enclosure type being sent to the server. The default is `application/x-www-form-urlencoded`. The only time you'll want to use `multipart/form-data` is if you're asking your visitors to upload a file.

✔ Tips

■ Make sure that all your form fields are inside your form; if they are not, their contents won't be sent to the server.

■ If you try to add a form field to a page that doesn't have a form, you'll be asked if you want to add a form tag. You might think from this that it's not worth bothering to add a form tag manually first, but it is. You'll have better control over where the form is placed, and what ends up going inside it.

■ No, that red border around the form won't actually display on your site. It's just there in Dreamweaver so that you'll know where the form begins and ends.

The Uncovered Fields

There are nine items in the Insert panel that aren't covered in this chapter:

◆ **Jump Menus:** We cover these in Chapter 13, "Using Behaviors and Navigation Objects."

◆ **File field:** If you need to upload a file to a server, you'll want to use this type of form field. It's fairly self-explanatory, but you'll need to talk to your server administrator about how they've set up their server to accept files.

◆ **Spry Validation:** These seven buttons help you use Spry, Adobe's Ajax user interface library, to validate form entries. We cover Spry in Chapter 14: "Building Dynamic Pages with Spry."

Adding Text Fields

The simplest type of form field you can have is a single-line text field. Your average form will have several of them, allowing people to enter anything from their name to their phone number to their shoe size.

To add text fields:

1. Choose where in your form you want your text field to appear (by clicking in the document), and click the Text Field button on the Insert panel. The new text field appears on your page (**Figure 11.4**).

2. If the text field hasn't been automatically selected, select it, and you'll see the options you can change for your new field in the Property Inspector (**Figure 11.5**). From there, you can change the fields:

   ▲ **TextField:** This field contains the name of the field, which can be used by JavaScript behaviors and by CGI scripts on the server.

   ▲ **Char width:** This is the width of the text input area on your page. The larger this number, the wider the space it needs. And because it's the number of characters allowed, the larger the font you've set (usually with CSS), the wider the space will be.

Figure 11.4 The first text entry field added to the form.

Figure 11.5 Set a text field's properties using the Property Inspector.

▲ **Max chars:** This is the maximum number of characters that someone visiting your site can enter into this field. For instance, you might want to limit a phone number to ten characters, or a credit card to 16.

▲ **Type:** This has three values: *Single line*, *Multi line*, and *Password*. Multi line is covered in the next section, "Adding a Text Area." The only difference between Single line and Password is what the user sees when they enter something into this field: if the type is Password, no matter what your visitor types, it will appear as black dots. The correct value will be sent back to the server, though.

▲ **Init val:** The initial value of the field. This text is displayed when the page is loaded.

✔ Tip

■ There's another type of field that's similar to a text field called a *hidden field*. It's used when there's information that a CGI needs to get from a form, but which a user doesn't enter—so the field itself contains a value, but isn't seen in the document. Adding a hidden field is virtually identical to adding a text field: just click the hidden field button in the Insert panel (obviously, where it's put on the Web page doesn't matter) and then set the value and unique field name in the Property Inspector.

Labeling Your Fields

When you click a button in the Insert panel to add a form field to your page, the Input Tag Accessibility Attributes dialog may appear (**Figure 11.6**). This dialog allows you to set certain attributes that can enhance accessibility for people with disabilities. These fields are:

◆ **ID:** This is same as the field name in the Property Inspector. It's used by JavaScript to manipulate the contents of fields, and also by the CGI that processes the form.

◆ **Label:** Figure 11.6 shows a label of "First Name:" being entered. Figure 11.4 shows the result: that text is displayed just to the left of the new text field.

◆ **Style:** There are three style options: *Wrap with label tag, Attach label using 'for' attribute*, and *No label tag*. If you choose *Wrap with label tag*, Dreamweaver surrounds your new <input> tag with a <label> tag:

```
<label>First Name: <input type="text"
name="textfield" /></label>
```

Figure 11.6 To enable your site to be accessible for people with disabilities, set the label attributes here. The default position for a text field label is before the form item.

If you choose *Attach label using 'for' attribute*, Dreamweaver writes the <label> tag based on what you enter for *position* (covered below):

```
<label for="textfield">First Name: </label><input type="text" name="textfield"
id="textfield" />
```

Unfortunately, Dreamweaver doesn't offer full WYSIWYG support for this option— you can then change the name and id attributes of your new text field (by changing the TextField), but the label's for attribute, which should change to match, doesn't. There isn't any way to change it short of going into the markup and changing it by hand.

If you choose *No label tag*, the text you enter appears, but it'll be just that: text.

The <label> tag helps make your site more accessible in two ways: it tells voice browsers that this is the text associated with this field, and it allows users with certain browsers (such as Firefox) to click the text label as an alternative to only clicking inside a check box. This gives your visitor a larger space in which to click. Accessibility is important, and using the <label> tag helps make your site more accessible—but if you want to use it with Dreamweaver's Design view, stick with the *Wrap with label tag* option.

Labeling Your Fields *continued*

◆ **Position:** The label for a form field can be either before or after the field. For text fields, you'll usually see the label before the field. For check boxes and radio buttons, you'll usually see the label afterwards. The default value of the position changes depending on the type of field (**Figure 11.7**).

◆ **Access key:** Some browsers allow users to enter keyboard shortcuts to select form fields. If you want this option, enter the keyboard shortcut for the field here. For instance, if I entered *g* in **Figure 11.7**, the user with Internet Explorer for Windows could click that check box by pressing Alt-G.

Figure 11.7 For a check box, the label's default position is usually after the form item.

◆ **Tab Index:** If you want users to be able to tab from form field to form field in a particular order, you'll want to assign each field a tab index. This is the numbered order in which the user can tab through your form's fields. It's especially useful to set this when your form fields are inside table cells, as the default can be quite different from what you actually want to occur. The numbers need to be between 0 and 32767, and they don't have to be in sequence: you can make your fields be (for instance) 100, 200, and so on, leaving room for future changes to your form.

If you don't use labels, access keys, or tab indices, and are annoyed at seeing this dialog come up every time you add another form field, you can get rid of it by clicking the link at the bottom. This opens Dreamweaver's preferences, and turning off "Show attributes when inserting Form objects" makes the dialog go away for good. If you later decide you want it back, go back into Preferences, choose the Accessibility category, and you can turn it back on again.

You can also add a label afterwards by clicking the Label button on the Insert panel, but it doesn't do what you expect. Instead of bringing up the Input Tag Accessibility Attributes dialog, Dreamweaver adds a `<label>` tag around whatever you selected and throws you into Split view. If you are markup-phobic, stick with adding labels along with their associated fields.

Adding a Text Area

It's possible that you want your visitors to enter more than just a single line of text—maybe they have a lot to say, or you just want them to have a free-form area in which to enter their comments. If that's the case, you'll want to use a text area.

To add a text area:

1. Choose where in your form you want your text area to appear, and click the Textarea button on the Insert panel. The new text area appears on your page (**Figure 11.8**).

2. If the text area isn't automatically selected, select it, and you'll see the options you can change for your new field in the Property Inspector (**Figure 11.9**). From there, you can change the same values that you could for text fields, with some small differences:

   ▲ **Num Lines:** This is the number of lines that you want the field to take up on the page. If you only want a single line, use a text field instead.

   ▲ **Disabled** and **Read-only:** These check boxes do similar, but not identical things. Disabled displays the text area, but makes it so that the user can't select or change it. You might use this when you have a conditional JavaScript on the page that would make the text area active if the user performed a particular action. Read-only makes the text area unchangeable by the user, but they can still select and copy the field's contents.

Figure 11.8 A text area lets your visitors enter multiple lines of text, and it will scroll when necessary.

Figure 11.9 Use the Property Inspector to set the dimensions and initial value of the text area.

I am interested in learning more about:

☐ Recipes

☐ Wine

☐ Cookware

☐ Cooking News

☐ Deals

Figure 11.10 Check boxes are an easy way to get exact information from your site's visitors.

Adding Check Boxes

Check boxes are one of the most commonly used form fields, and you're likely to want several on your forms. They're particularly useful when you want specific responses from your site visitors, and you don't want them to have to enter data into text fields (and possibly misspell their entry).

To add a check box:

1. Choose where in your form you want your check box to appear, and click the Checkbox button on the Insert panel. A new check box appears on your page (**Figure 11.10**).

2. If the check box isn't automatically selected, select it, and you'll see the options you can change for your new field in the Property Inspector (**Figure 11.11**):

   ▲ **Checkbox name:** This is the name of the field, and it's used by any JavaScript validation as well as any server-side CGI.

   ▲ **Checked value:** This is the value that's passed to the server (and JavaScript client-side code) when the user has checked the check box.

   ▲ **Initial state:** This refers to the appearance of the check box when the page is first loaded—is the box checked or unchecked?

✔ Tip

■ Just a reminder: the difference between check boxes and radio buttons is that for a group of radio buttons, only a single option can be picked. When you have a group of check boxes, however, the state of each check box is not dependent on the other check boxes, so you can select multiple check boxes.

ADDING CHECK BOXES

Figure 11.11 Set the name and value of the check box in the Property Inspector along with the checked status of the box when the page is loaded.

Adding a Fieldset

A *fieldset* is HTML's way of grouping fields on your form together to add additional meaning for the user. How a fieldset displays on a Web page depends on the browser being used, and you can't control that: Dreamweaver's Design view shows it as a thin gray line around a fieldset's contents. Compare Figure 11.10 with **Figure 11.12**: it's easier to see that those check boxes are grouped together, and all have a similar function.

To add a fieldset:

1. Choose where in your form you want your fieldset to appear, and click the Fieldset button on the Insert panel.

2. The Fieldset dialog appears (**Figure 11.13**), asking you to enter a *legend*—that's the text that appears at the beginning of the fieldset (Figure 11.12). Enter that text, click OK, and the fieldset box appears in the document.

3. If you're adding a fieldset to an existing form, drag the related fields into the fieldset. If it's a new form, click inside the fieldset and create its fields.

✔ Tips

- If the fieldset contains no form fields, the legend appears inside the box. When form fields are added, the legend is displayed as part of the box.

- If you're dragging fields inside the fieldset, be careful when selecting—make sure (for example) that all of a label is selected.

- You can't change a fieldset or a legend using the Property Inspector. You can change the legend by modifying the text in the document window, and change the fieldset by going into Code view.

- A fieldset can contain any type of form fields, not just check boxes.

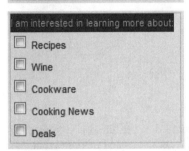

Figure 11.12 Adding a fieldset to your form helps group together related form fields, making your form easier for your visitors to understand. Dreamweaver puts a thin gray line around the fieldset in the document (top). Selecting the <fieldset> tag in the Tag Selector shows you the items in the fieldset (middle) and selecting the <legend> tag in the Tag Selector highlights the fieldset's legend (bottom).

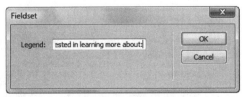

Figure 11.13 Enter the legend text in the Fieldset dialog.

Figure 11.14 The Radio Group dialog lets you enter all of your radio buttons in a single dialog.

Adding a Radio Button Group

Radio buttons don't exist by themselves—they always come in a group. And of that group, only one option can be chosen: your visitors can pick rock *or* paper *or* scissors.

To add a radio button group:

1. Choose where in your form you want your radio button group to appear, and click the Radio Group button on the Insert panel.

2. The Radio Group dialog appears (**Figure 11.14**), asking you to enter several fields:

   ▲ **Name:** A radio group needs a name that associates all of the radio buttons together. In this example, your visitor is choosing whether or not to subscribe to a newsletter, so the name is "newsletter." This name will not appear in the finished form.

   ▲ **Radio buttons Label:** Each radio button needs a label to distinguish it from its neighbors. In this example, the labels are "Yes" and "No."

   ▲ **Radio button Value:** Each radio button needs a value, which will be passed back to the server CGI and/or JavaScript. The example values here are, again, "yes" and "no."

continues on next page

ADDING A RADIO BUTTON GROUP

▲ **Lay out using:** Radio buttons are normally aligned vertically, so here you make your choice of how you want that layout to be done in the HTML markup. Your choices are "Line breaks" and "Table." Line breaks will almost always be sufficient.

The Radio Group dialog starts with two fields, which you can overwrite to say whatever you want. If you want to add more radio buttons, click the + on the left side. If you want to delete buttons, in the list, select the one you want to remove, and click the -.

To rearrange the order of buttons, in the list, select the name of the button to move, and then click the up/down arrows to move that button.

3. Click OK to accept your entries, and your new radio button group is added to your document (**Figure 11.15**).

Would you like to subscribe to our newsletter?

○ Yes ○ No

Figure 11.15 Here's your radio group. Only one item can be clicked.

✔ Tips

- If you want your buttons to all be on the same line (as in this example), select "Lay out using: Line breaks," and then remove the line breaks. Sadly, Dreamweaver doesn't include an option of "just leave them on the same line, okay?"

- There's also an option on the Insert panel to add a single radio button (Radio Button): It's unlikely, though, that you'll ever want to have only a single radio button on a page. If you add a single radio button to an existing radio group, be sure to copy the name of the group exactly into the Property Inspector (**Figure 11.16**). In fact, your best bet is to click one of the existing radio buttons, copy the name from the Property Inspector, click the new radio button (if it already exists; add it if it doesn't), and then paste the name in from the clipboard.

- If you want one of your radio buttons to be set as checked, click that button in your document, and then change the Initial state in the Property Inspector from Unchecked to Checked.

- Dreamweaver will happily let you set multiple radio buttons with their initial state checked even though browsers won't display it that way. Each kind of browser may display this error in a different fashion, so don't make the mistake in the first place. Be careful that you're only setting one (or no) radio button to be checked.

Figure 11.16 When setting the properties for an individual radio button, set the name of the group carefully—it has to match other radio buttons to work correctly.

Adding a List/Menu

Another common form element is what's referred to in the Forms category of the Insert panel as a *List/Menu*. It's actually the two forms of the HTML `select` tag: either a pop-up menu or a scrolling list of options. If it's the latter, you can decide whether the user can click a single option or multiple options.

To add a pop-up menu:

1. Choose where in your form you want your pop-up menu to appear, and click the List/Menu button on the Insert panel.

2. The List Values dialog appears (**Figure 11.17**). Enter your desired options. The Item Label is what appears in the pop-up, and the Value is what's sent to the server-side CGI/JavaScript.

3. Click OK, and your new pop-up appears on your page (**Figure 11.18**).

Figure 11.17 You'll enter all the values for pop-up menus and scrolling option lists in the List Values dialog.

Figure 11.18 The new pop-up menu is now on your form.

4. If the pop-up menu isn't automatically selected, select it, and you'll see the options you can change for your new field in the Property Inspector (**Figure 11.19**):

▲ **List/Menu:** This is the field name that will be passed back to the server-side CGI/JavaScript when it processes the form.

▲ **Type:** The choices are Menu or List; for a pop-up menu, choose Menu.

▲ **Initially selected:** You can choose one of the menu options to be the default that's shown when the page loads.

▲ **List Values:** Clicking this button causes the List Values dialog (**Figure 11.20**) to reappear, so you can easily change the list contents.

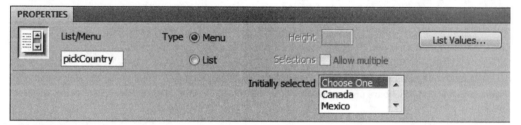

Figure 11.19 You can change the existing pop-up menu into a scrolling option list by clicking the List button in the Property Inspector.

Figure 11.20 You can return to the List Values dialog to view or change the items by clicking the List Values button in the Property Inspector.

To add a scrolling option list:

1. Follow steps 1-3 above to create a pop-up menu, and select the pop-up menu.

2. In the Property Inspector (**Figure 11.21**), change Type to List. You'll notice that even though you've changed the type to list, your field still displays as a pop-up menu.

3. Change the Height to show the number of items you want displayed at any one time in the scrolling list. Changing this causes the field to display as a scrolling list (**Figure 11.22**).

4. If desired, change the Selections option to allow multiple choices. When you do this, visitors to your site will be able to pick several options in the scrolling list at one time.

✔ Tip

■ If you leave the Height set to 1, and change Selections to "Allow multiple," you'll also see your pop-up menu change to a scrolling list. But a scrolling list with a height of one isn't much of a scrolling list—it's too difficult for your users to see what's available.

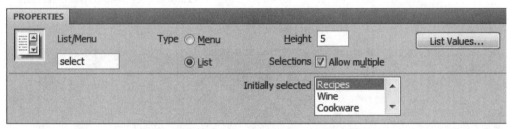

Figure 11.21 If you change from a pop-up menu to a scrolling list, you'll get a couple of new options in the Property Inspector.

Figure 11.22 And here's the new scrolling list above a pop-up menu.

Styling Forms

How forms should be styled is a matter of hot debate among leading Web designers: are tables acceptable, or should you try and stick to CSS-only solutions?

The grim reality is that it's unlikely that you'll get 100% of what you want from CSS, which is why we've used tables in this example—browsers such as Microsoft Internet Explorer 6 for Windows still can't do what's required. On the other hand, a simple form with a simple layout such as this one still comes across differently in browsers, even with the entire layout designed with tables. Looking at **Figures 11.23, 11.24,** and **11.25,** you can see that each browser has its own quirks, and no two look exactly the same.

Figure 11.23 Our new form, as it appears in Firefox on Windows.

Figure 11.24 The same form, in Microsoft Internet Explorer 7 for Windows.

Figure 11.25 And finally, the same form in Safari on the Mac. Even when you use CSS to style form fields in a certain way, Safari often uses its own Mac-like fields instead (even on Safari for Windows!).

Adding a Button

A form on your site doesn't do you much good unless you can get the information that's entered into it, and that's the primary use of a button. A Submit button triggers the action specified in the form tag (described earlier in this chapter). Another type of button is the Reset button, which allows a user to go back to a form's original state.

To add a button:

1. Choose where in your form you want your button to appear, and click the Button icon on the Insert panel. The default value—the Submit button—appears on your document (**Figure 11.26**).

2. If the button isn't automatically selected, select it, and you'll see the options you can change for your new button in the Property Inspector (**Figure 11.27**):

   ▲ **Button name:** This is the name of the button; generally, you'll use "Submit" to specify that it's a Submit button, and "Reset" to show that it's a Reset button (**Figure 11.28**).

   ▲ **Value:** This is the message that is displayed on the Submit button itself. It's common for it to say "Submit," but it can also say, "Place order," "OK," or whatever you think your users will understand.

   ▲ **Action:** There are three possible actions. *Submit form* and *Reset form* do what you'd expect. *None* creates a generic button, which can later be set to trigger a JavaScript action (covered in Chapter 13).

Figure 11.26 Add a Submit button to your Web form so you can receive your visitor's completed form.

✔ Tip

- There is actually one other type of button: an image button. It is created by clicking the Image Field button on the Insert panel. You'll be prompted to browse for an image file in your site, and the image then appears in your document. When a visitor comes to your site and completes the form, clicking that image triggers an immediate submission of the form.

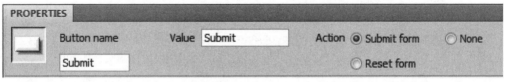

Figure 11.27 The buttons you'll usually use are Submit and Reset; this one's a Submit button.

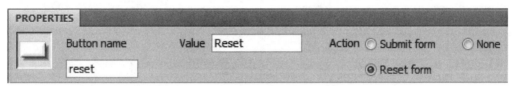

Figure 11.28 A button can be changed to a Reset button using the Property Inspector.

Submit/Reset or Reset/Submit?

If you want to start a fight in a group of designers, just ask which order your Submit and Reset buttons should be in. There are two vocal schools of thought, and they tend to break down into Windows advocates versus Mac advocates.

In a nutshell, Windows users expect to find the OK/Submit button as the first button in a group, while Mac users are accustomed to always seeing it as the right-most button. As shown in **Figures 11.29** and **11.30,** interface designers who work on cross-platform applications are able to change the order depending on the user's platform. While this is the same General Preferences dialog on both platforms, notice that where Mac and Windows users click to accept their changes is very different.

If you're working on a Web site you don't have that flexibility, but you should be aware that visitors to your site will have expectations about how your forms should work—and at least some of those expectations may be different than yours. We're not going to make the call here as to which is preferable; that call should be made based on your visitor logs and your own personal preferences.

Figure 11.29 Dreamweaver's General Preferences on Windows show the buttons as OK and Cancel at the bottom right and Help at the bottom left.

Figure 11.30 The General Preferences on the Mac also has Help at the bottom left, but uses the order Cancel and OK at the bottom right.

12

Adding Frames

Normally a Web page fills an entire browser window. However, a browser window can be split into two or more smaller individual panes called *frames*. Each frame contains an individual Web page.

Frames are used to define areas of a page, such as a navigation bar or a masthead, that remain constant as the user moves through the site. They are also used to define content areas where the content changes each time a navigation link is clicked. Frames allow you to have a site where the navigation part of the window only loads a single time (reducing your bandwidth needs), but the content part of the window changes whenever the user requests a new page.

In this chapter you'll learn how to create framed layouts, insert individual Web pages into the frames, and manage the navigation for a framed site.

How Frames Work

When you look at a framed site, you are actually seeing multiple pages (**Figure 12.1**). You've seen the site in Figure 12.1 before, but not in frames. At first glance you might not notice the site is framed. But once you start scrolling you'll realize the difference. Notice the scrollbar in Figure 12.1. See how it starts about halfway down the side of the page? That's because there are actually three framed pages shown, and only the frame on the lower right has a scrollbar.

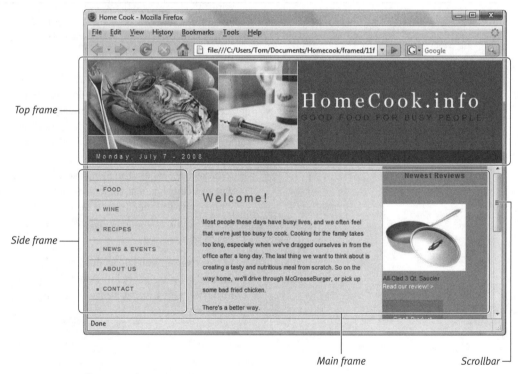

Top frame

Side frame

Main frame   *Scrollbar*

Figure 12.1 The HomeCook.info site in a framed layout looks much like the other layout.

The arrangement of the individual frames is determined by the *frameset document*. The frameset document contains one or more *frameset* tags which set up the number of frames, how they will be arranged, and which individual Web pages will be displayed when the page is opened for the first time.

No matter how many frames a browser window displays, there is usually only one frameset document for a site. A Web page with three frames actually needs four separate documents to display correctly: the frameset document and the three individual documents that fill the three frames.

A frameset divides a window into either columns or rows, but not both at once. Luckily, framesets can be *nested*, or put one inside another. A frameset of columns can be nested in a row of another frameset. Or, a frameset of rows can be nested in a column of another frameset. In Figure 12.1, the frameset has two rows. The top row holds the site identification. The bottom row splits into two columns with a nested frameset. One column holds the navigation, and the other holds the content. The content frame is the one with the scrollbar.

The frameset document is invisible to the user. It sets up the arrangement of the visible pages shown in the frames. The user sees the results of the frameset document, but not the actual frameset document itself.

But wait, there's an accessibility issue. Not all browsers work with framesets. For example, really old browsers didn't understand frames, and even today, browsers built into mobile devices may have problems with framesets. Therefore, each frameset document contains a *noframes* section. Use the `noframes` section to provide basic information in case the user's browser cannot display frames. Links to your content pages are an example of good information to include in a `noframes` section. That way every user can find your valuable content.

Dreamweaver lets you set up the frameset and then work on the individual Web pages for the frames separately. Or you can work on the individual Web pages while they are displayed in the frameset. Both are perfectly valid choices; for instance, an individual might manage a site with only a few pages inside the frameset, while a larger site might have numerous people handling different content pages.

HOW FRAMES WORK

Should You Use Frames?

Using frames is often a poor choice for layout. Although frames do have some advantages, they're outweighed by the disadvantages, to the point that few professional/commercial sites now use frames. For every advantage of frames, there are usually ways to achieve the same effect without frames. For example, most modern sites use CSS for layout.

The use of frames isn't recommended as a best practice for creating Web sites, but Dreamweaver has many tools for creating framed pages and sites, so it's important to know those tools are there if you need them. The most common reason for using frames is navigation. A navigation bar displayed in a frame is always visible no matter how much you scroll in other frames. Some disadvantages of using frames are:

◆ Not all browsers provide good frame support. Cellphone browsers, PDA browsers, and browsers for users with disabilities may have problems with frames. A noframes section helps, but it's a poor substitute for the good browsing experience you hope users have at your site.

◆ It's not possible to bookmark framed pages. The URL of a framed page doesn't appear in the browser's address bar.

◆ It's difficult to get graphic elements to line up precisely between frames.

◆ Testing the navigation is time consuming.

◆ Search engines may not be able to properly navigate and index a framed site.

◆ Visitors who come to your site from search engines will load an unframed page, as search engines will send visitors to your content pages and skip your navigation. To work around that requires some way to get to the "real" version—the content page they want, inside the proper frameset.

Some advantages of using frames are:

◆ Static frames such as navigation bars or graphical banners don't have to be reloaded each time the content changes, making your site load faster. But with broadband increasingly available, this argument is much less important than in the past.

◆ Each frame has its own scrollbar and can be scrolled individually.

Sometimes frames are the best layout choice in spite of their disadvantages. When that is the case, be extra careful to:

◆ Provide helpful noframes content, such as a list (with links) of your content pages. See "Adding noframes Content," later in this chapter.

◆ Use the title attribute to give each frame a descriptive name. This helps with frame identification and navigation. See "Creating a Frameset" for details.

◆ Provide a friendly way for visitors arriving from a search engine to get into your framed site. This could be a link to the frameset, or you could use a JavaScript to force the user's browser to load the frameset. There's no built-in behavior in Dreamweaver to do this, but we cover it in our book *JavaScript & Ajax for the Web, Seventh Edition: Visual QuickStart Guide*.

Figure 12.2 Dreamweaver's New Document dialog has numerous predefined framesets.

Figure 12.3 The Frame pop-up menu lets you select each frame to give it a title attribute.

Creating a Frameset

Dreamweaver comes with several predefined framesets that include the most commonly used frame layouts. For example, the HomeCook.info site needs a top frame for the masthead, a left frame for the navigation, and a right frame for the changing content. Dreamweaver has a predefined frameset that fits these specifications.

If you like, you could create a custom frameset from scratch, by manually drawing frames into a page. Dreamweaver gives you the tools to create and resize frames.

To use a predefined frameset:

1. Choose File > New.

   The New Document dialog appears.

2. In the left-most column, click Page from Sample, then click Frameset in the second column.

3. In the Sample Page column, select a layout.

   For example, you can choose Fixed Top, Nested Left (**Figure 12.2**). This layout uses a frameset with two rows. A second frameset with two columns is nested in the bottom row.

4. Click Create.

   Dreamweaver opens the new framed window, and the Frame Tag Accessibility Attributes dialog appears, if you have your Preferences set for Frames Accessibility (**Figure 12.3**). (You do have Preferences set for Frames Accessibility, right?)

   continues on next page

CREATING A FRAMESET

In the dialog, select each frame from the Frame pop-up menu and give a descriptive `title` attribute to each frame by typing it into the Title field.

In Figure 12.3, we replaced the default suggestion for mainFrame with the more descriptive title "content." A good `title` for the topFrame is "site identification." A good `title` for the leftFrame is "site navigation." Remember, `title` attributes help users whose browsers can't display frames understand and navigate your site, so be informative.

✔ Tips

■ You can also create a frameset using the Layout category of the Insert panel. First create a blank HTML document, then use the Frames button in the Insert panel to choose the frameset layout you want (**Figure 12.4**).

■ You can preview a thumbnail of each frame layout by clicking its name in the Sample Page column; the thumbnail appears in the right side of the New Document dialog.

To create a custom frameset:

1. Create a new HTML document by choosing File > New, then in the resulting New Document dialog, click Blank Page, then double-click HTML in the Page Type column.

2. Choose View > Visual Aids > Frame Borders (**Figure 12.5**).

   This turns on a dotted border around the frame edges.

Figure 12.4 The Insert panel has numerous predefined framesets as well.

Figure 12.5 One of the Visual Aids you can view is Frame Borders.

3. Click and drag the dotted border to insert frames. The cursor changes to a double-headed arrow cursor to drag (**Figure 12.6**).

If you drag from the top or bottom, the document splits horizontally. If you drag from the left or right, the document splits vertically. If you drag from a corner, the document splits into four frames.

✔ Tip

■ You can also add frames to a frameset by choosing Modify > Frameset > Split Frame Left, Split Frame Right, Split Frame Up, or Split Frame Down.

To delete a frame from a frameset:

1. Choose View > Visual Aids > Frame Borders (Figure 12.5).

2. Click and drag the dotted border to the edge of the document window to delete a frame.

or

Click the frame border and drag it until it meets another frame border.

Figure 12.6 The dotted line around the outside of the document window indicates the frame borders. Drag to create frames, as shown here.

CREATING A FRAMESET

Frame Name vs. Frame Title

Frame navigation won't work unless you can point to a frame by name. (See "Targeting Frames with Links" a little later in this chapter.) Every frame needs a name. Dreamweaver assigns a default name based on location or assumed purpose, for example, `topFrame`, `leftFrame`, `mainFrame`.

The *Frame name* displays at the left on the Property Inspector when a frame is selected. If you don't like Dreamweaver's choice of name, you can type a different one in the Frame name field. If you use a name of your own choosing, there are a few rules:

◆ No spaces are allowed in a frame name.

◆ The name must begin with a letter or number.

◆ It's okay to mix uppercase and lowercase letters.

Frame names work behind the scenes to make the frameset function. They don't make any difference to your users.

Frame titles, on the other hand, do make a difference to at least some of your users. As we mentioned previously, the `title` attribute provides important identification and navigation help for users with certain types of browsers. Dreamweaver suggests `title` attribute text for you as a prompt in the Frame Tag Accessibility Attributes dialog. This is your one chance to enter `title` information if you work in Design view.

The rules are different for `title` attribute text. More than one word, spaces, even sentences can go into a `title` attribute. For example, the `title` attribute for the `topFrame` might be something like "Site identification and a link back to the home page."

Look at the markup for `topFrame` to see where `name` and `title` are used:

```
<frame src="masthead.html" name="topFrame" scrolling="No" noresize="noresize"
id="topFrame" title="site identification and a link back to the home page" />
```

Everything in that code snippet can be modified from the Property Inspector except `title`. That's why you need to grab your chance to write a great blurb for the `title` text when the Frame Tag Accessibility Attribute dialog prompts you for a title.

Figure 12.7 A thick border indicates the selected frameset.

Figure 12.8 The nested frameset in the bottom row is outlined with a thick border, indicating that it is selected.

Figure 12.9 The black border indicates the selected frame. Note that the border for a frame is not quite as thick as the border for a frameset.

Using the Frames Panel

You've probably noticed by now that Dreamweaver has a panel for everything. Frames are no exception. If the Frames panel isn't visible, choose Window > Frames to bring it into view.

It's a good idea to keep the Frames panel in view when working with a framed site. It gives you a miniature view of the frames within a frameset. It also gives you an easy way to select either an individual frame or an entire frameset.

To select frames and framesets with the Frames panel:

1. In the Frames panel, click the outermost border around the frameset (**Figure 12.7**).

   The selected frameset displays a thick black border.

2. Do one of the following:

   ▲ To select a nested frameset, click the white border around the frameset (**Figure 12.8**).

   The selected frameset displays a thick black border.

   or

   ▲ To select an individual frame, simply click inside the frame (**Figure 12.9**).

   The selected frame displays a black border, thinner than the one used for the frameset.

USING THE FRAMES PANEL

✔ Tips

- When you select a frame in the Frames panel, the corresponding frame is selected in the document window. A dotted border highlights the selected frame in the document window (**Figure 12.10**). The Tag Selector displays the appropriate element—in this example it's `<frameset<frame#topFrame>`.

- When you select a frameset in the Frames panel, the corresponding frameset is selected in the document window. A dotted border highlights the frameset (**Figure 12.11**). The Tag Selector displays the appropriate element—in this example, it's `<frameset><frameset>`.

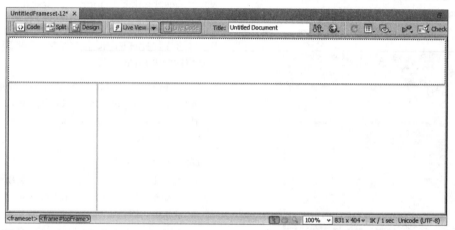

Figure 12.10 In the document window, the selected topFrame is indicated by a dotted border.

Figure 12.11 The dotted border indicates that the nested frameset in the bottom row is selected.

To adjust rows or columns of the frameset:

1. Select the frameset in the Frames panel.

2. Make adjustments with the Property Inspector (**Figure 12.12**).

   The Property Inspector displays options for Borders, Border width, and Border color. You can also set either the row height or column width, depending on which is selected. Enter a value, and then choose pixels, percentage, or relative units.

If the selected frameset contains rows, the rows are miniaturized on the Property Inspector. The selected row is indicated in a dark gray. Clicking a row in this miniature display on the Property Inspector selects it. Set the Row Value (that is, the height) for each row as needed.

If the selected frameset contains columns, the columns are miniaturized on the Property Inspector (**Figure 12.13**). The selected column is indicated in a dark gray. Clicking a miniature column in this display on the Property Inspector selects it. Set the Column Value (that is, the width) for each column as needed.

Figure 12.12 The Property Inspector shows a miniature frameset with rows when a frameset with rows is selected. Options to adjust the frameset are displayed.

Figure 12.13 The Property Inspector with a column frameset selected. You see a miniature frameset indicating which column your adjustments will affect.

USING THE FRAMES PANEL

✔ Tips

■ Row height and column width can be set in exact units (pixels), as a percentage of the frameset, or as relative. If you choose relative, the row or column takes up whatever space is available. Relative rows and columns can shrink or grow, depending on the size of the browser window. Relative units are considered the most accessible.

■ As you work with frames, you'll see that Dreamweaver provides many visual cues, such as dotted borders around selected framesets in the document window and thick borders around selected framesets in the Frames panel. These visual cues are important to watch because it is easy to accidentally change something you don't intend to change in a complicated frameset if you don't pay attention to the selected element. These cues also help you make sure you have the right element selected when it is time to save your work. Remember that these visual cues won't show up in the Web browser.

■ Selecting a frame or frameset in the Frames panel is not the same as placing an insertion point in a frame by clicking within a frame in the document window.

To adjust frame properties:

1. Select the frame you want in the Frames panel.

2. The Property Inspector displays properties for that frame (**Figure 12.14**). Make changes in one or more of the properties:

   ▲ **Frame name** gives a needed identifier to the frame (see the sidebar "Frame Name vs. Frame Title"). Each frame must have a name. If you create a custom frameset, you need to supply the name for the frameset yourself. (Dreamweaver supplies a default name for each frame in the preset framesets.) A name that helps you make sense of your layout such as leftFrame, navFrame, or menuFrame is what you want here. No spaces are allowed in the name.

   ▲ **Src** is the URL of the page that initially is displayed in the frameset. Setting this field is covered in "Inserting Pages Into Frames."

continues on next page

Figure 12.14 With a frame selected, the Property Inspector displays options for adjusting and naming the frame.

▲ **Scroll** options are No, Auto, and Default. *No* means that particular frame will not have a scrollbar ever, even if not all the contents of the frame are visible. *Auto* means a scrollbar appears automatically if the contents of the frame are larger than the frame can display. *Default* is the browser's default, which is usually Auto. Scrollbars can be horizontal or vertical, depending on which is needed to see all the contents of a frame.

▲ Normally a frame can be resized in the browser. Checking the **No resize** check box means that there will be no way to resize a frame in the browser. If you leave it unchecked, users can drag the frame borders in the browser window. This is useful for users who prefer to have especially small or especially large browser windows.

▲ **Margin width** and **Margin height** refer to the margin surrounding an individual frame.

▲ **Borders,** which can be set at the frameset level, can also be set individually for each frame.

▲ **Border color** allows you to set the color for the frame borders. Click the color well to bring up a color picker to help you set the color.

✔ Tips

■ If you click inside a frame in the document window, the Property Inspector displays the standard text properties for that frame's document. To change the properties of the frame itself, use the Frames panel to select the frame.

■ Monitor size and screen resolution can vary widely among users. Some users must enlarge the text with the browser controls in order to read it. It is a good idea to test your framed site with various browser configurations. Only testing shows you whether scrollbars or resizing are needed so that all your content is viewable.

■ Size issues can also lead to printing problems in some situations. You may need to provide special printer-friendly pages for a framed site.

■ One of the reasons that frames got such a bad reputation was due to the tacky look of sites after frame border colors were applied. If you're considering changing your frames site's border colors, please reconsider unless you've got a darned good reason.

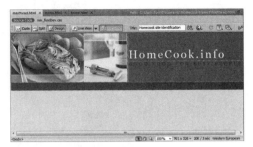

Figure 12.15 This individual HTML page will be placed in the topFrame of the frameset.

Figure 12.16 This individual HTML page will be placed in the leftFrame of the frameset.

Figure 12.17 This individual HTML page will be placed in the mainFrame of the frameset.

Inserting Pages Into Frames

Now that you've got your frames set up, you'll need to create pages to fill every frame. These pages are normal Web pages in every way except that they contain just a part of what appears in the overall window. To prepare the HomeCook.info example, it took four individual pages: masthead.html (**Figure 12.15**), menu.html (**Figure 12.16**), home.html (**Figure 12.17**), and the frameset document.

To add a prepared page to a frame:

1. Click anywhere in the frame.

2. Choose File > Open in Frame.
   The Select HTML File dialog appears.

3. Browse to select the file you want to insert, then click OK (Choose).

continues on next page

INSERTING PAGES INTO FRAMES

4. Repeat the steps to add files to other frames (**Figure 12.18**).

5. When every frame has its opening file, choose File > Save Frameset.

The inserted files are now the Src documents for the various frames in the frameset.

For more about saving framesets, see "Saving Framesets and Frames."

✔ Tip

■ Naming a "home" page is slightly different with framed sites. You'd normally name the home page `index.html`. But in a framed site, you need that file name for the `frameset`. With a framed site, think of the initial set of files displayed when the frameset opens as Home. The page in Figure 12.17 is named `home.html` because it's in the opening content frame before any links are clicked.

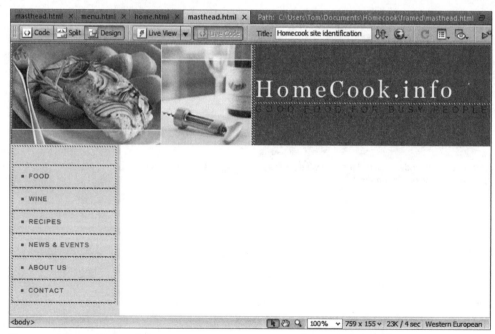

Figure 12.18 The `topFrame` and the `leftFrame` have files inserted, but the `mainFrame` is still unfilled.

To add content to a page in a frame:

1. Click anywhere in the frame.

2. Insert text and images with your normal Web content creation verve (**Figure 12.19**). If you need a refresher, take a peek at Chapter 3, "Building Your First Page" or Chapter 4, "Adding Text to Your Pages."

3. Choose File > Save Frame.

   For more about saving frames, see "Saving Framesets and Frames."

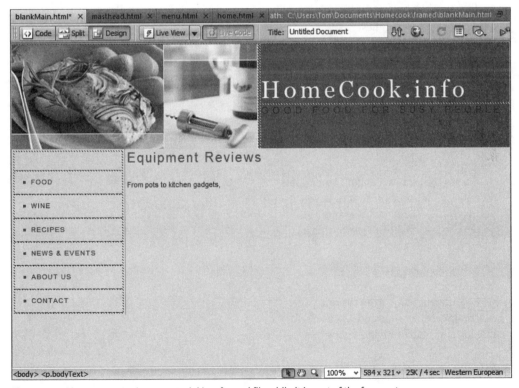

Figure 12.19 You can type or insert material in a framed file while it is part of the frameset.

Saving Framesets and Frames

As soon as you create a frameset it's selected in the document window. But if you've been working with frames and files, it can get tricky to know just what file you're working on. Sometimes the option to save that you want is grayed out. This could mean that the file was already saved. If you know it wasn't, then recheck all the visual clues to figure out what you have selected. Be sure you have the frame or frameset you intend to save selected.

To save a frameset:

1. To select the frameset, click the outer border of the frameset in the Frames panel.

The thick border indicates the selected frameset, as in Figure 12.7.

2. Choose File > Save Frameset.

If the frameset document has never been saved before, you'll be prompted to give the file a name. The frameset document is the file that is opened when a visitor first arrives at a URL, so frameset files are often saved as `index.html`.

or

Choose File > Save All.

This saves the frameset and all other open files at once. If this is the first time you are saving the files, Dreamweaver prompts you to name each file prior to saving it.

or

Choose File > Save Frameset As.

This prompts you to save the frameset with a different name from the one you might already be using, and it is useful for making a backup or saving a copy.

To save a frame:

1. Click anywhere in an individual frame.

2. Several File menu options related to frames are now available:
   ▲ Choose File > Save Frame to save the currently selected frame.
   ▲ Choose File > Save Frame As to save the current frame with a different name.
   ▲ Choose File > Save Frame As Template. This creates a template you can use to create similar pages (see Chapter 15, "Making Life Easier: Using Templates, Libraries, and Snippets").

Page Title and Frame Title

Every document you create in Dreamweaver has a Title field in the toolbar at the top of the document window. The `frameset` page `title` may be the only title a user ever sees for your framed site, so make it count. However, it's a good idea to give each individual document in the site a `title`, too.

We need a little semantic clarification here, because there are `title` elements, and then there are `title` attributes. You first heard about `title` elements in Chapter 3, "Building Your First Page." There you learned how to create the document `title` in the Title field at the top of the window. This is the title that appears in the title bar of a Web browser when the page is loaded.

In this chapter, we talk a lot about `title` attributes for frames. Now, `title` attributes are very important, but they're not the same thing as the `title` elements that give a document a title.

Attributes describe elements. An element is made with an HTML tag. If you wrap some text with an HTML tag, you've got an element. HTML elements are things like paragraphs, lists, images, headings, and frames. All those elements have attributes like `size`, `color`, `border`, `margin`, and possibly `title`. A `title` attribute tells you some characteristic about its element. In this chapter, `title` attributes give information about the `frame` element.

If all this semantic talk is too much for you, just remember this: if Dreamweaver gives you a chance to put a title anywhere, do it!

✔ Tips

- Double-check the document window to verify that the frameset or frame you want to save is what's selected. Dotted borders outline the selected frameset (**Figure 12.20**). In the figure, because the selected frame is inside a nested frameset, the tag selector at the bottom of the window displays <frameset> <frameset><frame#mainFrame>

- If you're working on an internal content page of your site while typing in a frame in the frameset document window, be careful when you save. You only want to save the file in the frame, not the entire frameset. If you inadvertently save the frameset, you'll be accidentally changing the Src file in the frameset document to that of the file you just saved—probably not what you wanted. Make sure that you're saving the frame file, not the frameset file.

Figure 12.20 Check for the dotted lines indicating a selection to be sure about what you are saving.

Figure 12.21 When you create a link while working in the frameset document, Dreamweaver provides the Target options in the Property Inspector.

Targeting Frames with Links

You probably surfed the Web for all of a minute and a half before you first realized that if you click a link the current page goes away and a new page fills the window. That's a great system—except for framed sites. Often, when a link is clicked in one frame, the new file should open in some other frame entirely. You can make that happen by using a *target* attribute in the link. The target names the frame where the new file will open. Yep, that's why you named the frames.

To make a target link while working in the frameset:

1. Open the frameset with the page where you want the link visible.

2. Highlight the text for the link.

3. The Property Inspector link options appear.

   Browse for the file you want the link to open.

   or

   Click the Point to File icon and point to a file in the Files panel to create the link.

   Choose the target frame from the Target menu (**Figure 12.21**). Dreamweaver already knows which frames are in the frameset.

4. Choose Save > Frame to save your changes.

To make a target link while working on an individual page:

1. Open the page where the link will be.

2. Highlight the text for the link.

3. The Property Inspector link options appear.

   Browse for the file you want the link to open.

   or

   Click the Point to File icon and point to a file in the Files panel to create the link.

   Type the frame name in the Target field (**Figure 12.22**). Spelling and capitalization of the frame name must be exactly right.

4. Save your changes.

✔ Tip

■ While it's definitely handy to have the pop-up menu of frame targets right there in the Property Inspector when making links in the frameset document window, it's not without peril. Inadvertent improper saves can play havoc with the frameset. If you create the individual pages for the site independently, outside of the frameset document, you do have to do a bit of extra typing to get the Target field filled in. However, when you save an individual page, you can't possibly save anything besides the individual page.

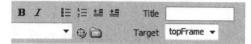

Figure 12.22 When you create a link in an individual document, you must manually type the target in the Target field of the Property Inspector.

Working with Frames and CSS

You won't use CSS to lay out a framed site, but what about for everything besides layout? CSS works just fine with framed sites to control the various display properties of the individual pages.

In Chapter 9, "Managing Styles," you learned how to attach a style sheet to a document. To use CSS with a framed site, you simply attach a style sheet to every individual page that will be inserted in your frameset.

Adding noframes Content

Some wireless users who access the Web with mobile phones, PDAs, or pocket PCs can't view frames. Nor can users with disabilities who have specialized browsers. These folks need noframes content—unless you want them all to go away and leave your site alone, never to return.

The content in a noframes element could be an entire alternate Web page, providing all the information a frames-capable user would find in the framed site. A less ambitious noframes element might contain an invitation for the user to click through to a site navigation page or a site index page so that the content you offer could still be accessed.

Search engines also make use of noframes content. Use it to describe the site's key information and provide links for the search engine robots (or other users) to follow.

Working with iframes

An *iframe* is an inline frame or an inline subwindow. In much the same way that you can insert an image into a page of text, you can insert an iframe. The iframe element inserts an entire miniature view of an HTML page into another page. This is handy when you want some small bit of content to come from somewhere else, in a page that otherwise isn't framed. For instance, those ubiquitous Google AdSense ads you see on many sites are done with iframes.

Dreamweaver is only minimally equipped to create iframes fresh out of the box, but you can get an extension to add more capabilities. For instance, one named iFrame Suite contains five extensions for working with iframes. It, along with other extensions related to iframes, are available at the Adobe Exchange at www.adobe.com. Appendix B, "Customizing and Extending Dreamweaver," has more information about how to install and use extensions.

To add noframes content:

1. Select the frameset in the Frames panel.

2. Choose Modify > Frameset > Edit NoFrames Content (**Figure 12.23**).

3. A blank page appears in the document window, replacing the framed pages (**Figure 12.24**).

   Type or paste the noframes content in this blank window (**Figure 12.25**).

4. To return to the frameset, choose Modify > Frameset > Edit NoFrames Content again.

✔ Tips

- If you preview your site in a regular browser (which has no trouble displaying frames), you won't see the noframes content.

- Apple's iPhone comes with a version of the Safari browser that has no problem with framed sites. Expect other manufacturers over time to follow suit to improve the mobile browsing experience on their units.

Figure 12.23 To set what will be displayed for non-frames-supporting browsers, choose Edit NoFrames Content from the Frameset submenu of the Modify menu.

Figure 12.24 The Edit NoFrames Content command brings up an empty NoFrames Content document.

Figure 12.25 Site information and links are added to the NoFrames Content document.

USING BEHAVIORS AND NAVIGATION OBJECTS

13

Dreamweaver provides a number of JavaScript actions you can easily add to your pages. No prior knowledge of JavaScript is required to use them. Adobe calls these JavaScript actions *behaviors*. Behaviors can add interactivity to your site. Many times the behavior is triggered by some action of the user; for example, the behavior will happen when the user clicks a link or hovers over a link. Other behaviors happen without any overt action from the user, such as a browser check for a needed plug-in as a page loads.

In Dreamweaver, you add many behaviors with the Behaviors tab of the Tag Inspector panel. There are also some behaviors available in the Insert panel. And finally, Dreamweaver imports behaviors from other Adobe software such as Fireworks.

In this chapter you'll learn how to use behaviors to add rollovers, open new windows, check for plug-ins, validate forms, insert jump and pop-up menus, and add navigation bars. **Table 13.1** gives a list of some of the available behaviors.

Table 13.1 The primary behaviors available through Dreamweaver. Only the most commonly used are covered in this chapter, but you can add any of these to your page.

Dreamweaver Behaviors

BEHAVIOR	DESCRIPTION
Call JavaScript	Specify that a custom JavaScript should execute for a specific event. You can write the custom JavaScript yourself, or use one from the many available JavaScript libraries.
Change Property	Change the value of an object's properties. Only certain properties can be changed, and only in certain browsers.
Check Plugin	Send visitors to specific pages based on whether they have certain plug-ins installed. This only works in certain browsers.
Drag AP Element	Set up movable elements that users can drag. Attach this behavior to the document to make interactive puzzles, games, or sliders.
Effects	Add one of seven visual effects, including Appear/Fade, Blind, Grow/Shrink, Highlight, Shake, Slide, and Squish.
Go To URL	Open a new page in a specified window or frame or change the contents of two or more frames with one click.
Jump Menu	Create or edit a Jump Menu. Normally, you create a Jump Menu using Insert > Form Objects > Jump Menu, and merely use the Behaviors panel to edit it.
Jump Menu Go	Like Jump Menu, but adds a Go button to the menu to activate or re-activate the menu choice.
Open Browser Window	Open a URL in a new window. You can set the properties for the new window.
Popup Message	Create a JavaScript alert with the message you specify, usually a brief informative statement.
Preload Images	Preload images that won't be seen right away, for example, images for rollovers. That way, there's no wait to see the image when the action is triggered.
Set Nav Bar Image	Edit the properties of navigation bar images. Normally, you create the nav bar using Insert > Image Objects > Navigation Bar. Use the Behaviors panel to control the display and actions of images in a navigation bar.
Set Text	Change the text display in a frame to the new content and formatting you specify. The new content can include text, HTML, and JavaScript functions.
Set Text of Container	Replace the content and formatting of an existing absolutely positioned element with new content. The new content can include text, HTML, and JavaScript functions.
Set Text of Status Bar	Put a message in the browser's status bar.
Set Text of Text Field	Replace the content of a form's text field with new content. The new content can include text or JavaScript functions.
Show-Hide Elements	Show, hide, or restore the default visibility of one or more absolutely positioned elements.
Swap Image	Swap one image for another to create rollover effects or even swap more than one image at a time.
Swap Image Restore	Restore the last set of swapped images to their previous source files. If you leave the Restore option selected when you attach a Swap Image action, this action gets automatically added.
Validate Form	Check the contents of specified text fields to be sure the user has entered the proper type of data. You can also check whether the user entered something in a required field.

Figure 13.1 The Behaviors are shown in black if they are available for the particular element you chose, and in gray if they aren't. You can't select a grayed-out behavior.

Figure 13.2 The Go To URL dialog is nice and simple. If you're using frames, frame names appear in the Open in box.

Using the Behaviors Panel

In order to add interactivity to your site, you'll want to add *behaviors* to the objects on your pages, such as images and links. You'll use the Dreamweaver Behaviors tab of the Tag Inspector panel to add, modify, and remove behaviors (in this chapter, we'll usually just refer to the "Behaviors panel"). Objects can have multiple behaviors attached, so you'll also need to know how to rearrange their order.

To add a behavior:

1. If the Behaviors panel is not visible, choose Window > Behaviors (Shift-F4).

2. Select an object on the page such as an image or a text link.

3. Click the plus button on the Behaviors panel to see the list of available actions for the selected object (**Figure 13.1**). If a choice is grayed out, that action is not available for the object selected. Click to choose an action.

4. The dialog for the chosen action opens (**Figure 13.2**). Enter the requested information in the dialog.

continues on next page

5. The default event for that action is displayed in the events column on the left side of the Behaviors panel (**Figure 13.3**). If you want a different event, select it from the pop-up menu in the events column (**Figure 13.4**) by clicking the default.

To edit a behavior:

1. Select an object with a behavior attached.

2. Double-click the behavior name in the behaviors column of the Behaviors panel.

   or

   Select the behavior name and press Enter (Return). The dialog for the behavior opens.

3. Change any parameters and click OK.

To change the order of behaviors:

◆ If more than one behavior is attached to an object, the behaviors run in the order listed in the Behaviors panel, from the top to the bottom (**Figure 13.5**). Select an event and use the up or down arrow to change the order.

Figure 13.3 The Behaviors panel shows the event handler and the behavior name.

Figure 13.4 If you want to change the event handler, click the event. An arrow appears, and clicking it brings up the pop-up menu.

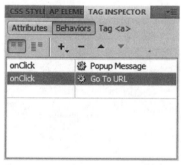

Figure 13.5 Any behaviors attached to an element execute in the order they are listed in the Behaviors panel.

To delete a behavior:

1. On your Web page, select an object with an attached behavior.

2. In the Behaviors panel, select the name of the behavior you want to delete.

3. Click the minus button.

   or

   Press Delete.

✔ Tips

- You can extend Dreamweaver by adding additional behaviors from the Adobe Dreamweaver Exchange. See "Finding and Installing Extensions" in Appendix B for more information about extending Dreamweaver.

- JavaScripts you write yourself can be inserted in Dreamweaver. To learn more about JavaScript, check out another of our books: *JavaScript and Ajax for the Web: Visual QuickStart Guide* (now in its seventh edition) (Peachpit Press).

- If you're familiar with older versions of Dreamweaver, you might be wondering where some of your other behaviors, such as Play Sound, disappeared to. They're still there; they're just hiding in the ~Deprecated submenu. This is Dreamweaver's way of telling you that using those behaviors is a bad idea and that they aren't guaranteed to work in some browsers. If you're using them in existing sites, consider removing them or replacing them with other functionality.

- Whether or not you've worked with previous versions of Dreamweaver, you might be wondering about those behaviors in the Effects submenu. We'll cover them in Chapter 14, "Building Dynamic Pages with Spry."

USING THE BEHAVIORS PANEL

Events and Browsers

JavaScript includes many *event handlers* such as onClick or onDblClick, as seen in Figure 13.4. The name of the event handler is usually pretty descriptive of the user event involved.

Not every browser understands every event. Dreamweaver gives you a say as to the browsers you want to choose events for (**Figure 13.6**). For instance, onPaste is available when you pick IE 6.0, but not when you choose HTML 4.01. Choose Show Events For in the Behaviors panel list of actions to specify your choice of browser or browsers.

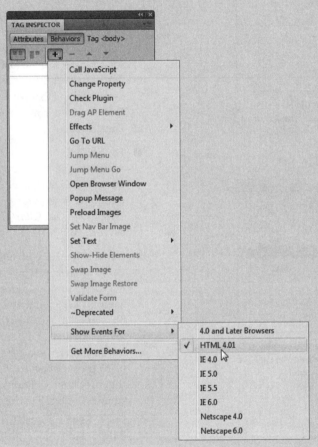

Figure 13.6 When you select Show Events For, you can choose from a list of browsers.

Events and Browsers *continued*

Events can only be applied to certain tags. See **Table 13.2** for specific event names and associated tags.

Table 13.2 Not all events available in Dreamweaver are listed. Some event handlers available in JavaScript are not available in Dreamweaver.

Dreamweaver Event Handlers

Event	Triggered when	Associated with
onAbort	The user stops the browser from completely loading the object	document, images
onBlur	A field loses focus	form fields
onChange	The user changes a default value on the page	form fields
onClick	The user clicks an object	links, form
onDblClick	The user double-clicks an object	links, images
onFocus	A field gains focus	form fields
onHelp	The user clicks F1 or something labeled Help	links, images
onKeyDown	The user presses a key on the keyboard	form fields
onKeyPress	The user presses any key	form fields
onKeyUp	The user releases a key	form fields
onLoad	When a page, frameset, or image finishes loading	document, images
onMouseDown	The user presses the mouse button	links, images
onMouseMove	The user moves the mouse	links, images
onMouseOut	The user moves the mouse off a selected object	links, images
onMouseUp	The user releases a mouse button	links, images
onMouseOver	The user points the mouse at an object	links, images
onReset	The user clicks a form reset button	forms
onResize	The user resizes the browser window	document
onScroll	The user scrolls up or down	document
onSelect	The user selects text in a form field	form fields
onSubmit	The user clicks the Submit button in a form	forms
onUnload	The user leaves a page	document

Adding Rollovers

Web users love *rollovers*, sometimes called mouseovers. There's something endlessly pleasing about running a mouse over a page and watching things change. A color changes, an image changes, an image somewhere else on the page changes or pops up. Web users also expect rollovers—if they move their mouse over an image and nothing happens, they'll assume that it's not a link and move on to something else.

To add a rollover:

1. Prepare two images, such as those in **Figures 13.7** and **13.8**, for the rollover's Up and Over states.

2. Position the insertion point in the document where you want the rollover to appear.

3. In the Common category of the Insert panel, click the arrow beside the Images icon (**Figure 13.9**).

4. Select Rollover Image.

   or

   Select Insert > Image Objects > Rollover Image.

5. The Insert Rollover Image dialog appears (**Figure 13.10**). Fill out the fields:

   ▲ **Image name:** This is the name that JavaScript uses internally to refer to this image.

   ▲ **Original image:** The path to the Up state of the image, which is what displays when the page is loaded.

   ▲ **Rollover image:** The path to the Over state of the image, which is what displays when the user's cursor is over the image.

Figure 13.7
An example of an Up state image.

Figure 13.8
An example of an Over state image.

Figure 13.9
The Images icon on the Common category of the Insert panel has a pop-up menu with several options.

Figure 13.10 Specify both the up and over images to insert a rollover image.

Figure 13.11 Be sure the Swap Image Restore behavior is added along with the Swap Image behavior.

▲ **Preload rollover image:** This should be selected so the Over version of the image is in the browser's cache when it's needed. Don't make the users wait for the Over image to download—they might think the page isn't working and give up on your site.

▲ **Alternate text:** This is the alternate information for users with non-graphical browsers.

▲ **When clicked, Go to URL:** This is the URL of the Web page you want to open when the user clicks the image.

6. Click OK to accept the changes.

7. Check the newly created events in the Behaviors panel to be sure it's what you want (**Figure 13.11**).

✔ Tips

■ To preview the rollover, click the Live View button at the top of the document window, then rollover the image with your cursor. You can also preview the page in a browser to see the rollover.

■ Select the behavior in the Behaviors panel if you want to change the mouse events or edit the parameters of the Insert Rollover Image dialog.

■ To create multiple rollovers, use the Set Nav Bar Image behavior instead, as described later in this chapter.

■ Adding a single rollover adds two events to the Behaviors panel: one for the action of moving the mouse over the image, and one for the action of moving the mouse off the image. Check to make sure that both parts are added or your rollover won't work the way you expect it to.

Image States

To understand rollovers, buttons, and navigation bars, you need to know something about image states. An image state corresponds with a mouse event. The most common image states are:

◆ **Up:** This image appears when the page first loads. It's the default image, in that it's what is displayed unless the user is interacting with this image.

◆ **Over:** This image appears when the user moves the mouse over the image.

◆ **Down:** This image appears when the user clicks the image. Down state images are often used in navigation bars to indicate the current page.

◆ **OverWhileDown:** This image appears when the user moves the mouse over an image after clicking.

Most rollovers only use the Up and Over states.

Adding Navigation Bars

A Dreamweaver navigation bar (nav bar) consists of a set of images that change in response to a user action. Before you use the Insert Navigation Bar command, you must prepare the image sets for each individual image (or button) that will appear in the navigation bar. If you want to use four image states, you'll need four images for each button similar to the four variations on the FOOD button you see in **Figure 13.12**.

To add a navigation bar:

1. Position the insertion point in the document window where the navigation bar goes.

2. Select Insert > Image Objects > Navigation Bar.

   or

   Select Navigation Bar from the pop-up menu next to the Images icon in the Common category of the Insert panel.

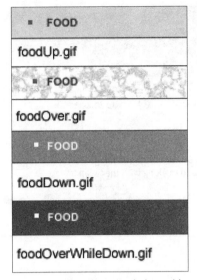

Figure 13.12 Save image variations with names that relate to the image state they represent.

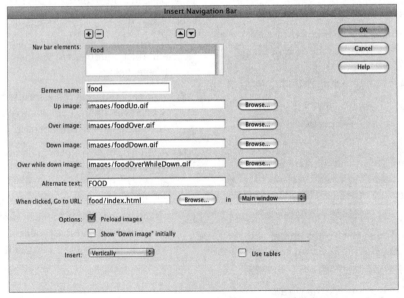

Figure 13.13 Those helpful image names come in handy when you're trying to manage four images for each button.

(side margin) ADDING NAVIGATION BARS

3. The Insert Navigation Bar dialog opens (**Figure 13.13**), and displays the following fields:

▲ **Nav bar elements:** Don't enter anything here. As you add each element to your nav bar, this list grows automatically.

▲ **Element name:** This is the unique name that identifies the object. JavaScript objects must have unique names. On a nav bar, it makes sense to use a name that's the same or similar to the menu choice on the button. Remember, no spaces are allowed in the name.

▲ **Up image:** This is the path of the Up (default) version of the image.

▲ **Over image:** This is the path of the Over version of the image.

▲ **Down image:** The path of the image displayed when the user clicks the image.

▲ **Over while down image:** The path to the version of the image that appears when the user moves the mouse after clicking the image.

▲ **Alternate text:** This is what displays for users with non-graphical browsers.

▲ **When clicked, Go to URL:** This is the page the user sees when the menu is clicked. Specify the window in which you want the URL to open. If you're using frames (see Chapter 12, "Adding Frames"), put the name of one of the frames here. If you're not using frames, leave it at "Main window."

continues on next page

▲ **Options:** Always check Preload images. Select Show "Down image" initially on a page-by-page basis only if you're using the down version of the image to indicate the current page. When this option is selected, an asterisk appears after the element in the Nav bar elements list.

▲ **Insert:** This pop-up menu lets you choose either a horizontal or vertical layout for the nav bar.

▲ **Use tables:** If this check box is selected, the nav bar uses a table layout.

4. Click the plus button to add other elements and complete the dialog for each new element.

5. When you're done adding elements, click OK to accept your entries.

6. Check the default actions in the Behaviors panel to be sure they're the ones you want.

✔ Tips

■ If you want a navigation bar with only Up and Over image changes, leave the "Down image" and "Over while down image" fields blank.

■ Remember, alternate text appears when the image isn't visible. Write text that replaces the image effectively. If the button says "FOOD," for example, it's a good idea to use the word "FOOD" as the alternate text.

■ You can save some time if you copy and paste your navigation bar onto other pages. If you want to change the parameters for the navigation bar on individual pages, use the Modify > Navigation Bar command or the Set Nav Bar Image behavior.

■ You can save even more time by making your navigation bar into a reusable library item. (See Chapter 15, "Making Life Easier: Using Templates, Libraries, and Snippets," for more about library items.) You can't customize a library item on individual pages.

Modifying a Navigation Bar

No matter how often you think that you've got it just right when you first create your navigation, something's going to come along and make you change it. Some changes will be to the navigation bar itself, and some changes will be for only the images in the bar. How they're each changed differs slightly.

To modify a navigation bar:

1. Select the navigation bar in the document.

2. Select Modify > Navigation Bar. The Modify Navigation Bar dialog opens (**Figure 13.14**).

3. Make your changes as needed. This dialog's fields are set just like those in the original Insert Navigation Bar dialog.

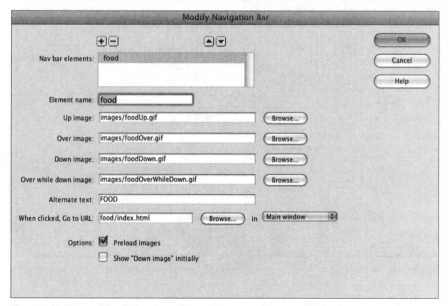

Figure 13.14 Some of the choices from Figure 13.13 are no longer available when you use the Modify Navigation Bar dialog.

To modify images in a navigation bar:

1. Select one of the image elements in your navigation bar and double-click one of the Set Nav Bar Image actions in the Behaviors panel (**Figure 13.15**).

2. The Set Nav Bar Image dialog opens (**Figure 13.16**). This dialog looks similar to the Insert Navigation Bar dialog, but there are some major differences. You're only dealing with a single object from the nav bar, and you have tabs for basic and advanced modifications.

On the Basic tab, you can modify any of the parameters for Element name, image URLs, Alternate text, and the URL for the page to open. The Options let you Preload Images and set the image to be in the Down state initially.

Figure 13.15 Double-click any behavior in the Behaviors panel to edit it. Alternatively, select it and press Return (Enter) to edit.

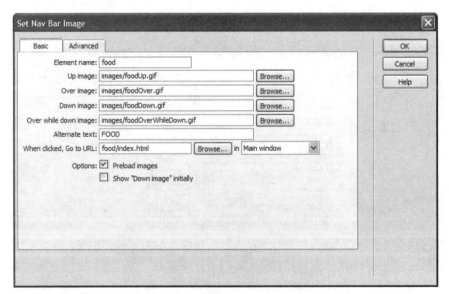

Figure 13.16 The Basic tab of the Set Nav Bar Image dialog deals with just one specific button.

MODIFYING A NAVIGATION BAR

With the Advanced tab (**Figure 13.17**), use nav bar image actions to swap additional images elsewhere on the page with "Also set image."

For example, an image of an entrée might appear somewhere on the page when the FOOD button is in the Over state, or an image of a wine bottle might appear somewhere on the page when the WINE button is in the Over state. This type of fancy footwork—called a *disjoint rollover* in Dreamweaver—allows you to have multiple images that change due to a single event.

✔ Tip

- A default opening image must be in place in the document before you can use the Advanced tab in the Set Nav Bar Image dialog to create a swap image behavior.

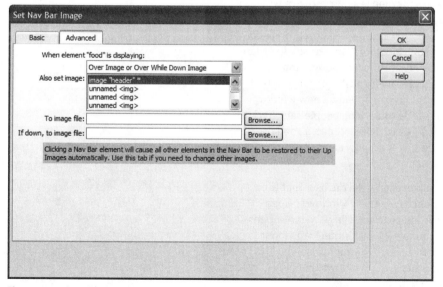

Figure 13.17 The Advanced tab has options to change other images besides just the selected button.

Opening a New Browser Window

It isn't a good idea to open a new browser window unless you really, really need one. Some users may not realize that a new window opened. Users may become lost or confused by the grayed-out Back button. Users may not realize they must close the new window to get back to the original page. Certain browsers, particularly those used by people with accessibility needs, may not deal with new windows in a way that helps the user understand what's happening. Depending on the action you use to trigger the opening of the new window, some users may not see it at all. For example, setting a new window to open during an onLoad event is the trick to getting a pop-up ad in a user's face. Therefore, many users set their browsers so pop-up windows won't open, ever.

Given all that, when is a new browser window justified? Consider it if the content of the new window is a small example or elaboration on one idea. Small means smaller than a normal-sized browser window. Small also means small in concept: if the main content of your page is clear already, a new window can add a little something people can check if they're interested. For instance, a good use of a new window is to show an enlarged image of a product.

You should explicitly tell the user that their click would cause a new window to open: "Click the image to see a larger view—opens in new window." Leave the decision about whether to click up to your users—don't blindside them with windows that automatically open without warning.

Figure 13.18 When you open a new browser window, you have all kinds of control over how that new window will appear.

To add the Open Browser Window action:

1. Prepare an HTML page or an image to appear in the new window.

2. Select an object such as a link or image in the document window.

3. In the Behaviors panel, click the plus sign to add a new behavior. Choose Open Browser Window from the pop-up menu, and the Open Browser Window dialog appears (**Figure 13.18**).

4. Fill out the following fields:

   ▲ **URL to display:** This is the HTML page or image that will appear in the new window.

   ▲ **Window width** and **Window height:** Set an exact pixel size for the new window.

   ▲ **Navigation toolbar:** Checking this box adds Back, Forward, Home, and Reload buttons.

   ▲ **Location toolbar:** Checking this box adds a location text box with the page URL showing.

   ▲ **Status bar:** Checking this box adds a display at the bottom of the browser window showing status information.

   ▲ **Menu bar:** Checking this box adds browser menu items, such as File, Edit, View, Go, and Help. This option only applies to Windows users; Mac users always have access to the menu.

   ▲ **Scrollbars as needed:** Checking this box adds scrollbars (horizontal or vertical) only if needed. If unchecked, there will be no scrollbars. It's a good idea to always check this.

continues on next page

OPENING A NEW BROWSER WINDOW

▲ **Resize handles:** Checking this box adds a gripper in the lower-right corner of the window for the user to drag, and a maximize button at the top of the window. If unchecked, the user can't resize the window by either method. This is another good attribute to routinely include.

▲ **Window name:** This is a required identifier needed by JavaScript. Remember, no spaces are allowed in this name.

5. Click OK to accept.

6. Check the default event. If it isn't the event you want, select another event from the pop-up menu.

✔ Tips

■ If the new window contains only an image, the pixel dimensions of the image and the pixel dimensions of the window aren't an exact match. For better control, many designers put the single image on an HTML page and link to the HTML page.

■ Dreamweaver can be extended with an action to add a "Close Window" script to an HTML page. It's a good idea to give users an obvious way to close the new window. See "Finding and Installing Extensions" in Appendix B for more information about extending Dreamweaver.

■ The event choices are determined by the targeted browsers. If an event you want is not available, check to see what's selected in the Show Events For submenu of the Add behavior menu.

Figure 13.19 You can check for any plug-in, if you know the correct name for it. In this case, we're looking for the Flash plug-in, which is in the pop-up menu.

Checking for Plug-ins

The Check Plugin behavior sends users to different pages depending on whether they have particular plug-ins. For example, if a user has Flash installed, you might send them to one page; otherwise, you might send them to a page where they get the same information but without Flash.

You can depend on most Dreamweaver behaviors to work on a wide variety of browsers, but the Check Plugin action smacks into some browser issues. You can't detect plug-ins in Internet Explorer for Windows using JavaScript. Dreamweaver adds a VBScript plug-in detector when you select Flash or Director. This only works with Internet Explorer on Windows.

To add the Check Plugin action:

1. In the document window, use the tag selector to select either the document (the body tag) or a link (the a tag).

2. In the Behaviors panel, click the plus sign and select the Check Plugin action from the pop-up menu. The Check Plugin dialog opens (**Figure 13.19**) and shows the following:

   ▲ Choose a plug-in from the pop-up menu: Flash, Shockwave, Live Audio, QuickTime, or Windows Media Player.

   or

   ▲ Click the Enter radio button and type the name of a plug-in in the text box. The name must be exactly the same as the name in bold on the About Plug-ins page in a Mozilla-based browser such as Firefox. To see the About Plug-ins page, enter about:plugins in the Firefox address field.

continues on next page

▲ **If found, go to URL:** Enter the URL in this text box. This field is optional; if you leave it blank the user stays on the same page if the plug-in is detected.

▲ **Otherwise, go to URL:** Enter the alternate URL in the text box. If you leave this field blank, users *without* the plug-in stay on the same page.

▲ **Always go to first URL if detection is not possible:** If detection is impossible, the user is sent to the URL in the "Otherwise, go to URL" box. If you select this check box, then the user instead goes to the first URL (the one labeled "If found, go to URL"). If this is checked, users may be prompted by the browser to download the plug-in.

3. Click OK to accept changes.

4. Check the default event in the Behaviors panel to be sure it's the one you want.

✔ Tips

■ All Netscape browsers since version 2.0 can detect plug-ins. By "Netscape browser," we mean Netscape Navigator, Communicator, Mozilla, Firefox, and other browsers based on any of these.

■ The old Microsoft Internet Explorer for Mac does allow checking of plug-ins via JavaScript; however, Dreamweaver doesn't allow it to work for this one browser. Why they did this, we don't know. We also don't know why Microsoft was able to put real plug-in detection into their Mac browser but not their Windows browser. If you're on a Mac, though, you should be using Safari or Firefox, in which case this would not affect you.

Figure 13.20 Here's a brand-new Insert Jump Menu dialog, ready for you to add as many items as you want.

Using Jump Menus

A jump menu is a pop-up menu listing links to documents or files. When a user chooses an item, they "jump" directly to the new URL.

Jump menus save space on the page. For example, to find a retailer in your area for a particular product, you might be asked to select your state or country. A list of states or countries could be very lengthy. Putting the links in a jump menu saves you from listing them in full as part of the page layout.

In addition to the required list of linked items, a jump menu can optionally include a menu selection prompt, such as "Select one," and a Go button.

To insert a jump menu:

1. Place the insertion point in the document.

2. Select Insert > Form > Jump Menu.

   or

   In the Form category of the Insert panel, click the Jump Menu button.

   The Insert Jump Menu dialog appears (**Figure 13.20**). Fill it out as follows:

   ▲ **Menu items:** Don't type anything in this list. As you add items to the menu, they automatically appear.

   Move items up or down in the Menu items list by selecting one and using the up or down arrow to change its order.

   ▲ **Text:** Type the text you want for the menu item. You can type a prompt such as "Choose one" here. For text to be a prompt, leave the URL blank.

   ▲ **When selected, go to URL:** Browse for or type the URL to go here.

   continues on next page

▲ **Open URLs in:** Select the window where you want the URL to display. If you're using frames (see Chapter 12, "Adding Frames"), choose one of the frames here.

▲ **Menu ID:** Type a name in here for JavaScript to use; as always, it cannot contain any spaces.

▲ **Insert go button after menu:** Select this if you want a Go button. The Go button isn't required to make the menu work for users with JavaScript enabled in their browsers. If the user's browser doesn't use JavaScript or if the site uses frames, the Go button is needed.

▲ **Select first item after URL change:** If you use a prompt, select this.

3. Click OK to accept your changes, and the jump menu shows up on your page.

To edit a jump menu:

1. Double-click the behavior name in the Behaviors panel. The Jump Menu dialog opens (**Figure 13.21**).

2. Make any changes as needed.

3. Click OK to accept the changes, and the revised jump menu appears in your document.

Figure 13.21 When you edit a jump menu, some of the original options are missing, particularly the "Insert go button after menu" choice.

Figure 13.22 Make sure your new button has a value and that it doesn't have an action.

Figure 13.23 The Jump Menu Go dialog attaches a Go button to an existing jump menu of your choice.

To insert a jump menu Go button:

1. Select an insertion point in the document window. A jump menu must already exist in the document.

2. Insert a button from the Forms category of the Insert panel. In the Property Inspector, set the button's Action to None and its Value to Go (or something similar, as in **Figure 13.22**).

3. In the document, select your new button. In the Behaviors panel, click the plus button and select Jump Menu Go. The Jump Menu Go dialog opens (**Figure 13.23**).

4. Select a menu for the Go button to activate. A Go button needs to be associated with a jump menu in order to work. If you only have one jump menu on the page, you can take the default.

5. Click OK to add the behavior to the button.

✔ Tip

- A jump menu requires a form, which Dreamweaver adds automatically. You'll notice the red form indicator bordering the jump menu in the document window and you'll see a form tag in the tag selector bar.

Validating Forms

Dreamweaver behaviors can check up on how users complete forms. You can require certain fields, check to make sure that a user has entered a value in a required field, or check to make sure that the user entered the correct type of information in a field.

With the Validate Form behavior you can set parameters for an entire form. You can also use the Validate Form behavior on individual fields. See Chapter 11, "Using Forms and Fields," for more information about making a form with Dreamweaver, and Chapter 14, "Building Dynamic Pages with Spry" for the new Spry form validation routines.

To validate a form:

1. In the document window, select the Submit button.

   or

   Select the form tag from the tag selector at the bottom of the document window.

2. On the Behaviors panel, click plus and select Validate Form. The Validate Form dialog opens (**Figure 13.24**):

   ▲ **Fields:** Select a field in the box.

   ▲ **Required:** Select this if the user *must* enter data in this field in order for the form to be accepted.

   ▲ **Anything:** Check this radio button if any combination of text and numbers is acceptable.

   ▲ **Number:** Check this if you want the user to enter a zip code, phone number, or other strictly numerical data.

   ▲ **Email address:** Choose this if you want to check for an @ symbol within the entered data.

   ▲ **Number from:** Select this if you need to check for a number within a specified range.

Figure 13.24 One form validation option is to require an email address from the user. You can also see here why you should always name your form fields; it makes it easier to know which field is which in this dialog.

Figure 13.25 The user sees an alert if the form validation requirements aren't met.

3. Select the remaining fields in the Fields box and set the parameters for each until you have completed the dialog for each field in the form.

4. Click OK to accept your changes.

✔ Tips

■ You can also select an individual form field and add a validate form behavior. The dialog is the same but the event handler (that's the real name for those fields on the Behaviors panel) is different. Check the Behaviors panel to be sure it's the correct event (onBlur or onChange) when setting validation parameters field by individual field. Be careful with this method, because it can get annoying to a user who wants to skip certain questions and come back to them later. Saving the validation for last, when the user finally clicks the Submit button, is a better idea.

■ When a user enters something incorrectly or neglects to fill in a required field, a JavaScript alert box similar to **Figure 13.25** pops up with a message about the error.

■ It's good practice to give users an explicit cue when a field is required. An asterisk next to a required field is a common visual cue, along with a note to the user that the asterisk denotes a required field. You may have colorblind users, so merely formatting the required field labels in a different color isn't considered adequate.

■ The Dreamweaver behaviors for validating forms are different from server-side scripts used to handle submitted information. The same validity checks on user data you add with Dreamweaver should also be done with server-side scripts. Why both? The server-side checks are necessary because not everyone has JavaScript. The client-side JavaScript checks added here are also useful because they give faster feedback to users.

Inserting Fireworks Pop-Up Menus

If you own Fireworks, you can use it to create a pop-up menu. When you insert a Fireworks pop-up menu into a Dreamweaver document, it's best to use the round-trip editing feature to edit the menu in Fireworks. You will be able to edit the pop-up menu in Dreamweaver, but if you do, you lose the ability to edit it in Fireworks later. Stick with Fireworks.

When you have the Fireworks pop-up menu completed, simply export it. Fireworks creates all the image and HTML files for you and adds them to the Dreamweaver site root folder. With the files in your site folder, you're ready to insert the menu in Dreamweaver.

To insert a Fireworks pop-up menu:

1. Place the insertion point in the document where you want the menu.

2. Choose Insert > Image Objects > Fireworks HTML.

or

Select Fireworks HTML from the pop-up menu by the Images icon in the Common category of the Insert panel (**Figure 13.26**).

The Insert Fireworks HTML dialog opens (**Figure 13.27**).

Figure 13.26
You can choose to add Fireworks HTML from the Image icon in the Common category of the Insert panel.

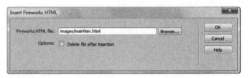

Figure 13.27 Getting Fireworks HTML into Dreamweaver is as easy as pointing to the HTML file.

3. Browse for or type the name of the Fireworks HTML file.

4. (Optional) Select the "Delete file after insertion" option if you no longer want the Fireworks HTML to be stored as a separate file. Selecting this option won't affect the source PNG file associated with the HTML file, or your ability to use round-trip editing to edit the pop-up menu in Fireworks.

5. Click OK to insert your menu. All the HTML, image links, and JavaScript connected to the pop-up menu are inserted in the appropriate areas in the document.

✔ Tip

■ Deleting the HTML file after insertion has its pros and cons. You might want to keep it around to use elsewhere, or you might want to delete it to clean up after yourself. Either way, you can re-create it inside Fireworks, so if you delete it accidentally, it's not the end of the world.

INSERTING FIREWORKS POP-UP MENUS

BUILDING DYNAMIC PAGES WITH SPRY

14

If you spend much time building Web sites, or even just reading about current styles of online design, then you've heard of "Web 2.0." In Dreamweaver CS3, Adobe added a library of the most common "Web 2.0"-ish widgets, to enable Web builders to make their sites look and act like cutting-edge destinations.

This library—also referred to as a *framework*—is named *Spry*. Spry is a collection of HTML, CSS, JavaScript, and graphics, the relevant pieces of which are automatically added to your site when you add any of the Spry elements. No, you don't need to know anything about CSS or JavaScript to use Spry; in fact, you don't even need to know much about design to create pages that work well and look good.

In Dreamweaver CS4, Adobe has added several new Spry elements that help you validate user entries in forms and provide tooltips for items on your pages.

What Is Spry?

To use Spry's full functionality, it helps to know a little bit more about what Spry is and how it works behind the scenes.

A (brief) history of frameworks

When people first started adding JavaScript to pages, they quickly realized that a lot of the work they were doing was the same stuff, over and over and over again. Just about every JavaScripter has their collection of code snippets that they've already debugged and now reuse regularly.

In recent years, it's become common to let JavaScript handle more and more of the user interface (UI) duties. This means that Web sites have become smarter and more flexible, but it's also been a lot more work for people who write code. Programmers tend to be lazy by nature, and hate to write something when they know someone else has already solved that particular problem. Instead, they go looking for free code offered by others, and in return offer their own snippets. The result is shared libraries of code that can handle most of the usual user interface requirements.

However, programmers also tend to have definite opinions about the "right" way to write code, and the result of that has been the creation of many different frameworks. If you've ever heard of libraries such as Dojo, YUI, jQuery, or Prototype, they're all the same thing, built by developers who thought that *their* way of doing things was better than what already existed.

Spry is Adobe's answer to this same challenge, geared to work with Dreamweaver and to stand on its own. It's not an application; instead, it's a collection of code snippets (both CSS and JavaScript) that when added to your pages creates some standard effects.

What's in Spry

Spry contains three types of components:

◆ **Widgets:** These elements let you create a more interactive Web site. There are two main types of widgets: UI widgets (such as the accordion, menu bar, and collapsible panel), and form validation (such as text fields and text areas).

◆ **Effects:** Unlike widgets, effects don't so much interact with the user as just look good on their own. You can use effects to visually highlight transitions or to emphasize elements on your page. Some examples of effects are highlight, shrink, and squish.

◆ **XML data sets:** If you want data on your page that's read from an external file, or you want users to be able to sort displayed information without having to reload the page, or you want to show some detailed information when the user selects various options, then you're looking at using Spry data sets.

Ajax and more

One of the hot buzzwords of modern day Web design is *Ajax*. Unfortunately, that term has come to mean different things to different people, to the point where it's almost a meaningless term.

On the one hand, Jesse James Garrett, who invented the name, says that it stands for "Asynchronous JavaScript And XML"— meaning that Ajax-enabled pages are those where JavaScript is used to read data off a server, allowing you to update Web pages on the fly without your browser loading an entirely new document.

On the other hand, some people only care that the page is updating, not what technology it's using to do it. To those people, any time you use CSS to change the content of a page, or to hide or show different areas, it's Ajax in action.

But no matter what definition you use, if you want to add Ajax to your pages with Dreamweaver's built-in tools, the Spry framework is what you'll be adding to your site.

If after working with Spry you decide that you really want to learn more about asynchronous JavaScript, we recommend another book we've written, *JavaScript & Ajax for the Web, Seventh Edition: Visual QuickStart Guide* (Peachpit Press).

WHAT IS SPRY?

Dynamic Data

Working with XML data is beyond the scope of this book, but that doesn't mean that you can't check out Spry data sets. Take a look at the examples at Adobe's online Spry site (`http://labs.adobe.com/technologies/spry/`); they should give you some good idea of what's possible.

Adding Spry Elements

By now, you've surely noticed the Spry category (**Figure 14.1**) in the Insert panel. It's just one of the many places where you can find Spry elements to add to your page.

To add a Spry element:

◆ **For widgets and data objects:** With the Spry category showing in the Insert panel, choose where on your page you want to add the element, and then click the desired Spry button.

or

For widgets and data objects: Choose Insert > Spry from the menu bar and then choose which Spry element you want to add from the submenu (**Figure 14.2**).

or

Figure 14.1
Spry widgets are found in the Spry category of the Insert panel.

Figure 14.2 Spry commands can be found in several locations in the Insert Menu, as shown in this composite illustration.

Figure 14.3 Spry effects are considered behaviors, so they're found in the Behaviors tab of the Tag Inspector panel.

For form validation widgets: choose Insert > Form from the menu bar and then choose which Spry widget you want to add from the submenu (Figure 14.2).

or

For UI widgets: choose Insert > Layout Objects from the menu bar and then choose which Spry widget you want to add from the submenu (Figure 14.2).

or

For effects: select the element on the page you want the effect to affect, click the plus button on the Behaviors tab of the Tag Inspector panel, and choose an action from the Effects submenu (**Figure 14.3**).

✔ Tips

- If you've added a widget, you'll see the object on the page outlined with a bright blue border and the name of the widget. If you've added an effect, you'll see it listed in the Behaviors panel tab of the Tag Inspector.

- Believe it or not, these aren't all the places where you can find options to add Spry elements in Dreamweaver.

Using the Menu Bar Widget

One of the most common user interface items you're likely to add to a site is the common menu bar. As mentioned in Chapter 13, you can build complex menu bars in Fireworks—but what if you don't have Fireworks, or its menus aren't quite what you want? Spry menu bars are simple, flexible, and powerful.

To add a menu bar widget:

1. Decide where you want the menu bar on your page, and click the Spry menu bar button in the Spry category of the Insert panel. The Spry Menu Bar dialog appears (**Figure 14.4**).

2. Decide if you want a horizontal menu bar (a pull down, where the main menu options go across, and submenu options go down) or a vertical menu bar (a flyout, where the main menu options go down, and submenu options go across). Click OK to accept.

3. The Spry menu bar appears on your page, with default data displayed in the Property Inspector (**Figure 14.5**).

4. To change the name of items in the menu bar, click any item name in the first column of the Property Inspector (**Figure 14.6**) and change the Text field on the right. Items in the second column are submenus of the selected item in the first column, and items in the third column are submenus of the selected item in the second column. To delete an item, select it, and click the minus button at the top of the column. To add items, click the plus button at the top of the column, and then change the name from the automatically named default. And to change the order, select an item, then click the up or down arrow at the top of the column.

Figure 14.4 The Spry menu bar can be horizontal or vertical.

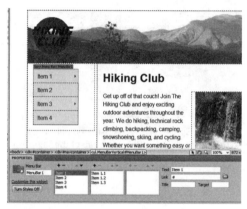

Figure 14.5 The brand-new Spry menu bar on our page starts off with some default values.

Figure 14.6 After you've created the menu bar you'll set its values using the Property Inspector.

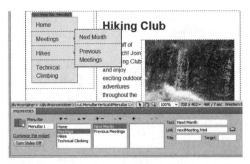

Figure 14.7 Set the link for each menu bar item in the Property Inspector.

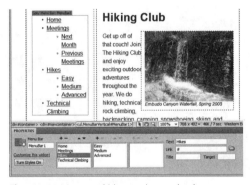

Figure 14.8 It's a good idea to always check to see how your Spry elements appear without styling.

5. Turn menu options into links by selecting the option and changing the link field to the URL of the desired page (**Figure 14.7**).

6. Click the Turn Styles Off button in the lower left of the Property Inspector to see how the menu bar appears when CSS isn't available (**Figure 14.8**). Click the Turn Styles On button to make the styles reappear.

7. When you first save the page, or when you view the page in a browser, you'll see the Copy Dependent Files dialog (**Figure 14.9**). This lets you know that the required Spry files are being added to your site. They'll all be in a directory named SpryAssets at the root of your site, and you'll need to upload that directory and the files it contains to your server so your site works correctly.

8. When you view your site in a browser (**Figure 14.10**), you'll see your new flyout (or pull-down) menu.

However, what we see is the menu in Dreamweaver's default menu style, which isn't quite what we wanted, so we'll need to edit the widget's styles.

Figure 14.9 Every Spry command has associated JavaScript, CSS, and graphics. Dreamweaver warns you that it's adding them to your site.

Figure 14.10 And here's our Web page with its new cool flyout menu.

To edit a menu bar widget:

1. This page is similar to one we used earlier in the book, which means we've already got a style sheet defined with our desired appearance. To use it, we need to change the menu bar's `id` by changing its name in the Property Inspector, from `MenuBar1` to `navlist` (**Figure 14.11**).

2. As you'll also see in Figure 14.11, the `SpryMenuBarVertical.css` file contains the CSS rules for the Spry menu bar. All that's left is to go through the different rules that apply to `navlist`, see which ones change the color, and delete them—that lets the `navlist` colors display the way we designed them. The easiest way to see which rules apply to `navlist` is to use the Code Navigator on the rule (see Chapter 7 for more about using the Code Navigator).

Figure 14.11 You can modify the way the menu looks by changing the styles, as seen in the CSS Styles panel.

Figure 14.12 The new cool flyout menu looks even cooler when its design matches the rest of the site.

3. And finally, when we view the page in the browser, we see our new flyout menu just the way we wanted it to appear (**Figure 14.12**).

✔ Tips

■ You can also see the new SpryAssets folder and its files in Figure 14.11. They're automatically added to your site when you accept the Copy Dependent Files dialog.

■ The Turn Styles Off button on the Property Inspector is also useful to verify that you've set up all your menus and submenus correctly, as it causes them to display all at once on the page.

■ Be sure to always test your pages in a browser, though you can also get a good idea of how the menu will look by clicking the Live View button on the document toolbar inside Dreamweaver.

■ To delete the widget, make sure the entire menu bar is selected, and then press Delete.

■ When using any Spry widget, be careful to test your pages for accessibility for those users who don't have JavaScript, those with older browsers, and those with disabilities. Your sites need to work for everyone, not just people with the latest and greatest browsers, and the current version of Spry doesn't always create widgets that work when (for instance) a visitor to your site sees it on a mobile device.

■ In Figure 14.7, you can add a tool tip to any link simply by typing text into the Title field.

Using the Tabbed Panels Widget

Another common user interface element is tabbed panels, which make a Web page look similar to an application. Creating tabbed panels was a time-consuming and difficult process until Spry came along, but not any more.

To add a tabbed panel:

1. Decide where you want the tabbed panel on your page, and click the Spry Tabbed Panels button in the Spry category of the Insert panel. A Spry tabbed panel with defaults and the Tabbed panels Property Inspector display (**Figure 14.13**).

2. To change the default tab names and panel content, simply type over them in the Dreamweaver document. The first tab is shown by default when the page first loads; you can change that by re-setting the Default panel field in the Property Inspector.

3. To delete tabs, select the tab in the Property Inspector and then click the minus button. To add tabs, click the plus button. And to change the display order of the tabs, select a tab, and then click the up or down arrow.

4. To view a specific panel inside Dreamweaver, hover over the tab until you see an icon of an eye. Click the eye, and that panel displays (**Figure 14.14**).

5. As always, be sure to test your Spry widget in a browser and Dreamweaver's Live View to see how it actually works (**Figure 14.15**).

Figure 14.13 Tabbed panels can be a way to show a lot of information in a limited space (although not all at once).

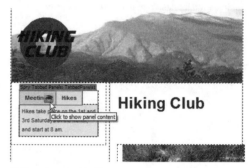

Figure 14.14 Inside Dreamweaver, you can see how each tab and panel will appear in the browser window.

✔ Tips

- As with the menu bar widget, you can use Dreamweaver to modify the CSS that applies to the tabbed panel widget to make it match the rest of your site design. If you want detailed information on a widget's CSS properties, click the Customize this widget link in the Property Inspector to launch the Adobe Help Viewer.

- You can use the Code Navigator to figure out what CSS rules apply to the widget. See Chapter 7 for more about the Code Navigator.

- Unless you change the applicable CSS, the tabbed panel widget takes up as much room as is available horizontally. There wasn't much room available in this design, so as Figure 14.15 shows, the tabs wrapped. Dreamweaver makes that happen automatically, but if that's not what you're looking for, you may want to try an accordion widget instead, as described next.

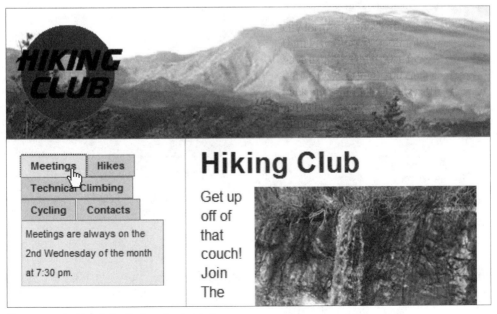

Figure 14.15 And here's the final version in a browser.

Using the Accordion Widget

An accordion widget is a set of panels, where one (and only one) is displayed at a time. It's a handy way to present several discrete chunks of information in a limited space.

To add an accordion widget:

1. Decide where you want the accordion on your page, and click the Spry Accordion button in the Spry category of the Insert panel. A Spry accordion widget with defaults and the Accordion Property Inspector display (**Figure 14.16**).

2. To change the default labels and content panels, simply type over them in the Dreamweaver document. The first panel is always shown by default when the page first loads.

3. To delete panels, select the panel in the Property Inspector and then click the minus button. To add panels, click the plus button. And to change the display order of the panels, select a panel, then click the up or down arrow.

4. To view a specific panel inside Dreamweaver, hover over the label until you see the eye icon. Click the eye, and that panel displays (**Figure 14.17**).

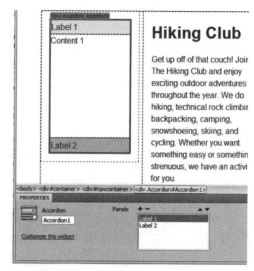

Figure 14.16 The accordion widget might be a better match for the type of information that we're trying to display, so we've added one here.

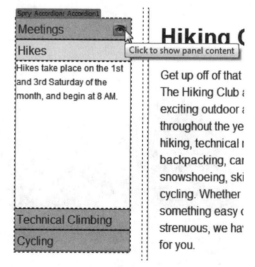

Figure 14.17 The panels can be set to display or hide inside Dreamweaver.

USING THE ACCORDION WIDGET

Figure 14.18 And here's the final accordion in the browser.

5. Here's your new accordion as seen in a browser (**Figure 14.18**). Simply click the label, and the currently open panel closes and the desired panel opens. In this example, we've decreased the height of the accordion panels (see the tip below), as they don't need to be as tall as the default (shown in Figure 14.17).

✔ Tips

■ To change the height of an accordion panel, we first needed to discover which CSS rule controlled the panel's height. We clicked in the panel's content, and chose View > Code Navigator (see Chapter 17 for more on that feature). The Code Navigator window showed a rule named `.AccordionPanelContent`, which had a default height of 200 pixels. We clicked the rule in the Code Navigator window, which changed the document window to Split view, highlighting the rule in the code pane. We then changed the value of the `height` attribute to 100 pixels, and saved the file.

■ When adding a widget to an existing page, be careful about moving text that's already on the page into the widget. Widgets can be fragile, and if you don't drag and drop the text into exactly the right spot, you can end up with a mess. We've had better luck just deleting text and re-typing it directly into widgets.

Using the Collapsible Panel Widget

If the accordion widget is almost, but not quite, just what you want, then the collapsible panel widget is probably what you're looking for. Where the accordion widget allows you to have one—and only one—open panel, the collapsible panel widget lets you have as many or as few open as you and your visitors want.

To add a collapsible panel widget:

1. Decide where you want the collapsible panel on your page, and click the Spry Collapsible Panel button in the Spry category of the Insert panel. A Spry collapsible panel widget with defaults and the Collapsible panel Property Inspector display. **Figure 14.19** shows a document with two collapsible panel widgets.

2. You can set each panel to be open or closed when the page loads. Toggle the display by changing the Default state in the Property Inspector from Open to Closed or vice versa.

3. Choose whether or not the panel contents are viewable inside Dreamweaver by toggling the Display value in the Property Inspector from Open to Closed and back again.

   or

   Hover over the label until you see the eye icon, as seen in Figure 14.19. If the panel is closed, the eye icon is open. Click it to open the panel (**Figure 14.20**). If the panel is open, the eye icon is closed, and clicking it closes the panel.

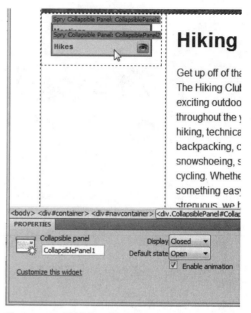

Figure 14.19 Multiple collapsible panels is another UI approach, allowing us to have multiple panels display at one time.

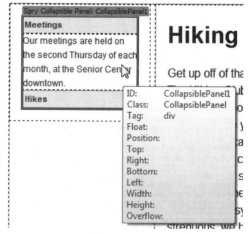

Figure 14.20 Again, panels can be seen and hidden inside Dreamweaver without affecting how they will appear in the browser.

Figure 14.21 Here are the two panels—both closed— in the browser window.

Figure 14.22 Click each label, and its panel slides open so you can see all the information at once.

4. Change the default labels and content panels by simply typing over their current values in the Dreamweaver document.

5. Finish up by checking the display in Dreamweaver's Live View or a browser. **Figure 14.21** shows the panels in their collapsed state, and **Figure 14.22** shows them in their open state.

✔ Tip

■ The Property Inspector also contains a checkbox to enable (or disable) animation. If it's on, visitors to your site see a brief animation when they open and close panels. If you think that people might get impatient, turn the animation off.

Validating Forms with Spry

Figure 14.23 should look familiar, as it's the same form example used earlier in this book. But if you look at **Figure 14.24**, it's actually a little different—you can see that Spry has added some smarts to it. The addition of the new error messages tell people filling out the form more about what kind of data they need to enter where.

New to Dreamweaver CS4 is the ability to validate a group of radio buttons, validate password fields, and require the user to enter a password twice for verification.

To add Spry validation to a text field:

1. Select an existing text field and click the Spry Validation Text Field button in the Spry category of the Insert panel. The usual blue box appears around the field, and the Spry TextField Property Inspector appears (**Figure 14.25**).

2. Using the Property Inspector, you can make your text fields require a wide range of input types. Figure 14.25 shows a text field that requires that something (anything) be in the last name field. That's done by checking the Required check box, and setting the Min chars field to one.

Figure 14.26 shows the email address field, which is a little more complex. Here, the Type drop-down menu is set to Email Address, which rejects the user's entry unless it matches the format of an email address.

The last name field is set to show the field required error, and the email address field is set to show the invalid format error. These are done via the Preview states drop-down menu in the Property Inspector, which lets you see how each possible error message displays inside

Figure 14.23 This contact form doesn't look particularly intelligent.

Figure 14.24 But once a visitor sees the error messages, they have a better idea of what's required.

Figure 14.25 Text fields can be set to require some value before the form can be submitted.

Figure 14.26 Text fields can also be set to require very particular data, such as this email field, before submission is allowed.

Figure 14.27 This pop-up menu is now set to require visitors to make a choice.

Figure 14.28 Checkboxes can be validated individually or in groups.

Dreamweaver. And along with the error messages, the entry field itself has a pink background, showing that the current entry is insufficient.

To add Spry validation to a select field:

◆ Select an existing pop-up menu and click the Spry Validation Select button in the Spry category of the Insert panel. Once again, you'll see the blue box appear with its associated Property Inspector (**Figure 14.27**).

A pop-up menu can be set to have a required value or to only allow certain selections. You can also preview the various error messages inside Dreamweaver.

To add Spry validation to checkboxes:

1. Select where you want your new checkboxes to be placed and click the Spry Validation Checkbox button in the Spry category of the Insert panel. The Input Tag Accessibility Attributes dialog appears, which was covered in Chapter 11. Enter the appropriate data and click OK. Your new check box appears in its standard blue box, and the Property Inspector displays the Spry Checkbox (**Figure 14.28**).

2. If you want the validation to apply to a group of checkboxes instead of a single checkbox, add them inside the Spry region at this point or drag existing checkboxes into the region.

3. The Property Inspector allows you to require a single checkbox to be set, or to require a certain minimum number of checkboxes to be set. In this example, we want them to click at least one checkbox of the five, so the minimum is set to one and the maximum is five. Figure 14.28 shows the error message that displays when they submit the page without picking any of the checkboxes.

To add Spry validation to radio buttons:

1. Select where you want your new radio buttons to be placed and click the Spry Validation Radio Group button in the Spry category of the Insert panel.

   The Spry Validation Radio Group dialog appears (**Figure 14.29**). This is similar to the Radio Group dialog discussed in Chapter 11.

2. Fill out the dialog, then click OK.

   The radio buttons appear on the page, and you see the Spry Radio Group in the Property Inspector (**Figure 14.30**).

✔ Tip

■ A radio button group must have one of its choices selected, but Dreamweaver doesn't know which button you want selected, so you must do it yourself. Click the button that you want to use as the default choice, and the Property Inspector will change to show that button's properties. In the Initial state section, choose Checked.

To add Spry validation to a text area:

1. Select an existing text area field and click the Spry Validation Textarea button in the Spry category of the Insert panel. You'll see the usual blue box and Property Inspector (**Figure 14.31**).

2. In the Property Inspector, you can set it so the text area is required, and set it to have a minimum or maximum length. Additionally, you can choose to display a counter of characters filled in or characters remaining, so that users know how close they are to the limit. And finally, the Hint field puts optional text into the field when the form loads, telling the user what type of information you're requiring them to enter.

Figure 14.29 Begin adding your validated radio button group by entering the button values.

Figure 14.30 By default, a radio button group is set to have a required value.

Figure 14.31 Text area boxes can require that at least a certain amount of data be entered, and give a hint to the visitor as to what's necessary.

Figure 14.32 The form looks straightforward when it's first loaded in the browser.

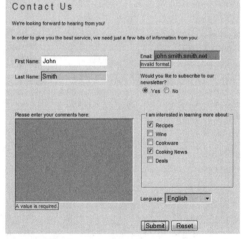

Figure 14.33 But this form won't let us get away with trying to submit it without the required fields.

3. Figure 14.32 shows how the form appears in the browser when the page first loads. **Figure 14.33** is an attempt to validate our bad input, showing the five error messages we've received.

✔ Tips

- Any field can be set to validate on blur, change, or submit, where the default is submit. *Blur* refers to when the user exits the field, whether or not they've actually changed its value.

- The text area Hint text automatically clears itself when the user enters the field. Hint text also doesn't count as characters towards the entry requirements/limits.

To add Spry validation to a password field:

1. Click to place the insertion point where you want to add your password field, and click the Spry Validation Password button in the Spry category of the Insert panel.

   The Input Tag Accessibility Attributes dialog appears (**Figure 14.34**).

2. Enter the appropriate data and click OK.

   The password field appears in the document, and the Property Inspector changes to reflect the Spry Password choices (**Figure 14.35**).

3. Set the requirements for the password in the Property Inspector. You can specify the minimum and maximum number of characters; how many letters and numbers must appear in the password; whether or not letters must be uppercase; and whether special characters are allowed or required.

To add a Spry confirmation field:

1. Confirmation fields require the user to re-enter the same value as another field in the form. They're usually used with password fields. Begin by placing the insertion point where you want to add your confirmation field, and click the Spry Validation Confirm button in the Spry category of the Insert panel. The Input Tag Accessibility Attributes dialog appears.

2. Enter the appropriate data and click OK.

   The confirmation field appears in the document, and the Property Inspector changes to reflect the Spry Confirm choices (**Figure 14.36**).

3. In the Validate against pop-up menu, choose the field you want to validate against. If there is only one field and one form on the page, it will appear in the pop-up menu automatically.

Figure 14.34 You need to give the password field an ID and a label.

Figure 14.35 Set the password's requirements in the Property Inspector.

Figure 14.36 The confirming password field is set to validate against the original password field.

VALIDATING FORMS WITH SPRY

Tooltip trigger goes here.

Tooltip content goes here.

Figure 14.37 If you don't select an element before adding a tooltip widget, you get boilerplate text for the tooltip's trigger and content.

Adding Spry Tooltips

New to Dreamweaver CS4, you can add a Spry-powered tooltip, which is a short bit of text that appears when you hover over an area on your page. Tooltips have two parts: the *trigger*, which is the part of your page that serves as the hotspot for the user's cursor, and the *content*, which is the tooltip's text.

To add a Spry tooltip:

1. Click to place the insertion point where you want to add the tooltip, and click the Spry Tooltip button in the Spry category of the Insert panel.

   Default trigger text and a field for the content appear in the document (**Figure 14.37**).

   or

   Select an element on the page and click the Spry Tooltip button in the Spry category of the Insert panel.

   The field for the tooltip's content appears in the document. When you first select an existing element, Dreamweaver assumes that you want the element to be the tooltip's trigger.

   The Property Inspector changes to reflect the Spry Tooltip choices.

2. If you did not select an element before you inserted the tooltip, type over the default trigger text with the text you want to appear on the page. If you did select an element, skip to step 3.

continues on next page

3. Type over the default text in the tool-tip content field, replacing it with your desired tooltip text.

4. In the Property Inspector, choose from the Trigger pop-up menu (**Figure 14.38**).

5. (Optional) Choose how the tooltip will appear to the user in the browser by setting its horizontal or vertical offset and whether there will be a delay or a visual effect as the tooltip appears or disappears (**Figure 14.39**).

Figure 14.38 You need to set the tooltip's trigger and visual effects (if you want them) in the Property Inspector.

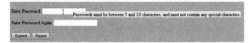

Figure 14.39 The tooltip appeared when I hovered the cursor over the password field.

Figure 14.40 The Appear/Fade dialog lets you control that effect.

Figure 14.41 The Blind dialog might sound scary, but in reality it makes an element on your page look like it's a window shade.

Figure 14.42 The Grow/Shrink dialog allows you to make objects on your page get larger or smaller.

Adding Spry Effects

You can use Spry to add cool visual effects to elements on your page with behaviors. As shown in Figure 14.3, Spry Effects are found in the Behaviors tab of the Tag Inspector panel. There are seven Spry effects: Appear/Fade, Blind, Grow/Shrink, Highlight, Shake, Slide, and Squish. You can see them in action at `http://labs.adobe.com/technologies/spry/demos/effects/`.

If you need a refresher on behaviors, please review Chapter 13. Remember to be careful setting which events trigger behaviors; if you want an effect to take place when an element is clicked, it should happen on the `onClick` (for instance), not `onMouseOut`.

Appear/Fade

The Appear/Fade effect makes an element appear or fade away. **Figure 14.40** shows the dialog, which allows you to set the element, duration, effect (appear or fade), start and end percentages, and whether you want the effect to be reversible.

Blind

The Blind up/down effect works like a window blind that hides or shows the element. **Figure 14.41** shows the dialog, which lets you choose the element, duration, effect (blind up or down), start and end values, and whether you want the effect to be reversible.

Grow/Shrink

The Grow/Shrink effect makes the element larger or smaller. Use the dialog (**Figure 14.42**), to set the element, duration, effect (grow or shrink), start and end values, whether you want the element to move towards the center of the page or its upper-left corner, and whether you want the effect to be reversible.

Highlight

The Highlight effect changes the background color of the element, causing it to stand out on the page. The Highlight dialog (**Figure 14.43**) is where you set the element, duration, start and end colors of the highlight, color you want displayed after the effect has completed running, and whether you want the effect to be reversible.

Figure 14.43 The Highlight effect changes the background color for the target element.

Shake

The Shake effect does just what it sounds like—it makes the selected element shimmy in place. As **Figure 14.44** shows, all you can set is the target element.

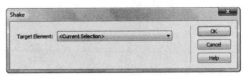

Figure 14.44 The Shake effect does just what it sounds like.

Slide

The Slide up/down effect moves the selected element up or down on the page. The Slide dialog allows you to set the target element, duration, effect (slide up or down), beginning and ending values, and whether you want the effect to be reversible (**Figure 14.45**).

Figure 14.45 Make an element slide up or down your page with the Slide effect.

Squish

The Squish effect makes the selected element disappear into the upper-left corner of the page. The element is set in the Squish dialog, as shown in **Figure 14.46**.

✔ Tips

- Not all effects can be applied to all elements. Play with them to see which behaviors work with particular objects on your page.

- You can combine effects as well; all you have to do is keep adding behaviors to a given element. Be careful, though, to keep from getting *too* tacky!

Figure 14.46 The Squish dialog lets you make elements on your page appear smooshed.

The Future of Spry

As mentioned at the beginning of this chapter, it's possible to get Spry as a free download and use it with your sites even if you don't have Dreamweaver. As this is a book on Dreamweaver, we're not going to get into how Spry is used outside of Dreamweaver—but one side effect is that Adobe plans to update Spry much more often than the every couple of years that a new Dreamweaver version is released.

Dreamweaver CS4 was shipping with Spry 1.6.1 when this book went to press.

You can check to see if there's a newer version of Spry by going to the Adobe Labs page at `http://labs.adobe.com/technologies/spry/`. There, you'll find Spry demos, forums, and documentation of what's possible to create with Spry. The Spry team even has a blog, which you can find at `http://blogs.adobe.com/spryteam/`.

To get newer versions of Spry (when available), use the Extension Manager, described in Appendix B.

Making Life Easier: Using Templates, Libraries, and Snippets

The first thing you do when you begin a site in Dreamweaver is define a site root folder, as discussed in Chapter 2. You tell Dreamweaver where you're keeping all your site files. Dreamweaver rewards you for sharing the information by making all sorts of cool site-wide tools available to speed up your workflow and make your life easier. In seconds, Dreamweaver's site management tools can make changes to every file in your local site root folder—changes that would take you much longer done one file at a time.

We'll cover two of those timesaving whole-site tools—templates and libraries—in this chapter. In addition, you'll learn how to create timesaving bits of reusable code called *snippets*. You access templates and Library items from the Assets panel. Snippets have a separate panel.

Before getting into the details, some brief definitions are in order. *Templates* are like master page designs. They create a uniform page design for a site while allowing certain material on each page to be customized for individual pages. *Library* items are not full pages, but reusable objects with text, code, images, or other elements that you insert in documents. For example, you can create a navigation bar as a Library item. Updating either a template or a Library item results in the automatic updating of any page in the entire site that is attached to the template or library. *Snippets* are custom-built code samples that you find useful and save for quick insertion. Changing a snippet doesn't have any site-wide effects.

MAKING LIFE EASIER

They Can't Break Your Sites!

Pages made from templates are perfect for use in organizations that want relatively unskilled people to be able to make changes and updates to sites without the possibility of accidentally "breaking" the site. In fact, Adobe has a program, Adobe Contribute, that works hand-in-hand with sites built using Dreamweaver templates to allow people to add content and make changes to Web sites without being able to mess up the site's design elements. With Contribute, the site designer can assign site contributors to *user roles*, which specify the editing tasks the user is allowed. For example, you can have a user who can add and change text to a page, but can only style that text with CSS styles you supply, or you can prevent the user from styling text at all. You can also require that users send their changed pages to a supervisor for review before making the page live on the site. Many other permissions and restrictions are possible if people who work on your site use Contribute.

With the launch of the CS4 suite, Adobe is also introducing a hosted service, called InContext Editing, that acts somewhat like Contribute, but works entirely in a Web browser. With InContext Editing, inexperienced users can make simple changes to Web sites, again without the possibility of breaking the site. You'll find more information about using Dreamweaver to work with Contribute and InContext Editing in Chapter 16.

Figure 15.1 The pop-up menu for the Template icon in the Common category of the Insert panel covers the basic commands you'll need.

Creating a Template

Templates are perfect for many situations. For example, let's say you have a large site where many different individuals change content and add pages. Using a template provides control over the page layout and design by restricting changes only to certain *editable regions* on a page. Other areas on the page are *locked regions*, which can't be changed by people working on an individual page. Locked regions can only be edited in the original template file. This kind of control guarantees a consistent look and feel for a site, and prevents any accidental changes to locked regions.

When a change is made to a template, every page made from, or *attached* to, the template is automatically updated throughout the entire site. You can create a template from scratch, but it is simpler to use an existing page as a model for the template, and that's what we'll explain here.

Before you save a document as a template, make sure you've already included any needed `<meta>` tags, style sheets, behaviors, or other underlying parameters. These page elements are located in the locked regions of a template. There's no way to add things like style sheet links to individual pages made from a template—they must exist in the template already.

To create a template from an existing page:

1. Open the document you want to turn into a template.

2. Choose File > Save as Template.

   or

   Choose Make Template from the Templates pop-up menu in the Common category of the Insert panel (**Figure 15.1**).

   continues on next page

The Save As Template dialog appears with the Site pop-up menu set to the current local site (**Figure 15.2**).

3. Enter the requested information in this dialog.

  ▲ **Existing templates:** You don't enter anything in this field. Dreamweaver lists any existing templates for the site automatically.

  ▲ **Description:** Type a brief description of the template.

  ▲ **Save as:** Type the name of the template.

4. Click Save.

  If it doesn't already exist, Dreamweaver adds a Templates folder to your site files. Your new template will be inside this folder, with the file extension .dwt, indicating that the document is a Dreamweaver template.

Figure 15.2 Any page can be saved as a template. The name you type in the Save as field will be followed by the file extension .dwt in the Assets list.

✔ Tips

■ Templates are for local use; they're never loaded in a browser. The Templates folder and its .dwt files don't need to be uploaded to the server. Just upload the individual HTML pages made from the template. To make this easier, you can cloak the Templates folder, which prevents Dreamweaver from uploading it to the remote server. See "Cloaking Files," in Chapter 2, for more information. On the other hand, you might choose to upload your Templates folder to the server so that you always have a handy backup of your templates.

■ It's possible to create a template from scratch. Choose File > New and select Blank Template in the New Document window. Or you can start one using the New Template button in the Templates area of the Assets panel.

Figure 15.3 Use the pop-up menu for the Template icon in the Common category of the Insert panel to designate editable regions in the template.

Figure 15.4 A short, descriptive name is best for a template region. Don't use spaces in the name; instead, use the underscore character, as shown.

Adding Editable Regions

Once you've saved the `.dwt` file, you will want to open it and define any regions you want to be editable. Regions on the page that you don't specifically mark as editable will be locked and can't be changed by anyone working on pages made from your template—hey, that's the whole point!

To add an editable region:

1. Open the template document.

2. Select the element to make editable, for example `<div>`, `<img>`, or `<td>`, with the Tag Selector in the document window.

   or

   Select the text to make editable. This choice is most useful when the text is within a div. Selecting the entire div, rather than just the text within it, makes everything about the div editable, including its position. You probably don't want your users being able to change anything other than the text, so just select that text and it will be the only editable part of the div.

3. Choose Editable Region from the Templates pop-up menu in the Common category of the Insert panel (**Figure 15.3**).

   or

   Choose Insert > Template Objects > Editable Region.

   The New Editable Region dialog appears (**Figure 15.4**).

4. Type a name for the region.

   continues on next page

5. Click OK.

The editable region will be outlined in green in the document window. A tab at the upper left of the region displays the region name (**Figure 15.5**).

6. (Optional) Delete the text that was in the region and replace it with some general instruction regarding the region, for example, "This region is for main content." If you don't do this, it's okay—anyone making a page from the template can replace the text later.

Region name

Figure 15.5 In the document window, the editable region is indicated with a visible tab giving the region name.

✔ Tips

■ You can make an entire table editable, or the table header, a table row, or individual cells within a table. But you can't put a table column or multiple noncontiguous table cells in a single editable region.

■ Don't use special characters in region names: no ampersands (&), single quote marks ('), double quote marks ("), or angle brackets (<) and (>).

■ Page titles are editable by default on pages that are created from templates.

■ When you name your editable regions, give them region names that make their purpose clear for the people who will eventually be entering content into the region, such as main_content in this example.

Figure 15.6 To remove an editable region from a template, choose Remove Template Markup.

Removing Editable Regions

If you make a region editable and later decide you want to lock it instead, it's easy to remove the editable region. This doesn't remove the content within the region; it removes the ability of the user to edit anything in the region. As the designer, you can still put any content you want in the region. But that content won't be editable by the user.

To remove an editable region:

1. Click the tab in the upper left of the region to select the region.

2. Choose Modify > Templates > Remove Template Markup (**Figure 15.6**).

3. The region is locked.

Other Kinds of Template Regions

Dreamweaver can create more complex editable areas in addition to the basic editable region. These kinds of editable regions are used less frequently, but they're still useful when you need them. You probably noticed the options in the Templates pop-up menu in the Common category of the Insert panel (Figures 15.1 and 15.3). They are:

◆ **Repeating Region:** Repeating regions can be duplicated by the user as often as needed. They're useful for things that vary from page to page, for example a chart of product colors or sizes or a list of recipe ingredients. Repeating regions aren't editable until you define the editable areas of the region.

◆ **Optional Region:** You set conditions for optional regions, indicated by the word *if* in the tab showing the region name. Optional content can be either hidden or displayed, depending on whether the conditions are met. For example, let's say that you have a page of upcoming events. You have an image that says, "Coming Soon!" that you want to appear next to events that will occur in the next month. You can write code that checks the date, then displays the "Coming Soon!" image in an optional region when the code expression is true.

◆ **Editable Optional Region:** As with optional regions, you can decide whether or not to display content in these regions. Editable Optional Regions are, well, editable.

◆ **Repeating Table:** Repeating tables are actually repeating regions, but they automatically include table tags, so you can easily use them for tabular data.

REMOVING EDITABLE REGIONS

Building Pages Based on a Template

Most of the time you will create new pages based on your template. This is the easiest and least confusing way to make templates work for you. It's also possible to take an existing page, say from an older site that you're completely redesigning, and apply a template to that page. That method is a bit trickier.

Figure 15.7 If you begin a new page from a template with the File > New command, you must choose the site, then the template.

To make a new page from a template:

1. Choose File > New.

   The New Document dialog appears.

2. Click the Page from Template tab, then click the site you are working on in the Site column.

   The existing templates for that site appear in the Template for Site column.

3. Select the template you want from the Template for Site column.

   A preview of the template appears in the dialog (**Figure 15.7**).

4. Click Create.

   A new page, based on the template, appears.

5. Add content to the editable regions and save the new document with an appropriate file name and location in your site.

✔ Tip

- You can create a new page from a template faster once you get used to working with templates. In the Assets panel, click the Templates category, then right-click the template name and choose New from Template from the shortcut menu (**Figure 15.8**).

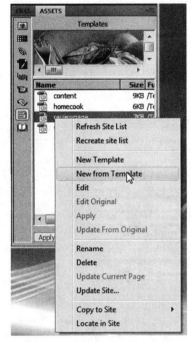

Figure 15.8 Fewer steps are involved in starting a new page from a template if you right-click the template name in the Assets panel.

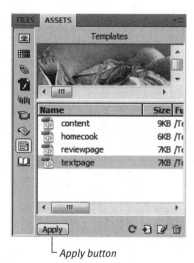

Apply button

Figure 15.9 Modify an existing page to fit into a template page by selecting the template and clicking the Apply button.

Figure 15.10 When retrofitting an existing page to work with a template, you must decide where to put the content. The pop-up menu shows possible regions.

✔ Tip

- Dreamweaver expects the Templates folder to be at the top level of your site structure. Don't move it into a subfolder. If you do, Dreamweaver won't display the template files in your Assets panel or in the New Document template list.

To apply a template to an existing page:

1. Open the existing document to which you want to apply the template.

2. In the Assets panel, select the template you want and click the Apply button at the lower left (**Figure 15.9**).

   or

   Drag the template from the Assets panel to the document window.

   or

   Choose Modify > Templates > Apply Template to Page. The Select Template dialog appears. Click a template in the list to choose it.

   The Inconsistent Region Names dialog appears (**Figure 15.10**). This dialog allows you to tell Dreamweaver in which region of the new page it should place the document's existing content.

3. In the Inconsistent Region Names dialog, do the following:

   ▲ In the scrolling list, select an unresolved region.

   ▲ Use the "Move content to new region" pop-up menu to select an editable region for the content.

   If you choose Nowhere from the pop-up menu, the content is removed from the document. If you click the "Use for all" button, all the unresolved content is moved to the selected region.

4. Click OK.

5. The resulting document probably needs some cleaning up to work seamlessly with the template. For example, you may need to restyle some text, or move a bit of content manually. After that is completed, save as usual.

Modifying a Template

Templates give you tons of control over what can be edited and what can't. Sure, that's important. But what happens if you make lots of pages from your template and then something changes? Maybe you need to add a new item to the menu, or you need a new editable region on the page. The answer is that something really cool happens when a Dreamweaver template is modified: Dreamweaver automatically changes all the pages you've already made using that template. So you can make changes to just one page (the template) and have those changes automatically ripple through the site.

Normally, you'd start your modification directly in the template file. But you can also start from any document that is attached to the template. You can pick and choose the attached pages to which you want the changes to apply.

To modify a template file:

1. In the Assets panel, click the Templates button to display the templates, then double-click the template file you want to edit.

   or

   In the Assets panel, click the Templates button to display the templates, then highlight the template file and click the Edit button at the bottom of the panel.

   The template file opens in the document window.

2. Edit as desired, then choose File > Save, or press Ctrl-S (Cmd-S).

   The Update Template Files dialog appears. Each file attached to the template is listed in the dialog (**Figure 15.11**).

   If you click Update, every file attached to the template will update. If you click Don't Update, none of the files attached to the template will update.

Figure 15.11 Here's the powerful part of using templates. Dreamweaver offers to update template-based pages when you change a template.

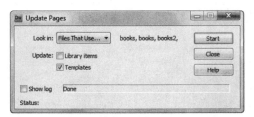

Figure 15.12 If you allow Dreamweaver to update template-based pages, it reports the results when it's finished.

You can't choose to modify just one page here (it's all or nothing), but it's possible to do that elsewhere. See the section below, "To modify an individual template-based page" for details.

3. Click Update.

The Update Pages dialog appears (**Figure 15.12**). Dreamweaver sorts through all the files in your site and makes the updates, showing you the progress in the Update Pages dialog.

This dialog also allows you to update all the pages in the site to their corresponding templates, or just update files based on a specific template. If you don't need any additional updates other than the ones Dreamweaver already made, go to Step 7.

4. (Optional) From the "Look in" pop-up menu, choose Entire Site or Files That Use.

The first choice reapplies all the templates in the site to files made from those templates. The second choice, which is what you will want to do most of the time, just updates the pages based on the template you just edited.

When you make a choice from the "Look in" pop-up menu, the inactive Done button becomes active, and its label changes to Start.

5. (Optional) Make sure that the Templates check box is selected.

6. (Optional) Click Start.

When the process is complete, the Start button changes to Done and becomes inactive.

7. Click Close to dismiss the Update Pages dialog.

8. Close the template file.

To modify a template attached to a current document:

1. With a document based on a template open, choose Modify > Templates > Open Attached Template.

The template opens in a separate window.

2. Make your modifications as described in the previous section.

When you save the template, you'll be prompted to update pages attached to that template, including the page you started with.

To modify an individual template-based page:

1. Change a template file as described above. In the Update Template Files dialog (Figure 15.11), click Don't Update.

2. Open a document attached to the same template.

3. Choose Modify > Templates > Update Current Page.

The page updates with the changes you made to the template. No other pages in the site will update.

✔ Tips

■ When your template links to a CSS file, all your template-based pages link to it as well. If you change your CSS rules, the pages created from the template automatically reflect those changes in exactly the same way non-template-based pages reflect CSS changes.

■ HTML pages changed by the update of a template file need to be uploaded to the server for the change to be visible to your site's visitors. The easiest way to do this is to synchronize the local and remote sites. See "Synchronizing the Local and Remote Sites" in Chapter 2 for more information.

MODIFYING A TEMPLATE

Creating a Library Item

For someone working alone, the restrictions imposed by using a template may be unnecessary or even annoying. For example, when you use templates, you have to set up the editable and locked regions, and then when you go to modify a page based on the template, you don't have access to page elements in the locked regions. These restrictions are great if you're a designer who is giving pages to co-workers to modify. But on sites where you want to exercise total control over editing every page, Library items offer some of the same timesaving abilities as templates, including the ability to update pages and maintain consistency, but with far fewer restrictions.

Library items aren't full pages. They're small bits of text, images, or code that you insert when needed. Good material for a Library item might be a navigation bar, copyright notice, list of links, graphic masthead, or perhaps a search box. If you want to use something frequently, have it display consistently on any page, and update all instances of it at one time, a Library item fits the bill. And Library items are easy to create and use.

To create a Library item:

1. Open a document.

2. Select an element in the document <body>. It can be anything you want to reuse: text, tables, forms, navigation bars, images, or other elements.

continues on next page

3. Do one of the following:

Choose Modify > Library > Add Object to Library.

or

In the Library category of the Assets panel, click the New Library item button.

or

Drag the selection into the Library category of the Assets panel.

4. The item appears in the Library category of the Assets panel (**Figure 15.13**). Type a name for the item.

In the document window, the item will be highlighted with a color, indicating that it's a Library item.

Figure 15.13 Type a name for your new Library item here.

✔ Tips

■ The color used to highlight a Library item is yellow by default. If desired, you can change this color in Dreamweaver's Preferences in the Highlighting category.

■ If it doesn't already exist, Dreamweaver creates a `Library` folder at the top level of your site. Library items are stored in this folder, with the file extension `.lbi`. The folder is for local use and doesn't need to be uploaded to the server.

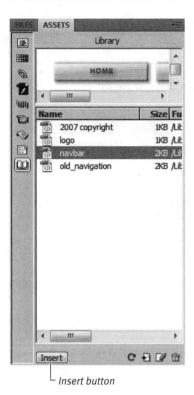

Insert button

Figure 15.14 A quick way to insert a Library item into a document is with the Insert button at the lower left of the Assets panel.

Using a Library Item

All you have to decide is where you want to use your Library items on your pages. The rest is easy.

To insert a Library item:

1. Position the insertion point in the document.

2. Drag the Library item from the Library category of the Assets panel into the document.

   or

   Highlight the Library item and click the Insert button at the lower left of the Assets panel (**Figure 15.14**).

   The Library item appears in the document.

To delete a Library item:

◆ **From a document:** select the Library item in the document window and press Backspace (Delete).

◆ **From a site:** choose the Library item in the Library category of the Assets panel and press Backspace (Delete). This step cannot be undone.

✔ Tip

■ Library items become part of the page's code and are subject to any CSS rules in style sheets linked to the page. For example, if your Library item contains a paragraph, and you have a CSS rule for the p selector, the inserted item will reflect the rule.

USING A LIBRARY ITEM

Editing a Library Item

You need to be a bit careful when you edit Library items, because when you change a Library item, Dreamweaver changes all instances of that item throughout all the pages of your site, in any documents that are not currently being edited. This can take some time if you have a large site, and you have to edit the item again to undo a mistake; the Undo command won't save you in this case. It's nothing to worry about; just be aware that changes can have far-reaching effects.

To edit a Library item:

1. Do one of the following:

   Double-click the item in the Library category in the Assets panel.

   or

   Highlight the item in the Library category in the Assets panel and then click the Edit button in the lower right of the Assets panel.

   or

   Highlight the item in the document window. The Property Inspector shows information for the Library item (**Figure 15.15**). Click Open.

2. A window much like a document window appears, but it contains only the Library item (**Figure 15.16**).

3. Edit the item as needed.

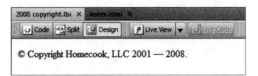

Figure 15.15 When you select a Library item in the document window, you can use the Property Inspector to open the Library item.

Figure 15.16 An open Library item window is rather like a normal document window, except there's nothing there but the Library item.

Figure 15.17 The benefit of using Library items comes from the ability to update any instances of the item in your site with one click of the Update button.

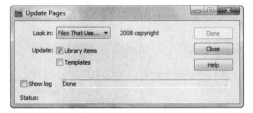

Figure 15.18 If you Update Library items, Dreamweaver reports on what it did.

4. Choose File > Save, or press Ctrl-S (Cmd-S). The Update Library Items dialog appears (**Figure 15.17**).
   - ▲ **Update:** Updates every instance of the Library item used in your site.
   - ▲ **Don't Update:** No Library items are updated.

   See the following section, "To update a Library item only in the current document," if you want to select individual pages to update.

5. Click Update to have Dreamweaver open the Update Pages dialog, run through all the files containing the Library item, update them, and report "Done" to you in the dialog when it's finished (**Figure 15.18**).

6. Click Close to dismiss the Update Pages dialog.

To update a Library item only in the current document:

1. Edit the Library item, then click Don't Update in the Update Library Items dialog (see the previous section, "To edit a Library item").

2. Open a document containing the Library item.

3. Choose Modify > Library > Update Current Page. The Library item on this single page updates.

4. Save the document.

To rename a Library item:

1. Highlight the name of the Library item in the Library category of the Assets panel. Do one of the following:

   Right-click and choose Rename from the shortcut menu.

   or

   Click the item name, wait a second, and click it again.

   The Library item's name is selected and becomes editable (**Figure 15.19**).

2. Type the new name for the item.

3. The Update Files dialog appears (**Figure 15.20**). Click Update to change the name of the Library item on every page where it is in use.

✔ Tips

■ Library items can't contain any head elements, so you don't have access to the CSS panel when editing a Library item (internal CSS style sheets appear within the <head> tag).

■ Library items can't contain a <body> tag, so you don't have access to the Page Properties when editing a Library item.

■ HTML pages changed by the update of a Library item need to be uploaded to the server for the change to be visible to your site's visitors.

■ If a document is open when a Library item updates, you'll have to save the document manually. Updates save automatically in a closed document.

Figure 15.19 Need a better name for a Library item? You can change it here.

Figure 15.20 When you change a Library item name, Dreamweaver asks you if you want to change all the instances of the item in the site to reflect the new name.

Figure 15.21 The Property Inspector can be used to detach a Library item from the source, or to re-create a Library item that's lost or missing.

Working on Library Items with the Property Inspector

As we mentioned in the previous section, "Editing a Library Item," the Property Inspector offers some options for working on Library items. We saw how to edit the Library item using the Open button, but there are two as yet unexplained buttons on the Property Inspector, Detach from original and Recreate.

Detaching a Library item doesn't remove the item from the page. It breaks the connection between the copy of the Library item on the current page and the original source in the site's Library folder. If you later update the original Library item, the current page's code won't be changed by the update. You might want to do this if you have a Library item that you want to be based on, but slightly different from, the original Library item.

Sometimes you can have a page that contains the code from a Library item that was removed from the site's Library folder (or never existed there). For example, let's say that you copied a page (that contained a Library item) from one of your sites to a different site. The site that now contains the page will not, of course, have a corresponding Library item in its Library folder. You can use the code in the current document to re-create the Library item in the new local site.

To detach the Library item:

1. Select a Library item in the document window.

2. On the Property Inspector, click Detach from original (**Figure 15.21**). Dreamweaver displays a dialog asking if you're sure you want to detach the item. Click OK. The link between the item on the page and the original in the Library is broken.

To re-create a missing or deleted Library item:

1. Open a document containing code for a Library item that is missing from the Library category of the Assets panel.

2. Highlight the item. The tag selector should display `<mm:libitem>`.

3. On the Property Inspector, click Recreate. The item is re-created using the name it has on this page. The re-created item appears in the Library category of the Assets panel.

✔ Tips

■ If you detach a Library item from a page, the highlighting in the document window that indicated that the element was a Library item disappears along with the broken connection to the Library item source. But the detached Library item still remains on the page; all you've done is sever its link to the original item.

■ Right-clicking a Library item in the document window reveals a shortcut menu with the same options available on the Property Inspector to Open, Detach, or Recreate.

New Snippet Folder

New Snippet

Remove

Edit Snippet

Figure 15.22 The Snippets panel comes preloaded with many useful snippets.

Figure 15.23 There's a brief description of a snippet to the right of its name.

Using Dreamweaver Snippets

The Snippets panel is used to store useful bits of code, or *snippets*, that can be inserted anytime, anyplace. In that way snippets are like Library items. But there's a big difference between snippets and Library items. If you change or update a snippet, there's no sitewide update to previously inserted versions of the snippet. There's no connection between the code in an inserted snippet and the original snippet.

Dreamweaver comes with many useful pre-built snippets already loaded and ready to use. You'll find them in the Snippets panel. If the Snippets panel is not already visible, choose Window > Snippets to bring it forward.

In the Snippets panel (**Figure 15.22**), the snippets that come with Dreamweaver are nicely organized into folders for you. Inside the folders you find individual snippets. Click an individual snippet to see a preview in the preview pane at the top of the panel. You can also see a description of the highlighted snippet. If you work with a narrow window, as in Figure 15.22, you may have to scroll to the right with the horizontal scrollbar at the bottom of the Snippets panel to see the description. Expand the width of the panel (**Figure 15.23**) to read the description without scrolling.

You've probably already figured out that any custom snippets you save appear in the Snippets panel, too. Your snippets and Dreamweaver's snippets are used in the same way. We'll explain how to save a new snippet first, and then how to use it.

To save a snippet:

1. Open a document containing the material you'd like to make into a snippet. Select the snippet (**Figure 15.24**). Be sure you get all the surrounding material needed by clicking the tag in the tag selector.

2. Click the New Snippet icon in the bottom right of the Snippets panel. The Snippet dialog appears (**Figure 15.25**). Complete the following fields:

   ▲ **Name:** Type a name for the new snippet. See the Tip at the end of this section regarding rules for naming snippets.

   ▲ **Description:** Type a description. This is helpful, but optional.

   ▲ **Snippet type:** Click Wrap selection if the snippet is meant to wrap around a selection. Click Insert block if the snippet is meant to be inserted as a block.

   If you choose Wrap selection, you will be asked to choose the parts of the snippet to insert before or insert after the wrapped selection.

   ▲ **Insert code:** The code you selected in the document is displayed here. This is an editable field.

   ▲ **Preview type:** Choose either Design or Code.

3. Click OK.

4. The snippet appears in the Snippets panel (**Figure 15.26**). The preview displays in the preview pane.

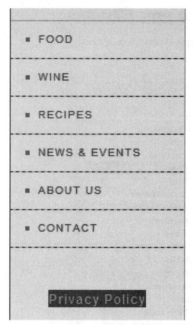

Figure 15.24 Select something on a page to save as a snippet.

Figure 15.25 When you save your own snippets, you decide on a name, description, and other basics.

Figure 15.26 Snippets you save appear in the Snippets panel. You can drag them into existing folders or organize new folders of your own.

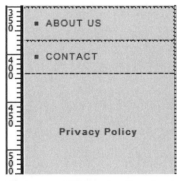

Figure 15.27 When you insert a snippet into a document, the text or other element the snippet contains appears on your page.

To use a snippet:

1. Position the insertion point in the document.

2. Highlight the snippet in the Snippets panel and do one of the following:

   Click the Insert button at the lower left of the Snippets panel.

   or

   Double-click the snippet name.

   or

   Drag the snippet from the Snippets panel onto the document.

3. The snippet appears in the document. Replace any dummy text with correct content (**Figure 15.27**).

✔ Tips

■ The snippet preview pane won't display the snippet with any CSS shown. The snippet must be on a page before CSS rules take effect.

■ Delete or modify snippets by highlighting them and using the Edit Snippet or Remove button at the lower right of the Snippets panel.

■ Organize your snippets by dragging them into preexisting folders or creating new folders of your own naming.

■ Don't use any special characters such as ampersands (&) or angle brackets (< and >) in snippet names.

USING DREAMWEAVER SNIPPETS

WORKING WITH OTHER APPLICATIONS

16

When building a Web site, no single application can stand alone; to get the best results, you must orchestrate elements from a variety of programs. For example, you might get your text from Microsoft Word, data for a table from Microsoft Excel, and the site's images from Adobe Photoshop, Adobe Fireworks, or any other image editing program.

Dreamweaver can help you expertly tie together these disparate elements into a unified Web site. It has special features that allow it to work with other programs, making it easy to incorporate files from those other programs in your pages.

In Chapter 5, we covered how Dreamweaver integrates with Photoshop to work with images. In this chapter, you'll learn how you can use other programs to edit elements on a page you're working on in Dreamweaver; use Dreamweaver's integration with Fireworks to edit and optimize images; and import and modify Microsoft Office documents. You'll also learn how Dreamweaver, Adobe Contribute, and Adobe InContext Editing work together to make editing your Web site easy, even for people who aren't Web savvy.

Assigning External Editing Programs

When you are working on your Web pages, you can launch another program to edit files that Dreamweaver can't edit itself, such as graphics and media files. For example, if you want to edit a JPEG file, you can have Dreamweaver use Fireworks or Photoshop or even something like Windows Paint. You specify an external editor for a particular file type.

Dreamweaver can use any programs that you have on your machine to edit files, but you'll need to tell Dreamweaver about these programs first. You do that in Dreamweaver's preferences.

To assign an external editor:

1. Choose Edit > Preferences (Dreamweaver > Preferences) or press Ctrl-U (Cmd-U). The Preferences dialog appears.

2. Click the File Types/Editors category. The File Types/Editors pane appears (**Figure 16.1**).

3. The field at the top of the pane, Open in code view, has extensions of all kinds of files that Dreamweaver automatically opens in Code view. If you will be working on code files of a type not listed, enter one or more extensions in the field, separated by a single space.

4. If you want to assign an external code editing program, click the Browse button, navigate to the program you want, and click OK (Choose).

   If you assign an external code editor, Dreamweaver changes the Edit > Edit with External Editor menu choice to Edit > Edit with *[program name]*.

Figure 16.1 Use the File Types/Editors category of the Preferences to set which programs you want to use to edit particular kinds of files.

ASSIGNING EXTERNAL EDITING PROGRAMS

Figure 16.2 When you add a new file extension, you enter it at the bottom of the Extensions column.

5. From the Reload modified files pop-up menu, choose what you want Dreamweaver to do when it detects that changes have been made in another program to a file that is open in Dreamweaver. Your choices are Prompt (Dreamweaver will ask you whether it should reload the page), Always, or Never.

6. From the Save on launch pop-up menu, choose whether Dreamweaver should always save the current document before starting the external editor, never save the document, or ask you if it should save the document.

7. If you have Adobe Fireworks on your system, tell Dreamweaver its location: click the Browse button, navigate to Fireworks in the resulting Select External Editor dialog, and click OK (Choose).

   Dreamweaver uses Fireworks by default to edit most graphic files, and Fireworks has special features that allow it to update images directly on Dreamweaver pages.

8. The Extensions column has a list of graphic and media types. Click to select the media type for which you want to assign an external editor.

   If the media type has an editor already assigned, that editor appears in the Editors column.

   or

   To add a media type, click the plus (+) button above the Extensions column. A new entry appears at the bottom of the Extensions column. Type a new extension for the new media type (**Figure 16.2**).

   continues on next page

9. To add an editor, click the plus (+) button above the Editors column.

The Select External Editor dialog appears. Navigate to the program you want to use and click OK (Choose).

10. Repeat steps 8 and 9 for the rest of the media types in the Extensions column.

11. Click OK to dismiss the Preferences dialog.

✔ Tips

■ If you prefer to use Adobe Photoshop as your image editor, set it to be the external image editor for JPEG, GIF, and PNG files.

■ Dreamweaver can make some edits to graphic files itself, including resizing, adjusting brightness and contrast, cropping, and more. See Chapter 5 for more information.

■ On the Mac, Dreamweaver can use Bare Bones Software's BBEdit, a popular text editor, as its external code editor. In the File Types/Editors pane of Preferences, there is a check box labeled Enable BBEdit Integration (**Figure 16.3**). Select this check box to make BBEdit the external code editor. This also changes the Edit > Edit with External Editor menu choice to Edit > Edit with BBEdit. For more information about using BBEdit to edit your code, see Chapter 17.

Open in Code View: .js .asa .css .cs .config .inc .txt .as .asc .asr .vb .htacce
☑ Enable BBEdit Integration

Figure 16.3 On the Mac, a single check box enables integration with BBEdit.

Figure 16.4 Click the Edit button in the Property Inspector to begin modifying an image with Fireworks (top). If Photoshop is set as the external file editor for the kind of image file you have selected, the Photoshop icon appears in the Property Inspector instead (bottom).

Editing Images with Fireworks

You can use Adobe Fireworks to edit images on your Dreamweaver pages, and the two programs work together to make it easier. When you start editing an image in Dreamweaver, Dreamweaver hands the image off to Fireworks. It's in Fireworks that you'll make the changes you want. Then you tell Fireworks that you're done editing the image and you want to go back to Dreamweaver. Fireworks saves the image and sends it back to Dreamweaver, which then updates the Web page with the modified image.

You can also have Fireworks objects on your Web pages, and Dreamweaver opens Fireworks when you need to make any changes to those objects. For example, in Fireworks you can create navigation bars complete with links and rollover effects. Fireworks saves these navigation bars as HTML and CSS, with associated images. Fireworks makes it easy to export its navigation bars to Dreamweaver, and Dreamweaver recognizes that the navigation bar was created in Fireworks, so that when you attempt to edit the navigation bar in Dreamweaver, Fireworks automatically launches.

In order to edit images in Fireworks, it must be selected as the external editor in Dreamweaver's Preferences for the particular image file type you want to edit. See "Assigning External Editing Programs," earlier in this chapter, for more information.

To edit images with Fireworks:

1. Select the image on the Dreamweaver page.

2. Click the Edit button in the Property Inspector (**Figure 16.4**).

continues on next page

Fireworks launches and displays the Find Source dialog. This gives you the choice to edit a PNG file that could be the original Fireworks file (**Figure 16.5**). That's because PNG is Fireworks' native format, and files that you create in Fireworks are saved as PNGs, and they are then, if necessary, exported to JPEG or GIF for use on your Web site. Fireworks provides more editing options for PNG files than it does for other formats. So if you create images in Fireworks, you can often have two copies of the image: the PNG source and the exported JPEG or GIF.

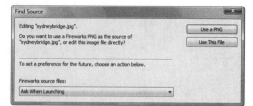

Figure 16.5 Fireworks gives you the choice to edit the file in the Dreamweaver page, or edit a Fireworks PNG source file.

3. If you originally created the image in Fireworks and want to edit the PNG, click Use a PNG.

   The Open dialog appears. Navigate to the PNG file, select it, and click OK (Choose).

   or

   If you want to edit the file itself, click Use This File.

   The image opens in Fireworks (**Figure 16.6**).

   Note that a status bar appears in the Fireworks document window and includes a Done button and the notation "Editing from Dreamweaver."

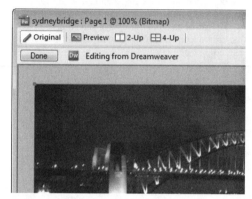

Figure 16.6 When you are editing an image from Dreamweaver, Fireworks lets you know in a status bar at the top of the Fireworks document window and includes a Done button.

4. Make your changes in Fireworks.

5. Click Done in the Fireworks window.

   Fireworks saves and closes the image. Behind the scenes, it has told Dreamweaver to update the image on the Dreamweaver document page.

6. Switch back to Dreamweaver to continue your work.

   The updated image will be on the page.

Figure 16.7 This navigation bar in Fireworks is destined for Dreamweaver.

Figure 16.8 Use the Export feature to begin sending the navigation bar to Dreamweaver.

Figure 16.9 Select your local site folder as the destination for the navigation bar.

To export Fireworks HTML to Dreamweaver:

1. In Fireworks, prepare and save the document (such as a navigation bar) that you want to export to Dreamweaver (**Figure 16.7**).

2. Choose File > Export (**Figure 16.8**). The Export dialog appears (**Figure 16.9**).

3. Navigate to the place in your local site folder where you want to save the Fireworks HTML file.

4. (Optional, but recommended) Click Put images in subfolder, then click Browse and select the images directory, so the different images that make up the Fireworks table don't clutter up the root directory of your site.

5. Click Save.

   Fireworks saves the HTML and associated images in your site folder.

EDITING IMAGES WITH FIREWORKS

To edit a Fireworks image or table:

1. In Dreamweaver, select the image or table that was originally created in Fireworks.

   Dreamweaver shows you in the Property Inspector that the object came from Fireworks, and shows you in the Src field the name of the original Fireworks PNG file (**Figure 16.10**).

2. Click the Edit button in the Property Inspector.

   or

   Right-click and choose Edit in Fireworks from the resulting shortcut menu.

   Fireworks launches and displays the PNG file for the object you wish to edit (**Figure 16.11**). A status bar appears in the Fireworks document window, with a Done button and the notation "Editing from Dreamweaver."

Figure 16.10 The Dreamweaver Property Inspector recognizes objects from Fireworks, and shows you the name of the original Fireworks source file in the Original field.

Figure 16.11 When you click the Edit in Fireworks button, the original PNG file opens for editing in Fireworks.

Figure 16.12 We've selected the borderless table that contains the navigation bar's components to show the slices that Fireworks creates.

3. Make the changes you want in Fireworks.

4. Click Done in the Fireworks window.

Fireworks saves and closes the object or table. Behind the scenes, it has told Dreamweaver to update the object on the Dreamweaver document page.

5. Switch back to Dreamweaver to continue your work.

The updated object will be on the page.

✔ Tips

■ When Fireworks creates a navigation bar (or any complex image that uses scripts), it slices the PNG file into many different pieces, some of which are buttons and some are spacers. Some of these pieces also have JavaScript associated with them, for functionality such as rollovers. When Fireworks exports the navigation bar to Dreamweaver, Fireworks converts the format of the slices to many different JPEG files and creates a borderless table to contain all the slices (**Figure 16.12**).

■ Fireworks exports its images to JPEG or GIF formats, which are less flexible to edit than PNG files. For example, once you have exported an image from Fireworks' native PNG format, you can't easily go back and edit text, effects settings, or paths in the artwork. That is why it's important to keep the original PNG files, so that you can easily go back and edit your work. We recommend that you save your original Fireworks PNG files in the same folder with the exported files, which usually means your site's images folder.

Using Adobe Bridge

When you install Dreamweaver (or most other CS4 programs), Adobe Bridge CS4 is also installed. Bridge works with most of the CS4 components, and acts as a central repository for project files such as graphics. The Bridge window shows thumbnails of your images, and you can drag images from Bridge and drop them on your Web pages in Dreamweaver (or other CS4 program document windows). Bridge provides many tools for organizing your project files, including searching, sorting, and keywords. You can also use Bridge to search for, preview, and purchase stock photos from online vendors.

To copy images from Bridge to Dreamweaver:

1. In Dreamweaver, open the page that will receive the image from Bridge, and click to place the insertion point where you want the image to appear.

2. Launch Adobe Bridge by choosing File > Browse in Bridge.

The Bridge window appears (**Figure 16.13**).

3. In Bridge, navigate to the folder that contains the image you want.

4. In the Content panel, click the image's thumbnail to select it.

Figure 16.13 The Adobe Bridge window lets you browse your computer in the left column, shows you thumbnails of your content in the center, and shows details of the item you have selected on the right.

Figure 16.14 Content from Bridge will almost always be outside of your local root folder, and Dreamweaver alerts you and offers to copy the file there.

Figure 16.15 Give the file a name, and place it in your images folder (unless it's not an image!).

Figure 16.16 It's a good idea to always enter alternate text for images.

5. Drag the thumbnail from Bridge into the Dreamweaver document window.

Dreamweaver alerts you that the file is outside your local root folder, and offers to copy it there for you (**Figure 16.14**).

6. Click Yes.

The Copy File As dialog appears (**Figure 16.15**).

7. Give the image a name, and navigate to where you want to save it (usually inside your site's images folder).

8. Click Save.

The Image Tag Accessibility Attributes dialog appears (**Figure 16.16**). This is another dialog where you can enter descriptive alternate text.

9. Enter the description for the image, then click OK.

The image from Bridge appears on your Web page.

✔ Tip

- You can use Bridge to organize other file types besides images. If you insert a non-image file, such as HTML, mp3, PDF, or a file with an unknown file type, Dreamweaver inserts a link to the source file.

Cleaning Up Word HTML

Back in Chapter 4, you learned how to bring content from Microsoft Word into Dreamweaver with the Paste Special command, which allows you to preserve varying amounts of the formatting from the Word document. By using the Paste Special command, you will get very good results.

There's another way to get content from Word into Dreamweaver, though we don't recommend it. We are only telling you because you might have to deal with it anyway. Word can export its files as HTML documents, which can then be opened in Dreamweaver. The problem is that when Word (and other Microsoft Office applications) saves a document as a Web page, the HTML code created includes lots of excess or Microsoft-specific code that is designed to enable these Web pages to be brought back into Word or Excel more easily, but that most browsers don't need. This excess code can easily bloat the size of a Web page to two or three times the size of a Web page created entirely in Dreamweaver.

Happily, Dreamweaver has the ability to import a Word HTML document and clean up its code. It does this by eliminating Word-specific styles, removing nonstandard CSS, getting rid of empty paragraphs, deleting Microsoft-specific XML tags, and more. In short, if you have been given Word documents that were exported to HTML, Dreamweaver has the means to clean them up.

Figure 16.17 Use the Clean Up Word HTML command to optimize the HTML from Word documents that were exported as Web pages.

To clean up a Word HTML document:

1. Open the Word HTML document.

   The document appears on the screen.

2. Choose Commands > Clean Up Word HTML.

   The Clean Up Word HTML dialog appears (**Figure 16.17**). Dreamweaver automatically detects whether the HTML was produced by Word 97/98 or Word 2000 or later.

Clean up word HTML results:
6 meta tags removed
55 instances of word XML removed
6 word [if...]'s removed
39 empty paragraphs removed
5 margin defines removed
107 word-only "mso" style properties removed
6 instances of non-Standard CSS removed
Source formatting applied

Figure 16.18 Dreamweaver lets you know the changes it made in the Word document.

3. Choose to turn on or off any of the options on the Basic or Detailed tabs of the dialog.

By default, all of the options are turned on. We recommend that you leave things this way, unless you know that there are specific options you don't need.

4. Click OK.

Dreamweaver processes the Word HTML document, then displays a dialog summarizing the results of the process (**Figure 16.18**).

5. Click OK.

The converted document appears in the Dreamweaver document window.

✔ Tips

■ The Paste Special command does a better job of preserving the original formatting and styling of the Word document than the Clean Up Word HTML command.

■ Long Word documents may take more than a minute to complete processing, depending on the size of the document and the speed of your computer.

■ There is a third way to bring Word or Excel documents into Dreamweaver for Windows, but again, we don't recommend it. You can choose File > Import > Word Document or File > Import > Excel Document. After choosing the document you want from an Open dialog, Dreamweaver converts the document and inserts its contents into the current page. Unfortunately, you get approximately the same quality results as you would get if you exported the Word or Excel document to HTML, imported it into Dreamweaver, then used the Clean Up Word HTML command, which is to say, not as good as if you used Paste Special.

Using Content from Excel

There are two kinds of information that you might want to use from Microsoft Excel on your Web pages. First, you may want the information in the worksheet—the data and calculations that make up all or part of the worksheet. Second, you may wish to place a graph taken from an Excel worksheet on a Web page.

In both cases, you'll copy and paste the information from Excel into your Dreamweaver document.

To import Excel worksheet data:

1. In the Excel worksheet, select the information you want to bring into Dreamweaver (**Figure 16.19**).

2. Choose Edit > Copy, or press Ctrl-C (Cmd-C).

3. Switch to Dreamweaver.

4. Click in the document at the insertion point where you want the Excel information to appear.

5. Choose Edit > Paste Special.

   The Paste Special dialog appears (**Figure 16.20**). This dialog has four choices. The first choice, "Text only," pastes all the information from the worksheet into a single line. This jumbles all the information together, so don't use it. The next three choices paste the worksheet information as a table, retaining increasing amounts of formatting information from the original worksheet. In most cases, you'll find that the best choice is "Text with structure plus full formatting."

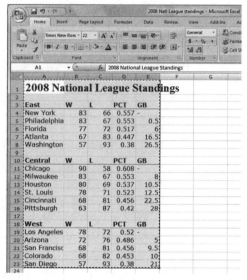

Figure 16.19 Begin importing Excel worksheet data into Dreamweaver by selecting and copying the information in Excel.

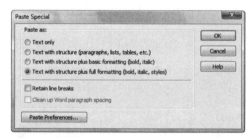

Figure 16.20 Use the Paste Special dialog to control how much formatting you want to maintain from the Excel worksheet.

2008 National League Standings

East	W	L	PCT	GB
New York	83	66	0.557	—
Philadelphia	83	67	0.553	0.5
Florida	77	72	0.517	6
Atlanta	67	83	0.447	16.5
Washington	57	93	0.38	26.5
Central	**W**	**L**	**PCT**	**GB**
Chicago	90	58	0.608	—
Milwaukee	83	67	0.553	8
Houston	80	69	0.537	10.5
St. Louis	78	71	0.523	12.5
Cincinnati	68	81	0.456	22.5
Pittsburgh	63	87	0.42	28
West	**W**	**L**	**PCT**	**GB**
Los Angeles	78	72	0.52	—
Arizona	72	76	0.486	5
San Francisco	68	81	0.456	9.5
Colorado	68	82	0.453	10
San Diego	57	93	0.38	21

Figure 16.21 The Excel worksheet data appears in Dreamweaver as a table.

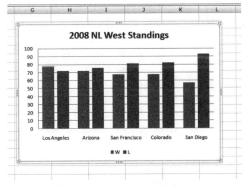

Figure 16.22 Begin bringing an Excel chart into Dreamweaver by selecting and copying the chart in Excel.

6. Choose the formatting option you want.

7. Click OK.

Dreamweaver pastes the Excel information into the document as a table (**Figure 16.21**).

✔ Tip

■ If you want to style the worksheet in Dreamweaver after import, you should use the "Text with structure plus basic formatting" choice in the Paste Special dialog. The reason is that the "Text with structure plus full formatting" choice creates CSS styles in your Dreamweaver document that make it difficult to restyle the table.

To import an Excel chart:

1. In the Excel worksheet, select the chart you want to bring into Dreamweaver (**Figure 16.22**).

2. Choose Edit > Copy, or press Ctrl-C.

3. Switch to Dreamweaver.

4. Click in the Dreamweaver document to set the insertion point where you want the Excel chart to appear.

continues on next page

5. Choose Edit > Paste, or press Ctrl-V.

The Image Preview dialog appears (**Figure 16.23**).

6. Make any adjustments you want in the Image Preview dialog.

7. Click OK.

The Save Web Image dialog appears.

8. Give the image a name, and navigate to where you want to save it (usually inside your site's images folder).

9. Click Save.

The Image Description (Alt Text) dialog appears. Alternate text is used by screen reading programs utilized by the disabled.

10. Enter the description for the image, then click OK.

11. The chart appears in the Dreamweaver document (**Figure 16.24**).

Figure 16.23 You can make adjustments to the chart image in the Image Preview dialog.

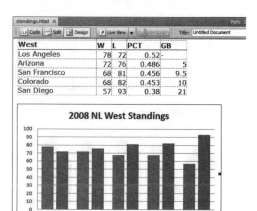

Figure 16.24 The Excel chart ends up on the Dreamweaver page as a graphic.

Working with Contribute

One of the difficulties faced by Web designers is the problem of maintaining a Web site in good order after you launch the site. Because Web sites need constant changing to remain vital, there is a need to update content throughout the site on a regular basis. But as a designer, you are probably reluctant to let everyday users make changes and updates to your Web sites for fear that minor mistakes will cause major problems.

That's where Adobe Contribute comes in. With a combination of Dreamweaver templates and Contribute, you can allow virtually anyone who can use a word processor to make changes to your Web sites, without the possibility of accidentally breaking the site. Contribute users can only change page content within the template's editable areas, and the Contribute site administrator can restrict the Contribute user's editing abilities. Contribute allows designers to get back to the job of designing sites (rather than maintaining pages) and allows clients to maintain sites themselves (rather than trying to track down the designers to make small changes).

In Dreamweaver, besides designing your pages using Dreamweaver templates (see Chapter 15 for more information about templates), you need to set some Dreamweaver preferences so that your site is ready for the Contribute user. You can also launch Contribute to perform site administration from Dreamweaver.

✔ Tip

■ For lots more information about using Contribute, we recommend another book, *Macromedia Contribute 3 for Windows and Macintosh: Visual QuickStart Guide*, and an online or DVD video training program, *Contribute 3 Essential Training* (www.lynda.com), both by Tom Negrino.

To set your site to use Contribute:

1. Choose Site > Manage Sites.

   The Manage Sites dialog appears (**Figure 16.25**).

2. From the list of sites, select the site that you want to enable for Contribute.

3. Click Edit.

   The Site Definition dialog appears, set to the Advanced tab (**Figure 16.26**).

4. In the list on the left side of the dialog, click the Contribute category.

   The Contribute pane appears (**Figure 16.27**).

5. Select the Enable Contribute compatibility check box.

6. In the Site root URL text box, the URL of your site should appear. If it does not, enter it now.

7. Click the Test button.

   Dreamweaver connects to the Web site and confirms that the connection is working. Dreamweaver puts up an alert box letting you know the connection was successful.

8. Click OK to dismiss the confirmation alert.

9. Click OK to dismiss the Site Definition dialog.

Figure 16.25 In the Manage Sites dialog, choose the site for which you want to enable Contribute compatibility.

Figure 16.26 The Site Definition dialog allows you to make many settings that are associated with the particular site you chose in the Manage Sites dialog.

Figure 16.27 You enable Contribute compatibility in the Contribute pane of the Site Definition dialog.

Figure 16.28 Begin administering the Contribute site by entering your administrator password.

Figure 16.29 Use the Administer Website dialog to adjust user roles and permissions.

To administer a site in Contribute:

1. Choose Site > Manage Sites.
   The Manage Sites dialog appears.

2. From the list of sites, select the site that you want to enable for Contribute.

3. Click Edit.
   The Site Definition dialog appears.

4. In the list on the left side of the dialog, click the Contribute category.
   The Contribute pane appears (Figure 16.27).

5. Click the Administer Site in Contribute button.
   You must also have a copy of Contribute on your hard disk. The Administrator Password dialog appears (**Figure 16.28**).

6. Enter your Contribute administrator password, and click OK.
   The Contribute Administer Website dialog appears (**Figure 16.29**).

7. Make any administrative changes you desire, then click Close to dismiss the Administer Website dialog.

Rollback and the Contribute Publishing Server

When you enable Contribute compatibility in Dreamweaver, you are setting up Dreamweaver to take advantage of two Contribute features. The first feature is *rollbacks*.

Contribute has the ability to rollback published pages—that is, revert to previously published versions of the pages. You can think of it as a sort of "Super Undo" for your Web page. The Contribute user can roll back to the last published version, or to any saved version, up to 99 previous versions. Enabling Contribute compatibility in Dreamweaver tracks page changes (using Dreamweaver's Design Notes feature) and marks pages as eligible for rollback, whether they are changed in Contribute or Dreamweaver. However, only Contribute users can rollback pages; that functionality isn't built into Dreamweaver.

The other feature is the Contribute Publishing Server (CPS), an Adobe product designed for enterprises that have many Contribute users. CPS is a server application, created as a J2EE application, that provides central administration, tracks users and user access, and handles publishing activities for a Web site. The CPS can be installed on Windows, Linux, Mac OS X, or Solaris server machines.

The CPS server allows enterprise-sized organizations to deploy Contribute to dozens or hundreds of users. The CPS works with standard user directory systems, such as LDAP and Active Directory, to easily assign users to what Contribute refers to as *user roles*, which are the editing permissions granted to individual users. The CPS server also keeps track of page graphs and allows the Contribute site administrator to implement a publishing flow for pages. For example, administrators can force writers to submit pages to editors for review and approval before publishing the pages to the live Web site.

When you enable Contribute compatibility in Dreamweaver, and if you're using the CPS, Dreamweaver notifies the CPS every time you do a network operation such as checking in or checking out a file.

Working with InContext Editing

InContext Editing (ICE) is a hosted, subscription service from Adobe that allows relatively inexperienced users to make simple edits to Web pages using nothing more than a Web browser. Users can load specially prepared pages into their Web browser (at press time the only supported browsers were Firefox 3 or Safari for Windows or Mac, or Internet Explorer 6 or 7 for Windows), make changes, and save the edited pages to the Web site. Dreamweaver CS4 has features that allow you to prepare pages for ICE.

As the Web designer creating the initial ICE pages in Dreamweaver, you can specify what editing privileges the user has, such as font styling, alignment, and more. If this sounds a lot like Adobe Contribute, that's no surprise; just as Adobe is offering Photoshop Express (part of the Photoshop.com Web site) as a lightweight Web application to edit images, InContext Editing is designed to allow users simple Web page editing abilities without needing to purchase a separate program. See the "Contribute versus ICE" sidebar for more differences between the two.

When you prepare a page for ICE, you define sections on the page as editable regions, just as you might with any Dreamweaver template. However, ICE editable regions aren't quite the same as regular editable regions; they can't be edited by Contribute users.

We're not going to cover how you edit pages with ICE (when this book went to press, the ICE interface was still changing, so any instructions we give you will probably be inaccurate by the time you read this); instead, we'll focus on how you prepare a page in Dreamweaver CS4 for use with InContext Editing.

To add ICE editable regions:

1. Open an existing page, or create a new page from a template, that you want to prepare for ICE.

2. Select content on the page, or select a div on the page using the Tag Selector (**Figure 16.30**).

3. From the InContext Editing category of the Insert panel (**Figure 16.31**), click the button for the kind of region you want to add:

   ▲ **Create Repeating Region** inserts regions that can be duplicated by the user as often as needed. They're useful for things that vary from page to page, for example a chart of product colors or sizes. Inside a repeating region, users can create and remove regions, and move regions up and down within the overall region container.

   ▲ **Create Editable Region** is the choice you'll use most often. This wraps a div around the selection, with the ice:editable attribute, which is understood by the Web-based ICE application (but ignored by browsers, so the page will display just fine).

If you selected content, Dreamweaver will show a dialog letting you know that it will be wrapping a div around the selection (**Figure 16.32**). If you selected a div in Step 2, this dialog will not appear.

Dreamweaver outlines your selection in blue with a tab that says Repeating Region or Editable Region at the top (**Figure 16.33**).

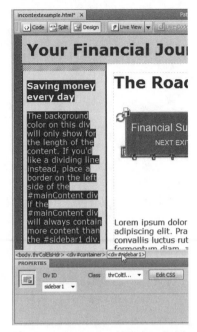

Figure 16.30 To begin adding an editable region for InContext Editing, select a div with the Tag Selector, as shown here, or select some page content.

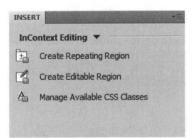

Figure 16.31 Choose the kind of ICE region you want in the Insert panel.

Figure 16.32 Dreamweaver lets you know it will add a div around a selection to make it an editable region.

Figure 16.33 The editable region appears outlined in blue.

4. In the document window, click the tab at the top of the new region to select it.

   The Property Inspector changes to show the editing options that you can allow the user.

5. Check or uncheck the editing options that you want the user to have available for this region (**Figure 16.34**).

   You can speed things up by clicking the Check all or Uncheck all button.

continues on next page

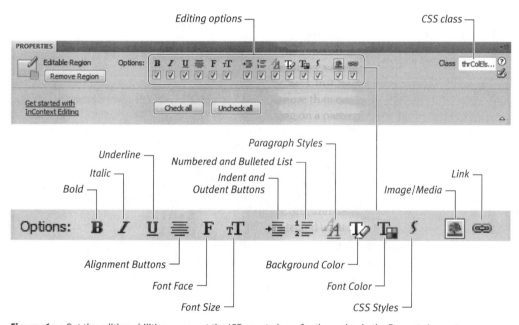

Figure 16.34 Set the editing abilities you want the ICE user to have for the region in the Property Inspector.

6. Repeat steps 2 through 5 for the rest of the regions that you want to put in the document.

7. Save the file.

If this is the first time that you have added an ICE page to your site, Dreamweaver lets you know that it will need to copy a new folder called `includes` to the root level of your local site, and that you will have to upload this folder and its contents to your server in order for the page to be editable by ICE (**Figure 16.35**).

Figure 16.35 Dreamweaver lets you know it needs to upload a folder containing JavaScript and HTML files to your server to make the ICE page work correctly.

✔ Tip

■ In order to test the ICE-enabled page, you must upload it to a Web server, load the page in a browser, then invoke the InContext Editing interface by pressing Ctrl-E (Cmd-E). You'll be asked to log in to the ICE service, then the page will appear in the InContext Editing interface. You can't test ICE by previewing the page from the local copy on your hard disk.

Contribute versus ICE

You might think that using ICE to edit Web pages in a browser would make Contribute obsolete. However, there are important differences between the two programs, and Contribute remains more powerful. For example, InContext Editing users can't edit pages based on Dreamweaver templates if those pages haven't been prepared by a Dreamweaver user with the special ICE markup. Contribute CS4 can't edit Web pages that use ICE markup, as there is no way for Contribute to be sure that the page isn't being edited by another user simultaneously with ICE.

Other limitations of ICE that are not shared by Contribute include:

◆ Can't edit pages hosted in intranets

◆ Limited user access to CSS styles

◆ Can't create new pages based on the site's templates

◆ Doesn't create Contribute-style rollback pages, so there's no easy backup or page reversion

◆ Requires the latest Flash Player to be installed

◆ Subscription service, so you can lose editing access to pages

Using Device Central

When you install Dreamweaver, whether by itself or as part of one of the Creative Suite packages, another program called Device Central is also installed. This program helps you design pages for mobile devices, such as cellphones. It does this by keeping a database of device profiles. You should be able to preview a Web page that you are working on in Dreamweaver in Device Central and see how your page would render on the device. And that's how it works; you create a page in Dreamweaver and preview it in Device Central as you would preview in any other browser, with the content appearing on the screen of the phone. On Windows, Device Central is installed in `\Program Files\Adobe Creative Suite CS4\Device Central CS4\`. On the Mac, you'll find the Device Central CS4 folder inside your Applications folder.

Less Than it Appears

The devil in the details with Device Central is that it doesn't maintain separate emulators of all of the different Web browsers built into the many phones available in the program. Instead, Device Central uses a single rendering engine, Opera Small Screen Rendering, to preview Web content for all devices, which may look wildly different from how the content may really render on a particular phone. So at best, you only have a vague idea of how your content will appear.

Another big problem is that when we wrote this, Device Central didn't include profiles for any of the smartphones, such as the iPhone, Blackberry, Treo, or Windows Mobile phones, which are the very phones most people use to surf the Web on the go. Here's hoping that Adobe updates Device Central soon to be actually useful for Web designers who want to deploy their sites on mobile devices, because while right now it's better than nothing, it's not by much.

Device Central is really intended for Flash developers who are creating mobile Flash applications, targeting Flash Lite, the version built into many phones.

To preview a Web page in Device Central:

1. In Device Central, open the mobile device profile that you want to use to view your Web page, then click the Emulator tab.

A representation of the mobile device appears in the Device Central window.

2. In Dreamweaver, open the page that you want to preview.

3. Choose File > Preview in Browser > Device Central.

The Device Central window comes to the front, and displays your Web page's content (**Figure 16.36**). You can scroll the page by clicking buttons on the emulated device, just as you would if you were pressing buttons on the real device.

✔ Tips

■ If you don't like the way your page looks on the emulated mobile device, you'll need to change it in Dreamweaver, then preview it again in Device Central.

■ A how-to on design for mobile devices is beyond the scope of this book, and there's not a lot of information on it; it seems as though it is still largely a trial-and-error process. Look for tutorials on the Web by doing a search for "designing Web pages" and "mobile devices."

Figure 16.36 Device Central CS4 allows you to get a feel for how your Web pages will look on mobile devices.

USING DEVICE CENTRAL

17

EDITING CODE

Dreamweaver is what's known as a *WYSIWYG* application; *WYSIWYG* is an acronym for "What You See Is What You Get." Given Dreamweaver's strengths as a design tool, why would anyone ever want to bother looking at code, much less editing it?

Believe it or not, there are people who purchase Dreamweaver who then spend most of their time in Code view. There are a number of reasons why; some of the more common we hear are:

◆ "It's perfect for control freaks like me who just want to change that one character or move things one pixel."

◆ "I learned tags before good WYSIWYG editors existed, so it's faster for me to make changes this way."

◆ "There are things I can do this way that can't be done any other way in Dreamweaver."

These are all perfectly valid reasons to want to use Code view (and there are plenty of other reasons). If you haven't before, check it out. You might find that Code view works best for you, or that it's useful when you simply want to tweak one small thing on your page.

Using the Coding Toolbar

Yes, it's another toolbar in Dreamweaver, but the Coding toolbar is a little different: it only shows up when you're in Code view, and it only acts on those things that you would deal with when you're in Code view.

To use the Coding toolbar:

1. If you're in Design view, click the Code button in the Document toolbar. This switches you into Code view, so you'll now see the tags (instead of the WYSIWYG appearance of your page) and the Coding toolbar. For instance, **Figure 17.1** shows a page in Design view, while **Figure 17.2** shows the same page in Code view.

Figure 17.1 Here's the familiar Design view that you've grown to know and love.

Figure 17.2 The Code view shows the exact same page but in a whole new light.

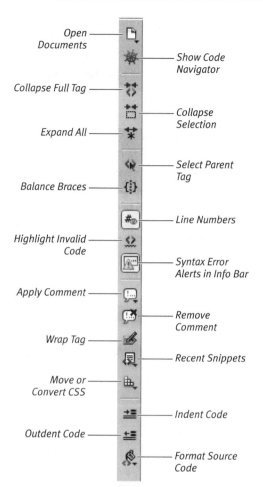

Open Documents

Show Code Navigator

Collapse Full Tag

Collapse Selection

Expand All

Select Parent Tag

Balance Braces

Line Numbers

Highlight Invalid Code

Syntax Error Alerts in Info Bar

Apply Comment

Remove Comment

Wrap Tag

Recent Snippets

Move or Convert CSS

Indent Code

Outdent Code

Format Source Code

Figure 17.3 The Coding toolbar provides everything you need to manage text and tags.

2. On the left side of the document window, you'll see the Coding toolbar (**Figure 17.3**). Let's review its buttons, from top to bottom:

▲ **Open Documents:** The name of this button might make you think that it's a way to open documents, but that's incorrect; it actually offers a pop-up menu of all the items that are currently open.

▲ **Show Code Navigator:** Displays the Code Navigator window. Code Navigator is covered in Chapter 7.

▲ **Collapse Full Tag:** Collapsing code (and why you'd want to do it) is covered later in this chapter. For now, it's enough to know that this button will do it. Holding the Alt (or Option) key while clicking this button collapses everything outside the current tag.

▲ **Collapse Selection:** This button collapses the current selection of code, and holding down the Alt (or Option) key while clicking this button collapses everything outside the selection.

▲ **Expand All:** If any code on the page is collapsed, clicking this button expands it again.

▲ **Select Parent Tag:** This button causes the selection area to change to include the parent tag, based on the current cursor position.

▲ **Balance Braces:** If your current cursor position is inside a <script> or <style> tag, clicking this button causes the innermost set of braces ( ), { }, or [ ] to be selected. This also works inside external JavaScript and CSS files.

continues on next page

USING THE CODING TOOLBAR

▲ **Line Numbers:** Toggles the display of line numbers in the current document. If they're currently displayed, they'll be hidden, and if they're currently hidden, they'll display.

▲ **Highlight Invalid Code:** If you enter tags that Dreamweaver doesn't like and you've chosen this option, your mistake will be highlighted in yellow. If you click in the highlighted area, the Property Inspector will tell you more about the error (**Figure 17.4**).

▲ **Syntax Error Alerts in Info Bar:** Turns on or off an information bar that appears at the top of the page if Dreamweaver detects a code syntax error. The program also highlights the line of code containing the error.

▲ **Apply Comment:** The pop-up menu on this button gives several choices, each of which wraps comments around the selected text:

 ▪ **Apply HTML Comment:** Inserts <!-- and --!> before and after the selection (respectively).

 ▪ **Apply /* */ Comment:** Wraps this type of comment around the selected CSS or JavaScript.

 ▪ **Apply // Comment:** Inserts this type of comment at the beginning of each selected line of CSS and/or JavaScript.

 ▪ **Apply ' Comment:** Inserts this type of comment at the beginning of each selected line of VBScript.

 ▪ **Apply Server Comment:** If you're working on a server-side file such as PHP, JSP, or ColdFusion, Dreamweaver automatically detects the file type and inserts the correct type of comment.

▲ **Remove Comment:** Removes comment tags from the selected code.

▲ **Wrap Tag:** Opens the Quick Tag Editor (described later in this chapter) allowing you to wrap a tag around the selection.

▲ **Recent Snippets:** Allows you to insert a recently used snippet. Snippets are covered in Chapter 15: "Making Life Easier: Using Templates, Libraries, and Snippets."

▲ **Move or Convert CSS:** Here you can either convert inline CSS to a rule, or move CSS rules. CSS is covered in Chapters 7–9.

▲ **Indent Code:** Takes the selection and moves it to the right, based on your chosen indentation preference in the Code Format settings (covered in the sidebar "Text Editing Tips," later in this chapter).

▲ **Outdent Code:** Takes the selection and moves it to the left.

Figure 17.4 It's always a good idea to tell Dreamweaver to highlight invalid code, so you can see problems at a glance.

Figure 17.5 The View Options button on the Document toolbar contains some very useful settings.

Figure 17.6 If you have too many buttons for your screen size, you'll find they're still accessible once you learn where they're hiding.

▲ **Format Source Code:** From this pop-up, you can choose whether to apply formatting to the file as a whole, or to just the current selection. Whichever you choose will be formatted as set in the Code Format settings, which can also be accessed via this pop-up.

✔ Tips

■ Some of these options can also be set from the View Options button on the Document toolbar (**Figure 17.5**). There are a few extra ones there, also: Word Wrap, Hidden Characters, Syntax Coloring, and Auto Indent. Yes, this is different from the View Options button that you're used to in Design view; it changes its appearance based on whether you're in Design, Code, or Split view.

■ If you appear to be missing a button or two, don't fret—your document window may just be smaller than the Coding toolbar. If that's the case, you'll see a couple of downward-facing arrows at the bottom of the toolbar. Click on those arrows and the missing buttons appear off to the side (**Figure 17.6**).

■ If for some reason you don't like this toolbar and just want it to go away, you can do that just as you would with other Dreamweaver toolbars: choose View > Toolbars > Coding. And if you change your mind, that same command brings it back.

■ Dreamweaver opens files in Design view by default. If you want all your HTML files to open in Code view instead, open the preferences and choose the File Types/Editors category. In the "Open in Code View" text box, add a space followed by .html. You can add any other file types where you want to use Code view by default by adding those file extensions, too.

USING THE CODING TOOLBAR

Layout for Coders

In previous versions of Dreamweaver, you could choose between Designer layout and Coder layout the first time you launched the application. If you chose the latter, your screen looks a little different than our screenshots. It's also possible that after using Code view for a bit, you decide that that's the way you want to work in the future, and so you decide to check out Coder layout. **Figure 17.7** shows you what Figure 17.2 looks like if you change the layout by choosing Coder from the Workspace Switcher menu in the Application Bar (**Figure 17.8**).

Figure 17.7 Coder layout is for those who want to see lots of code with as few distractions as possible.

Figure 17.8 It's simple to switch between the different layouts with the Workspace Switcher menu.

Layout for Coders *continued*

Other preset workspaces of interest to codeheads include Coder Plus, which adds an icon bar to the right of the document window providing easy access to the Insert, CSS Styles, and AP Elements panels, and App Developer and App Developer Plus, which are useful for people setting up database-backed Web sites (**Figure 17.9**). The latter two workspaces display the document window in Split View, and show the Databases, Bindings, and Server Behaviors panels.

Figure 17.9 If you're setting up a database-backed Web site, check out the App Developer workspace.

Using Split View

Does losing your WYSIWYG view freak you out a little? Wish you had a way to see both Code and Design views at once? Well, that's exactly what the Split view is about. It splits the document window into two separate panes, so you can see both code and WYSIWYG at once. New to Dreamweaver CS4, you can now have a split code view, where both panes show code. This is really useful when you want to copy and paste code from one section of your page to another part of the same page.

Dreamweaver has always had the ability to split the document window horizontally, but Dreamweaver CS4 gives you the option to split the pane vertically instead. In both horizontal and vertical split modes, you can choose which panes contain the Code and Design views.

To use Split view:

1. Whether you're in Design view or Code view, click the Split button in the Document toolbar. Your document window splits into two: one part for Design view and one for Code view. By default the split is horizontal (**Figure 17.10**).

Figure 17.10 Split view is like training wheels for code—it lets you see how changing the design changes the code, and vice versa.

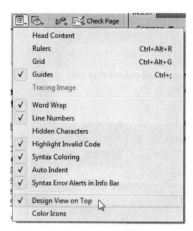

Figure 17.11 The View Options button has all of its choices visible when you're in Split view.

2. If you wish the two were reversed (you'd prefer Code on the top instead of Design or vice versa), use the View Options pop-up menu on the Document toolbar (**Figure 17.11**). You've already seen how the button changes depending on which mode you're in (Code or Design). When you're in Split view, you get all the choices from the other two, plus a choice of whether or not Design view should go on top.

3. (Optional) If you want to use the new vertical Split view, choose View > Split vertically. The display changes from the horizontal split to reflect the vertical choice (**Figure 17.12**).

4. (Optional) If you want the Code view in both panes, so that you can look at different parts of the same page in each pane, choose View > Split Code. The display changes to reflect the choice.

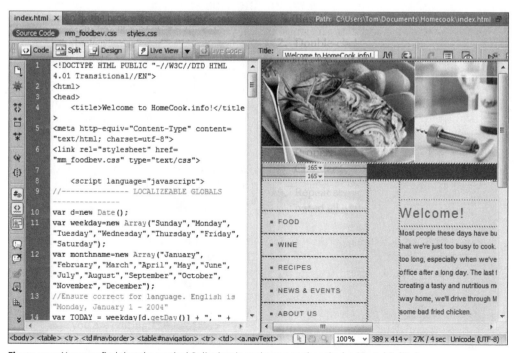

Figure 17.12 You may find that the vertical Split view is easier to use than the horizontal Split view.

✔ Tips

- If you update your page in Design view, Code view automatically updates in response. But if you update in Code view, the Property Inspector displays the message, "You have made changes to the code. To edit selection properties, click Refresh or press F5."

- When you're in Split view, the Coding toolbar only extends down the left side of the code pane, not down the full document window.

- If you select anything in one view, the document automatically scrolls to show and highlight the same selection in the other view.

- If you've never looked at HTML tags before, Split view can be a great way to familiarize yourself with which tags go with which elements of your design.

- If you switch to vertical Split view, the Design View on Top option in the View Options menu on the Document toolbar changes to Design View on Left. You can also find this option in the View menu.

- You can change the size of the panes by pointing at the border between them. When the cursor changes into a two-headed arrow, you can click and drag the border to resize the panes.

Text Editing Tips

When you start using Code view and see tags and markup for the first time, you'll find that there are a lot of things that Dreamweaver assumes you already know. In case you don't, here are a few handy tips:

- ◆ **Word Wrap:** You may want all of your paragraphs to be one long string of text, but if you have Word Wrap turned off, all your long lines will go off the right side of the document. Turn Word Wrap on using the View Options button on the Document toolbar (Figures 17.5, 17.11).

  When you're entering code, be careful about putting in hard returns (where you press Enter/Return) versus the soft returns that Dreamweaver displays even though you didn't type anything in. If you want soft returns, just keep typing and Dreamweaver will handle it for you. If you want hard returns, you might as well turn Word Wrap off.

- ◆ **Syntax coloring:** At first, you might wonder why the text in the code editor is *so* many different colors. If all the colors confuse you and make you think about turning syntax coloring off, give it a try with colors first. Syntax coloring is one of the best ways to learn what's what in code, as similar elements will have identical coloring.

  Wish there were fewer colors all at once? In the Code Coloring category in Preferences, you can change any color to any other color. And if for some reason you want to make things even more tasteless, you can add unique background colors to each different foreground color. But you shouldn't.

Text Editing Tips *continued*

◆ **Line numbers:** These are another matter of personal preference. Some people love them, while other people find them terribly annoying. What you'll want to note is how they work in conjunction with Word Wrap: soft-wrapped lines only get a single line number (you can see this in the Code pane in Figure 17.12).

◆ **Indentation:** If you haven't worked with code before, you might not immediately get why indentation is so useful. But if you're trying to figure out where your divs begin and end, you'll get it quickly when you can see them lined up with each other, with their contents indented.

There's no single "right" way to indent code. What we've found works best is to find one style that works for you, and then *stick to it*. It's the consistency that matters most, especially when you have multiple people working on a site.

If you want to manually indent/outdent your code, you can (with the Indent Code/Outdent Code buttons on the Coding toolbar; see Figure 17.3)—but we recommend instead turning on Auto Indent using the View Options button on the Document toolbar (Figures 17.5, 17.11).

◆ **Code formatting:** The last button on the Coding toolbar (actually a pop-up menu) lets you format your source code (Figure 17.3). If your tags are all over the place because your code came from here and there (as happens to all of us), "Apply Source Formatting" can be found in that pop-up menu. If you don't like the way that Dreamweaver formats your code by default, you can choose the Code Format Settings option from the pop-up menu, and you'll be presented with the Code Format category of the Preferences. Even if you don't know much about tags, it's easy to use this to put your text just where you want it (**Figure 17.13**).

Figure 17.13 Dreamweaver lets you format your code precisely the way that you want it.

Using Live Code View

New to Dreamweaver CS4, Live Code view is a version of Split view that complements Live View (see Chapter 1 for more about using Live View). Normally, when you're in Split view, you see the Design view in one pane and the Code view in the other. If you then click the Live View button, Dreamweaver changes the rendering in the Design view pane to show how the contents of that pane would look in a Web browser. The underlying code in the Code view pane remains the same. But what if your Web page uses JavaScript or Ajax for visual effects, such as rollovers? As the script executes, it's actually changing the HTML on the page, rewriting it under script control. Live Code view allows you to see how the HTML in the Code view pane changes as you interact with the page in the Design view pane. This is especially useful if you're trying to debug a script because it is not producing the effect that you want.

To turn on Live Code view:

1. In any view, click the Live View button on the Document toolbar.

   The page rendering changes to show what the Web page would look like in a Web browser (**Figure 17.14**).

2. Click the Live Code button on the Document toolbar.

   The document changes to Split view, with the code in the Code view pane highlighted to indicate that it is live (**Figure 17.15**). As you interact with the page in the Design view pane, the code in the Code view pane is updated.

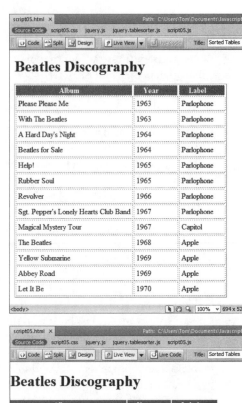

Figure 17.14 In Design view, Dreamweaver shows you the usual view (top). In Live View (bottom), you can see the application of the CSS styles, and the highlighting of the row under the cursor thanks to JavaScript.

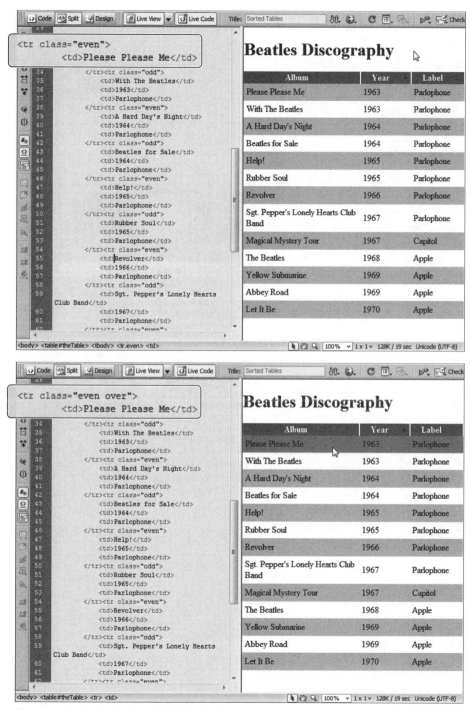

Figure 17.15 In Live Code view, the HTML code changes as you interact with the page in the Design pane (bottom).

Using the Quick Tag Editor

If you prefer Design view (as do most people who've bought a WYSIWYG editor, after all) but wish you could type a little bit of HTML now and then without switching back-and-forth between modes, there's an answer: the Quick Tag Editor.

To use the Quick Tag Editor:

1. With your page in Design view, put the cursor in the place where you wish to add a tag, or select the tag you wish to change, or select the element you wish to wrap a tag around.

2. Press Ctrl-T (Cmd-T).

   or

   Click the Quick Tag Editor button at the right edge of the Property Inspector.

3. The Quick Tag Editor appears, in one of its three modes: Insert, Edit, or Wrap. In any of these modes, start typing, and the possible options appear in the code hints menu below.

   Insert HTML: This mode allows you to place a new tag on the page (**Figure 17.16**).

   Edit tag: This allows you to modify an existing tag, either to change it or to add attributes to it (**Figure 17.17**).

   Wrap tag: In this mode, you can wrap a new tag around an existing element (**Figure 17.18**).

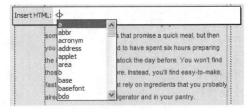

Figure 17.16 With the Quick Tag Editor, you can easily insert a new tag on the page.

Figure 17.17 The Quick Tag Editor also lets you edit existing tags.

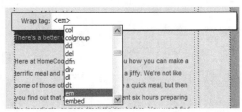

Figure 17.18 And lastly, you can tell the Quick Tag Editor that you want to wrap a tag around existing page elements.

USING THE QUICK TAG EDITOR

4. To accept your changes and leave the Quick Tag Editor, press Enter. To leave the Quick Tag Editor without making any changes, press Escape.

✔ Tips

■ Dreamweaver tries to guess which Quick Tag mode you want to be in. If it guesses incorrectly, you can cycle through the three modes by pressing Ctrl-T (Cmd-T) again. Be careful about what's actually chosen when you do that, though— sometimes, the selected area can expand. For instance, if you've selected the text of a link with the goal of modifying that link, but you've also (accidentally) selected something outside the <a> (link) tag, you can find that you're modifying the <p> (paragraph) around the text instead of the link itself.

■ If the Quick Tag Editor appears but it's covering an area you want to see, you can move it. Just click and drag in the area that displays the mode name to put it in the location you want.

Using the Tag Editor

You've seen the Quick Tag Editor; now here's the Tag Editor itself. It's not really slower than the Quick version, and it's handy for when you want more control than you can get in, say, the Property Inspector, but you don't want to deal with actual HTML tags.

To use the Tag Editor:

1. With your page in Design view, select an element where you wish to edit an existing tag. For instance, you can select an image, or the text of a link.

2. Right-click, and choose Edit Tag from the contextual menu.

   or

   Press Shift-F5.

   or

   From Dreamweaver's menu, choose Modify > Edit Tag.

3. The Tag Editor dialog for that particular tag appears. Every tag has a custom dialog of its own with a variety of categories in the left column. **Figure 17.19** shows the Tag Editor dialog for an <img> tag, while **Figure 17.20** shows the Tag Editor dialog for an <a> tag. Make any desired changes.

4. Click OK when complete.

✔ Tips

■ Near the bottom right of the Tag Editor dialog is the Tag info disclosure arrow. Click it, and the dialog size increases to include a description of the tag you're modifying. For more information about this description, see "Using the Tag Chooser" and "Using the Code Reference," later in this chapter.

■ You can also get into the Tag Editor from Code view by right-clicking on a tag (**Figure 17.21**).

Figure 17.19 The Tag Editor for images lets you modify every possible image attribute and event.

Figure 17.20 The Tag Editor for the *a* tag allows you to change attributes and events for links.

Figure 17.21 Right-click and this contextual pop-up appears with the available options.

Figure 17.22 The Tag Chooser lets you insert tags.

Using the Tag Chooser

If you're beginning to think that there are a lot of different ways to insert elements into a Dreamweaver page, you'd be right—except that you haven't even seen many of them yet. Here's a tool you might not have run across yet—Dreamweaver's Tag Chooser.

To use the Tag Chooser to insert tags:

1. With your page in Code view, put the cursor into the section of the document that you want to add to or edit.

2. Right-click, and a pop-up menu of the available options appears. Choose Insert Tag (Figure 17.21). The Tag Chooser dialog appears (**Figure 17.22**).

3. Click any of the icons or tag categories on the left side, and the matching tags will appear on the right.

4. Select one of the tags on the right, and click Insert. If the tag you chose contains angle brackets (< and >), it will be inserted into the page. Otherwise, a Tag Editor dialog appears, allowing you to enter the required information. For more about the Tag Editor dialog, see "Using the Tag Editor."

5. When you are done with the Tag Chooser dialog, click Close.

USING THE TAG CHOOSER

To use the Tag Chooser to get tag information:

1. With the Tag Chooser open (Figure 17.22), select a tag on the right side.

2. Click the Tag Info button that's just above the Help button on the bottom left. The Tag Info reference area appears, along with useful information about the tag you selected (**Figure 17.23**).

or

Click the <?> button directly to the right of the Tag Info button. The same information appears, but in the Code Reference panel. For more information about the Code Reference panel, see "Using the Code Reference," later in this chapter.

✔ Tip

■ You can also open the Tag Chooser by clicking on the bottom-most icon in the Insert panel when you're in the Common category. If you do this in Design view, Dreamweaver automatically switches to Split view.

Figure 17.23 Select a tag, click the Tag Info button, and Dreamweaver displays a reference guide to that tag.

Collapsing Code

If you've spent much time working with tags and code, you'll often find yourself in a situation where you wish you could hide just some of it. Thankfully, that's something you can do with Dreamweaver.

To collapse code:

1. In Code view, select the code that you want to collapse (**Figure 17.24**). The simplest way to do this is to click somewhere inside the area, and then click the Select Parent Tag button on the Coding toolbar (Figure 17.3).

continues on next page

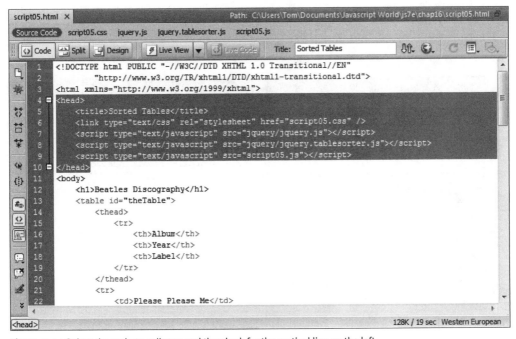

Figure 17.24 Select the code to collapse and then look for the vertical line on the left.

2. Just to the left of the code, you'll see a vertical line that goes from the beginning of the selected area to the end. Windows users will see a white box with a minus sign on each end and Mac users will see two gray triangles, the top one facing down and the bottom one facing up. Click one of these endpoints, and the selected code collapses (**Figure 17.25**). You'll now see the first part of the first line inside a highlighted box, plus a white box with a plus sign (Windows) or a right-facing gray arrow (Mac).

or

Click anywhere inside the tag you want to collapse, and click the Collapse Full Tag button on the Coding toolbar.

or

Select the code you want to collapse, and click the Collapse Selection button on the Coding toolbar.

or

Click in a particular location on the page, and press the Alt (Option) key while clicking the Collapse Full Tag button on the Coding toolbar. This collapses everything *but* the full tag around your particular cursor position.

or

Select a segment of code, and press the Alt (Option) key while clicking the Collapse Selection button on the Coding toolbar. This collapses everything *but* the current selection.

or

Right-click inside a tag on the page, and choose Selection from the pop-up menu (**Figure 17.26**). From there, you can choose to Collapse Selection, Collapse Outside Selection, Collapse Full Tag, or Collapse Outside Full Tag.

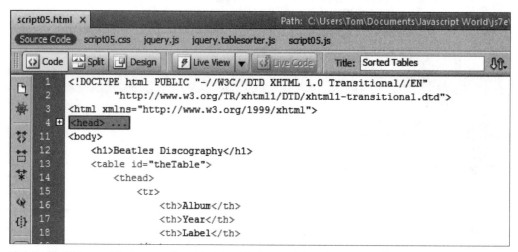

Figure 17.25 Click one of the icons on the endpoints of the line, and the selected text collapses to a single line.

COLLAPSING CODE

Figure 17.26 You can also collapse code by right-clicking on the selection and choosing one of the collapse options.

Figure 17.27 If you want to know what's collapsed, this tool tip gives you the info without actually expanding the code.

To work with collapsed code:

◆ Put your cursor over the highlighted box and a tip appears displaying all of the collapsed code (**Figure 17.27**).

◆ Collapse a section of code if you need to move it from one area of the page to another. You'll know that you're moving exactly what you want to move and no more.

◆ If you collapse a section of code and then save and close the page, the next time you open the page that section will still show as collapsed.

To expand code:

◆ Click the collapsed code symbol (the white box with a plus sign (Windows) or the right-facing gray arrow (Mac)) to the left of the code you wish to expand.

or

Double-click the highlighted box.

or

Click the Expand All button on the Coding toolbar, which expands *all* the collapsed code on the page.

or

Right-click on the page, and choose Selection from the pop-up menu (Figure 17.26). From there, you can choose to Expand Selection or Expand All.

Using Code Hints

When it comes to working with HTML, not all text editors are created equally—and Dreamweaver's code hints are one reason why text editor fans will use its Code view rather than someone else's garden variety notepad-like application.

To use code hints:

1. Click anywhere on the page that you want to add a tag. Start a new tag by typing <, and the code hints appear in a pop-up menu (**Figure 17.28**).

2. Type in the first character or two of the tag, and the code hints menu should change to reflect your typing (**Figure 17.29**). When the hinted value is the tag you want, press Tab.

3. To add an attribute to your new tag, press the spacebar and continue to type. The code hints pop-up menu will appear again, this time displaying just the valid attributes for that tag (**Figure 17.30**). Again, choose the one you want and press Tab to get the full attribute added to your tag.

4. If you select an attribute that needs to link to a file, the code hint changes to a Browse button (**Figure 17.31**). Click the button to browse to the file on your disk.

Figure 17.28 Start typing and the code hints pop-up menu appears.

Figure 17.29 As you continue to type, the code hints narrow down your choices.

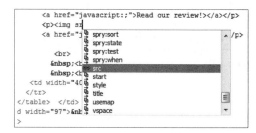

Figure 17.30 Code hints work for attributes as well as tags.

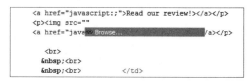

Figure 17.31 Code hints can tell you when the attribute needs a URL as its value.

Figure 17.32 You can add an attribute to an existing tag—just click inside the tag and start typing.

Figure 17.33 Dreamweaver lets you make code hints work just the way you choose.

5. If you want to add an attribute to an existing tag, click immediately after the tag name (for instance, right after the g in <img>), press the spacebar, and the attributes available will display (**Figure 17.32**).

6. To end a tag, type </, and the most recently opened tag will automatically be closed.

✔ Tips

■ If the code hints pop-up menu doesn't appear, press Ctrl-spacebar (Cmd-spacebar) to make it display.

■ You can use the arrow keys on your keyboard to move up and down through code hints to choose the tag or attribute you want.

■ If you're using XHTML and you end a tag with > rather than />, code hints will automatically change it to the proper format.

■ You can't modify an attribute with code hints; instead, delete the attribute and re-create it.

■ If you want a special character but can't remember the exact name of it (such as   for non-breaking space), just type in the first ampersand & and you'll get a code hint that lists all the possible characters you can enter.

■ If there's anything you don't like about how code hints work, you can change them to suit your taste by modifying the values in the Code Hints category of Dreamweaver's Preferences (**Figure 17.33**).

Using the Tag Inspector

If you prefer to stay in Design view but every so often you just want to tweak something, the Tag Inspector panel is one of the simplest ways to do so. Along with the Tag Editor and Quick Tag Editor (covered earlier), it's a great way to modify existing tags, and it's an easy way to get used to the attributes that exist for each tag.

To use the Tag Inspector:

1. If the Tag Inspector currently isn't displaying, choose Window > Tag Inspector.

2. If you're in Design view, click on an element on the page, or choose a tag from the tag selector. If you're in Code view, click anywhere inside a tag. The tag and its attributes appear in the Tag Inspector (**Figure 17.34**). Be sure the Attributes tab is selected.

3. There are two ways to view the attributes in the Tag Inspector: by category or as a list.

   ▲ To view by category, click the Show Category view button. Categories can be open or closed; to open a closed category, click the + button (Windows) or the right-facing triangle (Mac). To close an open category, click the - button (Windows) or the downward-facing triangle (Mac). When open, the list of attributes that fall into that category are displayed.

   ▲ To view as a list, click the Show List view button. This choice displays all the tag's attributes in an alphabetical list (**Figure 17.35**).

4. You can now modify, add, or delete attributes. There are different ways to edit different types of attributes:

   ▲ If you're adding or modifying an attribute with a value of a URL (**Figure 17.36**), you'll see the Point to File icon and a browse icon to the right of the

Show Category view
Show List view

Figure 17.34 The Tag Inspector can be found in the Attributes tab of the Tag Inspector panel. Here's the Category view.

Figure 17.35 Or optionally, there's also the List view, which shows all that tag's attributes in alphabetical order.

Figure 17.36 The standard Point to File and browse icons work the same way here as they do everywhere else in Dreamweaver.

entry field. Alternatively, you can type into the entry box, which is also the case for most attributes.

▲ If your attribute has particular defined values, clicking in the value column displays a pop-up menu containing the valid values (**Figure 17.37**).

▲ If the attribute contains a color, clicking on the small box in the value column brings up the standard color picker (**Figure 17.38**).

5. There's no OK or Accept changes button on the panel; simply clicking away from the attributes or off the panel implements your changes on your page.

✔ Tip

■ As you might remember from Chapter 1, it's also possible to change tag attributes in the Property Inspector. Because the Property Inspector only shows the most commonly used attributes, you'll want to use the Tag Inspector those times when you need to get at the others.

Figure 17.37 For those attributes that can only have certain values, Dreamweaver lets you know what those possibilities are.

Figure 17.38 Instead of having to remember odd codes for colors, the color picker lets you choose the color you want.

Using the JavaScript Extractor

Best practices for Web pages call for content to be separated from structure and behavior. So you should have, respectively, separate HTML, CSS, and JavaScript (.js) documents. Separating the functions like this makes it easier to make changes in any of the documents without accidentally breaking your site. And since CSS and .js documents can apply to many HTML pages on your site, changes you make in them are automatically applied to all the pages that reference those files.

Many older pages, and even pages that are created inside Dreamweaver, can have JavaScript that is embedded in the HTML page. This can be within the document's <head> tag, or can be in the <body>. Dreamweaver CS4 adds a new command that automates extracting this embedded JavaScript code and writing it out to an external .js file.

To extract embedded JavaScript:

1. Open a page containing JavaScript code.

2. Choose Commands > Externalize JavaScript.

   Dreamweaver will analyze the page, and the Externalize JavaScript dialog will appear (**Figure 17.39**).

3. In the dialog, choose "Externalize JavaScript and attach unobtrusively."

   This option extracts the JavaScript and adds a link to the external file to the head section of the HTML page. The external .js file will be named *filename*.js.

Figure 17.39 Choose which JavaScript you want to be extracted from the page.

Figure 17.40 When the JavaScript Extractor is done, it reports on what it accomplished.

4. Check or uncheck any of the proposed JavaScript edits in the dialog.

5. Click OK.

   Dreamweaver displays a dialog that gives you a rundown of what the Externalize JavaScript command did (**Figure 17.40**).

✔ Tip

■ Once you externalize Dreamweaver behaviors, you can't re-edit them in the Behaviors panel, because Dreamweaver doesn't have a way to read in JavaScript code from external files.

Using the Code Reference

It's often very handy to have a book close by when you're first starting to work with code (we recommend *HTML, XHTML, and CSS, Sixth Edition, Visual QuickStart Guide*, by Elizabeth Castro (Peachpit Press), by the way). If you don't happen to have a book nearby, don't fret—Dreamweaver's got several reference books built-in.

To open the Code Reference tab:

◆ Right-click the element on the page that you have questions about, and select Reference from the pop-up menu (**Figure 17.41**). The Reference tab of the Results panel appears (**Figure 17.42**).

or

Follow the directions in "Using the Tag Chooser," earlier in this chapter.

or

From Dreamweaver's menu, choose Window > Reference.

USING THE CODE REFERENCE

Figure 17.41 Picking Reference from this contextual pop-up menu displays the Reference tab of the Results panel.

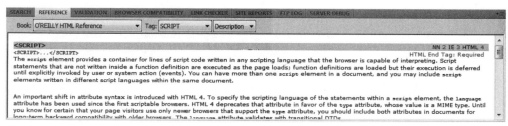

Figure 17.42 The Reference tab can display material about HTML, CSS, JavaScript, and more.

To insert code from the reference into your document:

1. In the Reference tab, find the code fragment you want, click it once, and the entire fragment will be selected (**Figure 17.43**).

2. Right-click the selected text and choose Copy from the pop-up menu.

3. Paste the copied code into your document wherever you want it.

✔ Tips

■ If you don't like the size of the text in the Code Reference tab, you can change it. Right-click anywhere inside the panel and you'll have your choice of small, medium, or large text.

■ The HTML, CSS, and JavaScript reference material included in Dreamweaver is all excerpted from Danny Goodman's book, *Dynamic HTML, The Definitive Reference* (O'Reilly Media). It's a darn good book, but for learning HTML, we still recommend the Visual QuickStart Guide.

■ Besides that material, the Code Reference tab also includes information on ColdFusion, ASP, JSP, PHP, SQL, XML, and XSLT (and probably a few other three-letter acronyms, too). Lastly, there's also the *UsableNet Accessibility Reference*, a great resource for learning how to make your sites more accessible.

USING THE CODE REFERENCE

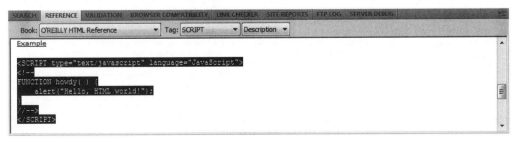

Figure 17.43 Click the code sample once, and it will be selected.

Validating Your Code

To *validate* your code is to make sure that it conforms to the W3C standards for whatever version of HTML or XHTML your page is in. There are a number of reasons for validating, but the most important is that if your page is valid, it's more likely to render better in more browsers—an amazing number of the page display errors we've seen could have been solved by making the site validate before it was uploaded to a live server.

To validate your page:

◆ From Dreamweaver's menu, select File > Validate > Markup (**Figure 17.44**).

or

Press Shift-F6.

or

Click the Validate Markup button on the Document toolbar. A pop-up menu appears; from it, choose Validate Current Document (**Figure 17.45**).

or

Click the green arrow in the top-left corner of the Validation tab of the Results panel. A pop-up menu appears; from it, choose Validate Current Document (**Figure 17.46**).

The validation report appears in the Validation tab of the Results panel (**Figure 17.47**).

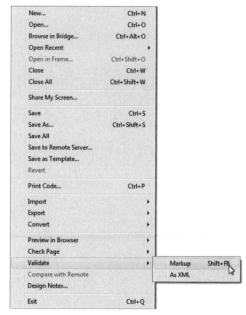

Figure 17.44 This menu lets you validate your pages.

Figure 17.45 This menu lets you validate both pages and sites.

Figure 17.46 The Validate button on the Validation tab can also check your HTML.

VALIDATING YOUR CODE

To use the validation report:

1. After you validate your page (by one of the above methods), the validation report appears in the Validation tab of the Results panel, displaying all of the errors and warning messages your page has generated (Figure 17.47).

   There are four types of messages:

   Errors ❶**:** These are things that you *have* to fix in order for your page to be valid.

   Warnings ⚠**:** These are things you should look at, but they aren't mandatory.

   Nesting errors 📄**:** This is still an error that has to be fixed, but it's a specific type of error: it's displayed when there's a problem with nested tags. If an end tag wasn't found to close an opened tag, or if an <img> tag didn't end with a /> in an XHTML file, a nesting error would be shown.

   Messages 💬**:** These are less serious than warnings, but things that Dreamweaver still thinks you should know about. If your page is error-free, you'll get a message saying so.

continues on next page

Validate

Stop

More Info

Save Report

Browse Report

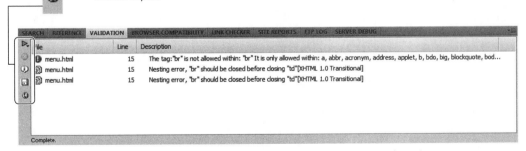

Figure 17.47 Validating this page resulted in a variety of different errors, messages, and warnings.

2. To go to the problem line, double-click the error, and focus shifts to that line in the document. If you were in Design view when you did this, you'll be placed in Split view.

3. To get more information about an error, or just to see it in a reasonably sized font, select the error in the Validation tab and then click the More Info button on the left toolbar of the panel. A Description dialog appears (**Figure 17.48**). Click OK to close the dialog.

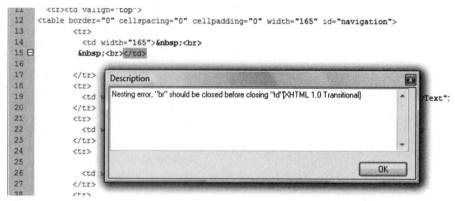

Figure 17.48 Clicking the More Info button gives you the error's Description dialog.

4. If you want to view the full report, click the Browse Report button on the left toolbar. A browser window opens displaying each error, along with its category, description, line number, and file location (**Figure 17.49**).

5. If you want to save the report for later, click the Save Report button on the left toolbar. You'll then see the standard Save As dialog, prompting you to save a new XML file.

✔ Tip

- As shown in Figures 17.45 and 17.46, you can also choose to validate the entire current local site or selected files in the site. If you start this process and then decide to cancel it, click the Stop button on the left toolbar.

Figure 17.49 Viewing the error report launches a browser and displays all the errors, warnings, and messages.

Using an External Editor

No matter how much you love Dreamweaver, there may be times when you want to use a different text editor. There are many possible editors you might use, but the two most common are Macromedia HomeSite+ (on Windows) and BBEdit from Bare Bones (on the Mac).

To use an external editor:

1. In Dreamweaver's Preferences, go to the File Types/Editors category. You'll see a dialog that looks like either **Figure 17.50** (Windows) or **Figure 17.51** (Mac).

2. If you're on a Mac and you want to use BBEdit as your external editor, click the Enable BBEdit Integration button, and you're done. Otherwise (on either platform), click the Browse button next to the External Code Editor text field, navigate to your application of choice, and click Open. Next, decide when you want to reload modified files, and when you want to save on launch. The choices for both are Always, Never, or Prompt.

3. Click OK to accept your changes.

Figure 17.50 With Windows, you can pick any text editor by browsing to it and selecting it.

Figure 17.51 You can do the same on the Mac, but it's easier to just choose BBEdit.

4. To switch to your chosen editor, select Edit > Edit with HomeSite+ from Dreamweaver's menu (Windows) (**Figure 17.52**) or Edit > Edit with BBEdit (Mac) (**Figure 17.53**).

continues on next page

Undo	Ctrl+Z
Redo	Ctrl+Y
Cut	Ctrl+X
Copy	Ctrl+C
Paste	Ctrl+V
Paste Special...	Ctrl+Shift+V
Clear	
Select All	Ctrl+A
Select Parent Tag	Ctrl+[
Select Child	Ctrl+]
Find and Replace...	Ctrl+F
Find Selection	Shift+F3
Find Next	F3
Go to Line	Ctrl+G
Show Code Hints	Ctrl+Space
Refresh Code Hints	Ctrl+.
Code Hint Tools	▶
Indent Code	Ctrl+Shift+>
Outdent Code	Ctrl+Shift+<
Balance Braces	Ctrl+'
Repeating Entries	▶
Code Collapse	▶
Edit with HomeSite+	
Tag Libraries...	
Keyboard Shortcuts...	
Preferences...	Ctrl+U

Figure 17.52 There's a new entry on this menu that lets you edit with your text editor of choice.

Edit	View	Insert	Modify
Undo			⌘Z
Redo			⌘Y
Cut			⌘X
Copy			⌘C
Paste			⌘V
Paste Special...			⇧⌘V
Clear			
Select All			⌘A
Select Parent Tag			⌘[
Select Child			⌘]
Find and Replace...			⌘F
Find Selection			⇧⌘G
Find Again			⌘G
Go to Line			⌘,
Show Code Hints			^_
Refresh Code Hints			^.
Code Hint Tools			▶
Indent Code			⇧⌘>
Outdent Code			⇧⌘<
Balance Braces			⌘'
Repeating Entries			▶
Code Collapse			▶
Edit with BBEdit			
Tag Libraries...			

Figure 17.53 And the Mac menu shows BBEdit now, too.

USING AN EXTERNAL EDITOR

If the application was closed, it will now launch, and the current page will open in the text editor and come to the front (**Figure 17.54**).

5. If you're in your chosen editor, and you want to switch back to Dreamweaver:

   ▲ **In HomeSite:** Click the Dreamweaver icon in the Editing toolbar.

   ▲ **In BBEdit:** Choose Markup > Misc > Dreamweaver.

✔ Tips

■ The best part of using an external editor is being able to open your Dreamweaver window in Design view while you've got the text visible in the external editor. You can then change the file in either application, and the other changes to match. In some ways, this is more powerful than Dreamweaver's Split view, where any time you make a change to the code, you have to manually refresh Design view. Yes, this does mean that you'll need either a very large monitor or multiple monitors, but take our word for it—there's no such thing as too much screen real estate.

■ If you haven't set an external editor, Figures 17.52 and 17.53 instead say Edit with External Editor. Choose that, and Dreamweaver opens the File Type/Editors Preferences, as in step 1.

Figure 17.54 With both applications open on the Mac, you can see both the code and the design.

About Roundtrip HTML and Automatic Code Correction

Dreamweaver features what they refer to as *Roundtrip HTML*, meaning that you can modify your file in Dreamweaver, then in an external editor such as BBEdit, and then in Dreamweaver again without Dreamweaver changing what you've done in the text editor. Except when it does change what you've done—but you can control this.

The Code Rewriting category of the Preferences (**Figure 17.55**) allows you to set what you do and do not want fixed. For instance, it can be handy to have Dreamweaver fix any badly nested or unclosed tags. Or maybe you want it to fix some types of files but not others (depending on their extension). That's all customizable here. We recommend turning on "Warn when fixing or removing tags" so that you're told what's being changed and when.

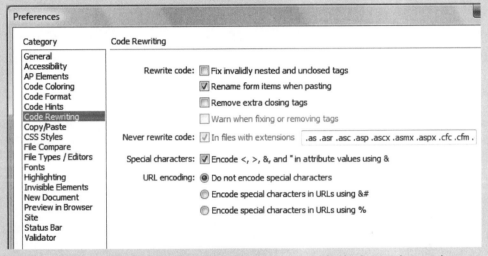

Figure 17.55 Use the Code Rewriting preference to tell Dreamweaver exactly what it can and cannot change.

18

MANAGING YOUR SITE

As you've seen in the rest of this book, building a site means creating dozens, hundreds, or even thousands of files that must work together to present a dynamic, exciting Web site. Keeping track of and managing all these files, a process called *site management*, may not be an exciting job, but it is essential.

The problem of site management gets even more complex when, as is extremely common these days, you are just one member of a team that is responsible for building and maintaining the Web site. Imagine, for example, that you have two or three people who could be responsible for making changes to page content. It would be easy for one person to overwrite the changes already made by a coworker on the same page. That's where Dreamweaver's collaboration features come in. With Check In/Check Out, members of the team are notified when another person is already working on a particular file on the site. New support for the open-source Subversion version control system allows Dreamweaver to be integrated into the largest sites.

In this chapter, you will learn how to manage the files and folders that make up your site; work with Dreamweaver's collaborative tools; and learn different ways to look at and work with your site.

Planning for Site Expansion

When you're designing a site, you take the time to think about the site navigation so that your site visitors have an easy time finding the information they need. But what about *your* needs? When you're building and maintaining a site, it's just as important for you to plan the folder structure so that you can easily and quickly find items you need to work on. Web sites have a disturbing tendency to grow, so when you set up your site, lay out your folder structure logically, and leave room for expansion in your site structure (**Figure 18.1**).

For example, if you have different sections of a site (as represented in the site's navigation), it's a good idea to create a folder for each section (which will contain all of the pages for the section). Then consider creating an images folder inside each section folder. After all, you will probably have images for each section that are used only in that section of the site. A separate images folder in the root of your site can handle images that are used globally throughout the site.

As your site grows, you can add additional folders for new sections from the site root, or you can add folders inside the existing section folders for new subsections.

Expand/Collapse button

Figure 18.1 You should create your site structure with logical sections (shown here as folders) and plan for growth.

✔ Tips

- Make sure that you name your files and folders understandably. While you are creating a site, you may remember what the `med_sec_hed.html` file is used for, but when you come back to the site four months later, you might not have a clue, at least without opening the file and looking at it. Instead, name the file something like `media_home.html`, and it makes it easier for you to pick up where you left off. This also helps make your site easier for other people to maintain.

- Don't forget that there are some characters that you can't use in file and folder names, including space, #, &, @, /, and most other punctuation. Use a hyphen or underscore as substitutes for a space.

- If you create images folders inside section folders, give those images folders descriptive names, too. We like to use the name of the section, followed by an underscore, then images, like so: `recipes_images`.

Expanding the Files Panel

The Files panel does an adequate job of showing you the files and folders in your site, but it has some drawbacks. The biggest of these is that it is cramped for space, especially for larger sites. You also can't see the Local Files and the Remote Files at the same time, making it difficult to compare items that are on your machine and on the server. Dreamweaver allows you to expand the Files panel to solve these problems. You can view the local and remote sites, and easily create, move, and delete files on either copy of the site. Of course, you can still use the Get, Put, Check Out, Check In, and Synchronize buttons at the top of the Files panel.

You can also select multiple files in the following categories:

◆ All files

◆ Checked Out files

◆ Newer Local files

◆ Newer Remote files

◆ Recently Modified files

To expand the Files panel:

1. At the top of the Files panel, click the Expand/Collapse button.

   On Windows, the Dreamweaver window will be replaced by the expanded Files panel (**Figure 18.2**).

   On the Mac, the expanded Files panel will appear in a new window (**Figure 18.3**).

2. Create, delete, rename, or move files and folders as you like. See Chapter 2 for more details.

3. When you're done with the expanded Files panel, click the Expand/Collapse button again to toggle the window back to the normal Files panel.

Figure 18.2 The expanded Files panel allows you to easily see both Remote (left) and Local (right) files. On Windows, the panel completely replaces the Dreamweaver window.

Figure 18.3 On the Mac, the Files panel expands into its own window.

Figure 18.4 On Windows, the Edit menu allows you to highlight specific groups of files.

To select multiple files in the expanded Files panel:

1. At the top of the Files panel, click the Expand/Collapse button.

2. On Windows, from the Edit menu, choose Select All, Select Checked Out Files, Select Newer Local, Select Newer Remote, or Select Recently Modified (**Figure 18.4**).

   or

   On Mac, right-click in the expanded Files panel, and from the Select menu choice in the resulting shortcut menu, choose Select All, Select Checked Out Files, Select Newer Local, Select Newer Remote, or Select Recently Modified.

   The files highlight.

EXPANDING THE FILES PANEL

What Happened to the Site Map?

All previous versions before Dreamweaver CS4 had the Site Map, which was a visual tool that helped you see the links and relationships between the files on your site. The Site Map was a different view in the Files panel, and it allowed you to see the links between the different files in the site in a tree display resembling an organizational chart, descending from the site's index page. Some people preferred the Site Map because it made it easier to visualize the site structure.

In August 2007, Adobe released a list of features that they planned to remove from Dreamweaver, because research revealed they weren't being used by many people. The Site Map was on this list. Some of the features on the list were also dated and didn't conform to current best practices, such as the old Table Layout Mode (modern sites use CSS for layout). Rather than continuing to put resources into maintaining unpopular or obsolete features, Adobe chose to relegate them to the mists of history.

✔ Tips

■ If you want the opposite selection of what is already selected, choose Invert Selection in step 2 above.

■ If you select a file or folder in either the Remote or Local panes and right-click, you can easily find the corresponding file in the other pane by choosing Locate in Remote Site (if your selection is in the Local pane) or Locate in Local Site (if your selection is in the Remote pane) from the shortcut menu.

■ Dreamweaver usually doesn't show the hidden files it places on the Remote Site. For example, when you check a file out, Dreamweaver creates a small file on the server called `filename.LCK`. These LCK files are how Dreamweaver knows that the file is checked out. If you want to see these hidden files, on the expanded Files panel in Windows, choose View > Show Hidden Files. On Mac, there doesn't appear to be a way to do this.

■ It's usually a good idea to do your file management in Dreamweaver, but you can easily show a selected file in Windows Explorer or the Macintosh Finder. Select a file, right-click, and from the shortcut menu choose Explore (Reveal in Finder).

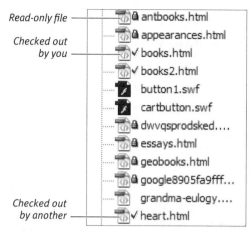

Read-only file

Checked out by you

Checked out by another

Figure 18.5 These files in the Files panel show their checked out status (though you can't tell the difference between the red and green check-marks in this figure).

Setting Up Check In and Check Out

In Chapter 2, you saw how to copy selected files or folders between the local and remote sites in the Files panel using the Get file or Put file buttons. Get and Put work fine when you are the only person working on a site, but you don't want to use them when you are working on a site with other members of a team. In that case, you would like to prevent one person from accidentally undoing or overwriting changes made by another member of the team when the page is transferred back to the remote site.

When you are working with other people on a Web site, you will come to rely on Dreamweaver's ability to keep track of and manage who is working on a file. Known as Check In/Check Out, this feature prevents more than one team member from working on a particular file at a time. The feature also lets all members of the team know who is currently working on what file. Check In/ Check Out replaces the use of Get and Put for sites that have Check In/Check Out enabled. When you want to work on a file, you check it out, and when you are done working on the file and want to send it back to the remote server, you check it in.

Dreamweaver shows the status of files in the Files panel. Files that are checked out to you appear with a green checkmark next to them, and files that are checked out by others appear with a red checkmark next to them. Files that are read-only (because they are files that Dreamweaver can't edit, or because the last time Dreamweaver connected to the remote server and checked their status they were checked out) appear with a padlock icon (**Figure 18.5**).

In order to get the Check In/Check Out system to work properly, there are two cardinal rules all members of the Web team must follow:

- ◆ All members of the team must enable Check In/Check Out and Design Notes in their site definitions.

- ◆ All members of the team must *always* use Dreamweaver or Contribute (and no other tools, such as an FTP program) to transfer files to and from the remote Web server.

✔ Tips

- ■ If Check In/Check Out is enabled for your site and you use the Get File or Put File button in the Files panel, rather than the Check In or Check Out button, Dreamweaver transfers read-only versions of the file to and from the remote server.

- ■ When any team member checks out a file, Dreamweaver places a small text file on the remote site with the name of the checked out file plus the extension .LCK. Dreamweaver uses this file to store the Check Out name and e-mail address of the person who is using the file. When the file is checked back in, Dreamweaver automatically deletes the .LCK file.

To enable Check In/Check Out for your site:

1. Choose Site > Manage Sites.

   The Manage Sites dialog appears (**Figure 18.6**).

2. In the list of sites, click to select the site for which you want to enable Check In/Check Out and click Edit.

   The Site Definition dialog appears, set to the Advanced tab.

Figure 18.6 Begin enabling Check In/Check Out in the Manage Sites dialog.

SETTING UP CHECK IN AND CHECK OUT

Figure 18.7 You enable Check In/Check Out in the Remote Info pane of the Site Definition dialog.

3. In the Category list on the left side of the dialog, click the Remote Info category.

The dialog changes to show the Remote Info pane (**Figure 18.7**).

4. Select the check box next to "Enable file check in and check out."

5. Select the check box next to "Check out files when opening."

6. Enter a check out name.

Because you may be working on a page using different programs or different systems, it's a good idea to use a name that describes the program and/or system you're working on. For example, the check out name `tom-dw-win` indicates "Tom, using Dreamweaver, on Windows." The check out name `tom-ct-mac` would indicate "Tom, using Contribute, on Macintosh."

7. (Optional but recommended) Enter your email address in the Email address text box.

This allows coworkers to easily send you email if they need to communicate with you about the status of a file.

8. Click OK.

The Manage Sites dialog reappears.

9. Click Done.

Checking Files In and Out

When Check In/Check Out is enabled for your site and you use the Check Out button at the top of the Files panel, Dreamweaver checks to see if anyone else is currently working on the file. If someone else has the file checked out, Dreamweaver displays a dialog asking if you want to override that check out (**Figure 18.8**). In general, it's a bad idea to do so, because it could lead to exactly the problems with multiple people working on the file that you want to avoid. On the other hand, if the person who checked out the file is you, just working on another machine, and you know the current state of the file, go ahead and override the lock on the file.

To check out a file for editing:

1. In the Files panel, from the Site pop-up menu, choose the site that contains the file you want to check out (**Figure 18.9**). The site must have Check In/Check Out enabled.

2. Click the Connect to Remote Site button. Dreamweaver connects to the remote site.

3. Choose the file (or files) you want to check out from the Files panel.

Figure 18.8 If someone else has already checked out a file, Dreamweaver lets you know and asks what you want to do.

Figure 18.9 You'll check files in and out with the toolbar in the Files panel.

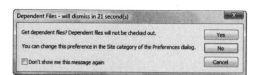

Figure 18.10 You can choose whether or not to download dependent files. If they haven't changed, don't bother.

4. Click the Check Out button in the Files panel toolbar.

   The Dependent Files dialog appears (**Figure 18.10**).

5. If you need to also edit the dependent files, such as images or external style sheets, click Yes. In most cases, however, you will click No.

   Dreamweaver transfers the selected files, and puts green checkmarks next to the files in both the Local Files and the Remote Site views in the Files panel.

6. Make the changes you want to the checked out files.

To check in a file to the remote server:

1. In the Files panel, select the checked out file or files.

2. Click the Check In button in the Files panel toolbar.

   If the files you're checking in have not been saved, Dreamweaver prompts you to save them. After you save the files, Dreamweaver removes the green check-marks from the files in the Files panel.

✔ Tips

- If you make a mistake and check out the wrong file, you can revert to the version of the file on the remote server, even if you modified and saved the checked out version on your machine. Just right-click the checked out file in the Files panel, then choose Undo Check Out from the resulting shortcut menu. Dreamweaver removes your check out lock from the remote server, replaces your local copy with the copy from the server, and that local copy of the file becomes read-only.

- You can have Dreamweaver automatically save unsaved files before checking them in by enabling the "Save files before putting" option in the Site category in Dreamweaver's Preferences.

- If you save and close a file without checking it in, the copy of the file on the remote site will not be updated. You should always check a file in when you are done working with it.

Using Design Notes

Dreamweaver's Design Notes are XML files that Dreamweaver places on the site that can be used by Web team members to annotate changes or note when a file was modified and by whom. A Design Note is associated with a file on your site, but it is a separate XML file with different fields that can be read by the Adobe programs (**Figure 18.11**). Design Note files aren't visible to your site's visitors.

You can create a Design Note yourself, and Dreamweaver and other programs in Creative Suite 4 can also make automated Design Note entries. For example, when you create an image in Fireworks, then export it to Dreamweaver, Fireworks creates (and places in the Dreamweaver site) a Design Note entry for the exported file, which could be in GIF or JPEG format. The entry records the name of the Fireworks source file (remember, the Fireworks file format is PNG) associated with the exported image in your site. That's how Dreamweaver, Fireworks, Photoshop, and other external image editors know how to integrate the source file with the exported site image when you go to edit it (refer to Chapter 5 for more information about editing images in Dreamweaver with external image editors).

Dreamweaver stores Design Notes in folders called _notes in each of the site folders that have files with associated notes. These folders don't appear in the Files panel, but you can see them if you use an FTP program to view your site (**Figure 18.12**). These notes folders contain one Design Note file for each site file that has a note.

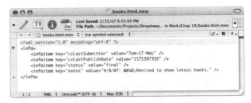

Figure 18.11 Design Notes are XML files that Dreamweaver knows how to read.

Figure 18.12 Design Notes appear in the special _notes folders Dreamweaver creates in your site, seen here using an FTP program.

Figure 18.13 Use the Design Notes dialog to enter your notes.

To add a Design Note:

1. Open the file to which you want to add a Design Note, then choose File > Design Notes.

   or

   In the Files panel's Local View, select the file to which you want to add a Design Note, then right-click and choose Design Notes from the resulting shortcut menu.

   The Design Notes dialog appears, set to the Basic info tab (**Figure 18.13**). This tab shows you the file name and the location of the file at the top of the dialog.

2. (Optional) From the Status pop-up menu, choose the status you want to set for the Design Note.

   The preset statuses are draft, revision1, revision2, revision3, alpha, beta, final, and needs attention.

3. (Optional) if you want to date stamp your note, click the calendar icon in the dialog.

   The current date appears in the Notes field.

4. Type your note about the file.

5. Click OK.

   Dreamweaver saves the Design Note, and the Design Notes dialog disappears.

✔ Tips

- Adobe Contribute also uses Design Notes to make note of when a Contribute user has updated a page. But Contribute doesn't have an interface to make specific notes; it just creates automated notes with the contributor's username and the page's modification date. Contribute Design Notes also keep track of rollbacks, which allow Contribute users to revert to previously published versions of pages.

- You must check out the file associated with a Design Note before you can add or modify the Design Note.

USING DESIGN NOTES

To modify a Design Note:

1. Open the file that contains a Design Note you wish to modify, then choose File > Design Notes.

   or

   In the Files panel, select the file whose Design Note you wish to modify, then right-click and choose Design Notes from the resulting shortcut menu.

   The Design Notes dialog appears.

2. Make changes to the Status pop-up menu, or enter a new note in the Notes field.

   If you click the calendar icon to add a new date stamp, the new note appears at the top of the dialog, and older notes appear below the newest entry, in reverse chronological order.

3. Click OK.

Figure 18.14 Begins setting up Subversion support in the Manage Sites dialog.

Setting Up Subversion

One of the new features of Dreamweaver CS4 is support for Subversion, which is a free, open-source *version control system* (VCS). A VCS is software that runs on the remote server and that manages multiple revisions of the same bit of information. Every time a file changes, a VCS server creates a new version of the file, handles users checking files in and out of the server repository, and flags possible conflicts (when more than one has made changes to the same file). Most VCS servers allow permitted users to get the latest versions of files, check in changed files, and revert files to an unmodified state or to a past version.

A Subversion setup would generally be used on large Web sites, or with Web sites maintained by very technically savvy users. Your site administrator will know whether or not your Web site uses a Subversion version control system.

The Subversion server support in Dreamweaver does not give the Dreamweaver user all of the capabilities of a true Subversion client; instead it's meant to allow users to use the Files panel to check files in and out of a Subversion repository without having to constantly switch from Dreamweaver to a separate Subversion client program.

To enable Subversion version control:

1. Choose Site > Manage Sites.

   The Manage Sites dialog appears (**Figure 18.14**).

2. In the list of sites, click to select the site for which you want to enable Subversion and click Edit.

   The Site Definition dialog appears, set to the Advanced tab.

continues on next page

SETTING UP SUBVERSION

3. In the Category list on the left side of the dialog, click the Version Control category.

   The dialog changes to show the Version Control pane.

4. From the Access pop-up menu, choose Subversion.

   The server settings appear in the pane (**Figure 18.15**).

5. From the Protocol pop-up menu, chose the communications protocol used by your Web site's Subversion server. Check with your site administrator if necessary.

   Your choices are HTTP, HTTPS, SVN, or SVN+SSH.

6. In the Server address field, enter the Subversion server's URL.

7. In the Repository path field, enter the path to the server's database. Again, you can get this from your site administrator.

8. Most of the time, the Default choice in the Server port section will be correct. If not, your site administrator will know the correct port. Click the Non default radio button, then enter the correct port number.

9. Enter your username and password, then click the Test button.

   If all is well, Dreamweaver reports a successful connection to your Subversion server.

10. Click OK.

    The Manage Sites dialog reappears.

11. Click Done.

✔ Tip

■ You cannot use both a Subversion server and Dreamweaver's built-in Check-In/Check-Out system on the same Web site. You must choose one or the other.

Figure 18.15 Enter the information you need to connect to the Subversion server.

Generating Site Reports

A large part of site management, especially if you are managing a team working on the site, is keeping up with all of the things that are happening to the site. For example, let's say that you want to know which pages each of your team members is working on at the moment. Dreamweaver allows you to get a report of the checked out pages and who has checked them out. Similarly, you can get reports on many other aspects of your site, listed in **Table 18.1**. Dreamweaver splits reports into two categories: Workflow, with reports detailing who has worked on the site and when; and HTML Reports, which search through files on your site looking for HTML errors.

Some reports will let you enter parameters for the report that allow you to widen or narrow the criteria used for the report. All the reports, however, allow you to report on just the current document; the entire current local site; just selected files in the site; or files within a selected folder in the site.

Table 18.1

Dreamweaver Reports	
Workflow Category	
REPORT NAME	DESCRIPTION
Checked Out By	Reports file name and the name of the team member who has checked it out.
Design Notes	Shows the contents of the Design Note for files that have them.
Recently Modified	Shows the last modified date for the selected files, based on search criteria you specify.
HTML Reports Category	
REPORT NAME	DESCRIPTION
Combinable Nested	Finds markup with Font Tags
Accessibility	Checks the selected pages for adherence to accessibility guidelines.
Missing ALT Text	Flags missing alternate text attributes for images on your pages.
Redundant Nested Tags	Reports unnecessarily repeated nested tags, i.e., `<b><b> example text</b></b>`.
Removable Empty Tags	Shows any empty tags that can be safely removed.
Untitled Documents	Reveals documents where you have forgotten to enter a title.

To get site reports:

1. Choose Site > Reports.

   The Reports dialog appears (**Figure 18.16**).

2. From the Report on pop-up menu, choose the scope of the report.

   Your choices are Current Document, Entire Current Local Site, Selected Files in Site, or Folder.

3. In the Select reports list, check the report or reports that you want to run.

   If the report you have selected allows you to choose report criteria, the Report Settings button becomes active.

4. (Optional) For reports that allow additional settings, click Report Settings, then complete the resulting settings dialog.

   Each report that allows additional settings has a different criteria dialog. **Figure 18.17** shows, for example, the criteria dialog for the Recently Modified report.

   After you click OK in the settings dialog, you return to the Reports dialog.

5. Click Run.

   Dreamweaver runs the report and shows the report output in the Site Reports tab of the Results panel below the Property Inspector (**Figure 18.18**) and also in an HTML page, which it opens in your default browser.

Figure 18.16 Specify the kind of site report you want in the Reports dialog.

Figure 18.17 The Recently Modified dialog, brought up by the Report Settings button, allows you to specify the scope of the report. Other reports have different Report Settings dialogs.

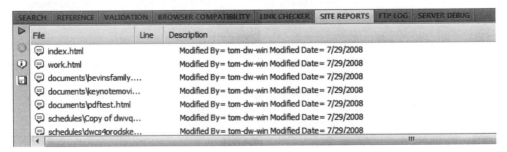

Figure 18.18 The report appears in the Results panel.

GENERATING SITE REPORTS

Figure 18.19 Files with broken links appear in the Results panel.

Figure 18.20 To fix the broken link, double-click one of the report results; the file with the broken link opens with the broken link selected, in this case to a media file.

✔ Tips

■ Dreamweaver only checks for the validity of links to documents within your site. If you have external links on your site (links that point to other sites on the Internet), Dreamweaver does not follow those links and make sure that those sites still exist and are reachable. If you need to validate external links, you need to follow those links manually, in a Web browser.

■ You can also check for broken links on just the page you are editing. Choose File > Check Page > Check Links, or press Shift-F8.

Checking for Broken Links

One of the more vexing problems with Web sites are broken links, that is, links that no longer point to valid destinations within your site. Dreamweaver usually does a pretty good job of updating links when you move or rename a page, but you can still end up with broken links if you cut or copy page content from one page to another on your site. Dreamweaver allows you to check all of the links on your site to make sure they are still valid and reports any broken links it finds. You can then easily open the file that contains the broken link to fix it.

To check for and fix broken links throughout your site:

1. Choose Site > Check Links Sitewide, or press Ctrl-F8 (Cmd-F8).

   Dreamweaver checks all the pages on your site and shows you files with broken links in the Link Checker tab of the Results panel (**Figure 18.19**).

2. Double-click one of the results.

   The file with the broken link opens, with the broken link highlighted (**Figure 18.20**).

3. Using the Property Inspector, fix the broken link.

   For more information about using the Property Inspector to work with links, see Chapter 6.

4. Repeat steps 2 and 3 until you have eliminated all of the broken links.

Finding External Links and Orphaned Files

You can get two other types of reports from Dreamweaver. The first is a list of links from your site to other sites, called *external links*, and the other is a report of *orphaned files*, which are files that have no links pointing to them. In the first case, after Dreamweaver finds the external links, you can (if needed) easily change them. In the case of orphaned files, you should create links to the files from your other Dreamweaver pages.

To find external links and orphaned files:

1. Choose Site > Check Links Sitewide, or press Ctrl-F8 (Cmd-F8).

   Dreamweaver checks all the pages on your site and shows you files with broken links in the Link Checker tab of the Results panel.

2. From the Show pop-up menu in the Results panel, choose External Links (**Figure 18.21**).

   or

   From the Show pop-up menu in the Results panel, choose Orphaned Files.

   Depending on your choice, the results appear in the Results panel.

3. (Optional) If you chose External Links in step 2, the Results panel shows a list of files and the external links that appear on them. Click one of the links to highlight it and make it editable. You can then enter a new destination for the link (**Figure 18.22**).

   or

   (Optional) If you chose Orphaned Files in step 2, the Results panel shows a list of files with no links pointing to them. Double-click a file name to open that file, or open other files in the Files panel to create links to the orphaned file.

Figure 18.21 Choose either External Links or Orphaned Files to obtain a report on those items.

Figure 18.22 You can change external links right in the Results panel.

Figure 18.23 Use the Check Page pop-up menu to make sure your pages appear correctly in different browsers.

Figure 18.24 Choose the target browsers for your compatibility check.

Checking Browser Compatibility

In terms of the HTML document type, Dreamweaver creates XHTML 1.0 Transitional files by default, as discussed in Chapter 3. These files are readable and valid for all commonly used modern Web browsers. So you could consider Dreamweaver's ability to check files for HTML browser support to be somewhat vestigial. But you may find you need to work on older pages that haven't been retrofitted for current browsers. Dreamweaver allows you to check your pages for errors with targeted browsers. It does this by keeping a database of browser profiles, which details how different browsers render pages. You can also check your pages for accessibility, to make sure that they comply with best practices for readability by screen readers used by people with visual disabilities. You can check the open page for browser and accessibility compatibility. Errors appear in the Results panel.

A similar feature, Check Browser Support, appeared in Dreamweaver 8, but the version found in Dreamweaver CS3 and CS4 is much more complete because it checks the CSS for possible rendering bugs, not just the HTML. For each bug that it finds, Dreamweaver provides an estimate of the bug's severity, and a link to a discussion about the bug on Adobe CSS Advisor, a Web site that offers solutions for fixing CSS bugs. See Chapter 9 for more about the CSS Advisor site.

To define browsers for checking:

1. Open any file in your site.

2. From the Check Page pop-up menu at the top of the document window, choose Settings (**Figure 18.23**).

   The Target Browsers dialog appears (**Figure 18.24**).

continues on next page

3. To enable a particular browser, select the check box next to its name. Choose from the pop-up menu next to the name to select the minimum version of that browser you want to check against.

4. Click OK to dismiss the Target Browsers dialog.

To check for browser compatibility:

1. From the Check Page pop-up menu at the top of the document window, choose Check Browser Compatibility.

If there are no errors found, a status line appears in the Results pane stating "No issues detected." Pop a cold one and relax.

2. If errors are found, a list appears in the Results panel (**Figure 18.25**).

There are three kinds of possible errors reported in the Results panel: *errors, warnings,* and *informational messages.* An error indicates a problem in the code that can cause serious visual problems with the page. A warning indicates that the page won't be displayed exactly correctly in the targeted browser, but the problem isn't serious. An informational message is used for code that isn't supported in a particular browser, but has no visual effect.

3. Double-click an error in the Results panel to change the document window to Split view, highlighting the error in Code and Design views.

4. Fix the error in Code view.

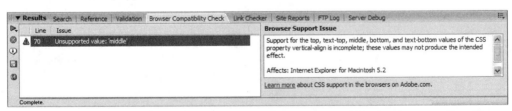

Figure 18.25 Errors in your document appear in the Results panel, along with names of the browsers affected by the errors.

To run an accessibility check:

1. From the Check Page pop-up menu at the top of the document window, choose Check Accessibility.

   Errors, if any, appear in the Results panel (**Figure 18.26**).

2. Double-click an error in the Results panel to change the document window to Split view, highlighting the error in Code and Design views.

3. Fix the error in Code view.

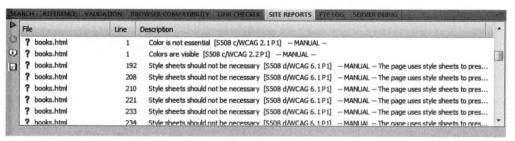

Figure 18.26 Accessibility problems are highlighted in the Results panel.

Deleting Sites

When you will no longer be working with a site (perhaps because the project has been taken over by another developer), you can delete its site definition. This removes the site from the Manage Sites dialog, and from the Site pop-up menu in the Files panel. Of course, all the settings for the site are also deleted. You should be careful when you delete site definitions, because there's no way to undo the action.

To delete a site from Dreamweaver:

1. Choose Site > Manage Sites.

   The Manage Sites dialog appears (**Figure 18.27**).

2. From the list of sites, click the site that you want to delete.

3. Click Remove.

   Dreamweaver alerts you that you cannot undo this operation (**Figure 18.28**).

4. Click Yes.

   Dreamweaver deletes the selected site.

✔ Tip

■ While Dreamweaver is asking if you want to delete the site, the site itself (that is, the files in the local site folder on your hard drive) aren't touched. The only thing that's deleted are the site definitions: what Dreamweaver itself knows about your site. And of course, nothing is changed on the remote site.

Figure 18.27 Begin deleting a site in the Manage Sites dialog.

Figure 18.28 When you try to delete a site, Dreamweaver needs you to confirm your action.

Exporting and Importing Site Definitions

When you create a local site on your machine, Dreamweaver creates a local site definitions file with all the information about the site's settings, including information about the server connection, your server password, and any site-specific preferences you may have set in the Site Definition dialog. If you need to move the site from one machine to another, or if you want to add members of your Web team and have them share the same site preferences, you must export the site definition. When you do that, Dreamweaver saves the site definition information as an XML file, with the .ste file extension.

Dreamweaver allows you to export the site definition in one of two ways. You can export it with your server username and password information (this facilitates you moving the site to a different machine), or you can export the site with the site preferences, but without your server login information (this is good for adding coworkers to the site).

You can, of course, also import a site definition file that you had previously exported or one you received from a colleague.

continues on next page

To export a site definition:

1. Choose Site > Manage Sites.

   The Manage Sites dialog appears.

2. From the list of sites, click the site you want to export.

3. Click Export.

   The Exporting site dialog appears (**Figure 18.29**).

4. Click "Back up my settings (includes login, password, and local paths)" if you plan to move the site to another machine.

   or

   Click "Share settings with other users (does not include login, password, or local paths)" if you want to create a site definition file that does not include your server login information.

5. Click OK.

   The Export Site dialog appears.

6. Navigate to where you want to save the site definition file, make sure that the name Dreamweaver has given the file is okay (by default it gives the file the name of your site and appends the .ste file extension), then click Save.

   Dreamweaver saves the site definition file onto your hard disk.

   You'll return to the Manage Sites dialog.

7. Click Done.

Figure 18.29 Choose whether or not you want to include your login information in the exported site definition file.

EXPORTING AND IMPORTING SITE DEFINITIONS

To import a site definition:

1. Choose Site > Manage Sites.
   The Manage Sites dialog appears.

2. Click Import.
   The Import Site dialog appears.

3. Navigate to and select the site definition file you want to import.

4. Click Open.
   Dreamweaver imports the site definition and adds it to the list of sites in the Manage Sites dialog.

5. Click Done to dismiss the Manage Sites dialog.

✔ Tips

- You can use the ability to export the site definition file as a way to back up your site's settings, but this is no substitute for a regular and comprehensive backup strategy covering all of the important documents on your hard drive.

- If you happen to work on multiple computers and multiple sites, and each of the computers has a copy of Dreamweaver, you can export your site definitions for all of your sites, then copy them to a USB flash drive. You could then plug in the flash drive on whichever computer you happen to be working on, and you will have your site settings, including your server passwords. Of course, you would need to resynchronize the remote site with a newly created copy that would then become the local site folder on the machine you are working on. See Chapter 2 for more information about synchronizing sites.

WHERE TO LEARN MORE

Once you've worked through this book, you should be well on your way to creating great Web pages with Dreamweaver. But Dreamweaver is such a broad and deep program that there is plenty more to learn about it and about building Web sites in general.

In this appendix, we'll point to several of the most helpful Dreamweaver-oriented Web sites, other sites where you can learn more about building standards-compliant Web sites, and even mention a few other books that will help you deepen your knowledge of not just Dreamweaver, but also of Web design and JavaScript.

As usual with products that can be found on the Internet, Web sites come, go, and change addresses with alarming regularity. The sites listed here were in existence when this book went to press (September 2008) and may be available when you check them out, or they may not. We are just reporting the URLs; we have no control over them. If you find a link that has become stale, we would appreciate it if you would drop a note to dwcs4@dreamweaverbook.com so that we can update the next edition of the book.

Find It Online!

You'll find an updated list of the sites and books in this appendix at this book's companion Web site, located at www.dreamweaverbook.com. We'll keep the Web site current with a list of Dreamweaver-oriented sites, and if eagle-eyed readers spot any errors in the book, we'll note them on the site, too.

Web Sites

Almost as soon as Dreamweaver came upon the scene, people began gathering online to discuss the program and help each other use it. There are several Dreamweaver community sites, informational sites, places where you can purchase premade Dreamweaver templates, and sites from developers who have created new Dreamweaver extensions. This list is by no means comprehensive, but it does include sites that we have found to be helpful.

Of course, Adobe has a variety of online support options as well.

Dreamweaver Documentation

http://www.adobe.com/support/
documentation/en/dreamweaver/

This should be your first stop when looking for answers to a Dreamweaver question (after this book, of course!). This site allows you to search Dreamweaver's LiveDocs (online manual) and the Product Support Knowledge Base (**Figure A.1**). The figure shows the CS3 site, as it had not yet been updated for CS4 when this book went to press.

Dreamweaver Exchange

http://www.adobe.com/exchange

This is the place to go when you're looking for Dreamweaver add-ons and extensions. At press time, there were more than a thousand items for download (**Figure A.2**).

Figure A.1 You can find the latest version of the Dreamweaver manuals, and search the Knowledge Base, at the Adobe Dreamweaver Documentation site.

Figure A.2 Dreamweaver Exchange should be your first stop when you are looking for a Dreamweaver extension.

Figure A.3 Adobe's weblog aggregator brings together interesting blog posts about Dreamweaver from all over the Web.

Figure A.4 Project Seven makes a variety of great Dreamweaver extensions, including ways to make customizable pop-up menus and automatic slide shows.

Dreamweaver Weblogs

`http://feeds.adobe.com`

Once you go to the URL above, click the link for the Dreamweaver category. This is an aggregator site that lists posts from many people's Dreamweaver-related weblogs (**Figure A.3**). It's a great way to keep up with the Dreamweaver community.

Dreamweaver Developer Center

`http://www.adobe.com/devnet/dreamweaver`

This site has tutorials and sample files focused on the new features of Dreamweaver CS4, and articles that will help you better use Dreamweaver to build your sites.

Project Seven

`http://www.projectseven.com`

Project Seven is one of the premier developers of Dreamweaver extensions and page templates (**Figure A.4**). Their Pop Menu Magic extension helps you build extensive pop-up navigation menus for your site with almost no effort. And their Page Packs are collections of great-looking page layouts with an interface that lets you easily add those pages to your site.

Besides the paid products, the Project Seven site also contains many tutorials covering CSS, images, navigation, and more.

WEB SITES

Community MX

http://www.communitymx.com

Tons of constantly updated content, page templates, tutorials, and extensions are available on a subscription basis at Community MX (**Figure A.5**), which not only covers Dreamweaver, but other Adobe products. Subscribers get the content at no extra charge; non-subscribers can purchase items à la carte; everyone can sign up for a free trial. The site also has support forums for subscribers, where the site partners guarantee a timely, useful response.

A List Apart

http://alistapart.com

A List Apart is not Dreamweaver-specific, but it's essential reading nonetheless. This Web magazine has been around since 1998, and it's still an invaluable resource for people who make Web sites (**Figure A.6**). You'll find great, well-written articles on virtually all aspects of building sites. Now, go check it out.

Figure A.5 Community MX provides a large number of articles and tutorials for its subscribers.

Figure A.6 If you're serious about staying on the bleeding edge of Web development and running a Web-based business, you should be reading the Web magazine A List Apart.

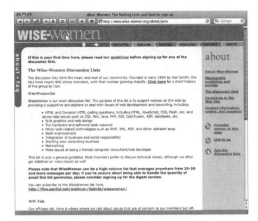

Figure A.7 The Wise-Women online community offers support and help for women and men alike.

Other Online Resources

You can find interesting and useful help with Dreamweaver and more about building Web sites if you look beyond just Web sites.

Dreamweaver Newsgroup

```
http://groups.google.com/group/
macromedia.dreamweaver
```

Adobe (under the old Macromedia name) has a lively newsgroup for Dreamweaver users that gets many messages every day. You can use a Web browser to view the newsgroup, but you'll get a better experience with a Usenet newsreader program. Good ones are Microsoft Outlook or Outlook Express on Windows, or Microsoft Entourage or Panic Software's Unison on the Mac. If you prefer to use a newsreader program, you can access the newsgroup with this URL:

```
news://forums.macromedia.com/
macromedia.dreamweaver
```

Wise-Women Mailing List

```
http://www.wise-women.org
```

Wise-Women is an online community with a Web site and an email discussion list (**Figure A.7**). The purpose of the list is to provide women on the Web with a supportive atmosphere to deal with issues of Web development, design and consulting. Wise-Women was founded in 1999 by one of the authors of this book (Dori) and is going strong today. You'll find lots of useful information on the mailing list about using Dreamweaver, among many other subjects. And in case you're wondering, the community is not just for women only.

OTHER ONLINE RESOURCES

Lynda.com
Online Training Library

`http://www.lynda.com`

If you're more of a visual learner, Lynda.com offers an excellent series of video training programs that cover Dreamweaver and the rest of the Adobe product line, as well as many other software packages (**Figure A.8**). You can purchase these training programs as CD-ROMs that you can view on your computer, or you can access the videos over the Internet through their Online Training Library, for which you'll need to purchase a subscription. Tom produced *Contribute 3 Essential Training* and *Quicken 2009 for Windows Essential Training* for Lynda.com, and Dori produced *JavaScript Essential Training* and *Ajax Essential Training*.

Figure A.8 The Lynda.com Online Training Library offers many hours of video training on Dreamweaver.

Other Dreamweaver Books

Though the authors would naturally like to think that the book you've got in your hands is all you'll ever need to become a Dreamweaver expert, we recognize that you might just want a bit more information after you've completely devoured this book. There are approximately a million different Dreamweaver books on the market; here are some of the books we think are the best.

Adobe Dreamweaver CS3 with ASP, ColdFusion, and PHP: Training from the Source

Written by Jeffrey Bardzell and Bob Flynn and published by Adobe Press, this book covers many of the aspects of Dreamweaver that aren't covered in the book you have in your hands. You'll find information on working with servers, setting up database connections, using SQL, and building database-backed Web sites with dynamic pages. It's not being updated for Dreamweaver CS4, but little has changed in this area, so the book should still be useful.

Dreamweaver CS4 Bible

Joseph Lowery is well known in the Dreamweaver community, and this massive reference, published by Wiley, shows why. At a whopping 1,100 pages, we think this is perhaps the best comprehensive Dreamweaver reference book available.

Mastering CSS with Dreamweaver

Our book has three chapters on CSS, and we've still only barely scratched the surface of the topic. The authors of this book from New Riders, Stephanie Sullivan and Greg Rewis, are two of the best-qualified people to get you to the next level.

Web Design and JavaScript Books

After our last edition of this book, we got email from readers asking for our suggestions for books about JavaScript and Web design. There are too many books to count about these subjects, so here are some of our favorites.

JavaScript & Ajax for the Web, Seventh Edition: Visual QuickStart Guide

Written by Tom Negrino and Dori Smith (hey, that's us!), this best-selling JavaScript book is a great introduction to the JavaScript language. When you want to find out more about using JavaScript than you can achieve by using Dreamweaver's behaviors and Spry widgets, our book is a good start.

Stylin' with CSS: A Designer's Guide, Second Edition

This book by Charles Wyke-Smith, published by New Riders, teaches you how to use CSS to style text and create page layouts, as well as create user interface components. It makes good use of case studies to tell you not just how things are done, but why you should do them that way, all delivered in an easy-to-understand style.

Designing with Web Standards, Second Edition

Jeffrey Zeldman was one of the earliest and strongest voices evangelizing Web standards, and this book for designers explains the gospel to designers in familiar terms that they understand. This book is best for readers who are already familiar with using CSS to build Web sites. It's another book from New Riders.

Transcending CSS: The Fine Art of Web Design

This is another beyond-the-basics book, written by Andy Clarke and Molly E. Holzschlag. Both authors have been involved with Web standards for many years (they and Zeldman have been long-time participants in the Web Standards Project, www.webstandards.org), and they bring that cross-platform, cross-browser sensibility to the problem of designing Web sites. This is a book for designers who want to learn how to use CSS to create beautiful sites with exceptional design.

CUSTOMIZING AND EXTENDING DREAMWEAVER

One of the best things about Dreamweaver is that it is both customizable and incredibly extensible. What's the difference? *Customizable* means that you can change the keyboard shortcuts to suit your style of working, and of course you can customize using Dreamweaver's Preferences. That's fine, but *extensibility*, the ability to add new features to the program, is where the real action is.

As you've seen in the rest of this book, Dreamweaver can do an awful lot. But just because Dreamweaver is amazingly capable doesn't mean that it does absolutely everything that people want it to do. Adobe allows software developers to write add-ons, called extensions, that add new features to Dreamweaver. These new features can range from the mundane (adding new Flash button styles) to the amazing (creating full site generators with associated page templates and navigation bars).

In this appendix, we'll show you how to customize Dreamweaver's keyboard shortcuts and how to find, acquire, and install Dreamweaver extensions.

Customizing Keyboard Shortcuts

Sometimes the keyboard shortcuts that come with Dreamweaver aren't quite what you want. For example, some shortcut keys used for editing code with BBEdit (on Mac) or HomeSite (on Windows) aren't the same as the shortcuts used for the equivalent commands in Dreamweaver CS4. No problem; you can change Dreamweaver shortcuts to match those in your favorite code editor. In fact, Dreamweaver comes with shortcut key sets for those two code editors, which makes it a snap to change shortcut keys and increase your productivity.

Of course, you can also change any keyboard shortcut, add shortcuts to menu items that may not already have them, or delete shortcut keys you don't like. You can also print out a cheat sheet of keyboard commands to help you learn them.

To change between shortcut key sets:

1. Choose Edit > Keyboard Shortcuts (Dreamweaver > Keyboard Shortcuts).

The Keyboard Shortcuts dialog appears (**Figure B.1**).

Figure B.1 Begin customizing your Dreamweaver experience in the Keyboard Shortcuts dialog.

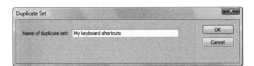

Figure B.2 Enter the name of your new keyboard shortcuts set.

2. Choose the keyboard shortcuts that you want from the Current set pop-up menu.

   Your choices are: Dreamweaver Standard, which includes the standard shortcut keys for Creative Suite 4; Dreamweaver MX 2004, a slightly different set found in a previous version of Dreamweaver; BBEdit, which modifies the code editing keyboard shortcuts to match those used by the popular Macintosh code editor; and HomeSite, which modifies the code editing keyboard shortcuts to match the popular (yet discontinued) Windows code editor.

3. Click OK.

   Dreamweaver changes its keyboard shortcuts to match the set that you chose.

To create a personalized set of keyboard shortcuts:

1. Choose Edit > Keyboard Shortcuts (Dreamweaver > Keyboard Shortcuts).

   The Keyboard Shortcuts dialog appears (Figure B.1).

2. From the Current set pop-up menu, choose the keyboard shortcuts set that you want to use as the basis for your personalized set.

   Dreamweaver won't let you change any of the included sets, so you must duplicate one of them, then modify the duplicate.

3. Click the Duplicate set button.

   The Duplicate Set dialog appears (**Figure B.2**).

4. Type the name for your duplicate set.

5. Click OK.

   Dreamweaver creates the duplicate set and makes it the active set. You can then personalize it, as shown next.

To add or change a keyboard shortcut:

1. In the Keyboard Shortcuts dialog, choose the kind of command you want to modify from the Commands pop-up menu (**Figure B.3**).

   This pop-up menu differs on Windows and Mac, with more choices (and more functionality) on Windows. Besides Menu commands, Code editing, Document editing, and Snippets keyboard shortcuts, Dreamweaver for Windows also allows you to set keyboard shortcuts for the Files panel options menu, the Site panel, and the Site window.

   Depending on what you chose, the Commands list changes.

2. In the Commands list, navigate to the command that you want to change. Click the + icon next to the name of the menu to expand the choices for that menu.

   The menu choices are shown with any existing shortcut keys (**Figure B.4**).

3. Click on the command that you want to change.

   The shortcuts assigned to the command appear in the Shortcuts text box (**Figure B.5**).

4. To add a shortcut, click the Add shortcut button (marked with a plus sign).

   A new blank line appears in the Shortcuts text box.

   or

   To change an existing shortcut, select it in the Shortcuts text box.

5. Click in the Press key text box.

Figure B.3 You can customize keyboard shortcuts for more items on Windows (top) than on Mac (bottom).

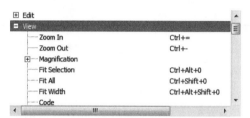

Figure B.4 Click the + buttons to display menu choices in an indented tree form.

Figure B.5 Select the shortcut key that you want to change.

Figure B.6 You can print your keyboard command cheat sheet from a Web browser.

6. Press the key combination you want to use for the shortcut key.

If the key combination is already in use, Dreamweaver lets you know with a message at the bottom of the Keyboard Shortcuts dialog.

7. Click Change.

The new shortcut appears in the Shortcuts text box.

8. Click OK to save your changes and dismiss the Keyboard Shortcuts dialog.

To export a keyboard command cheat sheet:

1. Choose Edit > Keyboard Shortcuts (Dreamweaver > Keyboard Shortcuts).

The Keyboard Shortcuts dialog appears (Figure B.1).

2. Click the Export set as HTML button.

The Save as HTML file dialog appears.

3. In the Save as text box, give the exported file a name, then navigate to where you want to save the HTML file.

4. Click Save.

Dreamweaver saves the list of keyboard commands to your hard disk as an HTML file. You can then open it in Dreamweaver or any Web browser (**Figure B.6**).

Finding and Installing Extensions

You add extensions to Dreamweaver using Adobe Extension Manager, a program that was installed when you installed Dreamweaver on your system. After you install an extension, it appears as part of Dreamweaver. Where it appears within the program depends on what kind of extension it is. For example, if you have installed an extension that allows you to easily add Google search boxes or maps, that extension would appear in the Insert menu. An extension that provides new ways to add pop-up menus may appear in the Commands menu. And extensions that add new scripting behaviors will appear in the Behaviors panel. Because Dreamweaver is almost infinitely extensible, the extensions you add can appear almost anywhere within the program.

You can find extensions in a variety of ways. Some extensions are free for downloading and others are paid products. Many extension developers have Web sites where they host (and sometimes sell) their extensions. A Google search for "Dreamweaver extensions" will result in a large number of useful results.

But the most common way to find Dreamweaver extensions (and also extensions for other Adobe products, such as Photoshop, Fireworks, Flash, etc.) is to use the Adobe Exchange site, at www.adobe.com/exchange/. The Dreamweaver Exchange portion of the site has lists and short descriptions of more than a thousand extensions.

Figure B.7 The Dreamweaver Exchange site lists more than a thousand extensions.

In Dreamweaver, it's easy to go to the Dreamweaver Exchange site. Just choose Help > Dreamweaver Exchange, and your default Web browser opens to the site (**Figure B.7**). From the Exchange site, or from an extension developer's site, download the extension file to your hard disk. Then you're ready to use Adobe Extension Manager to install the extension.

To install an extension:

1. If it's running, quit Dreamweaver by choosing File > Quit (Dreamweaver > Quit).

2. Launch Adobe Extension Manager by double-clicking its icon.

   On Windows, launch the program from the Start menu. On Mac, you'll find it in `/Applications/Adobe Extension Manager CS4/`.

   The Adobe Extension Manager window appears (**Figure B.8**).

continues on next page

Products list   Install extension   Go to Adobe Exchange

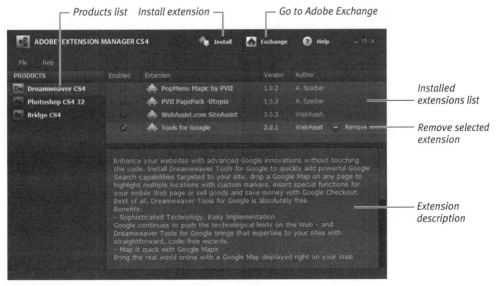

Installed extensions list

Remove selected extension

Extension description

Figure B.8 Use the Adobe Extension Manager program to install or remove extensions.

3. From the Products column on the left side of the window, choose Dreamweaver CS4.

Any extensions you have installed for Dreamweaver CS4 appear in the Installed extensions list.

4. Click the Install button.

The Select Extension to Install dialog appears (**Figure B.9**).

5. Navigate to and select the extension file you wish to install.

6. Click Open (Select).

A license dialog appears.

7. Click Accept.

The Extension Manager installs the extension and reports success with an alert dialog.

8. Click OK to dismiss the alert dialog.

The new extension appears in the Installed extensions list.

9. Choose File > Exit (Extension Manager > Quit Extension Manager).

10. Launch Dreamweaver to use the new extension (**Figure B.10**).

✔ Tips

- If you have more than one version of Dreamweaver installed (perhaps you didn't want to remove an older copy immediately when you upgraded to Dreamweaver CS3), you can have different sets of extensions installed for each version.

- Because each extension works differently, you need to refer to the instructions that came with the extension to discover how to access the extension from within Dreamweaver.

Figure B.9 Find and select the extension file that you want to install.

Figure B.10 Extensions can provide a complete user interface, as in this example, Tools for Google, which helps you easily create a Google search box on your site.

CASCADING STYLE SHEETS REFERENCE

This appendix lists the CSS 2.1 properties as defined by the W3C at http://www.w3.org/TR/CSS21.

The CSS 2.0 specification was standardized all the way back in May 1998, but as of this writing, some properties aren't implemented in any browser. The next version, CSS 2.1, was at the Candidate Recommendation stage at the time this was written. The goal of the CSS 2.1 specification is to clarify CSS2 so that it is closer to what browser makers have actually implemented. Dreamweaver CS4 properties mostly match those in CSS 2.1; those properties not in Dreamweaver are shown in italics.

This list is complete except for the aural properties (those used for speech synthesis for the visually disabled). Dreamweaver does not support aural style sheets.

If you want to learn more, we recommend *Cascading Style Sheets: The Definitive Guide, Third Edition,* by Eric A. Meyer. The book lives up to its name, with exhaustive descriptions of CSS through version CSS 2.1.

Table C.1

Basic Concepts

PROPERTY NAME	VALUE
In HTML	link
	<style>...</style>
	<x style="declaration; ">
Grouping	x, y, z {declaration;}
Contextual selectors	x y z {declaration;}
Class selector	.class
ID selector	#id
At-rules	@import
	@media
	@page
Important	!important

Table C.2

Pseudo-Elements and Pseudo-Classes

PROPERTY NAME	VALUE
after	:after
anchor	a:active
	a:focus
	a:hover
	a:link
	a:visited
before	:before
first	:first
first-child	:first-child
left	:left
paragraph	p:first-letter
	p:first-line
right	:right

Table C.3

Color and Background Properties

PROPERTY NAME	VALUE
background	<background-color>
	<background-image>
	<background-repeat>
	<background-attachment>
	<background-position>
background-attachment	scroll
	fixed
background-color	<color>
	transparent
background-image	<url>
	none
background-position	<percentage>
	<length>
	top
	center
	bottom
	left
	right
background-repeat	repeat
	repeat-x
	repeat-y
	no-repeat
color	<color>

Table C.4

Font Properties

PROPERTY NAME	VALUE
font	<font-style>
	<font-variant>
	<font-weight>
	<font-size> / <line-height>
	<font-family>
	caption
	icon
	menu
	message-box
	small-caption
	status-bar
font-family	<family-name>
	cursive
	fantasy
	monospace
	sans-serif
	serif
font-size	<absolute-size> (xx-small–xx-large)
	<relative-size> (smaller–larger)
	<length>
	<percentage>
font-style	normal
	italic
	oblique
font-variant	normal
	small-caps
font-weight	normal
	bold
	bolder
	lighter
	100 – 900

Table C.5

Generated Content Properties

PROPERTY NAME	VALUE
content	<string>
	<url>
	<identifier>
	<counter>
	open-quote
	close-quote
	no-open-quote
	no-close-quote
	none
	normal
counter-increment	<identifier>
	<integer>
	none
counter-reset	<identifier>
	<integer>
	none
quotes	<string>
	none

Table C.6

Text Properties

Property Name	Value
letter-spacing	normal
	<length>
text-align	left
	right
	center
	justify
text-decoration	none
	underline
	overline
	line-through
	blink
text-indent	<length>
	<percentage>
text-transform	capitalize
	uppercase
	lowercase
	none
white-space	normal
	pre
	nowrap
	pre-wrap
	pre-line
word-spacing	normal
	<length>

Table C.7

Box Properties

Property Name	Value
border	<border-width>
	<border-style>
	<border-color>
border-bottom	<border-width>
	<border-style>
	<border-color>
border-bottom-color	<border-color>
border-bottom-style	<border-style>
border-bottom-width	<border-width>
border-collapse	collapse
	separate
border-color	<color>
	transparent
border-left	<border-top-width>
	<border-style>
	<border-color>
border-left-color	<border-color>
border-left-style	<border-style>
border-left-width	<border-width>
border-right	<border-top-width>
	<border-style>
	<border-color>
border-right-color	<border-color>
border-right-style	<border-style>
border-right-width	<border-width>
border-spacing	<length>
border-style	none
	hidden
	dotted
	dashed
	solid
	double
	groove
	ridge
	inset
	outset
border-top	<border-top-width>
	<border-style>
	<border-color>

Table C.7 *continued*

Box Properties

PROPERTY NAME	VALUE
border-top-color	\<border-color\>
border-top-style	\<border-style\>
border-top-width	\<border-width\>
border-width	thin
	medium
	thick
	\<length\>
margin	\<margin-width\>
margin-bottom	\<margin-width\>
margin-left	\<margin-width\>
margin-right	\<margin-width\>
margin-top	\<margin-width\>
padding	\<padding-width\>
padding-bottom	\<padding-width\>
padding-left	\<padding-width\>
padding-right	\<padding-width\>
padding-top	\<padding-width\>

Table C.8

Visual Formatting Properties

PROPERTY NAME	VALUE
display	block
	inline
	inline-block
	list-item
	run-in
	table
	inline-table
	table-row-group
	table-header-group
	table-footer-group
	table-row
	table-column-group
	table-column
	table-cell
	table-caption
	none

Table C.8 *continued*

Visual Formatting Properties

PROPERTY NAME	VALUE
left	auto
	\<length\>
	\<percentage\>
right	auto
	\<length\>
	\<percentage\>
top	auto
	\<length\>
	\<percentage\>
bottom	auto
	\<length\>
	\<percentage\>
float	left
	right
	none
clear	none
	left
	right
	both
direction	ltr
	rtl
unicode-bidi	normal
	embed
	bidi-override
width	\<length\>
	\<percentage\>
	auto
min-width	\<length\>
	\<percentage\>
max-width	\<length\>
	\<percentage\>
	none
height	\<length\>
	\<percentage\>
	auto
min-height	\<length\>
	\<percentage\>
max-height	\<length\>
	\<percentage\>
	none

continues on next page

CASCADING STYLE SHEETS REFERENCE

Table C.8 *continued*

Visual Formatting Properties

PROPERTY NAME	VALUE
line-height	normal
	<number>
	<length>
	<percentage>
vertical-align	baseline
	sub
	super
	top
	text-top
	middle
	bottom
	text-bottom
	<percentage>
	<length>
position	static
	absolute
	relative
	fixed
z-index	auto
	<integer>

Table C.9

Visual Effects Properties

PROPERTY NAME	VALUE
overflow	visible
	hidden
	scroll
	auto
clip	auto
	<shape>
visibility	collapse
	visible
	hidden

Table C.10

List Properties

PROPERTY NAME	VALUE
list-style	<list-style-type>
	<list-style-position>
	<list-style-image>
list-style-image	<url>
	none
list-style-position	inside
	outside
list-style-type	disc
	circle
	square
	decimal
	decimal-leading-zero
	lower-roman
	upper-roman
	lower-greek
	lower-alpha
	lower-latin
	upper-alpha
	upper-latin
	armenian
	georgian
	none

CASCADING STYLE SHEETS REFERENCE

Table C.11

Table Properties

PROPERTY NAME	VALUE
caption-side	top
	bottom
table-layout	auto
	fixed
border-collapse	collapse
	separate
border-spacing	<length>
empty-cells	show
	hide
border-style	none
	hidden
	dotted
	dashed
	solid
	double
	groove
	ridge
	inset
	outset

Table C.12

Page Properties

PROPERTY NAME	VALUE
orphans	<integer>
page-break-after	auto
	always
	avoid
	left
	right
page-break-before	auto
	always
	avoid
	left
	right
page-break-inside	avoid
	auto
widows	<integer>

Table C.13

User Interface Properties

PROPERTY NAME	VALUE
cursor	<url>
	auto
	crosshair
	default
	pointer
	move
	e-resize
	ne-resize
	nw-resize
	n-resize
	se-resize
	sw-resize
	s-resize
	w-resize
	text
	wait
	help
	progress
outline	<outline-color>
	<outline-style>
	<outline-width>
outline-color	<color>
	invert
outline-style	<border-style>
outline-width	<border-width>

Table C.14

Units	
PROPERTY NAME	VALUE
Length Units	em
	ex
	px
	in
	cm
	mm
	pt
	pc
Color Units	#000
	#000000
	(RRR,GGG,BBB)
	(R%,G%,B%)
	<keyword>
URLs	<url>

INDEX

Symbols

\# (pound sign)
  using with anchors, 177
  using with divs, 189
  using with id selectors, 194–196
$ (dollar sign), using in searches, 125
( ) (parentheses)
  selecting in Coding toolbar, 451
  using in searches, 125
* (asterisk)
  using with fields, 369
  using with regular expressions, 125–126
. (period)
  before class selectors, 193
  in searches, 125
/ (slash), avoiding in file names, 73
// comments, applying from Coding toolbar, 452
/* */ comment, applying from Coding toolbar, 452
? (question mark), using in searches, 125
 [] (square brackets)
selecting in Coding toolbar, 451
using with regular expressions, 125
\ (escape) character, using in searches, 125
^ (caret), using in searches, 125
_ (underscore), preceding targets with, 174
{} (braces), selecting in Coding toolbar, 451
+ (plus sign) character, using in searches, 125
<!-- (HTML comment), using, 125
</, ending tags with Code Hints, 471
, (commas), using with keywords, 86
' comments, applying from Coding toolbar, 452

A

a:* CSS rules, using with links, 172
<a> tag, using to target links, 174
[abcde] and [^abcde], using in searches, 125
Absolute image alignment, advisory about, 137
absolute link, defined, 168
absolute positioning, applying to boxes, 221
access keys, using in forms, 307
accessibility attributes
  choosing for Image Tag, 131
  including in forms, 306
accessibility check, running for browsers, 509
Accessibility report, described, 503
accordion widget, adding, 384–385
Action menu, using with specific tags, 123–124
Action program, using with forms, 302
actions, undoing, 90
add-ons for Dreamweaver, obtaining, 516
Address bar, copying URLs from, 69
Adobe Bridge
  copying images from, 432–433
  organizing file types with, 433
Adobe Contribute program
  administering sites in, 441
  features of, 400, 439
  versus ICE (InContext Editing), 446
  rollbacks in, 442
  setting sites for use of, 440
  use of Design Notes with, 499
Adobe Extension Manager, launching, 529
Adobe Fireworks. *See also* Fireworks images
  copying and pasting images in, 140
  editing images with, 427–428
  using image placeholders with, 136
[a-e] characters, using in searches, 125

INDEX

INDEX

X

Z